These critical studies of US foreign policy in the Middle East cover America's involvement with the region and its peoples from the Founding Fathers to the Trump presidency. Gresh and Keskin bring together key experts from the US, Asia, the Middle East, and Europe in a wide-ranging assessment of how US foreign policy increasingly has been shaped by the cultural, economic, ideological, and strategic complexities of the Middle East after 1941. Accessible and engaging, it develops an excellent in-depth assessment of the geopolitical challenges that American foreign policy-makers face in this region during the 21st century.

Timothy W. Luke, Virginia Polytechnic Institute and State University

U.S. Foreign Policy in the Middle East provides critical analyses from multiple cultural perspectives of instabilities in the Middle East. It provides a comprehensive examination of American foreign policy for a strategically important part of the world that is in the midst of difficult and challenging transformations. The book is especially important because the efforts of U.S. leadership to foster global security are profoundly affected by the current upheavals in the greater Middle East. These diplomatic efforts require the participation, support, and knowledge of U.S. allies.

Andrew C. Hess, Professor of Diplomacy & Director of the Southwest Asia and Islamic Civilization Program, The Fletcher School, Tufts University

US Foreign Policy in the Middle East

The dawn of the Cold War marked a new stage of complex US foreign policy involvement in the Middle East. More recently, globalization and the region's ongoing conflicts and political violence have led to the US being more politically, economically, and militarily enmeshed – for better or worse – throughout the region.

This book examines the emergence and development of US foreign policy toward the Middle East from the late nineteenth century to the present. With contributions from some of the world's leading scholars, it takes a fresh, inter-disciplinary, and insightful look into the many antecedents that led to current US foreign policy. Exploring the historical challenges, regional alliances, rapid political change, economic interests, domestic politics, and other sources of regional instability, this volume comprises critical analysis from Iranian, Turkish, Israeli, American, and Arab perspectives to provide a comprehensive examination of the evolution and transformation of US foreign policy toward the Middle East.

This volume is an important resource for scholars and students working in the fields of Political Science, Sociology, International Relations, and Islamic, Turkish, Iranian, Arab, and Israeli Studies.

Geoffrey F. Gresh is Department Chair and Associate Professor of International Security Studies at the College of International Security Affairs, National Defense University in Washington, DC.

Tugrul Keskin is Associate Professor and member of the Center for Turkish Studies and Center for Global Studies at Shanghai University.

Routledge Studies in US Foreign Policy

Edited by Inderjeet Parmar, *City University*, and John Dumbrell, *University of Durham*

This new series sets out to publish high-quality works by leading and emerging scholars critically engaging with United States Foreign Policy. The series welcomes a variety of approaches to the subject and draws on scholarship from international relations, security studies, international political economy, foreign policy analysis and contemporary international history.

Subjects covered include the role of administrations and institutions, the media, think tanks, ideologues and intellectuals, elites, transnational corporations, public opinion, and pressure groups in shaping foreign policy, US relations with individual nations, with global regions and global institutions and America's evolving strategic and military policies.

The series aims to provide a range of books – from individual research monographs and edited collections to textbooks and supplemental reading for scholars, researchers, policy analysts and students.

For more information about this series, please visit: www.routledge.com/series/RSUSFP

US Foreign Policy in the Middle East

From American Missionaries to the Islamic State

Edited by
Geoffrey F. Gresh and Tugrul Keskin

LONDON AND NEW YORK

First published 2018
by Routledge
2 Park Square, Milton Park, Abingdon, Oxon OX14 4RN

and by Routledge
711 Third Avenue, New York, NY 10017

Routledge is an imprint of the Taylor & Francis Group, an informa business

© 2018 selection and editorial matter, Geoffrey F. Gresh and Tugrul Keskin;
individual chapters, the contributors

The right of Geoffrey F. Gresh and Tugrul Keskin to be identified as the
authors of the editorial material, and of the authors for their individual
chapters, has been asserted in accordance with sections 77 and 78 of the
Copyright, Designs and Patents Act 1988.

British Library Cataloguing in Publication Data
A catalogue record for this book is available from the British Library

Library of Congress Cataloging in Publication Data
Names: Gresh, Geoffrey F., 1979- editor. | Keskin, Tugrul, editor.
Title: US foreign policy in the Middle East : from American missionaries to
the Islamic State / edited by Geoffrey Gresh and Tugrul Keskin.
Description: New York, NY : Routledge, 2018. | Series: Routledge studies in
US foreign policy | Includes bibliographical references and index.
Identifiers: LCCN 2017050670 | ISBN 9780815347149 (hardback) | ISBN
9781351169646 (e-book)
Subjects: LCSH: United States--Foreign relations--Middle East. | Middle
East--Foreign relations--United States.
Classification: LCC DS63.2.U5 U17 2018 | DDC 327.73056--dc23
LC record available at https://lccn.loc.gov/2017050670

ISBN: 9780815347149 (hbk)
ISBN: 9781351169646 (ebk)

Typeset in Times New Roman
by Taylor & Francis Books

Contents

Illustrations

Figure

Map

Contributors

Editors

Geoffrey F. Gresh is Department Chair and Associate Professor of International Security Studies at the College of International Security Affairs, National Defense University (NDU) in Washington, DC. He is also former Director of the South and Central Asia Security Studies Program at NDU. Previously, he served as a Visiting Fellow at Sciences Po in Paris and was the recipient of a Dwight D. Eisenhower/Clifford Roberts Fellowship. He also received a US Fulbright-Hays grant to teach international relations at Salahaddin University in Erbil, Iraq. He has been awarded a Rotary Ambassadorial Scholarship to Istanbul, Turkey, and a Presidential Scholarship at the American University in Cairo, Egypt. Additionally, he has worked with Colombian refugees in Quito, Ecuador. Most recently, he was named as a US-Japan Foundation Leadership Fellow, an Associate Member of the Corbett Centre for Maritime Policy Studies at King's College in London, and a term member to the Council on Foreign Relations. He is the author of *Gulf Security and the US Military: Regime Survival and the Politics of Basing* (Stanford University Press, 2015) and editor of *Eurasia's Maritime Rise and Global Security: From the Indian Ocean to Pacific Asia and the Arctic* (Palgrave, 2018). His research has also appeared in such scholarly or peer-reviewed publications as *Gulf Affairs, World Affairs Journal, Sociology of Islam, Caucasian Review of International Affairs, Iran and the Caucasus, The Fletcher Forum of World Affairs, Turkish Policy Quarterly, Central Asia and the Caucasus, Insight Turkey, Al-Nakhlah, War on the Rocks,* and *Foreign Policy.* He received a PhD in International Relations and a MALD from The Fletcher School of Law and Diplomacy at Tufts University. He can be followed on Twitter via @ggresh.

Tugrul Keskin is an Associate Professor and member of the Center for Turkish Studies and the Center for Global Studies at Shanghai University. Keskin was the graduate director at the Department of Political Science and International Relations at Maltepe University in Turkey. He taught previously at the Department of International and Global Studies and as an affiliated faculty in Black Studies, Sociology and the Center for Turkish

Studies at Portland State University (PSU). He served as the Middle East Studies Coordinator at PSU for six years. His research and teaching interests include International and Global Studies, Social and Political Theory, African Society and Politics, Sociology of Human Rights, Islamic Movements, and Sociology of the Middle East. Previously, Dr. Keskin taught as an instructor of Sociology and Africana Studies at Virginia Tech University and was a Visiting Assistant Professor of Sociology at James Madison and Radford Universities. He received his PhD in Sociology from Virginia Tech, with graduate certificate degrees in Africana Studies, Social and Political Thought, and International Research and Development. He is the founder and moderator of the Sociology of Islam mailing list, and the founder and editor of the journal *Sociology of Islam*-BRILL and region editor of *Critical Sociology*-SAGE (Middle East and North Africa). His current research involves modern Uyghur nationalism, China and the Middle East, and US foreign policy and think tanks in the post-Cold War era.

Contributors

Mohamed-Ali Adraoui is a political scientist and historian working on international relations and Middle East politics. He received his PhD in Political Science from Sciences Po Paris (France) in 2011. In 2013–2015, he was a Max Weber fellow at the European University Institute (Florence), a Postdoctoral Researcher at Paris Saint-Denis University, and a part-time Lecturer at the Institute of Political Studies in Grenoble (France) in the field of History of Political Thought. His research is concerned with the history and development of Salafism, with a special focus on how the quietist approach to Salafism has impacted Western, particularly French, youth and has gone global over the last few decades (mainly from Saudi Arabia to the rest of the world). He has published *Du Golfe aux banlieues. Le salafisme mondialisé* (Presses Universitaires de France, 2013; with English and Arabic versions coming soon). He has also edited a volume dealing with the foreign policies of Islamist movements, *Les islamistes et le monde. Islam politique et relations internationals* (L'Harmattan, 2015). His current research is on the history of Jihadi thought. He is also involved in a project dealing with US foreign policy towards political Islam.

Hamad H. Albloshi is Assistant Professor of Political Science at Kuwait University. He holds a PhD in International Relations from the Fletcher School of Law and Diplomacy, Tufts University. He is the author of *The Eternal Revolution: Hardliners and Conservatives in Iran* (I.B. Tauris, 2016).

Elizabeth Bishop is Associate Professor of History specializing in Arab West Asia and North Africa at Texas State University (San Marcos, TX), researching nineteenth- and twentieth-century workers' movements and law in five jurisdictions, with particular emphasis on Hashemite Iraq. She edited *Imperialism on Trial: League of Nations Mandate States in*

Historical Perspective (Rowman and Littlefield, 2006) with Ray Douglas
and Michael Callahan. She is also editor, with Guy Beckwith, of *Technology and Civilization* (Pearson, 1997). Her scholarly research has appeared
in such peer-reviewed journals as *Studia Historica Gedanensia, International Journal of Contemporary Iraqi Studies, Al-Mawaqif, Africa and the
West, Arab World Geographer, Studia Europaea, Oriente Moderno,
Romano-Arabica, Studia Politica, Ab Imperio, Social and Human Sciences
Review*, and *Al-Tawasool*. She is also a former project editor at Brill Academic Publishers and Stanford University Press. Bishop received her PhD
in History from the University of Chicago and a BA in History/Political
Science from Earlham College.

Russell A. Burgos is Associate Professor of International Security Studies and
Academic Director at the College of International Security Affairs,
National Defense University (NDU) Ft. Bragg, NC campus. He joined
NDU in 2015 after ten years at the University of California at Los
Angeles (UCLA), where he taught courses in globalization and governance, globalization and international security, international relations
theory, American foreign policy, arms control and international security,
and homeland security, and gave seminars on human security, the Iraq
War, and American national security policy in the Persian Gulf. In 2013,
he received the UCLA Alumni Association's My Last Lecture award, the
university's only campus-wide teaching award based on the vote of the
undergraduate student body. He was also a Visiting Assistant Professor at
the University of Southern California, teaching courses on American
foreign policy in the Middle East, and a Visiting Assistant Professor at
Claremont McKenna College, where he taught on international relations
and Middle East politics and gave seminars on American foreign policy
and the Iraq War. For five years, Dr. Burgos was Director of the Middle
East Military-Security Track II dialog at University of California-San
Diego's Institute on Global Conflict and Cooperation, bringing together
senior Arab, Israeli, and North African military officers and security
ministry officials, senior officers from the United States and NATO partners, and international experts from research institutions, senior military
educational institutions, think tanks, and international organizations
(ranging from the Organization for Security and Cooperation in Europe
to the Multinational Force of Observers to the Lawrence Livermore
National Laboratory) for intensive biannual seminars on emerging and
enduring security challenges in the Middle East-North Africa region. His
research interests include human security, globalization and conflict,
borderlands, and American national security policy in the Middle East
and sub-Saharan Africa. He has published articles in scholarly journals
and chapters in edited book volumes, and he is at work on a book on
patterns in American foreign relations with Iraq from the nineteenth
century to the twenty-first century.

Ethan Corbin is currently Director of the Defence and Security Committee at the NATO Parliamentary Assembly. He is also an Adjunct Professor of International Relations at Vesalius College (VUB) in Brussels, where he teaches a course on US foreign policy in the Middle East. He completed his doctorate in International Relations at the Fletcher School of Law and Diplomacy at Tufts University in 2013. His dissertation developed a theory of state alignment with external armed groups, which he tested with a longitudinal case study of Syria's use of the Palestinian and Lebanese armed groups from 1963 to 2010. Prior to joining the NATO Parliamentary Assembly, Dr. Corbin was Lecturer in International Relations at Tufts University, teaching courses on US foreign policy and international security studies. His research interests include US foreign policy, international security, international organizations, and Middle Eastern politics. From 2011 to 2013, Corbin was a Research Fellow at the Belfer Center for Science and International Affairs at Harvard's Kennedy School of Government. He received his AB from Bowdoin College, a Master's in Middle Eastern history from Université de Paris-IV (La Sorbonne), and a MALD from The Fletcher School. He has published on topics ranging from Syrian foreign policy, NATO, peacekeeping operations, and insurgency and counterinsurgency warfare.

Suleyman Elik is an Assistant Professor at Istanbul Medeniyet University in the Faculty of Political Science and International Relations. After he completed his PhD at Durham University (UK), he worked at the Energy Institute of School of Government and International Affairs, Durham University, as a Visiting Research Fellow and taught on Middle East politics at Newcastle University in the politics department in addition to being the acting module leader for "The Politics of the Middle East" from 2009 to 2010. Dr. Elik is also an International Security Studies fellow at the Wise Men Center for Strategic Studies (BILGESAM). He is author of *Iran-Turkey Relations, 1979–2011: Conceptualizing the Dynamics of Politics, Religion and Security in Middle-Power States* (Routledge, 2011).

Sean Foley is Associate Professor of History at Middle Tennessee State University (USA) and specializes in the Middle East, Southeast Asia, and religious and political trends in the broader Islamic world. Previously, he taught at Georgetown University (USA), where he earned an MA in Arab Studies in 2000 and a PhD in History in 2005. He graduated with a BA in History with honors and distinction from University of California, Berkeley (USA) in 1996. He has held Fulbright fellowships with Damascus University (Syria), Istanbul University (Turkey), and the International Institute of Islamic Thought and Civilization (Malaysia). He has also done extensive research throughout Saudi Arabia and was based at King Saud University from April 2013 until the end of January 2014. From June until August 2014, he was a Visiting Fellow at the Centre for Arab and Islamic Studies, Research School of Social Sciences at the Australian National University.

Dr. Foley speaks Arabic and Bahasa Malaysian. He has published widely on Islamic history, Middle East and Gulf politics, Southeast Asia, Sufism, and Muslims in American and European history. His first book, *The Arab Gulf States: Beyond Oil and Islam*, was published by Lynne Rienner Press in March 2010. He has delivered over 70 papers to international conferences and to universities in China, Europe, India, the Middle East, North America, and Southeast Asia. In addition, he serves as an expert for the Middle East Institute (USA) and has contributed to *The Atlantic*, Australian Broadcasting Corporation Television, *The Daily Zaman*, al-Jazeera.net, al-Jazeera English Television, *New Straits Times, Tennessean*, and Voice of America Television.

Kelly Gleason is a Lieutenant Colonel in the US Army, in addition to being a Lecturer of Regional and Analytical Studies at the College of International Security Affairs at National Defense University in Washington, DC. He teaches courses on topics such as Building Narrative for Countering Violent Extremism, Foundations in Strategic Leadership, and Campaigns, Operational Advising, and Strategic Threats. He is a former Afghanistan-Pakistan Hands adviser, having served two tours in Afghanistan. During his first deployment to Afghanistan, he was the 1st Cavalry Division Key Leader Engagement Chief. In this capacity, he provided the strategic-level support for US general officers and Department of State senior civilian representatives in preparation for negotiations with Afghan military and government decision makers. His second deployment to Afghanistan provided him with the opportunity to work with Afghan special operations leadership as the Executive Officer for the Afghan Operations Coordination Group. He has received master's degrees from National Defense University, National Intelligence University, Central Michigan University, and Southern Illinois University.

Gökser Gökçay is Assistant Professor of Political Science and International Relations at Üsküdar University in Turkey. He completed his PhD, on the international history of the Turkish foreign aid experience in the postwar period, at Dokuz Eylül University in 2015. He received his MS in International Relations from Ege University and a BS in Political Science and Public Administration from Middle East Technical University in Ankara.

Fatma Aslı Kelkitli is an Assistant Professor in the Department of Political Science and Public Administration at Istanbul Arel University. She obtained her undergraduate degree in Management at Boğaziçi University and her master's degree in history from the Atatürk Institute for Modern Turkish History in Boğaziçi University. She holds a PhD in Political Science and International Relations, also from Boğaziçi University. Her academic research interests encompass international relations theory, Turkish foreign policy, and Balkan, South Caucasus, Central Asian politics as well as Middle Eastern affairs with special emphasis on Iran.

Michael McCall is Assistant Editor of the journal *Sociology of Islam* and currently an associate of the Issam Fares Institute for Public Policy and International Affairs at the American University of Beirut, where he is also a graduate student. He holds an MA in International Relations from Leiden University in the Netherlands. His research interests include Middle East foreign policy, political Islam, international political economy and Uyghur nationalism.

Ozlem Madi-Sisman majored in International Relations at Koc University in Istanbul and earned her MA in Political Science at Central European University, Budapest. She completed her PhD in Political Science at Bilkent University, Ankara. During her doctoral research, Dr. Madi spent two years at Harvard University as a special student, and two years at Furman University, where she also began teaching courses on Turkish politics, Middle Eastern politics and politics of the developing world. Since 2014, she has been serving as an Adjunct Professor of International Relations at Bahçeşehir University. In the fall of 2016, she began as an Adjunct Faculty member of the University of Houston-Clear Lake, where she teaches classes on American politics and other related subjects. Her forthcoming book, *The Reluctant Capitalists: Muslims, Money and Democracy in Turkey*, is under contract with Palgrave Macmillan.

Jeremy Pressman is Associate Professor of Political Science and Director of Middle East Studies at the University of Connecticut. He is co-director, with Professor Erica Chenoweth, of the Crowd Counting Consortium at crowdcounting.org. His research interests include international relations, the Arab-Israeli conflict, US foreign policy in the Middle East, and political crowds. He has written two books, *Warring Friends: Alliance Restraint in International Politics* (Cornell University Press, 2008) and *Point of No Return: The Deadly Struggle for Middle East Peace*, with Geoffrey Kemp (Brookings Institution Press, 1997). His articles have appeared in *Diplomatic History, International Security, International Studies Perspectives, Perspectives on Politics, Security Studies*, and elsewhere. His article "Throwing Stones in Social Science: Nonviolence, Unarmed Violence, and the First Intifada," was published in *Cooperation & Conflict* in 2017. Pressman has worked at the Carnegie Endowment for International Peace, and he received his PhD in Political Science from MIT. Pressman is on Twitter at @djpressman.

Ahmed Ali Salem is an Associate Professor at the Institute for Islamic World Studies, Zayed University, UAE, and a former Assistant Director of the Institute. He teaches courses on the Islamic world, including in the MA programs in Islamic World Studies, and Diplomacy and International Affairs. His research agenda includes theoretical and methodological debates in international relations, modern Islamic reform thought and movements, conflicts in Arab and African worlds, and modern history of

Arab-African and Islamic-Western relations. He has authored, edited, and translated more than 20 books, book chapters, journal articles, web articles, and conference papers in both Arabic and English since he received his PhD in Political Science from University of Illinois at Urbana-Champaign (UIUC) and joined Zayed University in 2006. He also earned an MA in African Studies from UIUC in 2002; another MA in Islamic Studies from the Graduate School of Islamic and Social Sciences (now Cordoba University), VA, USA, in 1999; and a BSc in Political Science from Cairo University, Egypt, in 1996. His most recent book is *What Is Constructivist About Realism? Constructivist Critiquing of the Realist Paradigm in International Relations* (Lambert Academic Publishing, 2012), an in-depth analysis of the classic works of leading theorists in the realist school of international relations. His first book was *International Relations Theories and International Organizations: Realism, Constructivism, and Collective Security in the League of Arab States* (VDM Verlag Dr. Müller, 2008).

Cengiz Sisman majored in Psychology at Boğaziçi University in Istanbul and earned his MA in Islamic and Jewish Studies at Temple University. He earned another MA in History and Middle Eastern Studies at Harvard University, where he also completed his PhD dissertation, entitled "A Jewish Messiah in the Ottoman Court: Sabbatai Sevi and the Emergence of a Judeo-Islamic Community (1666–1720)." During his doctoral research, Dr. Sisman spent a year at Hebrew University as a special student. After receiving his PhD, he returned to Turkey to teach at Boğaziçi, Koç, and Bilkent Universities. He later returned to the United States, where he taught at Brandeis University as a visiting Assistant Professor and then at Furman University as Assistant Professor. Since the fall of 2015, Dr. Sisman has been serving as an Assistant Professor of History at the University of Houston-Clear Lake. His book *The Burden of Silence: Sabbatai Sevi and the Evolution of the Ottoman-Turkish Donmes* was published by Oxford University Press in September 2015. His work is connected by his deep interest in the history of religions, religious conversion, irreligion, messianism, mysticism, crypto-double identities, and religion and modernity. Currently he is teaching courses on world history, Islamic empires, and the modern Middle East.

Nickolas A. Spencer is an independent researcher and lawyer. He received a BA and MA in International Studies from Texas State University and a JD with a concentration in international and comparative law from Chicago-Kent College of Law. His research focuses on law, policy, and international development as well as the confluence of development, conflict, and security.

MIDDLE EAST

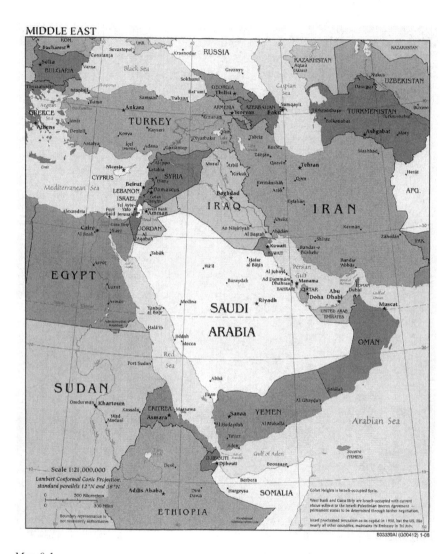

Map 0.1

Introduction

US foreign policy in the Middle East

Geoffrey F. Gresh

The swearing-in of US President Donald J. Trump in January 2017 provides an opportune moment to re-examine some of the pitfalls and perils of US foreign policy in the Middle East. The hope is to usher in new analysis and debates in addition to furthering both prior historical research and our understanding of how US foreign policy has shaped regional politics. Will US foreign policy in the Middle East change under President Trump, or will his administration maintain many of the policies of past US presidents? Will turbulence and warfare force President Trump and other regional actors to make drastic decisions that could have damning repercussions for domestic, regional, and global politics alike? Or are we experiencing new iterations of prior practices and policies associated with such regional and hegemonic actors as Iran, Saudi Arabia, and the United States? And perhaps most urgent: what effects has US foreign policy had on the broader Middle East during the past decade or more of war? These are some of the many important questions that the authors attempt to answer throughout this edited volume. Though there remains great uncertainty about what lies ahead for US foreign policy in the Middle East, it is important to take pause to see how we arrived at the current politics and instability of the day, and what can potentially be done about it.

Complex relationships

Before delving into the follow-on chapters that lay out the evolution and transformation of US foreign policy in the Middle East, it is important to first frame and contextualize some of the complicated origins of US foreign policy in the Middle East. Certainly, US regional interests date back to the nineteenth century with the spread of global US missionary movements in such countries as Egypt or Turkey, but the United States only began to play a more significant and influential role across the region following the end of the Second World War. To highlight this beginning, I start with the description of a series of meetings between President Franklin D. Roosevelt and King Ibn Saud of Saudi Arabia. The set of meetings aboard the USS *Quincy* near Ismailia, Egypt, in February 1945 is a symbolic anecdote that encapsulates many of the dynamic and complex themes addressed throughout the volume.[1] Though this story refers to Saudi Arabia, many other state and non-state actors can identify with how complicated and deep-seated many of the bonds and relationships are with the United States.

As the Second World War wound down in early 1945, President Roosevelt extended an invitation to meet with King Ibn Saud aboard his naval cruiser docking near the Suez Canal. The President was traveling to the United States after attending the Yalta Conference with British Prime Minister Winston Churchill and Marshal Josef Stalin of the Soviet Union. President Roosevelt wanted to talk with Ibn Saud about oil, the future of Palestine, and the Middle East's configuration after the war. Roosevelt was also concerned that the destruction of Europe during the Second World War might be exploited by the Soviet Union. The United States therefore needed to ensure the availability of energy resources from the Gulf for the reconstruction of Europe and Asia (Miller, 1980, pp. 129–131).

After traveling three days aboard the USS *Murphy* from Saudi Arabia with his 48-person entourage, King Ibn Saud arrived to meet with President Roosevelt aboard the USS *Quincy* on February 14 (Eddy, 1945 [1997], pp. 255–284; Miller, 1980, pp. 129–131; Holden and Johns, 1981, pp. 135–137). From the beginning, President Roosevelt and King Ibn Saud established a strong bond. The king spoke of Roosevelt as being his "twin" brother in age, in responsibility as head of state, and in physical demeanor. The President, who used a wheelchair due to his polio, replied, "But you are fortunate to still have the use of your legs to take you wherever you choose to go." The king replied, "It is you, Mr. President, who are fortunate. My legs grow feebler every year; with your more reliable wheelchair you are assured that you will arrive." The President then said, "I have two of these chairs, which are also twins. Would you accept one as a personal gift from me?" The king replied, "Gratefully, I shall use it daily and always recall affectionately the giver, my great and good friend" (Eddy, 1954, pp. 29–37; Memorandum of Conversation, 1945). Years later, the king reminisced with Colonel William Eddy, US Minister to Saudi Arabia, that, "This chair is my most precious possession. It is the gift of my good and great friend, President Roosevelt, on whom Allah has had mercy" (Memorandum for McGeorge Bundy, 1962; Eddy, 1954, pp. 29–37).

During the series of meetings, the king and President Roosevelt connected over their visions for the future of the region. President Roosevelt vowed that the US government would make no concrete decision on the future of Palestine "without consultation of both Arabs and Jews" (Roosevelt, 1945). Both leaders were pleased with the meeting and parted ways content with their newly established relationship (Holden and Johns, 1981, pp. 137–138). The Ibn Saud-Roosevelt meeting aboard the USS *Quincy* helped to fortify the future of US-Saudi relations and pave the way for the start of a more robust presence throughout the region that continues to this day.

As the United States transited increasingly between Europe and Pacific Asia toward the end of the war, the US military also recognized the growing geostrategic importance of the region. The United States had supplied approximately 90 percent of the oil used by the Allies during the Second World War, but by the end of the war resources had arguably become scarce (Yergin, 2008, pp. 395–396). In the end, the US military became a strong advocate, along with US oil companies, for the establishment of a US military regional basing presence in such countries as Saudi Arabia due to its location and easy access to vital natural resources (Rubin, 1979, pp. 253–254).

From here, regional events quickly unfolded: the declaration of Israeli independence in 1948, the subsequent rise of the Israeli-Palestinian conflict, the establishment of the North Atlantic Treaty Organization (NATO) in 1949, and Great Britain's waning influence and regional interest were some of the many essential triggering events and dynamics that created a string of political dilemmas for the United States as it was thrust increasingly into regional politics. At the dawn of the Cold War, it became harder for the United States to turn away from the Middle East as the emergence of the Soviet Union recast the US role from victor in the Second World War to defender of Allied nations against the spread of communism in a newly bipolar world. Thus, the beginning of the postwar era marked the start in earnest of a certain US dependence on and complex foreign policy in the Middle East from Turkey and Israel to Iran and the Gulf Arab states.

The intention of this introduction is not to rehash all events of the past half-century or more of complicated political dynamics and relationships between the United States and Middle Eastern countries. Instead, it serves to emblematically introduce and briefly contextualize one of the many long and complicated relationships that developed in the past century or more between the United States and all nations of the broader Middle East. The Ibn Saud-Roosevelt interaction cited here is just one tiny sliver of insight into how the Middle East would emerge as arguably one of the United States' greatest foreign policy challenges during the postwar period. This brief historical introduction is also meant to pay deference to the importance of the region's diplomatic and political history. Frequently today, much analysis of US foreign policy in the Middle East is taken out of context and neglects important historical pillars that have evolved over time.

The importance of historical context aside, the regional politics of today are nonetheless equally perplexing and gut-wrenching to watch, whether it is the rise of the Islamic State of Iraq and Syria (ISIS) or the spread of sectarian and ethnic violence. Despite recent attempts by the United States to pivot away from the region, the Middle East has again come into focus as the United States and its regional allies grapple with a way ahead. Due to the continued violent spillover from Syria, Iraq, Turkey, and Yemen of the past several years, US foreign policy has struggled to find its footing amidst revolution, war, and violence. Though much of the past few years marks an unprecedented period for the region, the United States has long been plagued by challenging choices with often grim outcomes that have shaped, for better or worse, the politics and future trajectory of the entire region. The intent of this volume is to strike a balance between re-examining some of the important events of the past in combination with analysing today's political situation. This volume also offers much-needed perspective from both regional and American scholars who offer important insights and critical analyses regarding how US foreign policy has evolved, in addition to examining many of the mishaps, obstacles, and struggles that the United States has confronted in the current age of instability and war.

Volume overview

To organize the volume, chapters have been divided into four main themes that help frame some of the larger challenges and issues tied to the evolution of US foreign policy in the Middle East over the past century or more: (1) Historical Cultural and Economic Interests; (2) Cold War Challenges; (3) Balancing Regional Alliances; and (4) Rapid Political Change and the Spread of Regional Instability. In addition to being broken down into themes, the chapters follow a more or less chronological timeline, beginning with a chapter on missionaries and ending the volume with chapters on both the US war against ISIS and an analysis of the current Trump administration. Certainly, and due in large part to space considerations, not every angle related to US foreign policy in the Middle East could be covered. That said, this volume provides a valuable interdisciplinary perspective on the evolution of US foreign policy in the Middle East that includes both US and regional scholars as well as historians, political scientists, international relations experts, sociologists, and practitioners.

To begin, Part I provides an historical retrospective on some of the cultural and economic interests of such vital non-state actors as Christian missionaries and US-owned international corporations. In Chapter 1, Ozlem Madi-Sisman and Cengiz Sisman write about the early days of the American missionary movement in the Middle East. Although early Americans viewed Muslims in relatively positive terms, they referred to North Africa and the Near East as the lands of "barbary" and "heathens," largely due of their lack of knowledge. By the turn of the twentieth century, American interest in Islam and its lands reached a more heightened level. Fueled by hopes of converting Muslims, Jews, and other "heathens," thousands of American missionaries flocked to the Near East, then ruled by the Ottoman Empire. For American revivalist Protestants, the late nineteenth century and beginning of the twentieth century was particularly important since they believed they were living at the "dawn of the millennium." As this chapter asserts, for more than a century the modern missionary movement helped to influence the perception of the modern West, especially that of Americans, vis-à-vis the Middle East. Moreover, the American missionary experience became one of the more important agents that shaped – often negatively – American foreign policy throughout the region.

This chapter is followed by a discussion on an often-overlooked element of foreign policy: the role of non-energy international corporations in the

Middle East and the case of the big tobacco industry. In Chapter 2, Sean Foley examines how American tobacco companies – with the aid of the US Department of Agriculture – defeated attempts in the 1970s and 1980s by Saudi political and religious leaders to ban smoking and popularized smoking cigarettes in the Kingdom. This chapter sheds new light on a little discussed but important aspect of the US-Saudi special relationship. These events are important today as Riyadh once again seeks to curb smoking and is fighting a war with Washington against ISIS, which prohibits all smoking. The combination of these chapters helps to lay a foundation of understanding for the historical cultural and economic forces that influenced larger strategic objectives of US foreign policy.

In Part II, the authors discuss some of the bigger challenges associated with the United States during the Cold War period and how the Middle East fit into a larger strategic perspective. In Chapter 3, Nickolas Spencer uses primary source material to re-examine the significance of ideology and geography in shaping US foreign policy. He looks at the work of George Kennan, for example, who helped shape US strategy and doctrine during the Cold War. Additionally, he examines how the United States used geography to its advantage in Turkey to help contain a rising Russia/Soviet influence across the region. Chapter 4, from Gökser Gökçay, acts as an important compliment to this with its empirical examination of US-Turkish relations during the Cold War through the use of previously unpublished archival material from American, British, and Turkish archives. The chapter focuses in part on Turkey's economic integration into the Western Bloc and the reorganization of its economic objectives domestically and alongside the US Marshall Plan of postwar reconstruction. The chapter argues that the formation of an integral US foreign policy towards Turkey in the postwar era was indeed shaped by an amalgamation of military–strategic planning and foreign economic objectives. Turkey was not just a military subject for US foreign policy; Turkey's inclusion in the postwar economic system was also essential for US foreign policy.

Chapter 5 rounds out this section with an examination of US atomic policy toward Hashemite Iraq. Elizabeth Bishop argues that the atomic era provided Great Britain an opportunity to re-colonize its wartime ally, the United States; turning its foreign policy responsibilities in the Arab world over to the United States. Winston Churchill's 1947 "Iron Curtain" speech marked a shift in US foreign policy toward the Arab States, from a wartime alliance to an atomic colonialism centered on London. During this important period of foreign policy transitions, the case of US policy toward Hashemite Iraq is analyzed in depth here.

Part III looks at the challenges that the United States has confronted in balancing many of the opposing forces and important alliances throughout the region. Jeremy Pressman in Chapter 6 begins with an examination of one of the United States' most critical regional allies, Israel. For the US decision to ally with Israel, the three most common explanations are: the idea that

Israel is a strategic asset to the United States; the idea that US domestic interest groups, often called the Israel lobby, press the United States to ally with Israel and support Israeli policy especially vis-à-vis the question of Palestine; and the idea that the two countries have shared values such as democracy or a shared biblical tradition. But as argued in this chapter, each of these explanations has shortcomings. On important policy issues, including the peace process and the definition of enemies or threats, the two countries have sometimes differed in stark ways. As Pressman asserts, the current domestic political changes in both countries raise important questions about the future of the alliance but in the end the alliance will likely remain strong.

This is followed in Chapter 7 with an analysis of Iran and Turkey. In juxtaposition to the more empirically oriented chapters of the prior section, Suleyman Elik takes a more international relations theoretical approach to explaining US relations with these two countries from the Cold War to the present. This chapter analyzes the patron-client and proxy power relations between the United States and each of the two nations respectively, explaining how great power or US security interests affected regional middle power relations through a systemic level of analysis framework.

Chapters 8 and 9 represent some of the essential relationships between the United States and Gulf Arab nations. In Chapter 8, Fatma Aslı Kelkitli analyzes the important US-Qatari partnership. She examines the small state and great power dynamic between the two countries, looking at the foundations of this relationship beginning in the early 1990s following the end of the First Gulf War. The elevation of this bilateral relationship has expanded through security, political, economic, and cultural elements but is currently under duress due to ongoing geopolitical and regional shifts. This is followed by Chapter 9 and Michael McCall's analysis of US-Gulf Cooperation Council (GCC) relations. This chapter analyzes the effect of the 'retrenchment' foreign policy towards the Middle East as implemented by the Obama administration. McCall argues that the nature of the partnership is undergoing a slow but fundamental shift towards less direct dependence as the United States changes its regional posture.

The final section of the volume, Part IV, provides salient analysis related to US foreign policy in the Middle East since 9/11, including the current age of rapid political change and instability. In Chapter 10, Russell A. Burgos looks at the Iraq War of the 2000s in an important historical context. As he argues, American foreign policy towards Iraq since the First World War has alternated between brief periods of intense interest and long periods of benign neglect. As a result, US policymakers never defined a specific foreign policy for Iraq; instead, the Iraq 'problem' was inevitably subordinated to some other set of national interests. Starting with the Iran-Iraq War, however, the lack of a defined Iraq policy set the stage for a recurring cycle of reactive policies that were less focused on carefully defined strategic objectives than they were on short-term domestic politics. This chapter thus asserts that that from 2003 to 2011, the Bush and Obama administrations were more concerned about domestic politics of the Iraq War than they were about the strategic implications of the war for US-Iraqi relations and for wider regional stability.

In Chapter 11, we move from Iraq to the Arab uprisings beginning in 2011. Here, Mohamed-Ali Adraoui analyzes the relationship between US foreign policy and political Islam during the Arab uprisings. This chapter highlights the difficulty of addressing the Muslim Brotherhood from a policy and more macro political perspective, especially at a time when it is hotly debated domestically in the United States. It sheds light, in the author's own framing, on the way the United States has conducted its policy of engagement with the Islamist movement and the dilemmas it has posed to US foreign policy. This chapter is complimented by Ahmed Ali Salem in Chapter 12 wherein he examines how the Obama administration handled the Arab uprisings from 2011 to 2012. The chapter begins by looking at the significant changes that Obama's first term introduced to US foreign policy, and reviews the opposing arguments of his critics and supporters as discussed in journals, magazines, and newspapers in the first six months after Obama assumed power. The second part of the chapter focuses on the Obama administration's policy on the Egyptian uprising and highlights the inconsistencies between its democracy-promoting words and status-quo-entrenching deeds.

In Chapter 13, Ethan Corbin examines another pressing contemporary issue: Syria. After almost 46 years in power, the Asad family continues to vex US administrations – earning them the moniker of the "Sphinxes of Damascus." Even before the uprising began in February 2011, Washington participated in various levels of sanctions against the Asad regime for state sponsorship of terrorism. Various levels of diplomatic, political, and economic coercion by the United States over the past decades, however, have led to very little behavioral change by the Syrian regime, and therefore proven to be of scant benefit to US regional interests. Throughout its history, a weak Syria has proven to be the bellwether for regional political disruption. As Syria crumbled to domestic political turmoil, regional and global powers sought to fill the resulting vacuum. The current civil war engulfing the country has proven once more the regional and global dilemma of Syrian instability. And once again the United States has failed to achieve almost any of its goals as it repeatedly tries to negotiate a democracy-friendly regime change in Damascus. Instead, the chaos and destruction of the Syrian Civil War have proven the durability of the Asad regime, the return of Russia to the region, and the enduring strength of Iran to disrupt a regional political order friendly to US interests.

In Chapter 14, Hamad H. Albloshi examines the contentious nature of the US-Iranian relationship. He analyzes the relationship from the perspective of hardline conservatives in Iran. Members of this faction do not support any rapprochement with the United States and strongly believe that Iran should not trust Washington. The chapter discusses the ideological roots of their position toward the United States and addresses some of consequences for the Iranian president Hassan Rouhani's government, in addition to the possible spillover implications for the current Trump administration.

In Chapter 15, Kelly Gleason examines the US propaganda war against the Islamic State of Iraq and Syria and what has gone wrong from the beginning. This chapter fits into a larger debate about the challenges faced by states when adopting communication or information strategies to combat or counter non-state actors promoting violent extremism. In other words, can a state actor successfully counter violent extremism from a strategic communications perspective? Gleason asserts that the United States has failed from the start, lacking any sort of integrative strategy across the inter-agency. Additionally, there remains a lack of any clear strategic communications direction or vision that could ensure full-spectrum coordination or synchronization efforts, whether covert or overt. ISIS is winning the online information war and it has only been aided in part by the United States' inability to support a strong counter-messaging campaign.

In the final chapter, Tugrul Keskin looks at the early days of the Trump administration's foreign policy in the Middle East, examining it from a political economic and sociological vantage point. Though Trump's administration is still in its relative infancy, President Trump's mark on Middle East politics has been influenced thus far by his coterie of economic advisors and many former or current military generals. There are still many unpredictable days ahead, but Keskin provides a beginning understanding of the frame of reference for the current administration's foreign policy.

Note

1 Parts of the anecdote have been excerpted and adapted from Geoffrey F. Gresh, *Gulf Security and the US Military: Regime Survival and the Politics of Basing* (Stanford University Press, 2015).

References

Eddy, W.A. (1945 [1997]). Eddy's account of Ibn Saud-Roosevelt meeting on February 14, 1945. In K.E. Evans (Ed.), *US Records on Saudi Affairs 1945–1959*, Vol. II (pp. 255–284). London: Archive Editions and University Publications of America.

Eddy, W.A. (1954). *F.D.R. Meets Ibn Saud*. New York: American Friends of the Middle East, Inc.

Holden, D. and Johns, R. (1981). *The House of Saud: The Rise and Rule of the Most Powerful Dynasty in the Arab World*. New York: Holt, Rinehart and Winston.

Memorandum for McGeorge Bundy, (1962, January 24). Subject: President's Call on King Saud of Saudi Arabia at Palm Beach. John F. Kennedy Presidential Library. *National Security Files*. Saudi Arabia. General Files. 11/20/61–1/31/62.

Memorandum of Conversation. (1945, February 15). Franklin D. Roosevelt Presidential Library Map Room Papers. *Naval Aide's Files*. Box 165. Crimean Conference.

Miller, A.D. (1980). *Search for Security: Saudi Arabian Oil and American Foreign Policy, 1939–1949*. Chapel Hill, NC: University of North Carolina Press.

Roosevelt, F.D. (1945, April 5). Letter from President Franklin D. Roosevelt to King Ibn Saud. Franklin D. Roosevelt Presidential Library. *President's Secretary's Files: Diplomatic Correspondence*. Box 5. Saudi Arabia.

Rubin, B. (1979, April). Anglo-American relations in Saudi Arabia, 1941–1945. *Journal of Contemporary History*, 14(2), 253–267.

Yergin, D. (2008). *The Prize: The Epic Quest for Oil, Money & Power*. New York: Free Press.

Part I
Historical Cultural and Economic Interests

1 From "heathen Turks" to "cruel Turks"

Religious and political roots of the changing American perception towards the Middle East

Ozlem Madi-Sisman and Cengiz Sisman

In his 2010 book *The Turk in America*, Justin McCarthy asserts that "From start to finish, the American missionaries viewed the Turks as their enemy. They carried their feelings to the American people" (p. 2). To McCarthy, this "constant image" almost never changed, as the eighteenth-century American geographers or nineteenth-century American journalists used virtually the same language in describing the Turks and, by extension, the Middle East-erners: "vindictive, jealous, haughty, intolerant, and full of dissimulation" (McCarthy, 2010, p. 18).

A closer look at the nineteenth century, however, suggests that the issue is more complex, that the century does not have a seamless, homogeneous, uninterrupted, and linear history with regards to the American perception of the Middle East. First of all, there were several individual exceptions who viewed the Turks, the Muslims, and Islam in positive lights, neutral at best. Second, a good number of Americans moderated their views about the Turks and Muslims after encountering them as merchants, diplomats, and missionaries in person. As a result, the American image of "heathen" and "tyrannical" Turks was transformed into "pluralistic" and "tolerant" Turks by the mid-nineteenth century and then into "cruel" and "bloodthirsty" Turks by the turn of the twentieth century. While the former image had been shaped by European (largely British) religious and political (read Orientalist) discourse, the latter image had been shaped by the increasing Protestant missionary activities in the Ottoman Empire in the nineteenth century. For example, 88 percent of the books on Islam in American libraries were written by missionaries in the nineteenth century (McCarthy, 2010). As a result of their intensified educational activities and increasing involvement in the Ottoman–Armenian conflict in the second half of the nineteenth century, American missionaries began to have some serious problems with the Ottoman authorities.

As shown by other scholars, long before oil interests, the American missionary experience had been one of the most important agents that set the tone of American foreign policy towards the Middle East until World War II. This chapter is an attempt to demonstrate the complexities of this picture and adumbrate the stages through which the American perception evolved over the nineteenth century and into the early twentieth century.

Following chronological order, we will first survey the pre-nineteenth-century American perception of the Middle East, focusing attention on the religious elite and founding fathers. Then we will examine the changing American attitude towards the Middle East with particular attention to merchants, missionaries, and diplomats. And finally, we will discuss the Ottoman–Armenian conflict at the end of the nineteenth century in relation to the changing American perception. Before we delve into our discussion, it is important to note that in premodern European and American context, the terms "Muslims" and "Near/Middle East" were used interchangeably with the terms "Turks" and "Ottoman Empire."

Early American perception of the Muslims, Turks, and the Middle East: Commoners, religious elite, and the founding fathers

Characterized by Orientalistic assumptions, early American perceptions of the Muslims and Turks were not so different than those of the Europeans, though with the major exception that the Americans' physical encounters with Muslims were very limited, if not absent, before the nineteenth century. Because of that, Americans were profoundly ignorant about the Turks, Muslims, and Islam before that time. John Ledyard, an explorer and adventurer, was the first citizen of an independent United States who traveled to the Middle East (Oren, 2008). On June 30, 1788, reflecting American interest in and knowledge of (and lack thereof) the region, Ledyard jotted down the following note in his journal before setting sail for his journey: "My path will be from here ... across the Mediterranean ... to Grand Cairo. ... Beyond is unknown, and my discoveries begin. Where they terminate, and how, you shall know, if I survive" (as cited in Oren, 2008, p. 6). Ledyard also wrote to Thomas Jefferson, thanking him for his friendship and trust and promising to honor them both (Oren, 2008).

As Spellberg (2014) states, "Americans had inherited from Europe almost a millennium of negative distortions of the faith's theological and political character" (p. 4). During interdenominational Christian violence in Europe in the early modern times, Muslims were chosen as a test case for the delineation of theoretical boundaries of Christian believers. Islam and fictional "oriental" figures such as Turks, Persians, and Arabs were used by the Europeans and Americans as vehicles to criticize falsehood and intolerances of other Christian denominations. Also, several books were published on fictional Muslim converts to Christianity in order to prove the veracity of Christianity over Islam. Islam and Muslims were debated in relation to how, and why not, to construct a society or religion with Muslims.

In fact, Islam and Muslims have been part of American history since the arrival of Europeans to the New World, but they almost always lived at the margins of the society and did not play prominent roles in the early colonies. Rumours suggested that Moriscos (forced Spanish Muslim converts to Christianity) and Marranos (forced Spanish Jewish converts to Christianity) were on board Christopher Columbus' ship during his accidental Atlantic crossing. It is estimated that between 15 and 20 percent of the African slaves brought to the Americas were of Muslim origin. Historical records indicate that New York/Manhattan had some European-origin-free Muslim residents since the mid-17th century. For example, Anthony Jansen van Salee (1607–1676), the son of Dutch convert to Islam Jan Janszoon van Haarlem (aka Murad Reis), was one of the most famous Muslims who settled in Manhattan in the 1630s, living there until his death. Known as the "Troublesome Turk," this rich and powerful creditor and real estate mogul was perhaps the first free American Muslim and was reported to have carried a Qur'an under his arm at all times (Hershkowitz, 1965). Marrying his children to the elite of Manhattan, Anthony became the great-grandparent of some prominent Americans, such as Cornelius Vanderbilt (1794–1877) and President Warren G. Harding (1865–1923) (Hershkowitz, 1965).

Until the nineteenth century, for the majority of Americans, the main sources of knowledge concerning Islam, Muslims, Turks, and the Middle East were religious texts, sermons, and rich, imaginative literature about the "orient" and "oriental" people. For example, *A Thousand and One Arabian Nights* was one of the most widely read texts in early modern America. As noted by McCarthy (2010):

> The Early American geography and history texts devoted very little attention to the Ottoman Empire and Islam beyond a few pages of insults and questionable history. ... These books gave often more space to camels than the Ottoman government. They usually dedicated a paragraph or two to the present government in which the words "cruel," "despotic," "arbitrary," and "brutal" featured prominently.
>
> (pp. 13–14)

As stated by Allison (2012), eighteenth-century American and European literature made the Muslim world a counterpoint to the idea of individual autonomy. In that period, wrapped in such heavy biases, American intellectuals and the public kept referring to the land of Muslims (North Africa and Near East) as the lands of "barbary," "tyrants," "exotics," and "heathens."

While the popular knowledge was shaped by imaginary literature, religious masses were exposed to Islam through religious texts and sermons that portrayed Muhammad as an impostor and evil and Islam as the religion of the devil. Despite the fact that the clergy class was the most educated segment of the society, their knowledge about Islam, Muslims, and Turks was quite limited. To these Protestant and evangelical masses, there was not much difference between Turks, Jews, papists, and heathens; in particular, Muslims and Turks were the universal bad example (McCarthy, 2010). They were either agents of the Antichrists or the Antichrist himself (McCarthy, 2010). These were the legacies of the European reformers from the sixteenth and seventeenth centuries, who defined the Antichrist in terms of Islam and Muhammad (Spellberg, 2014).

For example, American Puritan minister Cotton Mather (1663–1728) contrasted the liberty of Americans with the tyranny of Muslim societies. He asserted that heaven shone on "Our parts of the Earth" in allowing "Improvement of our modern Philosophy," while no followers of the "thick-skull'd Prophet" were permitted to question the scientific truths revealed to Muhammad (Allison, 2012, p. 317). An evangelical Baptist spokesperson denounced Muhammad as a "hateful" figure who spreads his religion with force of sword. For a Presbyterian preacher from South Carolina, "religion of Mahomet originated in arms, breathes nothing but arms, is propagated by arms" (Hutson, 2002, para. 6). According to Reverend George Bush (1796–1859), who wrote the first American biography of Muhammad, *The Life of Muhammad*, Muhammad was an impostor and "fanaticism, ambition and lust were his master passion" (McCarthy, 2010, p. 15). Bush's book on Muhammad was printed in America in 1830 and reprinted many times in the following years. Most of the school textbooks that educated masses of the time condoned the negative portrayal of Turks, Muslims, and Islam.

However, as argued earlier, there were some exceptions to this standard negative view of the Muslims in early modern America. For example, the Yale College president cited a study claiming that "Mohammadan" morals were superior to Christians (Hutson, 2002). In his book on Muhammad, Washington Irving (1783–1859) portrayed him as a good man who tried to reform the corrupt religion of his followers (McCarthy, 2010). Likewise, Samuel Goodrich (1779–1860), one of the most prolific American writers of the time, whose books on literature, geography, history, and religion were used in American schools, gave accounts of the Turks whereby they were even praised for their tolerance toward Christians (McCarthy, 2010). John Leland (1776–1841), a Baptist minister and champion of religious freedom and staunch ally of Jefferson, supported Muslim rights in his sermons and editorials published from 1790 until the end of his life. His principled support for the Muslims, like the views of other founding fathers, was mostly based on imaginary rather than real people (Spellberg, 2014). Leland's view on liberty and toleration is quite remarkable and surely way ahead of his time:

> The liberty I contend for is more than toleration. The very idea of toleration is despicable, it supposes that some have a pre-eminence above the rest, to grant indulgence, whereas, all should be equally free, Jews, Turks, Pagans and Christians. Test oaths and established creeds, should be avoided as the worst of evil.
>
> (As cited in Spellberg, 2014, p. 240)

Opinions of the American founding fathers constitute another exception to the standard negative American view on Islam and Muslims. One of the major themes for the founding fathers was whether to build an exclusively Protestant nation or a religiously plural state and society. In particular, George Washington, Thomas Jefferson, and John Adams were keen on the issues of citizenship and diversity. Their interest in Islam was not about it as a religion *per se*, but rather about "imaginary," and most probably "white," Muslims, who could be the future American citizens (Spellberg, 2014, p. 8).

In his *Autobiography*, Benjamin Franklin (1706–1790) relates that the English evangelical Rev. George Whitefield, having come to Philadelphia in 1739, was not allowed to preach in any of the churches. He proposed to build a place where everyone could gather and preach their faith and convictions. In this, one of the earliest American pluralistic, inclusivist, and somewhat secular documents, Franklin does not see any problem with including the Muslims in his imagined American society:

> It being found inconvenient to assemble in the open air, subject to its inclemency, the Building of a House to meet in was no sooner propos'd and Persons appointed to receive Contributions, but sufficient Sums were soon receiv'd to procure the Ground and erect the Building, which was 100 feet long and 70 broad, about the Size of Westminster Hall, and the Work was carried on with such Spirit as to be finished in a much shorter time than could have been expected. Both House and Ground were vested in Trustees, expressly for the use of any preacher of any religious Persuasion who might desire to say something to the People of Philadelphia, the Design [purpose] in building not being to accommodate any particular Sect, but the Inhabitants in general, so that even if the Mufti of Constantinople were to send a Missionary to preach Mahometanism [Islam] to us, he would find a Pulpit at his Service.
>
> (As cited in Metaxas, 2016, pp. 75–76)

In 1784, George Washington (1732–1799) wrote a letter to a friend, looking for a carpenter and bricklayer for his home: "If they are good workmen, they may be of Asia, Africa, or Europe. They may be Mahometans [Muslims], Jews or Christian of an[y] Sect, or they may be Atheists" (as cited in Spellberg, 2014, p. 5). Theoretically, Muslims could be part of a religiously free society. However, it would be hard to imagine that the founding fathers were visualizing a large free Muslim population in the country.

Thomas Jefferson (1743–1826), the principal author of the Declaration of Independence (1776) and third president of the United States (1801–1809), developed an even keener and somewhat positive interest in Islam and the Near East. His interest in Islam and Muslims began with his purchase of a Qur'an 11 years before the Declaration of Independence (Spellberg, 2014). A philosopher hero of Jefferson's was John Locke, who, in his seminal "Letter on Toleration" (1689), insists that Muslims and all others who believed in God be tolerated in England. Campaigning for religious freedom in Virginia, Jefferson followed Locke, demanding recognition of the religious rights of the "Mahamedan, the Jew and the pagan." He said, "Neither Pagan nor Mahamedan [Muslim] nor Jew ought to be excluded from the civil rights of the

Commonwealth because of his religion" (Jefferson, as cited in Spellberg, 2014, p. 3). As stressed by Spellberg (2014):

> Even earlier in his political life – as an ambassador, secretary of state, and vice president – Jefferson had never perceived a predominantly religious dimension to the conflict with North African Muslim powers, whose pirates threatened American shipping in the Mediterranean and eastern Atlantic.
>
> (p. 8)

Jefferson would insist to the rulers of Tripoli and Tunis that his nation harbored no anti-Islamic bias (Spellberg, 2014). In the Treaty of Tripoli in 1797, the American state explicitly announced that the United States of America was not founded on Christian religion and had no enmity against Islam as a religion:

> As the Government of the United States of America is not in any sense founded on the Christian religion; as it has in itself no character of enmity against the laws, religion, or tranquility, of Musselmen; and as the said States never have entered into any war or act of hostility against any Mehomitan nation, it is declared by the parties that no pretext arising from religious opinions shall ever produce an interruption of the harmony existing between the two countries.
>
> (Spellberg, 2014, p. 207)

From imagined to real Muslims: Merchants, missionaries, and diplomats

By the turn of the nineteenth century, the American perception of the Middle East began to change, with the increasing trade volume in the Mediterranean port cities and introduction of the missionaries to the Middle East.

The merchants were perhaps the first Americans who had direct encounters with the North Africans and Middle Easterners. Their ships had business ventures in the Mediterranean, first under the British flags and then under their own flags during the American conflict with the Barbary States, which lasted from the 1780s to the 1810s. The Barbary States were Tunis, Algiers, and Tripoli, all of which were semi-independent Ottoman territories by then. In the 18th and 19th centuries, the Barbary corsairs (also called Ottoman corsairs or Berber pirates) were attacking all the merchant ships, including the American ships, pillaging cargoes or asking them for tribute for their passage. They were capturing those who refused to pay for passage and holding them for ransom. While the Federalist President John Adams supported the idea of negotiation with the Barbary rulers, Vice President Jefferson was of the opinion that thorough measures should be taken against the pirates, showing the American prowess to them and also to the Europeans. John Adams' insistence won the day, and the American government and the Barbary rulers signed a treaty in London in 1797. The treaty did not end the conflict conclusively. Upon the capture of some more Americans, President Thomas Jefferson refused to pay tribute or ransom. Instead he chose to bombard various pirate cities along the coast in 1801. With the order of President Jefferson, the American navy, that was in the making, fought its first foreign war, which lasted until 1805. Although unsuccessful at first, these military campaigns ultimately secured concessions of passage from the Barbary rulers after the second Barbary war in 1815, led by the fourth American President James Madison (1751–1836) (Fremont-Barnes, 2006).

The turning point in the American interest in the Middle East came when the American missionaries developed a keen interest into the region. This missionary turn became instrumental in shaping American perception and foreign policy toward the Middle East almost until WWII (Sisman, 2015).[1]

Writing in 1929, Edward Mead Earle, an American diplomat and scholar, opens his article with a striking remark about American missionary activities in the Middle East:

> No other American activity in the Near East has been of such extent and consequence as Christian missions. No other has been so long and so earnestly supported by so numerous and so influential a constituency at home. No other has made such persistent claims upon Christian Americans for financial assistance and upon the Government of the United States for diplomatic support.
>
> (Earle, 1929, p. 398)

Once missionary activities in the Middle East are examined, it becomes clear that Earle's statement was not an exaggeration. For example, an Ottoman minister of education, Zuhdu Pasha, reports in a somewhat alarmed tone that hundreds of missionary schools, including 400 Protestant ones, had been operating in different parts of the empire in the 1880s (Cetin, 1980). Next to schools, dozens of missionary-run hospitals, orphanages, and printing presses had been active all over the empire, carrying Western material and spiritual values to the Ottoman society.

For revivalist Protestants, the late eighteenth and early nineteenth centuries were particularly important, because they thought that they were living at the "dawn of the millennium" and tried hard to accelerate the dawning of the new age. In earlier times, most of the missionary zeal was concentrated on conquering the Holy Land and Zion since, from Zion, the Kingdom of God would have spread over the earth (Kieser, 2010). Over time, however, missionaries gradually shifted their attention towards other parts of the world, including China, India, and the rest of the Ottoman Empire.

Especially stimulated by the American revivalist and millennial movements often described as Great Awakenings (1790–1840), members of dozens of different missionary organizations set out to evangelize the whole world. In the Ottoman Empire and the Eastern Mediterranean, the Boston-based

American Board of Commissioners for Foreign Missions (ABCFM), established in 1810, was the largest and most impactful missionary organization. Next to ABCFM, the American Presbyterian missionary organizations were laboring mainly in Syria, Lebanon, and Egypt, carrying American religious and imperial interests to the region.

The ABCFM's early missions were directed towards the American Indians, China, India, and Ceylon, but soon they shifted their interests towards the politically and economically challenged Ottoman Empire. As mentioned earlier, American missionaries came to the empire with certain preconceived ideas. In the millennial narratives in the early American Protestant imagination, powerful Ottoman armies were identified as apocalyptic forces of destruction, threatening Europe and the American evangelical way of life. The creation of these images was primarily the work of pre-millenarian Calvinist preachers and missionaries, who believed that they needed to do something to change the world before the Second Coming of the Christ.

John Calvin (1509–1564) identified the Antichrist in terms of Islam, but he assigned Muhammad rather than the Ottoman Sultan as the pope's evil partner in the "two horns of the Antichrist" (Spellberg, 2014, pp. 16–17). Because of that, Calvinist theology was by far the most influential on North American Protestant imaginations (Spellberg, 2014).

While China, India, and Africa were perhaps more promising in terms of the number of potential converts, the Holy Land was the most emotionally and symbolically important place for the missionaries. Jewish restoration in the Holy Land had been an integral part of Protestant millenarian thought since the 15th century. This legacy was reinterpreted within the American "Awakenings" framework and paved the way for increasing missionary activities towards the Jews and the Holy Land in the 19th century (Sarna, 1980, 1987). In those years, several fictional Jewish and Muslim first-person conversion narratives were published and republished in England and the United States in order to increase the missionary appetite and herald the coming of the millennial age. For example, *The Converted Jew, or, Memoirs of the Life of Joseph Samuel C. F. Frey* (Frey, 1815) and *The Conversion of a Mehometan, to the Christian religion, described in a letter from Gaifer, in England, to Aly-Ben-Hayton, his friend in Turkey* (Edwards, 1775) are just a few of those fictional narratives that were printed numerous times in the United States.

Pliny Fisk and Levy Parsons were the first ABCFM missionaries to be assigned to preparing the Holy Land for the Second Coming. In 1819, they sailed from Boston via Malta to Izmir, from where they traveled to Greece, Egypt, Palestine, and Syria. Without having accomplished much success, Parsons died in 1822 in Alexandria and Fisk in 1825 in Beirut, both as a result of fever. This fragile beginning did not dishearten the ABCFM administration. On the contrary, with the help of British missionary organizations, the ABCFM established a very effective network in the empire in the coming decades. William Goodell (1792–1867, missionary to the Armenians), Jonas

King (1792–1869, missionary to the Greeks), Elias Riggs (1810–1901, missionary to Greeks, Armenians, and Bulgarians), Daniel Bliss (1823–1916, missionary to Syria and founder of the American University of Beirut), William Schauffler (1798–1884, missionary to the Jews), and Cyrus Hamlin (1811–1900, founder and first president of Robert College) were perhaps the most important missionaries, each of whom learned local languages and labored in the empire for an average of 45 years. Unlike merchants and diplomats, these people lived in the empire, learned the language, culture, and history of the local people, and wrote extensive letters, reports, and books about them.

During their tenures, missionaries had constant communication with their headquarters. *Annual Reports* and the *Missionary Herald* published summaries of thousands of missionary reports and letters coming from all corners of the world. The main audience for these publications was missionaries at home and abroad. However, researchers, politicians, travelers, consuls, and businessmen were also regular readers of these summaries.

The missionary activities did not go without resistance, however. According to the Ottoman legal system, while the missionaries could not work among the Muslims, there was no legal barrier for them to work among the other religious minorities. But working among the minorities was not an easy task either. The Syrian, Greek, Rum, and Jewish religious authorities soon recognized missionary activities as a form of "cultural imperialism" and a threat to their traditions and sacred language. In a letter dated April 28, 1849, one of the missionaries, E. Maynard, mentions the indigenous resistance toward them but was still hopeful that "the day was not distant" (American Board of Commissioners for Foreign Missions, 1849, p. 102). Indeed, in the minds of the missionaries, Judaism, Oriental Christianity, and Islam were all examples of spiritual corruption that had to be eliminated.

Efforts to convert Jews by the Syrian and Greek Christians yielded only a handful of converts. In response to these multilayered challenges, the ABCFM abandoned its mission to the Greek Orthodox and Jews in the 1850s. It would have been more meaningful to channel all of their resources and energy to evangelizing the Eastern nominal Christians, which included the Armenians, Nestorians, Maronites, and Copts. Soon thereafter, however, they understood that converting the nominal Christians was not as easy as they had anticipated. With the exception of Armenians, they either abandoned or decreased the intensity of missions or switched their emphasis from converting local people to educating them. The first American colleges, such as Robert College and the American University of Beirut, were founded in the 1860s as a result of these changing priorities.

During this time period, corresponding to the American Antebellum period (1812–1861) and the Ottoman Tanzimat era (1839–1876), there were relatively peaceful relations between the American government, missionaries, and the Ottoman state and society. For example, in 1830, the United States and the Ottoman Empire signed a treaty, marking a historic turning point in the relationship between the two countries. David Porter was appointed as the first American consul to the Ottoman Porte in 1831. For the Ottomans, the United States was seen as a new economic, political, and military ally against the encroaching European colonialism and Russian expansionism. Although not ratified by the American Congress, one of the secret articles of the treaty was to build battleships for the Ottoman navy. In return, the treaty gave great privileges to the Americans, who wanted to open up embassies, engage in trade, and travel in the empire. This created a very favorable atmosphere for the American missionaries, who wanted to increase their activities.

During the Tanzimat era, the Ottoman Empire was in transition, literally reinventing itself as a modern state. The spirit of Ottoman economic, political, cultural, and legal reforms with regards to the Muslims and non-Muslims began to take root. For the first time in Islamic history, Muslims and non-Muslims were considered equal before the Islamic law. With the intense efforts of the British Ambassadors Stratford Canning and Lord Cowley, and heavy British and American diplomatic pressures on the Porte, Sultan Abdulmejid issued an imperial order (*irade*) on November 15, 1847, securing an official recognition of the Protestants as a separate religious minority, or *millet*. The decree was immediately translated and sent to the Protestant missionary headquarters, where it was met with great joy. It guaranteed that no one could interfere with Protestant prayers, churches, or graveyards or their religious and worldly affairs. This development was perceived as a threat by the other traditional Ottoman *millets* (Greeks, Orthodox, Armenians, and Catholics), as the Protestants had been trying to evangelize all the Eastern nominal Christians. The heads of the other churches tried everything possible, including violence, to stop the missionary activities, but to no avail.

Witnessing those days, Cyrus Hamlin (1878) wrote that the Tanzimat reforms were surprising and even shocking to some traditionalist Muslims, but represented the beginning of a new age for Christian subjects. Somewhat exaggeratedly, he also wrote: "You can anywhere converse with Mohammedans on religious matters, with a freedom impossible thirty years ago. Moslems treat Christians with a respect [he] never did before" (Hamlin, 1878, p. 320). In the classical Ottoman legal *dhimmi* framework, there was no legal regulation that allowed Ottoman authorities to interfere with missionary activities. As citizens of the most favored Western countries, missionaries were protected by the age-old Capitulation rights. They were free to exercise their activities under Ottoman protection as long as they did not labor among Muslims or own property. In 1867, when foreigners were allowed to own land in the empire, missionary organizations purchased properties in many cities and built missionary stations, schools, orphanages, and hospitals. Alongside Istanbul, other major missionary stations were established in Trabzon (1835), Erzurum (1839), Aintab (1849), Adana, Aleppo, Tarsus, Hadjin, Alexandretta, Kilis, Salonica (1850), Marash (1855), and Izmir (1859) (Erhan, 2001).

These economic and political developments created very positive sentiments among the American public towards the Ottomans. And the negative images about the Turks and Muslims began to soften after these direct encounters. For example, Pliny Fisk and Levy Parsons state that Muslims do not "induce others to embrace" their faith and respect Christian missionaries:

> As to any molestation from government, we feel almost as safe as we should in Boston. … We hear of no instance in which Turks have molested a Christian merely on account of his religion. There is reason to believe, that American missionaries will enjoy as much safety as merchants and other Christians who reside here and think of no danger.
>
> (Parsons & Fisk, 1820, p. 267)

Like Fisk and Parsons, others such as William Thomson praised Muslim ruler Muhammad Ali of Egypt and appreciated Muslim spirituality. These positive assessments were reflected even in the American religious texts. For example, the understanding that "Muhammad was the incarnation of evil" was moderated by the end of the nineteenth century, when he was seen as someone who was in error but not necessarily evil (McCarthy, 2010, p. 38).

From "heathen" to "cruel" Turks

Although the American mission failed from a conversionist point of view, it was, in a way, successful in that it contributed to the transformation and modernization of the Ottoman communities (Sisman, 2015). Through their publications, schools, hospitals, and orphanages, they began to leave deep impacts on local people, especially on Armenians. Their activities became the source of modernization and the rise of nationalism among the religious and ethnic minorities. And this very development was alarming for the Ottoman authorities, who began to take some measures against the missionary activities. In the larger scale of things, while the Americans had been struggling to recover from the impact of the Civil War, the Ottomans had been struggling to keep its integrity against the external colonial encroachments to its borders and internal nationalistic and separatist rebellions.

By the 1870s, the Ottoman authorities began to monitor the missionary activities more closely and wanted to curb their impact on the Ottoman religious and ethnic minorities. This created a major tension between the Ottoman government and the missionaries. As already discussed, no regulation existed in the classical Ottoman legal *dhimmi* framework that would allow Ottoman authorities to interfere with missionary activities. As long as they did not labor among Muslims or attempt to own property, missionaries were free to exercise their activities under Ottoman protection. In 1867, missionary organizations purchased properties in many cities and built schools, orphanages, and hospitals (Erhan, 2001). In the 1870s, the Ottoman authorities passed a law regulating missionary activities such as street preaching and missionary publications (Erhan, 2001).

Missionary schools, which were established by different Christian denominations and countries, created a new sphere of conflict among the superpowers with regards to their ambition for the Ottoman Empire and its Christian population (Erhan, 2001). All of these developments were quite alarming for the Ottoman authorities. As Erhan (2001) states,

> If the role of graduates from American colleges in the rise of Bulgarian, Armenian and Albanian nationalism in the last quarter of the nineteenth century is taken into consideration, one might understand the sensitivity of the Sublime Porte [towards the missionaries].
>
> (Para. 30)

For example, Sultan Abdulhamit II (r. 1876–1908) was quite keen on the issues of foreign intervention, missionaries, and missionary schools. He tried his best to cut all kinds of external support including the missionary support to the Ottoman non-Muslims. Expectedly, his resolute policies further radicalized the missionaries' growing negative perception of the sultan and the Ottoman Empire.

The major turning point in the changing American perception from bad to worse was the Ottoman–Armenian conflict, which led to Armenian rebellions, massacres, and intercommunal violence in the Eastern Anatolia in the 1890s. Until then, the American missionaries had been laboring heavily among the Armenians and played pivotal roles in heightening nationalistic and religious sentiments among them. In these chaotic years, the American colleges in Merzifon, Harput, and Marash and the houses of some American missionaries were greatly damaged by the Ottoman armies. In the meantime, some Armenian teachers were arrested under accusation of helping the rebels (Erhan, 2001). In February 1895, American missionaries in Bitlis informed American emissary Terrell that their lives were in danger (Erhan, 2001). The American Consul of Beirut, Mr. Gibson, reported that many American citizens were attacked in Maras, Hacin, Antep, and Urfa. Later, the Washington Embassy informed Istanbul that American schools in Maras and Harput were looted and their churches were arsoned.

These events furthered the tension between the Ottoman and American governments. American missionaries wanted the Ottoman government to pay an indemnity of 100,000 dollars for some of their damages. But the Ottoman government did not accept responsibility for the damage and refused to pay an indemnity. In order to resolve the issue, American President Grover Cleveland decided to send three battleships to the Ottoman shores as a deterrent force. The problem of indemnity remained unresolved until 1901, when an American cruiser was sent to the harbor in Izmir with orders to force the Ottomans to pay. Eventually the Ottoman government paid off the indemnity. When, in 1904, the Ottoman authorities closed some American schools and arrested some Armenians who were naturalized United States citizens, President Theodore Roosevelt sent another powerful fleet to the Izmir harbor. As a result, Armenians were released and the schools were reopened (Erhan, 2001). All of these incidents contributed to the already deteriorating American image of the Turks and the Middle Easterners. Although the Ottoman attitude towards the missionary activities became more tolerant after the deposition of the Abdulhamit II, that did not significantly change American attitude towards the Ottoman Empire, as the current events were paving the way to World War I when the Ottoman–Armenian conflict reached its apex.

By the end of the nineteenth century, except for a few examples, such as the case of Alexander Russell Webb, who converted to Islam, the dominant American feeling about the Middle Easterners was negativity. Webb traveled to Istanbul on special invitation from Abdulhamit II, who granted him the honorific title *Bey*. He was then appointed as the Honorary Ottoman Council General to New York.

When the Ottoman–Armenian conflict began in the 1890s, the American newspaper articles and missionary reports were filled with news about Turkish cruelties and Christian casualties. There was almost no mention of Turkish casualties in these news reports. A cursory look at the titles of some of the newspaper articles by the turn of the nineteenth century would demonstrate the establishment of the lasting negative image of Turks and Middle Easterners among the American public: from the *New York Times* – "Cruelty of the turks. Prof. Bryce describes the condition of Armenia" (1890), "Massacre of Armenians: Equals the Bulgarian butcheries which led to war. Over six thousand murdered" (1894), "The worst was not told; Armenian massacres described by the Rev. George H. Filian" (1895); from the *San Francisco Call* – "Shocking crimes of the terrible Turk" (1895); and from the *St. Louis Republic* – "Turkish policy is cruelty. Extermination of His Christian Subjects the Sultan's Deliberately Chosen Way of Settling Troubles" (1904). One could see the perpetuation of similar images about the Turks during the coming years, culminating in WWI when the American missionaries and diplomats had been extensively reporting to the American public about the 1915 Armenian affairs. As McCarthy (2010) asserts, American prejudices were to have a great impact on the Armenian-Turkish conflict of the 1890s and World War I. After World War I, the image of the terrible and cruel Turks was decisively established among the American public, as reflected in a 1920 newspaper article in *The Washington Times*: "How science cleansed her of the cruel Turk's brand of shame." The American image of the Turks and Turkey began to change slowly only during the Cold War era, when Turkey became an indispensable ally of the West against the real and imagined communist threats.

As stated earlier, the reports of missionaries and diplomats on the events in the Ottoman Empire and the then modern Middle Eastern states were the main source of the American perception of the Middle East. Missionaries may have assumed that they were delivering a message in a one-way stream of transmission, but a close study of their history shows that missionaries and missions came out transformed by their encounters with the local people. The missionary impact was reciprocal (Dogan & Sharkey, 2011). Religious, social, economic, and geographical studies by missionaries contributed not only to the modernization of the local people, but also to the shaping of the modern

West, especially the American perception of the Middle East. Kieser (2010) rightly maintains that long before oil interests, millennialism shaped American interaction with the region. Likewise, Makdisi states that the missionary experience was a "foundational encounter between Americans and Arabs" (2008, p. 1). Protestant missionaries outnumbered any other group of Americans in non-Western lands and accounted for the great preponderance of American thought about Asia and Africa prior to World War II. Bulliet (2004) argues that these Protestant missionaries harbored an ill-disguised contempt for Islam that shaped contemporary debates about Islam and the West.

As a result of these historical encounters and experiences over a century, the American image of the Turks (read Middle Easterners) changed over time from religiously constructed "heathen" Turks to historically grounded "cruel" Turks. While missionaries' religious and social labours contributed to the transforming of local people there, the experience and knowledge they gained from local people influenced the perception in the modern West, especially that of Americans, vis-à-vis the Middle East.

Note

1 For an extensive summary of the missionary interest in the Ottoman lands, see Sisman (2015). The summary in this chapter of the missionary history in the empire is mainly taken from this work.

References

Allison, R. (2012). Americans and the Muslim world: First encounters. In D. Lesch and M. Haas (Eds.), *The Middle East and the United States: History, Politics, and Ideologies* (pp. 315–317). Boulder, CO: Westview.

American Board of Commissioners for Foreign Missions. (1849). *40th Annual Report of the ABCFM*. Boston, MA: Press of Tr. Marvin.

Bulliet, R. (2004). *The Case for Islamo-Christian Civilization*. New York: Columbia University Press.

Cetin, A. (1980). Maarif Nazırı Ahmet Zühtü Paşa'nın Osmanlı İmparatorluğu'ndaki yabancı okullarla ilgili raporu. *Güney-doğu Avrupa Araştırmaları Dergisi*, 8–9, 189–219.

Dogan, M. and Sharkey, H. (Eds.) (2011). *American Missionaries and the Middle East: Foundational Encounters*. Salt Lake City, UT: Utah University Press.

Earle, E. (1929). American mission in the Near East. *Foreign Affairs*, 7, 398–417. doi:10.2307/20028702.

Edwards, J. (1775). *The Conversion of a Mehometan to the Christian Religion, Described in a Letter from Gaifer, in England, to Aly-Ben-Hayton, his Friend in Turkey*. New London, CT: T. Green.

Erhan, C. (2001). Ottoman official attitudes towards American missionaries. In A. Amanat and M.T. Bernhardsson (Eds.), *The United States and the Middle East: Cultural Encounters* (pp. 315–341). New Haven, CT: Yale University Press.

Fremont-Barnes, G. (2006). *The Wars of the Barbary Pirates: To the Shores of Tripoli: The Rise of the US Navy and Marines*. New York: Osprey.

Frey, S.C.F. (1815). *The Converted Jew, or, Memoirs of the Life of Joseph Samuel C. F. Frey.* Boston, MA: Samuel T. Armstrong.

Hamlin, C. (1878). *Among the Turks.* New York: Robert Carter & Brothers.

Hershkowitz, L. (1965). The troublesome Turk: An illustration of judicial process in New Amsterdam. *New York History*, 46(4), 299–310.

Hutson, J.H. (2002). The founding fathers and Islam: Library papers show early tolerance for Muslim faith. *Library of Congress Information Bulletin*, 61(5). Retrieved from https://www.loc.gov/loc/lcib/0205/tolerance.html.

Kieser, H.-L. (2010). *Nearest East: American Millenialism and Mission to the Middle East.* Philadelphia, PA: Temple University Press.

Makdisi, U. (2008). *Artillery of Heaven: American Missionaries and the Failed Conversion of the Middle East.* Ithaca, NY: Cornell University Press.

McCarthy, J. (2010). *The Turk in America: The Creation of an Enduring Prejudice.* Salt Lake City, UT: University of Utah Press.

Metaxas, E. (2016). *If You Can Keep It: The Forgotten Promise of American Liberty.* New York: Viking.

New York Times. (1890, November 6). Cruelty of the Turks, Prof. Bryce describes the condition of Armenia. Retrieved from http://query.nytimes.com/mem/archive-free/pdf?res=9A04E2D9113BE533A25755C0A9679D94619ED7CF.

New York Times. (1894, November 17). Massacre of Armenians: Equals the Bulgarian butcheries which led to war. Over six thousand murdered. Retrieved from http://query.nytimes.com/mem/archive-free/pdf?res=9D01E6D61131E033A25754C1A9679D94659ED7CF.

New York Times. (1895, January 14). The worst was not told; Armenian massacres described by the Rev. George H. Filian. Retrieved from http://query.nytimes.com/mem/archive-free/pdf?res=9800E4DC123DE433A25757C1A9679C94649ED7CF.

Oren, M.B. (2008). *Power, Faith, and Fantasy: America in the Middle East: 1776 to the Present.* New York: W. W. Norton.

Parsons, L. and Fisk, P. (1820). Letter of the Rev. Messrs. Fisk and Parsons to the corresponding secretary of the A.B.C.F.M. *Missionary Herald*, 16, 265–267.

San Francisco Call. (1895, November 19). Shocking crimes of the terrible Turk. Retrieved from http://chroniclingamerica.loc.gov/lccn/sn85066387/1895-11-19/ed-1/seq-9.pdf.

Sarna, J.D. (1980). The freethinker, the Jews, and the missionaries: George Houston and the mystery of Israel vindicated. *AJS Review*, 5, 101–114. doi:10.1017/s0364009400011879.

Sarna, J. (1987). The impact of nineteenth century Christian mission on Jewish community. In Todd Edelmann (Ed.), *Jewish Apostasy in the Modern World* (pp. 232–254). New York: Holmes & Meier.

Sisman, C. (2015). Failed proselytizers or modernizers? Protestant missionaries among the Jews and Sabbatians/Donmes in the nineteenth-century Ottoman Empire. *Middle Eastern Studies*, 51(6), 932–949. doi:10.1080/00263206.2015.1044526.

Spellberg, D.A. (2014). *Thomas Jefferson's Qur'an: Islam and the Founders.* New York: Vintage.

St. Louis Republic. (1904, May 9). Turkish policy is cruelty. Extermination of his Christian subjects the Sultan's deliberately chosen way of settling troubles. Retrieved from http://chroniclingamerica.loc.gov/lccn/sn84020274/1904-05-09/ed-1/seq-2.pdf.

Washington Times. (1920, September 5). How science cleansed her of the cruel Turk's brand of shame. Retrieved from http://chroniclingamerica.loc.gov/lccn/sn84026749/1920-09-05/ed-1/seq-23.pdf.

2   How big tobacco used Islam and modernity to conquer Saudi Arabia

Sean Foley

In 1986, Walter Thoma, a senior executive at Philip Morris (PM), briefed the company's board of directors about cigarette sales in Saudi Arabia, one of the company's most unlikely but most profitable markets in the world. Over the previous decade, PM had taken advantage of the tripling in size of the Saudi cigarette market during the oil boom, overcoming a government ban on cigarette advertising and the opposition of senior religious leaders, who labeled smoking *ḥaram* (forbidden) under Islamic law. Between 1975 and 1986 alone, the company increased the volume of its sales in Saudi Arabia sevenfold and increased its operating revenues from less than $1 million to $65 million (Thoma, 1986). During the same time period, PM nearly doubled its share of the Saudi market from 18 percent to 32.3 percent (Thoma, 1986).

However, Thoma warned that the company's profitable operations in the Kingdom were now in danger. The cigarette industry had lost significant volume in the late 1980s: Saudis' disposable incomes had evaporated and thousands of foreign laborers returned home as the economy contracted following the crash in the global oil market. The Saudi government, which earned much of its income from oil revenues, saw cigarettes as a new source of income. Riyadh had already increased its tariffs on imported cigarettes, forcing PM to raise prices by 18 percent to protect its margins (Thoma, 1986). In addition, Saudi health officials were renewing their drive to place health warnings on cigarettes (Thoma, 1986).

Thoma (1986) assured the board that the company had mounted a ferocious lobbying campaign to oppose these measures, building on contacts in the oil industry and the government of Saudi Arabia. Company executives had also enlisted the help of Vice President George W. Bush, who was then visiting Saudi Arabia, and other senior US officials to personally lobby King Fahd to reduce the new tariffs and not to accept the proposal to put health labels on cigarettes. In addition to these measures, the company was seeking to improve its market share and volume once Saudi Arabia's economy rebounded. Company officials had already dispatched teams of employees to work with distributors to improve efficiency and to refine PM's understanding of the market and its customers. Thoma (1986) concluded with an upbeat message about Saudi Arabia and the company's future: "I remain optimistic that

Philip Morris International will continue to earn a substantial proportion of its operating income in Saudi Arabia" (Thoma, 1986, p. 10).

More than a quarter century after Thoma gave his 1986 report, the Kingdom is one of the largest importers of cigarettes in the world (Kochhar, 2016); Saudis consume billions of cigarettes annually, a market worth $1.5 billion (Qusti, 2007). Despite higher tariffs and new restrictions on where Saudis can smoke in public, more Saudis are likely to smoke in the future since a third of the population is aged 14 or younger (Glum, 2015) – the age cohort that is most likely to produce new smokers ("Study: Teens most vulnerable to smoking," 2004). In fact, both the World Health Organization and the Saudi Diabetes and Endocrine Association have warned that the number of smokers will likely double from 5 million in 2015 to 10 million by 2020 ("10 million Saudi smokers by 2020," 2013).

Drawing on archival and field research conducted in America and in Saudi Arabia from 2013 to 2016, this chapter sheds light on the failure of the Saudi state and religious elites to deter the concerted campaign by multinational tobacco companies to make Saudis smokers. It argues that the rise of the new class of Saudi smokers reflects the nexus of four social factors: (a) a pragmatic tradition of informally permitting smoking in private or regions outside of Riyadh, (b) an oil-driven consumer spending boom in the 1970s, (c) a series of mass marketing campaigns that linked smoking to American freedom and modernity and Islam, and (d) a vision of society that highlights the Qur'an and the *hadith* over all other sources of revelation and Islamic law. These campaigns built on the tobacco industry's record of conducting detailed exhaustive surveys of smokers, overcoming social or religious impediments to smoking, and opening profitable new markets. Notably, while many Western social scientists highlighted the role of oil, autocracy, or religion in Saudi life (Haykel, Hegghammer, & Lacroix, 2015), researchers working for PM and other companies stressed a different set of factors as shaping politics and society; namely, dualism and the coexistence of what Westerners would perceive as oppositional or mutually exclusive forces.

Ultimately, this chapter sheds new light on the history and politics of the late 1970s and the early 1980s, an era widely seen as dominated in Saudi Arabia by the Kingdom's religious leaders, especially after the seizure of the Ka'aba in 1979. It also highlights the importance of smoking, a rarely discussed but critical aspect of contemporary Saudi society, and the history of America's special relationship with Saudi Arabia (Cooperman & Shechter, 2008). These issues are important today as Saudi political and religious leaders again seek to curb smoking in order to both improve public health and blunt the appeal of the Islamic State (ISIS), which has destroyed cigarettes and imposes draconian penalties on smokers (Hall, 2015).

"I never smoke in public and rarely do so in the presence of visitors"

For much of the 20th century, Western tobacco executives had little reason to view Saudi Arabia as a viable market. They knew that the 18th-century founder of Wahhabism, Muhammad ibn Abd al-Wahhab, had denounced smoking as *haram* and that King Abdulaziz ibn Saud denounced the "smoking of tobacco – *haram*, he said, a deadly sin which he deplored and strictly outlawed" (Lacey, 1981, p. 159). For decades, numerous Western academics had reinforced this worldview by linking Wahhabism to all forms of extremism in the Arab and Muslim worlds (Koskowski, 1955). As Princeton's John Willis once observed, the contemporary Saudi royal family in the 21st century is the logical successor to the Wahhabi worldview, including its "strict ban on the smoking of tobacco" (Willis, 2003, pp. 14–15). Indeed, Willis stated that a famous 1964 photo of King Hussein of Jordan, President Gamal Nasser, and other leading Arab leaders smoking "must have raised consternation within the house of Saud" (Willis, 2003, p. 15).

The founding King of Saudi Arabia, King Abdulaziz, reinforced this worldview. In meetings with foreign visitors, the Saudi king requested that those visitors present respect his religious views – a request that Britain's Prime Minister Winston Churchill flaunted but that US President Franklin Delano Roosevelt, a legendary chain-smoker, accepted as part of his legendary meeting aboard the USS *Quincy* in 1945 (O'Sullivan, 2012). It was also widely known that the *mutawwi'in* (singular *mutawi'*), what Westerners call the "religious police," rigorously enforced a ban on smoking in public in Jeddah, Riyadh, and other large settlements (Mouline, 2014, p. 208).

Visitors to the country and Saudis, however, understood that the rules (and practices) linked to smoking were more nuanced in the Kingdom. Cigarettes were produced in large quantities in Egypt (Schechter, 2006), a neighboring country whose ties with Saudi Arabia cannot be overstated, and tobacco was produced in commercial quantities in the neighboring Trucial Coast states (later the United Arab Emirates) (Zacharias, 2010). While foreign statesmen were asked not to smoke in their meetings with the king, it was not unusual for them to be provided cigarettes but with instructions to enjoy the gift in the privacy of their homes (Lacey, 1981). "In private," the Arab-American traveler Amin Al-Rihani noted, in the 1920s "one could smoke in Riyadh" (Rihani, 2002, p. 35). Even in the most sacrosanct neighborhoods of the Saudi capital, one was "likely to find some tobacco, hidden in the bottom of a chest" (Rihani, 2002, p. 35). In Qassim in the Najd, anyone could easily buy tobacco in private and smoke in public (Rihani, 2002). Tobacco sales were integral to the merchants of Mecca and to the taxes the Saudi state collected there – so integral that religious leaders did not object in 1925 when the king lifted a ban on tobacco in the city, which they had insisted he impose just a year earlier (Mackey, 2002). Even some of King Abdulaziz's personal bodyguards, the *Zhirt*, smoked when they were in the desert. As Rihani wrote, there was little that a pious Saudi could do in such settings except call on an individual to stop and repent:

> Once a *Zhirt* is in the open desert, he will light his pipe and raise his voice in song; and singing and smoking is banned in Najd, especially in

the new settlements, from one of which comes Nawwar. But our *Zhirt* would sing, and all that Nawwar could do was to repeat the CXII Sura of the Koran – *I fly for refuge unto God from the evil things he has created*, etc. But we saw him light a pipe as he leaped to the ground, exclaiming, "Deliver us, O God, from the devil! Deliver us, O God, from hell-fire!" Everyone laughed, but he continued to repeat the invocation.

(Rihani, 2002, pp. 210–211)

Critically, members of the *Zhirt* were not the only ones close to the Saudi king who smoked in the presence of strangers. No less a figure than Prince (and later King) Feisal – a man whose piety and aversion to alcohol and tobacco were a pillar of his public reputation – smoked (Hiro, 2013). When Edwin Plitt, an advisor to the American delegation to the United Nations, visited Feisal at the Hotel Waldorf in New York City in December 1952, the Saudi royal asked him to sit next to him and produced a package of cigarettes. Feisal then stunned the diplomat by saying, "I never smoke in public and rarely do so in the presence of visitors" (Plitt, 1952, para. 1). But Feisal, who Plitt observed was unusually agitated, went on to say that "he should like to consider him this morning as a member of my family circle and to join him in smoking for which I feel the need" (Plitt, 1952, para. 1). As the two men smoked, they had a frank but nonetheless warm discussion about regional politics (Plitt, 1952).

Feisal was hardly alone. His wife, Iffat, chain-smoked Turkish cigarettes and told the American physician Seymour Gray that she smoked "three packs a day, more or less" (Lippman, 2004, p. 261). As Gray later recalled, it would have been "useless to ask her to stop smoking" (Lippman, 2004, p. 261). Other highly educated Saudis, both royals and non-royals, also smoked. Even doctors smoked, while they advised their patients not to do so. Saudi men and women who did not smoke American or British cigarettes, which were relatively cheap at just $0.25, smoked the water pipe (*shisha*) at home or in cafés (Pace, 1971). As Rajaa al-Sanea observed in her novel, *The Girls of Riyadh*, "many Hijazi men and women" were addicted to *shisha* (Al-Sanea, 2007, p. 17). In the late 1960s, a café offering its customers water pipes opened in the Saudi capital of Riyadh, drawing fierce opposition from Saudi religious elites (Pace, 1971). It was one thing to smoke in Jeddah or a provincial city; it was something very different to smoke openly in public in the country's capital.

As religious elites sought to combat society's embrace of smoking cigarettes and *shisha*, they turned to Islamic law and *fatwā* (plural *fatāwā*) – a ruling on a given issue of Islamic law authored by a prominent cleric. These rulings, which are often presented in response to questions posed by society, are the same tools that their predecessors used to limit smoking when it was introduced to Muslims in the 16th century by European merchants operating in North Africa and West Africa (Batran, 2003). Throughout this era, leading Saudi jurists wrote a series of legal opinions that classified smoking as both *ḥarām* and *bid'a*, or a heretical practice unknown at the dawn of Islam.

Among the most important landmark opinions condemning smoking from this era is that of Abdur Rahman bin Nassir as-Sa'di against smoking. In the *fatwā*, this highly respected Wahhabi jurist from Qassim expressed his astonishment that doctors and other educated Saudis "who are intent on preserving their health" nonetheless "persist in smoking" (As-Sa'di, 2000, p. 33). In his eyes, these men, who had surrendered to their personal addictions, were far more committed to upholding "their lifestyle" (i.e., Western lifestyle) than their faith (As-Sa'di, 2000, p. 33). The Saudi jurist was especially bewildered by the Saudi doctors who smoked but also admitted that smoking was a "detriment to their health" (As-Sa'di, 2000, p. 33). While he never uses the word hypocritical in the *fatwā*, it is clear that As-Sa'di viewed any Saudi who smoked as insincere in his faith and a fraud as a Muslim.

As-Sa'di was not the only leading Saudi religious figure to condemn smoking as un-Islamic and to link it to a decadent Western lifestyle. Other religious scholars in Saudi Arabia invoked an even stronger taboo against smoking (Henderson to Bailey, 2004), especially in large public spaces, and the Saudi government imposed some of the earliest and most stringent restrictions in the world on public tobacco advertising – some imposed as early as 1971 (US Department of Health, Education, and Welfare, 1971). The punishments for breaking the laws on cigarette advertising were relatively severe; namely, "confiscation of ad material as well as possible jail sentences of two to six months" (Tobacco Institute, 1971, p. 3).

Although then Prince Fahd, the powerful interior minister and future king, backed these measures in 1971, they had little impact on Saudis. As income from oil sales rose in the 1960s and 1970s, cigarette use increased – sometimes by as much as 70 percent annually (World Health Organization, 1979). Between 1973 and 1977 alone, the number of American cigarettes consumed grew nearly threefold. While in 1962 Saudi Arabia was the fifty-second-largest market for US tobacco exports in the world by (P. Lorillard Company, 1963), the Kingdom had become the fourth-largest by 1978 (Economics, Statistics, and Cooperatives Service, 1979). A little over two decades later, Saudi Arabia was the third-largest export market for American cigarettes – behind Japan and Israel (Capehart, 2004). Among the many Saudis who became smokers during this era were some leading members of the royal family: Fahd (ironically given his long life) ("Fahd ibn Abdulaziz al-Saud died on August 1st, probably aged 81," 2005);[1] Prince Bandar, who was Saudi Ambassador to the United States from 1982 to 2005 (Lander, 2016); and Prince Abdullah, who was crown prince from 1982 until he succeeded Fahd as king in 2005 ("Saudi Arabia's crown prince: A man with a plan: A chain-smoking champion of the Arab world," 2002).

Naturally, Western tobacco corporations eagerly sought to understand a growing market that they had once written off as peripheral. As early as 1971, British American Tobacco petitioned, unsuccessfully, for the right to produce cigarettes in the Kingdom ("Minutes of the Committee of Directors, Benson & Hedges, held at Westminster House, London," 1971, p. 3). Certainly, rising numbers of expatriates from societies where smoking was common contributed to the increase in sales. But the rising population of young people (most smokers pick up the habit in their teens) and lack of taxation contributed even more to that rise (Hertog, 2011).[2] The US Department of Health reported in 1972 that Saudi children as young as eight to ten were often seen smoking and that cigarettes were prominently displayed at the front of groceries and super-markets (US Department of Health, Education, and Welfare, 1972). Detailed Western tobacco company studies of the Saudi market also suggested that there were correlations between smoking among Saudis of both genders and rising incomes and between smoking and education (Rodnight, 1978). In particular, Saudi smokers preferred American brands, which they saw as symbols of both Western modernity and openness to the world beyond the Kingdom (Pace, 1971; Rodnight, 1978). Indeed, anyone who smoked was implicitly challenging the authority of religious beliefs.

The same studies found that Saudis preferred to smoke at work or on the street – two settings where the use of tobacco had been strictly forbidden in the past – and that the most pious individuals could be reached through innovative advertising. For instance, in 1979, the British tobacco company Benson & Hedges introduced a limited edition of 50 gold pendants decorated with diamonds, valued at £750 each, to commemorate the first day of the 15th century of the Hijra Muslim calendar. This was a clearly manipulative ploy, admitted in the company's own internal documents, intended to circumvent bans on cigarette marketing by choosing an event that is central to the Muslim faith. Marketed in both large hotel foyers and in leading pan-Arab newspapers with the assistance of a "leading government dignitary," over 100 applicants bid on the pendants, including the governor of Mecca, Prince Fawwaz bin Abdulaziz (Emmerson, 1979, p. 12). A company report concluded that the offer allowed Benson & Hedges to "reach parts of the [tobacco] market ... which are closed to it by any other means" (Emmerson, 1979, p. 12).

"There is no ... Islamic text from the Qur'an or the Sunnah ... in this regard"

It would be tempting to characterize members of the Saudi royal family and pious Saudis who smoked as hypocrites, a word often used to describe Saudis and their relationship to the contemporary world. After all, while railing against the spread of Western culture in Saudi Arabia, the group of young men who briefly seized the Ka'aba in 1979 condemned Prince Fawwaz by name for his personal corruption. Echoing the words of As-Sa'di's *fatwā* and those of other Saudi jurists, the spokesman for the men, Sayid Abdullah al-Qahtani, called for a reformation of Saudi society. In particular, he argued that smoking, soccer, and other practices that had spread in the Kingdom in the 1960s and 1970s should have no place in a Muslim country governed by an interpretation of Sunni Islam overwhelmingly defined by the Qur'an and the Sunnah (Trofimov, 2007).

Notably, after the Saudi military dislodged Al-Qahtani and his followers from the Ka'aba by force, Saudi officials dismissed Prince Fawwaz as governor of Mecca and provided religious figures who agreed with Al-Qahtani's strict vision of Islam with substantial resources and power to shape Saudi social norms. Not only had the religious elites backed the government's campaign to retake the Ka'aba in 1979, but government officials and the royal family also believed that the stricter vision of Islam would define Saudi Arabia's future. As an unnamed senior Saudi prince told the British journalist Robert Lacey in 1980, Saudi society was likely to resist the seemingly "inevitable" push of modernization and secularization (Lacey, 1981, p. 519). "If anything," he said, "I think that our children will be stricter Muslims than we are" (Lacey, 1981, p. 519).

Despite this cultural change, the number of cigarettes imported to Saudi Arabia continued to grow, increasing from 27 million kilograms in 1977 to 42 million kilograms in 1984 (Albar, 1994). This growth in smoking in part reflected innovative advertising, including PM partnering with videocassette distributors, a booming industry in a country without movie theaters, and an influx of foreign workers who smoked. But it also reflected the view of a new young generation of stricter Saudi Muslims who saw smoking cigarettes as fully *consistent* with a vision of Islam that privileged the Sunnah and the Qur'an over other sources of religious law. We have a rich source of their views and the central role of smoking in their daily lives in the *fatāwā* collected by Saudi Arabia's General Presidency of Scholarly Research and Fatawwa (sic). Because the organization was created by a Royal decree in 1971, its jurists have answered hundreds of inquiries related to *fiqh, hadith*, and other issues posed by senior officials and citizens alike (Al-Atawneh, 2010). One of the most common themes in the inquiries revolved around smoking or smokers.

While many Saudis sought guidance on how to interact with smokers (The General Presidency of Scholarly Research and Ifta', n.d.g)[3] or businesses that sell tobacco products, (The General Presidency of Scholarly Research and Ifta', n.d.e), many others seeking guidance did not accept that smoking was necessarily *haram*. Is it permissible, for instance, for Muslims to pray behind an imam who smokes (The General Presidency of Scholarly Research and Ifta', n.d.c) or to smoke a cigarette while reading the Qur'an (The General Presidency of Scholarly Research and Ifta', n.d.a)? Could a child disobey a parent's request to buy them cigarettes (The General Presidency of Scholarly Research and Ifta', n.d.b)? There are also repeated requests for clarification on Islam's position on smoking (The General Presidency of Scholarly Research and Ifta', n.d.j), with some stating that they have heard that it is permissible to smoke in Islam or that smoking exists in a legal gray area (The General Presidency of Scholarly Research and Ifta', n.d.f). The answer in all of these cases is the same from Saudi jurists: Smoking and anything linked to it is *haram*.

Nonetheless, Saudis continued to present questions about smoking that assumed that it was permitted to smoke at least in certain situations – just as the *Zhirt* had done during Rihani's visits to the Kingdom decades earlier. One Saudi asked if it was permissible to smoke if one "found it hard to quit" or had learned it was *ḥaram* only after he had become addicted to smoking (The General Presidency of Scholarly Research and Ifta', n.d.h, para. 1). Some questioners boldly stated that there was no record of the Prophet Muhammad banning smoking and asked whether there were verses in the Qur'an or *hadīth* that addressed smoking (The General Presidency of Scholarly Research and Ifta', n.d.d). Among the statements made in this *fatwā* and other *fatāwā* were: "Although Islam permits smoking, what is your advice to those who smoke *Diamba* (marijuana) and consume intoxicants?" and "There is no evident Ayah (Qur'anic verse) or *hadīth* in the Qur'an and Sunnah" that smoking is illegal. To their credit, religious scholars did not evade the issue and freely admitted that "there is no ... Islamic text from the Qur'an or the Sunnah" prohibiting Muslims from smoking (The General Presidency of Scholarly Research and Ifta', n.d.i, para. 2). Instead, they called on Muslims to look to statements on human health in the Qur'an and the *hadīth* to understand why smoking was *ḥaram*. They also cited other sources of Islamic law, including judicial decisions and the consensus of the Muslim community (The General Presidency of Scholarly Research and Ifta', n.d.i).

In a society that values the literal word of the Qur'an and the *hadīth* above other forms of religious revelation, this was a relatively weak argument, especially when compared to the Saudi bans on alcohol and pork, both of which are clearly prohibited in the Qur'an and by the Prophet himself. Saudis could also readily access *fatāwā* produced by leading Muslim jurists in Africa, Asia, and the Middle East since the 17th century which viewed smoking as consistent with Islamic laws and norms (Grehan, 2006). This was the type of legal gray space that Western tobacco executives understood and sought to use to their advantage. For instance, in a memo written after a 1984 trip to Saudi Arabia, A. Courtier, who worked for the European division of Brown & Williamson Tobacco Company, informed his colleagues of new and "serious" developments in the Kingdom; namely, public pressure against smoking and "Friday sermons being delivered in the mosques stating that smoking is 'Harem' [sic]" (Courtier, 1984, p. 5). Still, the sermons were, in Courtier's eyes, "only rhetoric," for it is obvious that smoking "is not as clearly 'Harem' [sic] as alcohol, pork, etc. and will not therefore be banned" (Courtier, 1984, p. 5).

While Courtier (1984) was correct that smoking was not banned, that did not mean that Friday sermons had no impact on the demand for cigarettes, especially when they worked in tandem with a variety of direct (and indirect) anti-smoking measures undertaken by the Saudi government. In 1982, then Crown Prince Abdullah hosted the Islamic Conference to Combat Intoxicants and Drugs (Batran, 2003). The conference, which brought together leading Islamic scholars from around the globe, "declared the cultivation of tobacco, its sale, and consumption strictly *ḥaram*" (Batran, 2003, p. 34). Although no government implemented the conference's recommendations, the Saudi government continued to increase its cooperation with neighboring Arab

oil-producing states to combat tobacco sales, raised its own tariffs on imported tobacco products, and incorporated secular and religious anti-smoking
messages into the country's national school curriculum (ERC Statistics
International Limited, 1993; Ministry of Education, Kingdom of Saudi
Arabia, 1985).

These messages were reinforced by the rise of anti-smoking measures in the
United States and Western European societies in the 1980s and 1990s, in
countries where Saudis vacationed and studied. By 1989, these policies had the
intended impact; tobacco sales declined by 20 percent from 1986 throughout
the Kingdom and the Gulf. In one year alone, consumption of cigarettes
dropped from 17 million units (1988) to 15 million units (1989) (ERC Statistics
International Limited, 1993). Abdul Aziz al-Baban, a cigarette agent, told *The
Arab Times* in Kuwait that young people were a key factor in the decline: "The
new generation is more aware of the hazards to health posed by smoking as
compared to the earlier generation" ("Cigarette sales down twenty percent,"
1989, para. 7). Furthermore, Saudi Arabia's economy slowed considerably after
the oil market collapsed in 1986 and again in 1988.

In response, PM and other Western tobacco companies commissioned a
series of reports in the early 1990s to better understand the Saudi market. The
most comprehensive were written in 1993 by a European research team based in
Vienna: Denyse Drummond-Dunn and Claude-Alain Proz. They concluded
that the overriding characteristic of Saudi ideals and society was dualism and the
need to balance oppositional forces:

> The first, and perhaps most important finding, is that within individuals
> there exists a polarity of attitudes. There are therefore ideals that are
> contradictory – behaviour that seems to cut across ideals, and apparent
> conflicts which, if found in a study of Western populations, would be
> difficult to reconcile. This is best interpreted as a dualism, and in this
> particular case, as a dualism between the secular and spiritual values in
> the culture.
>
> (Drummond-Dunn & Proz, 1993, p. 9)

This seemingly "schizophrenic" vision of Saudi Arabia shaped everything in the
Kingdom, including the young men who were a core market for Western
tobacco companies. For them, the ideal of masculinity – a key theme for most
tobacco advertising – had little in common with an American ideal of a
rugged, self-sufficient individual living in the arid American West. Instead,
Saudi men operated in an environment in which (a) their peers defined their
personal worth and identity and (b) they had to uphold contradictory masculine
personas: they were expected to be always ready for action while simultaneously being seen as both calm and spiritual (Drummond-Dunn & Proz,
1993). Furthermore, in the eyes of Saudi men, smoking was not an activity
that an individual did but was something that had to be done with family and
friends – much like drinking coffee and tea, eating a meal, traveling to the

desert, or going to the beach (Drummond-Dunn & Proz, 1993). Indeed, there was considerable social pressure for groups of ordinary Saudis "to smoke the same brand, so that if one person runs out, he can take from the others" (Drummond-Dunn & Proz, 1993, p. 11).

Within this framework, Drummond-Dunn and Proz (1993) argued, the Marlboro Man, who embodied American masculinity, was an uneasy fit in the Kingdom and should be modified to appeal to local audiences. While many Saudis admired the image of a master horseman and saw the horse as a symbol of his power, they could not relate to many other defining aspects of the Marlboro Man, beginning with the persona of a cowboy living as a rugged individual in a desert setting. According to Saudis, this was a type of person who should be feared since he lacked social connections, and as desert dwellers they were unlikely to see dry climates as part of an escapist fantasy (Drummond-Dunn & Proz, 1993). Nor did they understand why the cowboys in ads appeared poor, wore tattered clothing, and used second-rate lighters (Drummond-Dunn & Proz, 1993). Consequently, the researchers recommended, future ads in Saudi Arabia should feature carefully chosen beautiful Arabian stallions and, above all, accentuate the relationships between them and their horsemen (Drummond-Dunn & Proz, 1993). By using this approach, Drummond-Dunn and Proz concluded, "some of the negatives concerning the lack of elegance can be overcome without turning the horseman into a 'Gucci cowboy'" (1993, p. 38).

Significantly, the argument of Drummond-Dunn and Proz (1993) bore no resemblance to Rentier theory – the academic model that dominated Western scholarship on the Kingdom in the 1990s. That theory stresses political economy and that oil is the defining factor in shaping Saudi society (Gray, 2011). By contrast, Drummond-Dunn and Proz (1993) drew on a source which no other scholar had ever used; namely, exhaustive interviews with hundreds of Saudis from all walks of life. For their part, PM executives recognized the value of this novel study and developed new strategies based on its recommendations. In 1993, the company's new creative guidelines for its ads in Saudi Arabia recognized a new broader (and softer) definition of masculinity (Marlboro Worldwide Creative Review Committee, 1993) and stipulated that all ads should feature more lush and green landscapes (Burnett, 1993) as well as "the power and beauty of horses" (Marlboro Worldwide Creative Review Committee, 1993, p. 4). In addition, senior PM executives decided that print ads in Saudi Arabia would stress "companionship," including companionship around food and coffee (Marlboro Worldwide Creative Review Committee, 1993, p. 3), and downplay the traditional "tough guy" Marlboro cowboy image (Philip Morris Tobacco, 1993).

It was a very wise decision as more than 40 percent of the Saudi population at the time was under the age of 15, a key target group for tobacco companies (Dymond, 1991). Many took up smoking, and consumption of cigarettes rose steadily in Saudi Arabia in the 1990s and the 21st century. Between the early 1990s and 2010, the overall numbers of smokers increased and the percentage of the male population that smoked rose from 21 percent to 35 percent (Al-Turki, 2014). In the first decade of the 21st century, Saudi Arabia ranked as the fifth-fastest-growing tobacco market in the world and the fourth-largest importer of tobacco in the world (Euromonitor, 2006). Further aiding the rise in cigarette consumption was the cheap price of cigarettes: $2.70 for a pack of Marlboro in 2015 (Moradi-Lakeh et al., 2015) despite rising tariffs on imported cigarettes (Euromonitor, 2006). For instance, in 2005, Saudi Arabia and its neighbors in the Gulf Cooperation Council raised the tariff on tobacco by 150 percent (Euromonitor, 2006). Throughout the era, PM's share of the Saudi market continued to rise, from 48 percent in the middle of the 1990s to 63 percent by 1999 (Philip Morris Tobacco, 2000). The company continued to dominate the market into the 21st century, exporting 9.8 billion cigarettes to Saudi Arabia in 2004 alone (Philip Morris Tobacco, 2004).

Many members of Saudi society continued to smoke, including prominent members of the royal family. In 1996, Prince Feisal bin Bandar, then the governor of Qassim, surprised a group of visiting American university professors by smoking at a formal dinner at his palace (Anderson, 2015). He apologized for exposing his guests to the secondhand smoke but noted that he had tried to quit multiple times from a habit his people had picked up from the West as a sign of "civilization" (Anderson, 2015, p. 187). As everyone in the room laughed at his joke, the prince added, "But now no one in the West is smoking. … I suppose by the time I quit smoking, the West will decide that nothing is wrong with it, so I think I'll continue smoking" (Anderson, 2015, p. 187).

Of course, the academics should not have been surprised that the prince (or anyone else) smoked in Saudi Arabia. The growth in smoking in Saudi Arabia represented the intersection of factors that had led to upsurges in smoking in the past. Between the late 1990s and early 2015, not only was there an increase in young people in the population (Murphy, 2012),[4] but there was also a sustained boom in oil prices and a concomitant era of prosperity similar to the one that had launched cigarettes in the Kingdom in the 1970s. Even health professionals smoked in large numbers (Al-Turki, 2006). In a study conducted in 2005, 13 percent of male students at the College of Medicine at King Saud University in Riyadh reported they were regular smokers and 38 percent reported they were passive smokers (Al-Turki, 2006). Equally important, King Abdullah, who, as noted earlier, was a chain-smoker, ascended to the throne in 2005. He oversaw a process of social liberalization and a reduction in the power that the religious elites had amassed since 1979. Both policies had broad popular support, in part because there was a consensus that religious elites had exceeded their authority. Ironically, one of the events that shaped that view – an infamous deadly fire at a girls' school in Mecca administered by clerics – was inadvertently started by a student who threw her still-lit cigarette into a pile of trash after she unexpectedly encountered a teacher in a school hallway (Weston, 2008).

As the peers of that young woman gravitated towards a new online culture in the second decade of the 21st century, PM adjusted its advertising to reach its core audiences – just as it had done in the past. In the large malls of Riyadh and the other cities where Saudi young people regularly hung out on afternoons and weekends, one could find young salesmen offering Saudi teenagers cards with free credits and ways to win points on PM-sponsored video games designed to be played on the new generation of smartphones.

Conclusion

But the innovative approaches and use of technology that PM pioneered could be used by others and could not protect the company and Western tobacco generally from the winds of change sweeping over the Kingdom and the Middle East. For instance, in January 2008, just as PM was in the process of launching a new brand in Saudi Arabia, Marlboro Filter Plus, an SMS text message campaign emerged against the brand and the company. The text message campaign alleged that the product was not safe, that someone had died from smoking the product, and that it was linked to Israel. After the launch of Marlboro Filter Plus failed and it did not meet its sales targets, PM conducted an investigation, with the aid of the US Embassy in Riyadh, to determine who was responsible for the text campaign. Remarkably, investigators concluded that the culprit was not a cleric or Islamic activist opposed to smoking, but one of PM's Western competitors, which had hoped to scuttle the launch of the new product and to gain a share of the Saudi market (personal communication, former official, US Embassy Riyadh, March 24, 2016).

Even more dangerous to PM's business model has been the shifting sands of the politics of the Middle East, especially the emergence of the Islamic State in Syria and Iraq. That new organization had considerable sympathy among Saudis on a host of levels – humanitarian, sectarian, and tribal. At least 2,500 Saudi citizens have reportedly gone to fight in Syria against the Syrian government (Williams, 2017). Following a deadly suicide bombing at a Shi'a mosque in Qatif in May 2015, it was clear that some Saudis were willing to kill their fellow citizens on their home soil for ISIS (Al-Shihri, 2015).

Critically, ISIS offers Saudis an opportunity to be part of a state community that has a substantial presence online, has proven itself on the battlefield repeatedly in Syria and Iraq, and upholds strict Islamic values without compromise. One should not discount the impact of the Islamic State's enforcement of public morality. While the Hai'a (religious police) can shape behavior in some public settings, and while Saudi religious leaders issue statements expressing their anger that "wrong matters" are allowed to exist in the Kingdom, the activists of ISIS have destroyed thousands of cigarettes and persecuted individuals found smoking (Mahmood, 2015; Malm, 2015). This type of state harkens back to the vision of the men who seized the Ka'aba in Mecca in 1979: an Arab-Muslim society that is not governed by the many factors that limit Salafi power in Saudi Arabia.

The policies of ISIS have impacted Iraq and Syria as well as other nations and organizations of the world. ISIS videos inspire fear of Arab Muslims in

America and Europe. In May 2015, Great Britain's Imperial Tobacco Corporation, the fourth-largest tobacco producer in the world, blamed ISIS for dramatic declines in tobacco consumption in ISIS-controlled territories in Syria and Iraq (Lewis, 2015). In the eyes of many conservative Saudis, the contrast between the regional and global roles of ISIS and Saudi Arabia – one of the world's largest importers of tobacco products – could not be clearer. Indeed, ISIS has been creating the very type of society that is assumed by much of the outside world to exist in Saudi Arabia.

For its part, the Saudi government has responded to this threat by participating in US-led military strikes on ISIS and by seeking to curb smoking within the Kingdom. Not only was smoking banned from most government offices and public places ("Saudi Arabia stubs out smoking," 2012), but government officials also sought to raise the price of cigarettes through new taxes and import fees ("Prices of cigarettes may go up by 30%," 2015). In March 2016, the government announced a doubling of the price of cigarettes throughout the Kingdom, and the price of a Marlboro cigarette pack immediately rose from 10 riyals to 15 riyals in some stores ("Tobacco off shelves amid price rise speculation," 2016).

Public reaction to anti-smoking measures in Saudi Arabia was mixed. Some Saudi health advocates even supported raising the price to 35 riyals, arguing it was essential to deal with the high costs of treating illnesses associated with smoking ("Price of a cigarette packet could go up to SR35," 2016). Others, however, reacted with anger at the new prices. The Twitter hashtag "rafaʻa_siʻr_al-dukān_b_20_riyāl" (raising the price of smoking to 20 riyals) trended in the Kingdom for weeks during spring 2016. Among those venting their anger on social media were young professionals and women, who make up an increasing share of the smokers in the Kingdom: nearly 22 percent of the total. Reportedly 1.2 million Saudi women smoked in 2012 ("Cigarettes off shelves as tobacco prices double," 2016).

As the Kingdom seeks to end its dependence on oil exports and realize the social and economic goals outlined by Muhammad bin Salman in April 2016 in Vision 2030 (Al-Dakhil, 2016), it is likely that cigarettes will remain part of the social landscape for many decades to come. Not only have Saudis been smoking since before the discovery of oil in the Kingdom, but also thousands of Saudi citizens of both genders and all ages, political opinions, and classes continue to smoke. In January 2015, Prince Feisal bin Bandar, a chain-smoker, was even appointed governor of Riyadh, one of the country's most important government posts ("Saudi monarch issues royal orders," 2015). Ultimately, few issues better illustrate the dualism of Saudi society and the need for Saudis to balance oppositional forces than smoking.

ISIS links "purity" to incredible cruelty and to violence. It promises people heaven if they will blow themselves up in its cause. Its response to oppositional forces is not to accommodate or balance them but to annihilate them. As Prince Feisal bin Bandar suggested, albeit with a trace of irony, Saudi Arabia retains its respect for "civilization" and for the complexities that civilization brings with it. In the actions of ISIS one can hear the infamous but fraudulent quotation from Hitler: "Yes, we are barbarians! It is an honourable title. We shall rejuvenate the world. This world is near its end" (Redles, 2005, p. 48).

Notes

1 Fahd reportedly smoked two cigarettes at a time – one for each hand – and had a separate ashtray for each hand.
2 In *Princes, Brokers, and Bureaucrats: Oil and the State in Saudi Arabia*, Steffen Hertog cited a 1970 report by Ramon Knauerhase that stated that a tobacco tax "was impossible to enforce" in Saudi Arabia; today, Saudi Arabia is one of the few nations in the world that does not impose an excise tax on cigarettes imported to the country (Hertog, 2011, p. 77).
3 This is one of dozens of *fatāwā* that deal with this subject. For more, see The General Presidency of Scholarly Research and Ifta', Fatwas of the Permanent Committee, Kingdom of Saudi Arabia at http://alifta.com/default.aspx?languagename=en#1.
4 Between 1990 and 2012, Saudi Arabia's population grew from 16 million to 28 million. By 2012, approximately 37 percent of the Saudi population was under the age of 14. Those under age 25 accounted for around 51 percent of the population, and when those under 29 were included, young people amounted to two-thirds of the Kingdom's population (Murphy, 2012, p. 3).

References

Al-Atawneh, M.K. (2010). *Wahhabi Islam: Facing the challenges of modernity: Dar al-Ifta in the modern Saudi state.* Leiden, Netherlands: Brill.

Albar, M.A. (1994). Islamic teachings and cancer prevention. *Journal of Family and Community Medicine*, 1(1), 79–86. Retrieved from www.ncbi.nlm.nih.gov/pmc/articles/PMC3437186/#ref47.

Al-Dakhil, T. (2016, April 25). Al Arabiya interviews Deputy Crown Prince Mohamed bin Salman [Video]. *Al Arabiya*. Retrieved from http://english.alarabiya.net/en/webtv/programs/special-interview/2016/04/25/Deputy-Crown-Prince-This-is-the-Saudi-vision-2030.html.

Al-Sanea, R. (2007). *The girls of Riyadh*. Trans. Marilyn Booth. New York: The Penguin Press.

Al-Shihri, A. (2015, May 24). Saudi king vows to punish those behind IS-claimed attack. *News OK*. Retrieved from http://newsok.com/article/feed/843546.

Al-Turki, K. (2014). *An investigation into the perceptions of male smokers and health care professionals in the smoking cessation clinics in Riyadh on the Tobacco Control Program in Saudi Arabia.* Doctoral dissertation, University of Huddersfield. Retrieved from http://eprints.hud.ac.uk/23794/1/kalturkifinalthesis.pdf.

Al-Turki, Y.A. (2006). Smoking habits among medical students in Central Arabia. *Saudi Medical Journal*, 27(5), 700–703.

Anderson, K. (2015). *Dreams of a Saudi princess and the Christians who believed in them.* Bloomington, IN: WestBow Press.

The Arab News. (2013, June 2). 10 million Saudi smokers by 2020. Retrieved from www.arabnews.com/news/453724.

The Arab News. (2015, September 13). Prices of cigarettes may go up by 30%. Retrieved from www.arabnews.com/saudi-arabia/news/805596.

The Arab News. (2016, March 15). Price of a cigarette packet could go up to SR35. Retrieved from www.arabnews.com/saudi-arabia/news/895401.

The Arab Times (Kuwait). (1989, June 13). Cigarette sales down twenty percent. British American Tobacco Records. Retrieved from http://industrydocuments.libra ry.ucsf.edu/tobacco/docs/zknx0196.

As-Sa'di, Abddur Rahman bin Naasir. (2000). The ruling concerning smoking cigar-ettes. In *Fataawwa concerning tobacco and cigarettes: Muhammad bin Ibraaheem Aal-ish-Sheikh Abdur-Rahmaan bin Naasir As-Sa'di Abdul-Azeez bin Abdullah bin Baaz* (pp. 29–36). Karachi, Pakistan: Vision Publications. Retrieved from https://d1. islamhouse.com/data/en/ih_books/single/en_Fataawa_regarding_Tobacco_and_Ciga rettes.pdf.

Batran, A.A. (2003). *Tobacco smoking under Islamic law: Controversy over its introduction.* Beltsville, MD: Amana.

Burnett, L. (1993, February 8–9). Marlboro Worldwide creative review meeting: EEMA brief. *Philip Morris Records.* Retrieved from http://industrydocuments.libra ry.ucsf.edu/tobacco/docs/hznp0110.

Capehart, T. (2004, April 22). *Tobacco outlook.* Washington, DC: United States Department of Agriculture. Retrieved from http://usda.mannlib.cornell.edu/usda/ers /TBS//2000s/2004/TBS-04-15-2004.pdf.

Cooperman, H. and Shechter, R. (2008). Branding the riders: "Marlboro Country" and the formation of the new middle class in Egypt, Saudi Arabia, and Turkey. *New Global Studies,* 2(3), 1–41. Retrieved from www.academia.edu/809435/Branding_the _Riders_Marlboro_Country_and_the_Formation_of_a_New_Middle_Class_in_Egy pt_Saudi_Arabia_and_Turkey.

Courtier, A. (1984, April 4). Trip report to Saudi 23–24 March [Interoffice memo]. Brown & Williamson Records. Retrieved from https://industrydocuments.library.ucs f.edu/tobacco/docs/#id=rxcv0136.

Drummond-Dunn, D. and Proz, C.-A. (1993, August). Marlboro qualitative image study Saudi Arabia: 1993. Philip Morris Records. Retrieved from https://idl.ucsf.ed u/tobacco/docs/#id=gnhd0110.

Dymond, H. (1991, July 19). Report on Saudi visit, June 24, 1991–July 5, 1991. British American Tobacco Records. Retrieved from http://industrydocuments.library.ucsf.ed u/tobacco/docs/xmlw0198.

Economics, Statistics, and Cooperatives Service. (1979, March 8). *Tobacco situation.* Washington, DC: U.S. Department of Agriculture. Tobacco Institute Records; RPCI Tobacco Institute and Council for Tobacco Research Records. Retrieved from https://industrydocuments.library.ucsf.edu/tobacco/docs/txyj0027.

The Economist. (2002, May 21). Saudi Arabia's crown prince: A man with a plan: A chain-smoking champion of the Arab world. Retrieved from www.economist.com/ node/1046748.

The Economist. (2005, August 4). Fahd ibn Abdulaziz al-Saud died on August 1st, probably aged 81. Retrieved from www.economist.com/node/4246122.

Emmerson, D. (1979, November/December). The house of Benson & Hedges in Arabia. *BAT Marketing News,* 9–10. British American Tobacco Records. Retrieved from https://industrydocuments.library.ucsf.edu/tobacco/docs/#id=rgfw0207.

ERC Statistics International Limited. (1993). The world cigarette market: The 1992 International Survey: Asia, Australasia & The Far East, Middle East & Africa.

Philip Morris Records. Retrieved from http://industrydocuments.library.ucsf.edu/tob acco/docs/qpxm0166.

Euromonitor. (2006). The world market for tobacco. Philip Morris Records. Retrieved from https://www.industrydocumentslibrary.ucsf.edu/docs/#id=yjyn0189.

The General Presidency of Scholarly Research and Ifta'. (n.d.a). Fatwas of the Permanent Committee, Kingdom of Saudi Arabia: Fatwa no. 1000, Part No. 22; Page No. 181. Retrieved from www.alifta.net/Fatawa/FatawaChapters.aspx?languagenam e=en&View=Page&PageID=8450&PageNo=1&BookID=7.

The General Presidency of Scholarly Research and Ifta'. (n.d.b). Fatwas of the Permanent Committee, Kingdom of Saudi Arabia: Fatwa no. 1914, Part No. 22; Page No. 187. Retrieved from http://alifta.org/Fatawa/FatawaSubjects.aspx?languagename= en&View=Page&HajjEntryID=0&HajjEntryName=&RamadanEntryID=0&Ramad anEntryName=&NodeID=3747&PageID=8454&SectionID=7&SubjectPageTitlesID =8573&MarkIndex=9&0.

The General Presidency of Scholarly Research and Ifta'. (n.d.c). Fatwas of the Permanent Committee, Kingdom of Saudi Arabia: Fatwa no. 16078, Part No. 9; Page No. 38. Retrieved from http://alifta.org/Fatawa/FatawaSubjects.aspx?languagename =en&View=Page&HajjEntryID=0&HajjEntryName=&RamadanEntryID=0&Ram adanEntryName=&NodeID=366&PageID=13553&SectionID=7&SubjectPageTitle sID=14200&MarkIndex=18&0.

The General Presidency of Scholarly Research and Ifta'. (n.d.d). Fatwas of the Permanent Committee, Kingdom of Saudi Arabia: The eleventh question of Fatwa No. 3056, Part No. 22; Page No. 201. Retrieved from www.alifta.net/Fatawa/fataw aDetails.aspx?languagename=en&View=Page&PageID=8459&PageNo=1&BookI D=7.

The General Presidency of Scholarly Research and Ifta'. (n.d.e). Fatwas of the Permanent Committee, Kingdom of Saudi Arabia: The first question of Fatwa No. 2512. Retrieved from www.alifta.net/Fatawa/FatawaChapters.aspx?languagename=e n&View=Page&PageID=5474&PageNo=1&BookID=7.

The General Presidency of Scholarly Research and Ifta'. (n.d.f). Fatwas of the Permanent Committee, Kingdom of Saudi Arabia: The fourth question of Fatwa No. 515. Part No. 22; Page No. 180. Retrieved from www.alifta.net/Fatawa/FatawaSubje cts.aspx?languagename=en&View=Page&HajjEntryID=0&HajjEntryName=&Ram adanEntryID=0&RamadanEntryName=&NodeID=3203&PageID=8449&SectionI D=7&SubjectPageTitlesID=8564&MarkIndex=16&0.

The General Presidency of Scholarly Research and Ifta'. (n.d.g). Fatwas of the Permanent Committee, Kingdom of Saudi Arabia: The fourth question of Fatwa No. 1788. Retrieved from http://alifta.net/Fatawa/FatawaSubjects.aspx?languagename=e n&View=Page&HajjEntryID=0&HajjEntryName=&RamadanEntryID=0&Ramad anEntryName=&NodeID=3004&PageID=9238&SectionID=7&SubjectPageTitlesI D=9451&MarkIndex=0&0.

The General Presidency of Scholarly Research and Ifta'. (n.d.h). Fatwas of the Permanent Committee, Kingdom of Saudi Arabia: The fourth question of Fatwa No. 6616. Retrieved from www.alifta.net/Fatawa/fatawaDetails.aspx?languagename=en &View=Page&PageID=8472&PageNo=1&BookID=7.

The General Presidency of Scholarly Research and Ifta'. (n.d.i). Fatwas of the Permanent Committee, Kingdom of Saudi Arabia: The second question of Fatwa No. 7924. Retrieved from www.alifta.net/Fatawa/fatawaDetails.aspx?languagename=en &View=Page&PageID=8468&PageNo=1&BookID=7.

The General Presidency of Scholarly Research and Ifta'. (n.d.j). Fatwas of the Permanent Committee, Kingdom of Saudi Arabia: The third question of Fatwa No. 36, Part No. 22; Page No. 179. Retrieved from www.alifta.net/Fatawa/fatawaDetails.asp x?languagename=en&View=Page&PageID=8448&PageNo=1&BookID=7.

Glum, J. (2015, January 23). Saudi Arabia's youth unemployment among King Salman's many new challenges after Abdullah's death. *The International Business Times*. Retrieved from www.ibtimes.com/saudi-arabias-youth-unemployment-proble m-among-king-salmans-many-new-challenges-after-1793346.

Gray, M. (2011). *A theory of "late Rentierism" in the Arab states of the Gulf*. Doha, Qatar: Center for Regional and International Studies, Georgetown University School of Foreign Service, Doha. Retrieved from https://repository.library.georgetown.edu/bitstream/ handle/10822/558291/CIRSOccasionalPaper7MatthewGray2011.pdf?sequence=5.

Grehan, J. (2006). Smoking and "early-modern" sociability: The great tobacco debate in the Ottoman Middle East (seventeenth and eighteenth centuries). *The American Historical Review*, 111(5), 1352–1377.

The Guardian. (2012, July 30). Saudi Arabia stubs out smoking. Retrieved from www. theguardian.com/world/2012/jul/30/saudi-arabia-stubs-out-smoking.

Hall, J. (2015, March 20). ISIS' feared religious police carry out another mass cigarette burning in Syria. *The Daily Mail*. Retrieved from www.dailymail.co.uk/news/a rticle-3003848/ISIS-feared-religious-police-force-carry-mass-cigarette-burning-Syria-unveil-shocking-new-anti-smoking-posters-showing-lungs-set-fire.html.

Haykel, B., Hegghammer, T. and Lacroix, S. (2015). Introduction. In B. Haykel, T. Hegghammer and S. Lacroix (Eds.), *Saudi Arabia in transition: Insights on social, political, economic, and religious change* (pp. 1–12). Cambridge: Cambridge University Press.

Henderson to Bailey. (2004, September 2). Ban on cigarette advertising and promotions [Diplomatic cable]. In L.P. Burdette (Ed.), *Records of Saudi Arabia Vol. 5, 1970*. London: Archive Edition.

Hertog, S. (2011). *Princes, brokers, and bureaucrats: Oil and the state in Saudi Arabia*. Ithaca, NY: Cornell University Press.

Hiro, D. (2013). *Inside the Middle East* (2nd ed.). New York: Routledge.

Kochhar, L. (2016). *Economic botany: A comprehensive study* (5th ed.). Cambridge: Cambridge University Press.

Koskowski, W. (1955). *The habit of tobacco smoking*. London: Staples Press Limited. Retrieved from http://industrydocuments.library.ucsf.edu/tobacco/docs/tyym01 78.

Lacey, R. (1981). *The Kingdom: Arabia and the house of Saud*. New York: Avon Books.

Lander, M. (2016). *Alter egos: Hilary Clinton, Barak Obama and the twilight struggle over American power*. New York: Random House.

Lewis, J. (2015, May 6). ISIS: Tobacco giant blames fall in cigarette sales on militant group. *The Daily Mirror*. Retrieved from www.mirror.co.uk/news/uk-news/isis-tobac co-giant-blames-fall-5646857.

Lippman, T. (2004). *Inside the mirage: America's fragile partnership with Saudi Arabia*. Boulder, CO: Westview Press.

Mackey, S. (2002). *The Saudis: Inside the desert kingdom*. New York: W. W. Norton and Company.

Mahmood, M. (2015, June 10). Life in Mosul one year on: ISIS with all its brutality is more honest than the Shi'a government. *The Guardian*. Retrieved from www.thegua rdian.com/world/2015/jun/10/mosul-residents-one-year-on-isis-brutality.

Malm, S. (2015, January 19). ISIS execute 13 football fans by firing squad for watching Iraq play Jordan on TV in Islamist controlled Mosul. *The Daily Mail*. Retrieved from www.dailymail.co.uk/news/article-2917071/ISIS-execute-13-football-fans-firing-squad-watching-Iraq-play-Jordan-TV-Islamist-controlled-Mosul.html.

Marlboro Worldwide Creative Review Committee. (1993). Marlboro worldwide creative issues and guidelines 1993. Philip Morris Records. Retrieved from https://indus trydocuments.library.ucsf.edu/tobacco/docs/#id=tppd0110.

Ministry of Education, Kingdom of Saudi Arabia. (1985). Programme of the protective guidance on the damage from smoking. Philip Morris Collection. Retrieved from http://industrydocuments.library.ucsf.edu/tobacco/docs/krpx0115.

Moradi-Lakeh, M., El Bcheraoui, C., Tuffaha, M., Daoud, F., Al Saeedi, M., Basulaiman, M., ... Mokdad, A.H. (2015). Tobacco consumption in the Kingdom of Saudi Arabia, 2013: Findings from a national survey. *BMC Public Health*, 15:611. doi:10.1186/s12889-015-1902-3.

Mouline, N. (2014). *The clerics of Islam: Religious autonomy and political power in Saudi Arabia*. Trans. Ethan S. Rundell. New Haven, CT: Yale University Press.

Murphy, C. (2012). *Saudi Arabia's youth and the Kingdom's future*. Washington, DC: Woodrow Wilson Center. Retrieved from https://www.wilsoncenter.org/sites/default/files/Saudi%20Arabia%E2%80%99s%20Youth%20and%20the%20Kingdom%E2%80%80%99s%20Future%20FINAL.pdf.

O'Sullivan, C.D. (2012). *FDR and the end of empire: The origins of American power in the Middle East*. New York: Palgrave Macmillan.

P. Lorillard Company. (1963, October 23). Lorillard international sales and market data. Lorillard Records. Retrieved from https://industrydocuments.library.ucsf.edu/t obacco/docs/#id=rtmx0013.

Pace, E. (1971, February 14). To many Saudis, water pipe is a drag. *The New York Times*, p. 20. Retrieved from www.nytimes.com/1971/02/14/archives/to-many-young-saudi-arabians-water-pipe-is-a-drag.html.

Philip Morris Tobacco. (1993, December 8). Saudi marketing plan 1994. Philip Morris Records. Retrieved from http://industrydocuments.library.ucsf.edu/tobacco/docs/sshc 0118.

Philip Morris Tobacco. (2000, May 10). CEMA region market sales report. Philip Morris Records. Retrieved from https://industrydocuments.library.ucsf.edu/tobacco/docs/#id=jxwc0170.

Philip Morris Tobacco. (2004, December 10). Export market analysis. Philip Morris Records. Retrieved from https://industrydocuments.library.ucsf.edu/tobacco/docs/#i d=msvk0150.

Plitt, E.W. (1952, November 4). Memorandum of conversation by Edwin Plitt, Adviser, United States Delegation to the General Assembly: Burami border dispute. Foreign Relations of the United States, 1952–1954, *The Near and Middle East*, Volume IX, Part 2; S/A (Jessup) files, lot 53 D 65, Arab-Asian Question, Miscellaneous File, UNGA 7th Session. Retrieved from https://history.state.gov/histor icaldocuments/frus1952-54v09p2/d1494.

Qatar News Agency. (2015, January 29). Saudi monarch issues royal orders. Retrieved from Lexis/Nexis Academic.

Qusti, R. (2007, September 12). Tobacco companies fail to show up; Hearings postponed. *The Arab News*. Retrieved from www.arabnews.com/node/303228.

Redles, D. (2005). *Hitler's millennial Reich: Apocalyptic belief and the search for salvation*. New York: New York University Press.

Reuters Staff (2016, March 13). Tobacco off shelves amid price rise speculation. *Reuters.* Retrieved from www.reuters.com/article/saudi-tobacco-idUSL5N16L04W.

Rihani, A. (2002). *Ibn Sa'oud of Arabia.* London: Kegan Paul.

Rodnight, E. (1978, January). Saudi Arabia [market analysis]. Brown & Williamson Records. Retrieved from https://industrydocuments.library.ucsf.edu/tobacco/docs/#id=pkyl0136.

The Saudi Gazette. (2016, March 14). Cigarettes off shelves as tobacco prices double. Retrieved from http://saudigazette.com.sa/saudi-arabia/cigarettes-off-shelves-tobacco-prices-doubled.

Schechter, R. (2006). *Smoking, culture, and economy in the Middle East: The Egyptian tobacco market, 1850–2000.* London: I. B. Tauris.

Thoma, W. (1986, May 27). Board presentation Saudi Arabia. Philip Morris Records. Retrieved from https://www.industrydocumentslibrary.ucsf.edu/tobacco/docs/nqfc0110.

Tobacco Institute. (1971, January 18). *Tobacco Institute Newsletter.* Tobacco Institute Records. Retrieved from https://industrydocuments.library.ucsf.edu/tobacco/docs/#id=jyjw0137.

Trofimov, Y. (2007). *The siege of Mecca: The forgotten uprising in Islam's holiest shrine and the birthplace of al-Qaeda.* New York: Doubleday.

UCSF. (1971, June 2). Minutes of the Committee of Directors, Benson & Hedges, held at Westminster House, London. British American Tobacco Records. Retrieved from https://industrydocuments.library.ucsf.edu/tobacco/docs/#id=hpvw0212.

United Press International. (2004, May 21). Study: Teens most vulnerable to smoking. Retrieved from www.upi.com/Science_News/2004/05/21/Study-teens-most-vulnerable-to-smoking/58231085168396/.

U.S. Department of Health, Education, and Welfare. (1971, December 8). *Smoking and health programs around the world.* Rockville, MD: Health Services and Mental Administration: Regional Medical Services; National Clearinghouse for Smoking and Health. R. J. Reynolds Collection. Retrieved from https://industrydocuments.library.ucsf.edu/tobacco/docs/rjfc0101.

US Department of Health, Education, and Welfare. (1972, December 30). *Smoking and health programs around the world.* Rockville, MD: Health Services and Mental Administration: Regional Medical Services; National Clearinghouse for Smoking and Health. R. J. Reynolds Records. Retrieved from https://industrydocuments.library.ucsf.edu/tobacco/docs/#id=yqjk0137.

Weston, M. (2008). *Prophets and princes: Saudi Arabia: From Muhammad to the present.* Hoboken, NJ: John Wiley and Sons.

Williams, B. G. (2017). *Counter Jihad: America's military experience in Afghanistan, Iraq, and Syria.* Philadelphia, PA: University of Pennsylvania Press.

Willis, J. (2003). Foreword. In A.A. Batran, *Tobacco smoking under Islamic law: Controversy over its introduction* (pp. 4–15). Beltsville, MD: Amana.

World Health Organization. (1979, December 13). Report of WHO consultation on smoking and health, Geneva, 12 and 13 December 1979. Philip Morris Records. Retrieved from http://industrydocuments.library.ucsf.edu/tobacco/docs/znyf0115.

Zacharias, A. (2010, January 13). Tobacco law threatens farms. *The National.* Retrieved from www.thenational.ae/news/uae-news/tobacco-law-threatens-farms.

Part II
Cold War Challenges

3 How geography and ideology shaped US foreign policy during the Cold War and beyond

Nickolas A. Spencer

"So as to strengthen the friendship between the two countries," begins the poem on the plaque that Sultan Abdulmecid gifted to the United States to help build the Washington Monument (Obama, 2009, para. 7). From time to time, the enduring relationship between the United States and Turkey has needed a great deal of strengthening. So long as the geographic and ideational realities that underpin the relationship endure, so too shall the relationship itself.

Like most nations, Turkey found its post-World War II place in international politics to be relative to the two superpowers of the era. The Soviet Union with its oft problematic geography would prove outcome determinative for Turkish foreign relations. The Soviet Union found its geopolitical position almost as hamstrung after World War II as it was before the war. With the Baltic easily blockaded, the North often frozen, and the West far away, Russia, in whatever guise, has often tried to break out of its geopolitical strait-jacket by southward expansion. Turkey, in whatever guise, has often blocked this route, leading to repeated armed confrontation. This is complicated by the idea of Russian strategic insecurity. During and after the Cold War, the United States took advantage of this geography and the idea Russia has of its strategic position to bolster its relationship with Turkey so as to contain the Soviet Union.

This chapter will examine primary and secondary sources to elucidate how the United States has managed US foreign policy with Turkey to contain the Soviet Union, and later Russia. Among other sources, it will include an exegesis of George Kennan's (1946) "Long Telegram" and its analysis of Soviet strategic thinking to "explain the past, describe the present, and predict the future" of US–Turkish relations (Bajema, 2010, p. 58).

The tug of history

Russia and Turkey have been geostrategic rivals for centuries. The substantial collapse that both nations suffered during and after World War I followed 350 years of conflict. These conflicts were occasioned by "overlapping territorial ambitions, the control of the Black Sea and the right of navigation through the Turkish Straits" (Yanik, 2015, p. 367). All of these occasions for conflict still exist in substantial measure. They inform Russian–Turkish relations today. This tension was seen as an opportunity by the United States as it resulted in a confluence of interests with Turkey. Turkey needed to protect itself from the Soviet Union. The United States needed a local foil to its greatest foe.

Russia

The root of the superpower rivalry lay in Russian insecurity. George Kennan was a foreign policy maven and Russian expert and was widely considered one of America's greatest foreign policy thinkers. He notes in his now famous "Long Telegram" that the Soviet Union's

> neurotic view of world affairs is [a result of] traditional and instinctive Russian sense of insecurity. Originally, this was insecurity of a peaceful agricultural people trying to live on vast exposed plain in [a] neighborhood of fierce nomadic peoples. To this was added, as Russia came into contact with economically advanced West, fear of more competent, more powerful, more highly organized societies in that area. But this latter type of insecurity was one which afflicted rather Russian rulers than Russian people.
>
> (Kennan, 1946, n.p.)

This view quite literally underpinned the US strategy to wage the Cold War. In its understanding of Russian insecurities, this view made manifest how patience and firmness could more safely secure US interests than could war. It also elevated Turkey from a land with interesting geography to an essential node in a US strategic network to check the Soviet expansionism fueled by insecurity.

Much of Russia's insecurity, as Kennan (1946) notes, is rooted in its geography or, rather, the reaction of its leaders to its geography. By most measures Russia's geography is favorable, even enviable. Russia's favorable geography has gifted it favorable geology. The Russian landmass sits atop a geological bounty. Blessed with abundant natural resources such as oil, natural gas, and precious metals and stones, Russia should have been able to use the near instant improvement in the world's security environment following the end of the Cold War to translate economic potential into practice, much as Germany has. Instead it has gotten itself caught up in the vicious cycle of the petro-state defined by its corruption and deteriorating institutions (Medvedev, 2009). As a consequence, Russia's post-Soviet experience has been characterized by increasing concentration of power in the hands of the president, political repression, and increased bellicosity towards its neighbors (Zudin, 2000). Poor governance has permitted Russia's gimlet-eyed view of its geography to rob it of the benefits its geology has bestowed upon it.

Admittedly, Russian geography is not charmed by all measures. From the perspective of security, Russian geography is quite simply wretched. Astride the Eurasian plain, Russia is a geographic colossus. It is the largest country on the globe by a considerable margin. It is also "one of the most insecure countries of the contemporary world" (Zeihan, 2014, p. 180). Peter Zeihan aptly describes the geographical causes for Russia's cultural insecurity. He states that Central Eurasia

> is a place of insecurity. The lack of reliable weather combined with the lack of local barriers to movement make it easy for any piece of civilization to fall to forces natural or man-made. Any people who rise in this harsh landscape crave what bits of security they can find or wrestle out of the earth – or from each other.
>
> (Zeihan, 2014, pp. 179–180)

Centuries of invasions have made Russian leaders distrustful of outsiders and ever in quest for greater security. This security has often been had by expansion. To the south, this has routinely occasioned conflict with Turkey. The Russian tug has often taken the form of violence or threats thereof.

Turkey

Turkey, by contrast, is both potentially capital-rich and important, to both the United States and Russia, because of its geography. Like Russia, Turkey is a Eurasian power. In antiquity,

> most land-borne trade between Europe and South Asia passed through the pair of double peninsulas that bracket the Sea of Marmara, while any waterborne trade between the Danube and Black Sea and the Mediterranean passed through the Sea of Marmara itself.
>
> (Zeihan, 2014, p. 188)

As an economic and cultural crossroads, Turkey has used its strategic location to garner wealth and importance and to leverage both into power. This fact is made manifest by its millennia-long relevance to international relations.

And Turkey *was* relevant to Russia. Like many Russian leaders, Stalin was afflicted by the insecurities that Kennan (1946) speaks of. Russia's insecurity led to Stalin's insistence that the Soviet Union have unfettered access to the Mediterranean. The Montreux Convention of 1936 governs the control over the strategic straits of Bosporus and the Dardanelles, which themselves control access from the Black Sea to the Mediterranean (Montreux Convention Regarding the Regime of the Straits, 1936). During World War II, the Soviet Union began demanding that it be allowed to defend and fortify the Turkish straits (Beisner, 2006). In short, it was demanding that Soviet troops be allowed to garrison Turkish territory, and its strategic territory no less. "Russian territorial demands and desires for changing some of the important terms of the Montreux Convention resulted in a worsening of relations and tension in Turkey about its relations with Russia," and this tension "increased with each demand from the Russian authorities" (Bayir, 2015, pp. 119–120). This naturally occasioned alarm in all quarters, not the least of which was Turkey itself. Comparatively weakened vis-à-vis the Soviet Union while occupying territory the Soviet Union coveted, Turkey found itself caught up in an ideological battle between an ancient rival and a promising protector. This was presumably not a difficult decision. The decision was to favor the American side in the geopolitical tug-of-war between the Soviet Union and the United States. This decision defined Turkey's postwar security.

Turkey's choice of the promising protector was surely impelled by its concerns about its ancient rival. Sir Winston Churchill gravely noted in 1946 that "Turkey and Persia are both profoundly alarmed and disturbed at the claims which are being made upon them and at the pressure being exerted by the Moscow government" (Churchill, 1947/1995, p. 299). During World War II, when Turkey still looked to the United Kingdom for its security concerns, "Ankara continued to fear that Britain might either be unwilling or unable to protect them from Soviet demands" (De Luca, 1977, p. 506). This of course left Turkey in need of external support. Turkey's need for external support coincided with the rise of the United States' doctrine of containment. It was at this point in their mutual relations that the United States began to tug.

The United States

The doctrine of containment has come to be synonymous with George Kennan. Though he eschewed such authorship, stating in his memoirs that he was misunderstood (Kennan, 1967), his words in an article in *Foreign Affairs* are unambiguous: "in these circumstances it is clear that the main element of any United States policy toward the Soviet Union must be that of long-term, patient but firm and vigilant containment of Russian expansive tendencies" (Kennan, 1947, p. 575). President Truman would accept this advice wholesale. Announcing the tenets of the doctrine which would bear his name, he informed Congress that "it must be the policy of the United States to support free people who are resisting attempted subjugation by armed minorities or by outside pressures" (McCullough, 1992, p. 649). In the ideological battlefield of the Cold War that was by then completely formed, this amounted to a declaration that the United States would assist states the world over in resisting communist subversion. Such was declared US policy. Consequently, Turkey would form the cornerstone of the United States' containment of the Soviet Union on its southern frontiers.

The tug of a promising protector: US foreign policy towards Turkey

From a US perspective, Turkey is a valuable strategic partner on its own. Nonetheless, the US–Turkish strategic relationship has been dominated by the needs of the US–Russian strategic relationship. There are essentially two fundamental aspects of the US–Turkish strategic relationship. The first aspect of that relationship is the US strategy of containing Russia, and Turkey's central role in it. The second aspect, and perennially the lesser of the two, is Turkey's role in bridging the West and the Middle East. From this it is clear that Turkey brings undoubted value to the relationship.

First, the Turkish role in the US strategy of containing Russia is a fundamental aspect of the strategic relationship. This role had early beginnings in the Cold War. By 1951, the United States was considering elevating this relationship to that of a formal treaty arrangement. The Central Intelligence Agency generated a Special Intelligence Estimate projecting Soviet reaction to this development. The assessment concluded that Turkey joining in a regional security alliance or inviting Turkey into the North Atlantic Treaty Organization (NATO) would be viewed by the Soviet Union as "an obstacle to Soviet expansion not only in the Near East but also in Europe" (United States Central Intelligence Agency, 1951, p. 1). The estimate further postulated that such an expansion would be viewed as "a threat to the USSR" and as evidence of "Western aggressive intent" (United States Central Intelligence Agency, 1951, p. 2). The estimate concluded that such an action would induce the Soviet Union to run the risks of a general war. Turkey thus joined NATO and stood with the alliance through to the present day.

The second aspect of the strategic relationship is Turkey's proposed role in bridging the West and the Middle East. With the fall of the Soviet Union, the world looked very different. Russia no longer posed the acute existential threat that the Soviet Union had. This meant that Turkey's value to the United States on the basis of its helping to contain the Soviet Union was necessarily lessened. Happily, another *raison d'être* existed for the alliance. Much hope was placed on Turkey's ability to serve as the gateway to the Middle East.

Nonetheless, the new role which was envisioned for Turkey was almost as important as the old one had been. Perpetually mired in conflict in the Middle East, the United States was eager for a new way of managing said conflicts. Consequently, "the possibility for Turkey to appear as the privileged interlocutor among the Islamic regimes only adds to its value, not least for US foreign policy" (Litsas, 2014, p. 133). This role is predicated on Turkish successes in democratic advancement. More still, it is based on Turkish economic successes.

It can be argued that Turkey stands on the cusp of rejoining the first rank of world powers. This is astonishing, considering that just 100 years ago Turkey was emerging from a long period of economic stagnation and perhaps even regression. So severe were the problems affecting Turkey's predecessor state, the Ottoman Empire, that it had earned itself the moniker of the Sick Man of Europe (Livanios, 2006). A clear line was not drawn under the disintegration of the Ottoman economy until its defeat in World War I led to the establishment of the Republic of Turkey. The macroeconomic reforms undertaken in 2001 are responsible for the more robust economy that Turkey enjoyed in the 2000s (Livanios, 2006).

The Justice and Development Party (AKP) was principally credited with the success of these reforms. More than anything, the AKP has been rewarded by the Turkish people for doing the right things in the right way. Much of this can be laid at the feet of Turkey's past hopes to join the European Union (EU). As Önis notes, in its early years, AKP

> demonstrated a firm commitment to the reform process, both in the economic and democratization realms. In spite of its Islamist roots, the party also appeared to be firmly committed to the goal of EU membership, with the EU proving to be a key long-term external anchor for the implementation of a series of important political and economic reforms.
>
> (Öniş, 2012, p. 136)

Prospective membership with the EU brought the promise of even greater economic growth through access to the EU's capital markets (Öniş, 2012). This made politically palatable the necessary structural reforms no matter their attendant pain. Moreover, it imposed strategic discipline on the AKP government. With a clear goal in sight and a clear path to achieve it, the AKP found it remarkably easy to stay the course.

Turkey was thus able to achieve remarkable economic success in the 2000s. She could therefore afford to seek an independent course in foreign policy. Coupled with the temporary absence of the Russian threat, Turkey was poised to reassess her own view of foreign policy and to have the United States assess its relationship with Turkey. Turkey is now a net possessor of what John J. Mearsheimer (2001) terms "latent power." Latent power is a state's ability to translate assets of population and wealth into military power. Enjoying increasingly great economic wealth and a population trending towards 100 million people, Turkey is indeed on its way to returning to the first rank of world powers. Turkey is perhaps not destined in the short term to again become a regional hegemon. In the intermediate term, the sorry saga of its belabored attempts to accede to the EU suggest that some of the members do not view Turkey fondly (Öniş, 2012). They are unlikely to wish to permit the establishment of an increasingly strong and recently slighted Turkey astride the Eurasian waterway. Turkey must be sure to be careful not to antagonize its rivals before it has achieved a stronger strategic footing.

Of late, hubris has led to an abandonment of early commitment to democratic reforms. The virtuous circle of economic growth underpinned by structural and regulatory reforms has left Turkey with great prestige built upon economic success and somewhat unmoored it from the strategic necessity of relying exclusively on the United States for its security. What US strategic planners want from Turkey is straightforward. As Flanagan and Brannen note, "Washington wants Ankara to be a reliable regional and global partner, at peace with its neighbors but not overly close to undemocratic regimes, and able to exert influence with its Muslim neighbors through its leadership and example" (Flanagan & Brannen, 2009, p. 82). In short, to use its geography and ideational similarity with its neighbors is to do Washington's bidding.

Testing the tug: the US–Turkish strategic relationship

The interplay of geography and ideas that animates the US–Turkish strategic relationship is built upon a solid foundation, but it still must be managed. The test of any successful relationship is not in how well it navigates times of ease and cooperation, but in whether it endures past difficult times. For this reason, much analytical information can be gleaned from the nadir of relations. For US–Turkish strategic relations, that nadir may well be the Cyprus dispute and its various flare-ups. Another nadir is undoubtedly the decision of the Turkish parliament not to authorize use of Turkish territory for the 2003 invasion of Iraq.

The Cyprus dispute

Regarding Cyprus, of particular note was the 1964 letter President Johnson penned to Turkish Prime Minister Inonu (United States Central Intelligence Agency, 1964). It was momentous. In this letter, the US president expresses his concern and displeasure to the Turkish prime minister about Turkish plans to invade Cyprus. Johnson was unstinting in his disapproval. He stated that he did not "consider that such a course of action by Turkey, fraught with such far-reaching consequences, is consistent with the commitment" of the Turkish government to consult fully with the United States (Johnson & Inonu, 1966, p. 386). This was particularly so because the actions of the Turkish government "posed the gravest issues of war and peace" (Johnson & Inonu, 1966, p. 388).

The Johnson letter contained both a chastisement and a warning. Its chastisement took the form of criticizing Turkish actions as inconsistent with its commitments as a NATO member. Johnson sternly admonished Turkey by stating that commitment to "NATO, in its very essence, means that NATO countries will not wage war on each other. Germany and France have buried centuries of animosity and hostility in becoming NATO allies; nothing less can be expected from Greece and Turkey" (Johnson & Inonu, 1966, p. 387). In any letter, this is strong stuff. It is all the more so in correspondence between two treaty allies.

The warning was more ominous still. Johnson noted that

> a military intervention in Cyprus by Turkey could lead to a direct involvement by the Soviet Union. I hope you will understand that your NATO allies have not had a chance to consider whether they have an obligation to protect Turkey against the Soviet Union if Turkey takes a step which results in Soviet intervention without the full consent and understanding of its NATO Allies.
>
> (Johnson & Inonu, 1966, p. 387)

Here Johnson is threatening to abrogate NATO commitments to Turkish security if unilateral Turkish actions prompt a military response from the Soviet Union. The consequences for Turkey could hardly have been graver.

Reaction in Turkey was instant. The Central Intelligence Agency opined that the letter "had done more to set back United States Turkish relations than any other single act" (United States Central Intelligence Agency, 1964). If Johnson's letter was chastising and bellicose, Inonu's response was aggrieved and prickly. It was also dismissive. In dismissing President Johnson's concerns about war with NATO allies, Prime Minister Inonu responded by saying:

> As to the concern you expressed over the out-break of a Turco-Greek war in case of Turkey's intervention in Cyprus … I would like to stress that Turkey would undertake a military operation in Cyprus exclusively under the conditions and for the purpose set forth in the agreements.
>
> (Johnson & Inonu, 1966, p. 391)

Consequently, the argument runs, any war between Greece and Turkey over this matter would be the fault of Greece, and by extension Johnson would be better served to make his concerns known in Athens rather than in Ankara.

Inonu's response to the threat was even more pointed. He replied:

> The part of your message expressing doubts as to the obligation of the NATO allies to protect Turkey in case she becomes directly involved with the USSR as a result of an action initiated in Cyprus, gives me the impression that there are as between us wide divergence of views as to the nature and basic principles of the North Atlantic Alliance.
>
> (Johnson & Inonu, 1966, p. 391)

The argument is well made. According to Inonu's view, aggression begets justification. Any alliance which spends its time litigating the aggression rather than defending against it is an alliance not worth joining.

What can be learned from this episode? Both parties must give due regard to the views and positions of the other side. The United States, for its part, could rightly expect consultation at a minimum in the foreign affairs of any state to which it extends explicit security guarantees. This point is essential, lest the tail be permitted to wag the dog. It cannot be expected that the United States be rushed headlong into war because the island of Cyprus cannot figure out how to govern itself in peace. President Johnson agreed. At the beginning of his letter he stated, "I must … first urge you to accept the responsibility for complete consultation with the United States before any such action is taken" (Johnson & Inonu, 1966, p. 386). This position seems more than reasonable.

Turkey too had cause for grievance. If the United States can insist upon a right to be consulted about the activities of a treaty ally, then Turkey, for its part, can rightly expect that its views would at a minimum be given the due regard of a trusted ally. In Prime Minister Inonu's response, he puts this point frankly and notes that his government's repeated attempts to get the United States to take this issue as seriously as his government does had been met with disinterest. Inonu stated:

> I think, I have thus reminded you how many times and under what circumstances we informed you of the necessity for intervention in Cyprus. I do remember having emphasized to your high level officials our due appreciation of the special responsibilities incumbent upon the United States within the alliance and of the necessity to be particularly careful and helpful to enable her to maintain solidarity within the alliance.
>
> (Johnson & Inonu, 1966, p. 389)

Turkey thus thought that it was in fact consulting the United States and that its concerns were not being taken seriously. It thus prepared to act unilaterally. It is indeed strange for the United States to insist upon consultation from Turkey while disregarding Turkish attempts to consult. Viewed thusly, one might be excused for thinking that what President Johnson was insisting on was not the United States' right of consultation, but rather a right of approval. Accepting this view, one can perhaps excuse the note of pique in Prime Minister Inonu's response. It is difficult not to conclude that the majority of the fault was American in this instance.

In the future, both countries will need to give greater regard to each other's concerns if the alliance is to continue to weather these difficulties. The United States considers that as the rock of the alliance, its core strategic interests must have primacy in the consideration of internationally significant actions such as the invasion of Cyprus. Turkey is quite simply beyond the point where it will accept being treated as the junior partner of an alliance managed from afar. The strength of the geopolitical bond is not a sufficient condition for the endurance of the alliance. It must be combined with a sustained effort to give each other the due attention strategic partners are owed. As can be seen by the fracas surrounding the second invasion of Iraq, it is not clear that either party learned this lesson.

The second invasion of Iraq

The Turkish decision not to approve the use of Turkish territory for the invasion of Iraq rocked the foundations of the strategic relationship. It caused another nadir in relations. Much useful information can be gained by analysis of this nadir as well. The Turkish decision placed much strain on the relationship at a time when the Russian threat, always the relationship's primary *raison d'être*, was less acute. That the relationship survived mostly intact is a testament to its strength. That the relationship was so seriously tried is a testament to the fact that neither party has fully learned the lessons the Johnson letter should have taught.

The failure of the Turkish parliament to approve US deployments in the run-up to the 2003 invasion of Iraq was a complete and unmitigated error. Blame abounds, and there is much to go around. Turkey, for her part, failed to give primacy to US core strategic interests. The United States failed to give Turkish interests the due regard owed to a strategic partner. In short, this conflict in the two states' mutual relations was entirely preventable. Both states need only learn the lesson of history. As they clearly had not by the time of the 2003 invasion, a greater study of how the same failures again afflicted the relationship is in order.

The first way in which it is clear that the parties failed to learn the lessons of the Johnson letter is Turkey's failure to give primacy to the United States' core strategic interests. On March 1, 2003, the Turkish parliament failed to pass a resolution permitting the United States use of its territory for the invasion of Iraq. This failing was a massive unforced error. That it was an unforced error was obvious at the time. Or, as will be seen, it was at least obvious to Turkish leaders in the immediate aftermath of the debacle that was to unfold. The primary reason that the Turkish government should have supported the US invasion and permitted the use of Turkey as a point of entry was that Turkey was not in a position to stop the invasion. It was therefore left with a decision to be involved and be decisive or not be involved and be divisive. General Hilmi Özkök, the Chief of the General Staff of the Turkish Armed Forces during the 2003 invasion of Iraq, is quoted as saying, "Our choice is between bad and worse" (Migdalovitz, 2003, p. 2). In this, he was correct.

Turkey was balancing legitimate concerns. It was seriously concerned about the harm the war would do to Turkey's economy. Suffice it to say this was a real concern that weighed heavily against supporting the invasion, or at least it would if it were possible to stop the invasion. As it stood, Turkey could not stop it. To therefore fail to participate would be to suffer the consequences of Turkish fears without realizing the offsetting benefits participation would bring. This would be the "worse" General Özkök spoke of. Unfortunately, General Özkök's sagacity only appeared after the decision had been taken in parliament to reject the approval of US use of Turkish territory (Migdalovitz, 2003). It does appear to be a clear indication that the folly of the course on which Turkey embarked was manifest.

General Özkök's worse option might have been a forgivable mistake if the Turkish government failed to appreciate the import the United States attached to the decision. Yet, the Turkish government was fully aware of the import of this decision both to the United States and to Turkey. Then Prime Minister Erdoğan stated that responding favorably to the parliamentary measure was in the national interest (Migdalovitz, 2003). This was because the United States defined the invasion of Iraq as in its core interests. As Turkey has hitched its national security fate to US might, whatever the United States defined as within its core interests becomes *a priori* Turkish core interests.

Having rightly determined that supporting the parliamentary measure was a core interest, Erdoğan failed to treat it as such. Astonishingly, the government permitted its party members a "free vote." This meant that party discipline was not in force for the vote. Members were thus relieved of the consequences of voting against the government's position. Passage of the measure required an "absolute majority of those present, or 267 votes ... but it got only 264 votes, failing by three. Ninety-nine members of the AKP voted against the measure; 19 abstained" (Migdalovitz, 2003, p. 2). This was a strange way to treat a measure deemed of national importance. Notably, the measure failed by just three votes. It is also noteworthy that three members of Erdoğan's own cabinet voted against the measure.

There can be no question that the government of Turkey, or at least its prime minister, was aware of the importance the United States attached to the passage of this measure. This is borne out by Erdoğan's own words. In the aftermath of the vote, one may have expected damage control to kick in. One could have expected the Turkish government to make whatever amends possible. Indeed, this may have been the point of General Özkök's post hoc support of the measure. His comments were said to have "laid a foundation for passage of a similar resolution if and when it were resubmitted. Immediately thereafter, politicians praised Özkök's statement and some members of parliament said that they would change their votes" if a new vote was called (Migdalovitz, 2003, p. 5). Coupled with the votes the government already had, this nearly ensured the passage of the measure were it to be resubmitted. It was not. Turkey thus underscored the message that it was unwilling to comply with US requests by conduct that made it clear that it could have done so.

Turkey further compounded these errors by dragging its feet on permitting use of its airspace. On March 19, the Turkish parliament voted to permit the United States access to air corridors through Turkish airspace for six months (Migdalovitz, 2003). Even after two weeks of roiling relations, the Turkish government still stalled. It was not until March 21 that Turkey permitted the United States unrestricted access to the air corridors approved by parliament, a full day after hostilities commenced. This is not how great powers expect to be treated by those whose security they guarantee.

It bears repeating that the measure of the strength of the US–Turkish strategic relationship can be gleaned from the fact that it survived this incident at all. In US governmental circles, officials were said to be "furious" with the Turkish government (Migdalovitz, 2003, p. 23). This is because Turkey's decision had real costs. The United States had wished to open a two-front war in Iraq. The northern prong of this strategy was predicated on Turkish cooperation. The two-pronged approach was considered of great import to US war planners. Undersecretary of Defense Paul Wolfowitz told Congress on March 27 that "There is no question if we had a US armored force in northern Iraq right now, the end (of the war) would be closer" (Migdalovitz, 2003, p. 23). In the deadly calculus of war, where every day can be measured in lives lost, Turkish intransigence was a deadly serious matter for the US government.

This entire episode is inexplicable. The Turkish government risked much with its strategy of insouciance and intransigence. By failing to support the chief guarantor of Turkish security in an issue which the said guarantor deems of critical importance, it imperiled not just its alliance with the United States but also five decades of Turkish security policy premised on that alliance. It is simply not clear why this risk was worth it to the Turkish government. What is clear is that it did not learn the lessons of the Johnson letter. For so long as Turkey depends on US security guarantees, US strategic concerns are necessarily Turkish strategic concerns. And yet, blame for this regrettable episode ought not be shouldered by Turkey alone. The United States too seems to have failed to learn the lessons of the Johnson letter.

The second example of the parties' failure to take heed of the lessons of the Johnson letter is the United States again failing to give Turkey the due regard that must be accorded to strategic partners. Turkish concerns about the prospect of war with Iraq were many. They included fear of the Kurds using the war as an opportunity to establish a separate state, concern for the fate of their ethnic kin the Turkomans, and apprehension that a humanitarian crisis would develop on its border as in the first coalition invasion of Iraq (Migdalovitz, 2003). All of these concerns were real and caused anxiety in Turkey. The most important concern, however, was economic. It has been said that "Turkey's highest priority was obtaining protection against the economic impact of a war" (Migdalovitz, 2003, p. 15). Here the United States would have been better served, and would have better served its ally, by explicitly agreeing to underwrite the impact of the war on the Turkish economy. This it did not do.

Turkish fears of the economic impact of the second invasion of Iraq were borne out of experience. That is to say that Turkish fears of the second invasion of Iraq were derived from the experience of the first invasion of Iraq. Turkish estimates of the economic impact of having to close the Iraqi border during the first invasion of Iraq range from $30 billion to $100 billion (Migdalovitz, 2003). The United States offered Turkey $6 billion. This is a paltry sum compared to the figures that concerned Turkey. While it must be said that the costs of the second invasion were costs Turkey would bear whether or not it accepted the offered US assistance and might be therefore thought of as sunk costs, one can certainly understand Turkey being less than impressed.

To be fair to the US side, it is necessary to note that this $6 billion was to be leveraged to get an additional $24 billion in debt relief (Migdalovitz, 2003). Steadfast support from the United States also permitted Turkey to receive $31 billion in support from the International Monetary Fund (Migdalovitz, 2003). This is laudable, even useful. It also missed the point. Turkey was concerned about the economic impact of another Iraqi war on its borders. US support was designed to assist Turkey with existing financial problems such as financing shortfalls. Turkey could undoubtedly put such funds to good use. But it could not be expected to accept such meager assistance in lieu of its actual needs in the event of war. Having made no effort to alleviate or even understand the ills that concerned Turkey, the United States appeared to give Turkish concerns the same short shrift that caused the Johnson Administration to ignore Turkish attempts to consult in 1964. The result was a similar seismic quake in the strategic relationship.

Moreover, the United States did not give much credence to Turkish concerns for the threat Iraq posed to Turkey in the event of a war. Turkish leaders viewed this refusal to give credence with their own shocked incredulity. General Özkök was quoted as having opined that he has "difficulty understanding those who claim there is a threat to them across the ocean, and when Turkey says the same threat exists on the other side of its border, this is found to be unbelievable" (Migdalovitz, 2003, p. 66). General Özkök's point is also well made. If Iraq posed a threat to the United States sufficient to justify a war, Turkish fears of a threat from Iraq, with which it shares a land border, must necessarily be more acute. At a minimum, Turkish concerns could not have been thought unreasonable. They surely merited the due regard of one ally for another.

Happily, the United States appears to be learning its lesson. It moved swiftly to overcome the inter-alliance fracas caused by the Turkish parliament's refusal to approve the resolution authorizing US troops to use Turkish territory to attack Iraq. On July 5, 2006, the United States and Turkey signed "Shared Vision and Structured Dialogue." This is apparently "the first important document confessing that USA realized that the course of events in Turkey changed and it was necessary to provide greater freedom to Turkey to conduct the primary negotiator role in the region" (Dağcı, 2012, p. 4). Additionally, one of President Obama's first trips abroad was to Turkey (Dağcı, 2012). Turkey is being accorded the formal consultations that are its due. It is also being treated as the trusted ally the alliance claims it to be. It remains to be seen if the US shift in perspective vis-à-vis Turkey is a long-term trend. As will be seen, Turkey's willingness to learn its portion of the Johnson letter lesson is even less clear.

Tug back: Turkey grabs the rope

Today Turkey is committed to a foreign policy strategy of "strategic depth." Promulgated by Ahmet Davutoğlu, formerly both Minister of Foreign Affairs and Prime Minister, strategic depth is the use of Turkey's historic ties "emanating from [Turkey's] geocultural, geopolitical and geoeconomics situation" to exercise greater influence in its immediate environs (Yalvac, 2012, p. 166). It is not a new strategy. As neo-Ottomanism, it formed the core of the foreign policy of Turgut Özal's various administrations and was summed up as "Peace at Home, Peace Abroad." Updated and refined, it represents the core of AKP's view of Turkish grand strategy and is often summed up as "Zero Problems" with neighbors (Flanagan & Brannen, 2009, p. 81).

Turkey's strategic depth policy proposes solutions and problems for US policymakers. Strategic depth's concern for the relations with neighbors makes Turkey better able to play the role of interlocutor to the Middle East. Yet, strategic depth represents a separate course for Turkey. It represents a Turkish view of its role, not a US view. What is clear is that "Turkey remains a pivotal country for advancement of many US interests, and Turkey still considers the United States its most important ally" (Flanagan & Brannen, 2009, p. 81). But Turkey is emerging from its century-long status as second-rate. This emergence will require careful balancing of both parties' concerns. It will also require due regard for Turkey's new role. At a minimum,

> Ankara would like fuller consultation from Washington on major US policies and initiatives vis-à-vis the Middle East, Russia, and the Caucasus. The worst surprise the United States could foist on Turkey would be to undertake a major move in the region without first consulting Turkey. Turkey also wants to be treated as a trusted ally even as it pursues distinct policies in advancing its interests.
>
> (Flanagan & Brannen, 2009, p. 82)

It may be that strategic depth is no longer in vogue in Turkish foreign policy circles, but the instinct to expand Turkey's role in world affairs is undoubtedly alive and well.

Conclusion

The chances of a major rupture in relations could be thought to be substantially ameliorated by the resurgence of the Russian threat to both parties. The resurgence of Russian expansionism once again demands containment from US foreign policy. It also requires that Turkey reaffirm the outside support it has enjoyed as a NATO member. It should be recalled that one of the main threats that the United States made to Turkey in President Johnson's letter was that any Soviet response to the unilateral actions of Turkey would not be covered under the US security guarantees. Now that Russian threat is once again acute.

Today Turkey appears to be precariously perched on a precipice fraught with danger. At least vis-à-vis Russia, Turkey has been attempting to strike a balance between its short-term economic interests and its long-term strategic interests. The tug-of-war between the United States and Russia over Turkey is again apparent. Turkey appears to be moving towards stronger relations with Russia. But events are fast-moving. On November 15, 2015, Turkey shot down a Russian jet that it said had strayed into Turkish territory (Mitchell & Weiner, 2015). This resulted in rapid deterioration in Turkish–Russian relations culminating in dueling sanctions. Yet, both states face severe economic pressures. Ending the mutual sanctions is a way to give their economies a jolt. To this end, Erdoğan, now Turkey's president, had been reaching out to

Russia in hopes of reviving relations. He has apologized for the shoot-down of the Russian jet after having steadfastly refused to do so. As can be seen, Turkish positions oscillate between near appeasement and outright bellicosity. Strategic depth, for all its acclaimed charms, appears not to have an answer for a centuries-long Russian rivalry.

In the midst of a diplomatic reset (Sahlin, 2016), Turkish–Russian rapprochement has serious consequences for US–Turkish relations. It is graver still for Turkey. Absent the Western alliance, which is Turkey's strategic bet to preserve its security, Turkey would be left strategically vulnerable to Russian whims to an even greater extent than it is now. While it is reasonably clear that hubris has been the driver of US failures to sufficiently take Turkish concerns into account, Turkey's reasons for failing to give sufficient regard for US strategic concerns is less obvious. It may be as a result of Turkish ambivalence towards the West, particularly NATO.

Turkish ambivalence to NATO is not especially new. While senior governmental figures have long seen it as the strategic lynchpin for Turkish security, the Turkish public has rarely been as convinced. Some of this is as a result of Turkey's experience with democracy. At times, autocratic governments have had to give very little attention to public opinion. This has led to a longstanding policy of failing to make the case for NATO specifically and the Western alliance generally. Evidence of this can be seen from polling done by the German Marshall Fund indicating that Turkish domestic support for the NATO alliance is the lowest of any NATO member (Flanagan & Brannen, 2009). In 2004 only 53 percent of Turks thought that NATO was an essential part of their country's security architecture. By 2007, this number was down to 34 percent (Flanagan & Brannen, 2009). If the Turkish government was working to counter these facts, the evidence suggests it has been unsuccessful.

Worse still, it seems that the ambivalence about the relationship has reached the highest quarters. While then Turkish President Ahmet Necdet Sezer stated that "there will not be any change in Turkey's attitude" towards the US alliance, and then Prime Minister Erdoğan was said to consider passage of the parliamentary resolution supporting US use of Turkish territory a matter of national importance, these sentiments were not evident in the Turkish government's handling of the vote (Migdalovitz, 2003, p. 24). Erdoğan's lackluster support for the measure was the principle cause of its demise.

Even more worrying is the attitude of the Turkish officer corps. Traditionally the great bastion of support for the alliance, many of the younger crop of officers "whose service has focused on Turkey's counterterrorism operations in the southeast see NATO as placing increasingly costly demands for expeditionary operations on the Turkish armed forces but providing few current benefits in return to Turkish security" (Flanagan & Brannen, 2009, p. 87). As a baseline, US expectations for Turkey's role in the strategic partnership must include an understanding that it is the responsibility of the Turkish government to undertake the task of convincing the Turkish people of the value of the alliance. The Turkish government might be well-served to expend a bit of effort convincing itself and those members of the government and military who have not yet been made to understand what role the alliance plays in Turkey's security arrangements. While the United States can certainly help in this effort, principally by treating Turkey with the respect it is due, convincing the Turkish people of the value of NATO must be a Turkish undertaking.

The tug of the future

The Turkish geopolitical position is under threat again, this time by the twin travails of a resurgent Russia and the effects of the Syrian civil war and migration crisis. The first must surely have reminded Ankara of the reasons for its deep strategic relationship with the United States, and the latter has surely knocked the sheen off the economic successes which fed the hubris in the first place. These two events should be used by those who favor the US–Turkish strategic relationship to cement the strategic partnership for at least the coming decade. This is so because the geography that animates Russia's insecurities and ideas about how to manage its security are the same, and Turkey is still best suited to contain it. The United States shall remain interested in Turkey so long as Russia remains a potent foe. Russia will continue to tug at Turkey in opportune times so as to chip away at the strategic bulwark to its south. In order to maintain the alliance between the United States and Turkey, both nations should be mindful of each other's needs "so as to strengthen the friendship between the two countries" (Obama, 2009, para. 7).

References

Bajema, N. (2010). Beyond the security model: Assessing the capacity of neoclassical realism for forecasting nuclear proliferation. In W.C. Potter and G. Mukhatzhanova (Eds.), *Forecasting Nuclear Proliferation in the 21st Century: A Comparative Perspective* (pp. 58–79). Stanford, CA: Stanford University Press.

Bayir, Ö.E. (2015). The perception of Russia in Poland and Turkey: A comparative analysis. *Polish Quarterly of International Affairs*, 24(1), 113–121. Retrieved from www.academia.edu/15151079/The_Perception_of_Russia_in_Poland_and_Turkey_A_Comparative_Analysis_The_Polish_Quarterly_of_International_Affairs_2015_No_1_p_113-121.

Beisner, R. (2006). *Dean Acheson: A Life in the Cold War*. Oxford: Oxford University Press.

Churchill, W. (1947/1995). The sinews of peace. In M.A. Kishlansky (Ed.), *Sources of World History* (pp. 298–302). New York: HarperCollins.

Dağcı, G.T. (2012). Turkey–US relations in Justice and Development Party's era. *Alternatives: Turkish Journal of International Relations*, 11(2), 1–11. Retrieved from http://alternatives.yalova.edu.tr/article/view/5000150689/5000136832.

De Luca, A.R. (1977). Soviet-American politics and the Turkish Straits. *Political Science Quarterly (Academy of Political Science)*, 92(3), 503–522. doi:10.2307/2148505.

Flanagan, S. and Brannen, S. (2009). *Turkey's Evolving Dynamics: Strategic Choices for US-Turkey Relations*. Washington, DC: Center for Strategic and International Studies.

Johnson, L. and Inonu, I. (1966). President Johnson and Prime Minister Inonu: Correspondence between President Johnson and Prime Minister Inonu, June 1964, as released by the White House, January 15, 1966. *Middle East Journal*, 20(3), 386–393.

Kennan, G.F. (1946). The charge in the Soviet Union (Kennan) to the Secretary of State [Telegram]. Retrieved from http://nsarchive.gwu.edu/coldwar/documents/episode-1/kennan.htm.

Kennan, G.F. (1947). The sources of Soviet conduct. *Foreign Affairs*, 25(4), 566–582. Retrieved from https://www.foreignaffairs.com/articles/russian-federation/1947-07-01/sources-soviet-conduct.

Kennan, G.F. (1967). *Memoirs, 1925–1950*. Boston, MA: Little, Brown.

Litsas, S. (2014). Bandwagoning for profit and Turkey: Alliance formations and volatility in the Middle East. *Israel Affairs*, 20(1), 125–139. doi:10.1080/13537121.2013.863085.

Livanios, D. (2006). The "sick man" paradox: History, rhetoric and the "European character" of Turkey. *Journal of Southern Europe & The Balkans*, 8(3), 299–311. doi:10.1080/14613190601004830.

McCullough, D. (1992). *Truman*. New York: Simon & Schuster.

Mearsheimer, J. (2001). *The Tragedy of Great Power Politics*. New York: W. W. Norton & Company.

Medvedev, D. (2009, November 12). Presidential address to the Federal Assembly of the Russian Federation. Retrieved from https://www.rt.com/politics/medvedev-annual-address-full/.

Migdalovitz, C. (2003). *Iraq: Turkey, the Deployment of U.S. Forces, and Related Issues*. Report for Congress. Washington, DC: UNT Digital Library. Retrieved from http://digital.library.unt.edu/ark:/67531/metacrs8186/.

Mitchell, A. and Weiner, C. (2015, November 30). U.S. confirms that downed Russian plane entered Turkish airspace. *NBC News*. Retrieved from www.nbcnews.com/news/world/u-s-confirms-downed-russian-plane-entered-turkish-airspace-n471481.

United Nations (1936). Montreux Convention Regarding the Regime of the Straits. *League of Nations Treaty Series*, Vol. 173, pp. 214–241. Retrieved from https://treaties.un.org/Pages/AdvanceSearch.aspx?tab=UNTS&clang=_en.

Obama, President Barack. (2009, April 6). Remarks by President Obama to the Turkish Parliament. Washington, DC: The White House. Retrieved from https://obamawhitehouse.archives.gov/the-press-office/remarks-president-obama-turkish-parliament.

Öniş, Z. (2012). The triumph of conservative globalism: The political economy of the AKP era. *Turkish Studies*, 13(2), 135–152. doi:10.1080/14683849.2012.685252.

Sahlin, M. (2016, August 9). Turkey's Erdogan unnerves West with Putin visit. *BBC News*. Retrieved from www.bbc.com/news/world-europe-37009931.

United States Central Intelligence Agency. (1951). *Probable Soviet Reaction to the Inclusion of Greece and Turkey in Western Defense Agreements*. Washington, DC. Retrieved from https://www.cia.gov/library/center-for-the-study-of-intelligence/csi-publications/books-and-monographs/listing-of-declassified-national-intelligence-estimates-on-the-soviet-union-and-international-communism-1946-1984/1951.htm.

United States Central Intelligence Agency. (1964, June 6). Turkish reaction to President Johnson's letter to Prime Minister Inonu [Intelligence Information Cable]. Retrieved from www.foia.cia.gov/sites/default/files/document_conversions/89801/DOC_0000615268.pdf.

Yalvaç, F. (2012). Strategic depth or hegemonic depth? A critical realist analysis of Turkey's position in the world system. *International Relations, 26*(2), 165–180. doi:10.1177/0047117811428331.

Yanik, L. (2015). Keep(ing) calm and carry(ing) on business? Turkey-Russia relations, as seen from Turkey. *Turkish Review, 5*(5), 366–375.

Zeihan, P. (2014). *The Accidental Superpower: The Next Generation of American Preeminence and the Coming Global Disaster.* New York: Twelve.

Zudin, A.I. (2000). Oligarchy as a political problem of Russian postcommunism. *Russian Social Science Review, 41*(6), 4–33. doi:10.2753/RSS1061-142841064.

4 The ties that bind

Postwar US foreign policy toward Turkey

Gökser Gökçay

Post-Second World War US foreign policy toward Turkey was shaped by the very events that were also considered among the origins of the Cold War. The crisis of the Soviet troops in Iran, the civil war in Greece, the Soviet demands toward Turkey, the British Aide-Mémoire of February 21, 1947, and the subsequent declaration of the Truman Doctrine were all major catalysts of the early Cold War. Because Turkey was at the center of all these crises, US officials placed particular emphasis on developing policies for Turkey. Despite the significance of Turkey in US foreign policy in the postwar period, it is a neglected case study in US-Turkey relations. The current literature regarding the history of US-Turkey diplomatic relations is full of discursive analysis and gestural diplomatic initiatives, such as the visit of the USS *Missouri* or the official statements of both countries. The analysis of US foreign policy toward Turkey has been based mainly on the declarations of political doctrines and security concerns. The so-called Soviet Union threat toward Turkey, the declaration of the Truman Doctrine, and Turkey's inclusion in the Marshall Plan are only studied within the limits of such discursive and descriptive framework. The reasons for the initiation of these policies and the economic and military motives behind them have been mostly neglected in the literature. In this chapter, by using primary documents from the National Archives and Records Administration at College Park, Maryland, United States, the National Archives at Kew, United Kingdom, and the Republican Archives at Ankara, Turkey, the author aims to conduct a structural analysis of the period and discuss the US foreign policy toward Turkey in the postwar period according to three themes.

One of the core problems of the era was the transition of power from the United Kingdom to the United States. Unable to fulfill its commitments in the region in the aftermath of the war, the United Kingdom gradually began to yield its influence in the Middle East to the United States. Despite the tacit acceptance of the British officials, this was not a smooth process, as demonstrated in the documents acquired at the National Archives at Kew. A concise story of this transition with regard to Turkey will be given. A second and more widely known aspect of the US foreign policy was the military-strategic planning for the defense of Turkey. Because this side of US-Turkey relations is much discussed by the scholars of US foreign relations, only the core aspect of the US strategy in Turkey, known as the Griddle Plan, will be addressed. Third, the process of Turkey's economic integration with the Western bloc and reorganization of its economic objectives in line with the Marshall Plan will be discussed as they were part of the foreign economic policy of the United States in the early Cold War.

It is argued that the formation of an integral US foreign policy toward Turkey in the postwar era was shaped by an amalgamation of these military-strategic planning and foreign economic objectives. Turkey was not just a military subject for US foreign policy; Turkey's inclusion in the postwar economic system was also essential. This chapter intends to analyze the development of this integral policy by explaining its political, military, and economic influence on Turkey's foreign policy choices as well as on the country's economic and political decision-making processes.

From Pax Britannica to Pax Americana

The decision makers of US foreign policy were hesitant to be involved in Near Eastern affairs in the immediate aftermath of the war. American policymakers considered the Middle East to be under the responsibility of the United Kingdom and therefore chose to withdraw themselves from direct involvement (U.S. Department of State, 1964). Still, this did not mean that they excluded themselves from the region completely. In the case of Turkey, they even feared that Turkey would be under the impression that the United States was "not interested in the country and [had] handed it over to British domination" (U.S. Department of State, 1964, p. 1100). On the other hand, while British officials accepted the upcoming US dominance in the region, they still wanted to be closely involved in the political decision-making processes, which created friction between the two countries' officials.

The United States had provided Lend-Lease aid to Turkey during the war – though from the Turkish perspective, the deliveries were made under the supervision of British officials. This process created friction among American, British, and Turkish politicians for several reasons. First, the Turkish government was suspicious of the British deliveries and assumed that some of the supplies were being withheld by the British in order to punish Turkey for not entering the war. Second, Turkey was afraid of making double payments in this process because itinerary lists were not properly documented. Lastly, the Turkish side wished to negotiate the terms of deliveries directly with the Americans, as the United Kingdom had failed to keep its promises in the Armaments Agreement of 1939.

The US administration tried to solve the crisis by negotiating directly with Turkey for the terms of the Lend-Lease agreement. On February 23, 1945, the same day that Turkey declared war against Germany and Japan, Turkey and the United States signed the Mutual Aid Agreement concerning the Lend-Lease aid program. The Mutual Aid Agreement and its supplemental agreements provided the basis for later foreign aid agreements between the United States and Turkey.[1]

Another case that got the attention of US decision makers was the diplomatic notes sent to Turkey by the Soviets. After denouncing the 1925 Treaty of Friendship and Nonaggression with Turkey in March of 1945, the USSR sent a diplomatic note on June 7, 1945, which called for a joint Turkish-Soviet condominium over the Straits. Truman and Churchill had agreed for a revision of the Montreux Convention at the Potsdam Conference (Leffler, 1985), but there had been no discussion of how this could be implemented. Following the success of the Red Army in the Second World War, the Soviet administration thought that they had a right to defend the Straits together with Turkey to ensure their safety in the event of another global war (Chuev, 2007).

The first note of the Soviets was not taken very seriously by the US administration. The Soviets were unable to start a new war after the colossal devastation of the Second World War. American defense officials were not expecting any Soviet attacks on Turkey and considered these demands as only intimidation, but they also feared that constant pressure on Turkey would force it to acquiesce to Soviet demands. Furthermore, the reports on Soviet troop deployments in Bulgaria were quite unsettling for both the US and U.K. administrations (Mark, 2005). Later, it was understood that the reports of Soviet formations in Bulgaria were incorrect. The Soviet note of August 7, 1946 repeated the same demands for a joint defense of the Straits. This time, the United States responded by rejecting the introduction of Soviet forces into the Straits (Mark, 2005). According to Secretary of State Dean Acheson, the President considered the "strong position" they had taken to be "the most important decision" since the bombing of Hiroshima (U.S. Department of State, 1974, p. 1649). While denying the Soviet demands for Turkey, the Truman administration secretly began to adopt a new strategy for the region. These preparations indicate that the United States was getting ready to act on its own in the region.

Documents in the National Archives and Records Administration show that the United States was still not ready to declare unilateral action in regards to Turkey. On November 18, 1946, in an interdepartmental meeting, the subject of aid to Turkey was discussed. We see from the recommendations of this meeting that the United States has been ready to initiate a large aid program for Turkey even before the declaration of the Truman Doctrine. However, it was also recommended that "the British government be informed in advance" of the plan and "its cooperation solicited" ("Aid to Turkey," 1946). The Truman administration was still hesitant to act by itself in the case of Turkey.

The Aide-Mémoire received by the US State Department on February 21, 1947 removed all hesitation in the administration. The British government declared in its note to the US government that it was no longer able to continue its obligations in Greece and Turkey (U.S. Department of State, 1971). The

State Department quickly began to prepare for a policy analysis of the situation. A month later, Truman delivered his famous speech and the United States declared its unilateral decision to intervene in the Greek civil war and supply Turkey with military assistance. The way in which this aid program was organized was a clear indication that the United States was ready to act on its own in the Middle East when it was able to provide the necessary justification for its intervention.

The subject of British responsibility in the region continued up until the first years of the 1950s. A British Foreign Office document dated February 14, 1951 stated that there was "no agreement between the US and UK on their respective roles in strategic planning in the Middle East" (Secondé, 1951). In the case of Turkey, US officials wanted to channel strategic guidance directly to the Turkish government, but the British administration rejected this position because it was in "conflict with the previous United States–United Kingdom Chiefs of Staff understanding that the Middle East should be a British responsibility" (Secondé, 1951). The same day that this British position was discussed in the Foreign Office, a conference gathered in Istanbul for the US mission chiefs in the Middle East. In the recommendations section of the concluding remarks of this conference, it was stated that

> the United States should seek an early clarification of the United States–United Kingdom military responsibilities for the Middle East. However, even though performance under such an agreement with the United Kingdom as to responsibilities be achieved through some regional arrangement, the present leading position of the United States in Turkey and Greece should be maintained.
>
> (U.S. Department of State, 1979, p. 56)

The US administration was aware that the British position in the Middle East was "weakened" (U.S. Department of State, 1979, p. 60). While refraining from a hasty takeover, the US foreign policy was to keep its influence in Turkey and slowly but surely convince the British to accept the new status quo. The accession of Turkey and Greece to NATO was one of the corner-stones of this transformation. In effect, Turkey was no longer under British responsibility, and despite the ongoing involvement of the United Kingdom in the regional security establishments, the United States became the major decision maker for the military strategy in the region.

Becoming the frontier country: The Griddle Plan

The military-strategic planning for the defense of Turkey was a key aspect of the US foreign policy. That is why the whole implementation of the Truman Doctrine was centered on military defense. At this point, it is necessary to make a clarification. The aid program that formed after the declaration of the Truman Doctrine was completely in the form of military supplies and equipment. Seemingly economic projects like the road program were in effect designed to support the military supply program (U.S. Department of State, 1971). The initial request for 150 million dollars of aid for Turkey later turned into a 100-million-dollar aid program, but together with additional appropriations, the total aid provided to Turkey under the Truman Doctrine was 158.6 million dollars (U.S. Agency for International Development, 2005).

The whole military assistance program was based on a series of contingency plans called Pincher. One of the area studies of the Pincher series was the Griddle Plan; the Truman Doctrine was used to legitimize the funds necessary to implement this strategic plan (Cohen, 1997). Accordingly, Turkey was to be used as "a base for Allied operations against the Soviet Union" (Leffler, 1985, p. 813). The plan was to bomb vital areas of the USSR such as the oil-producing areas of the Caucasus, while Turkish forces would hold back a Soviet attack on the Middle East (Cohen, 1997). The Pentagon knew that the Turkish forces would not hold for long against the Soviets, but the strategy was to slow down the Soviet army until B-29s in Cairo would bomb vital Soviet industries in the Urals (Mark, 2005). Therefore, Turkey's capability to resist the Soviet offensive was a crucial part of the US long-term strategy to prevent a Soviet invasion in the Middle East (Munson, 2012). The US administration was not concerned with "maintaining Turkish territorial integrity," but rather with "persuading the Turks to adopt a strategy that would cause the maximum delay to a Soviet offensive against the Middle East" (Cohen, 1997, p. 55). This strategy made Turkey one of the frontier countries of the containment policy in the Middle East, along with Iran.[2] General McBride, the mission chief of the military aid program JAMMAT (Joint American Military Mission for Aid to Turkey), explained their role in Turkey with these words:

> The purpose of the Aid Program is to increase the combat potential of the Turkish armed forces. The present Aid Program would not stop the Russians, but it would help. ... There is enough stuff here now so that the taking of Turkey by the Soviet Union would be an expensive proposition. A lot of Russians would be killed. That is the main idea. It is cheaper for us to make use of Turkish manpower by simply supplying equipment than to bring American boys over here to fight.
>
> (Robinson, 1948, p. 2)

As General McBride mentioned, it was far cheaper for the United States to use the Turkish forces, but the burden of this policy on the Turkish state budget was major throughout the 1950s. To ease the burden of the Turkish budget, the United States supplemented the military aid program together with economic assistance, which is the third and last theme of this chapter regarding U.S. foreign policy toward Turkey.

Economic integration via foreign assistance

Turkey's economic integration with the Western bloc and reorganization of its economic objectives in line with the European Recovery Plan (ERP), known as the Marshall Plan, were among its top priorities in the postwar period. At the end of the war, in October of 1945, the Turkish government requested 500 million dollars for its development plan ("Loan For Turkey," 1945). However, at the time, the United States was not ready to enter into such an obligation, and the amount requested by the Turkish government was far greater than the actual lending capacity of the Exim Bank. During the formation of the Marshall Plan, Turkey repeated a similar demand and presented a comprehensive development plan requiring more than 600 million dollars (Economic Cooperation Administration, 1949). Both requests were rejected by the United States and the members of the ERP. Those plans were viewed as incoherent and ineffective. As part of the Marshall Plan ideology, spending a good amount on underdeveloped sectors instead of focusing on the areas where the country had "comparative advantage" seemed unproductive and inefficient to the advisors. Charles Maier defined this perspective as "the politics of productivity," which "emerged as the American organizing idea for the postwar economic world depended upon superseding class conflict with economic growth" (1977, p. 629). The application of this policy in Turkey was based on a subset of inefficiency arguments seen in the advisory reports. The state institutions were defined as inefficient tools to provide economic development. So, the limitation of direct or indirect state control was perceived to be an obstacle to economic growth. In order to realize this objective, the Turkish economy had to be reorganized.

The reorganization of the Turkish economy began to be realized in four stages. First the economic planning of the republic was transformed into an agricultural-oriented one. Second, agricultural machinery was imported from both the United States and the European members of the Marshall Plan. Third, an agricultural extension plan was initiated by the American mission for the production of agricultural goods like wheat, which were badly needed by the European countries. Lastly, transportation and infrastructural investments like port development were funded via World Bank projects in order to sustain the continuous flow of agricultural products and raw materials from Anatolia to Europe. The American mission in Turkey summarized this policy in these words:

> The basic justification for Turkish participation in the ERP continues to be the development of her economy to increase the production and export of agricultural commodities and raw materials which Western European countries must otherwise purchase against dollars. ... While it is realized that the approach must not be negative and that American agricultural exports to Europe will probably be stabilized at a much higher level than pre-war, it also appears that substantial increases in

agricultural production within the ERP area will be necessary in order to restore a balanced economy disrupted by the war, the "Iron Curtain," and the gradually changing pattern of production in Eastern Europe. With the largest unrealized potential in agricultural production of any participating country, and considerable other natural resources, Turkey has an opportunity to contribute significantly toward general European viability.

(Dorr, 1950)

"The gradually changing pattern of production in Eastern Europe" (Dorr, 1950) was the result of the economic split between the two parts of Europe. Turkey was expected to close the dollar gap in these countries by exporting agricultural goods and raw materials. On the other hand, U.S. foreign economic policy toward Turkey was not limited to export products. The Marshall Plan and the foreign aid programs that followed belonged to "a particular model of development" which was linked with "the US campaign for multilateralism" (Wood, 1986, pp. 30–31). This model of development was proposed by U.S. officials as an alternative to the Soviet model in the Third World. They were aware that the Soviets were unable to conquer Eurasia by brute force. They were worried about a possible economic collapse in Europe and a possible accession of power by the communist parties. The Marshall Plan was designed to prevent such dangers from happening (Leffler, 2005).

The process of Turkey's economic adaptation to the Marshall Plan conditions and the corresponding reorganization of its economic objectives created several clashes with the American Mission for Aid in Turkey. The most striking of all was an agricultural equipment project agreement that resulted in a reshuffle of the Turkish government. The agreement in question was signed in March 1951 by the Acting Chief of the European Cooperation Administration's (ECA's) Special Mission to Turkey, Orren R. McJunkins, and three members of the Turkish government: the State Minister who was responsible for ECA relations, Fevzi Lütfi Karaosmanoğlu; the Minister of Agriculture, Nihat Eğriboz; and the Minister of Economy and Commerce, Zühtü Hilmi Velibeşe (Keith, 1951). The agreement dictated that "tractors and equipment … ordered in the future will be those suitable for cereal production and that no Marshall Plan tractors so imported will be allocated for sale or use in" regions where cotton and other export crops were specialized (Robinson, 1951, p. 1). There were also regions with some type of restriction to make certain that cereal production was prevalent. The common thing for all the restricted or limited provinces was that in all of these regions, big landlords were most prominent. With this agreement, the ECA mission aimed to control the allocation of Marshall Plan purchases and to make sure they were made in the spirit of the ERP, which in the case of Turkey was to provide necessary grain to European nations.

The restrictions for the cotton regions created a huge reaction from Prime Minister Menderes, who was also a substantial landowner in the Aydin region, one of the provinces to be excluded from the ECA tractor program (Robinson, 1951). Menderes quickly informed the mission that the agreement could not be considered valid, then dismissed the whole cabinet and reformed it in two days with the same members except for the three ministers who signed the Agreement (Keith, 1951). The mission found it "interesting that the three who were let out were those who were the ones to sign a project agreement for agricultural equipment" (Keith, 1951) and provided several problems within the cabinet that might have caused the reshuffle. Still, it was obvious that the government perceived this agreement as a violation of its sovereign rights and an interference with its domestic policies. This was a typical example of how the American advisors' recommendations and reports were acknowledged only if they neglected the inherent structural problems in the economy. When the reports suggested unfavorable policies that would hamper the ostensible performance of the Turkish government in domestic politics, sensitivities toward political independence and sovereignty became instrumental in their harsh rejection. The annulment of the agreement was clearly a political choice based on the economic balance of power in Turkey. The US mission was always aware of the fragile balance of interest in Turkish politics and refrained from any involvement that could lead to a shift in the socioeconomic system, especially in relation to agriculture.

The first four years of foreign economic assistance was quite successful for the Turkish economy, thanks to the good weather and harvests between 1948 and 1951. However, the defense budget could not be lowered below 35 percent, and Turkey's budget deficit remained an issue. When weather conditions were favorable and commodity prices for agricultural products were high (especially after the Korean War), Turkey's current account deficit did not seem to pose a threat to its economic stability. However, when the situation became reversed in 1953 and onwards, Turkey experienced severe foreign exchange problems, depleted its drawing rights in the European Payment Union, and began requesting foreign aid explicitly to cover up its balance of payments problem.

When these structural problems began to emerge in 1953, Hollis Chenery and his colleagues prepared a report under the auspices of the Foreign Operations Administration that recommended a structural change in the Turkish economy, aiming to fix the persistent balance of payments problem instead of saving the day with financial and monetary adjustments (Chenery, 1953). Especially irritated by the report's warnings about inflationary danger, the Turkish government completely rejected the premises of the report, confiscated copies, and even refused permission for the authors to enter the country. Interestingly enough, similar reservations about inflationary threat, structural change, and the balance of payments problem had already been mentioned in the Barker report two years earlier. But then the balance of payments problem was not so evident, and the prescriptions of the report were neglected by the government. When the problem became severe, the Turkish government perceived any criticism toward its policy as a threat to its sovereignty and an intervention in its domestic decision-making process, as if all the previous reports and conditions for the delivery of foreign aids were any different.

The Turkish government's eclectic approach to economic advisory was much more evident in the case of Dr. Pieter Lieftinck, former Dutch Finance Minister, who was sent to Turkey as a Special Representative of the World Bank (International Bank for Reconstruction and Development, IBRD) in 1954. During his tenure, Dr. Lieftinck wrote to Prime Minister Menderes and advised him to adopt stabilizing measures "to dampen internal inflationary pressures and to improve [the country's] external financial position" ("Economic and Financial Review," 1954). Menderes' reply to Lieftinck's letter was sent directly to President Black of the IBRD, and in it, Menderes rejected Lieftnick's criticisms about the lack of measures. Going further, Menderes accused the bank of delaying Turkey's loan applications unnecessarily, of interfering in the armaments credit question between the United Kingdom and Turkey, of exceeding its rights in seeking control over the activities of the Turkish Industrial Development Bank,[3] and of failing to understand Turkey's situation and problems as evident in the Barker Report ("Economic and Financial Review," 1954). According to the US Embassy in Ankara, after this incident, the IBRD decided to recall Lieftinck and close its office in Turkey. From then until the end of the 1950s, Turkey's relations with the IBRD were very limited.

The balance of payments problem created within this system was expected to be resolved with the introduction of newly designed stabilization programs of devaluation and controlled state expenditure, though still lifting the restrictions on the imports. In fact, these solutions were also part of the problem. The Turkish case was a prime example of this contradiction and the evident failure. However, Turkey was still advertised as a success story even after the 1958 Turkish Stabilization Program and the 1960 coup d'état. In spite of all these problems, the Turkish model had to be presented as a success story because the motives behind the formation of models had been economic as well as political. The success story of Turkey's market economy had to be promoted to the countries of the Middle East and Asia, despite the fact that the Turkish experiment did not go as planned.

On many occasions, representatives of the Turkish and US governments clearly expressed their disagreements about the funding of projects, their planning, or lack of it, and most important of all, the implementation of the economic program. The Turkish politicians' foremost objective regarding modernization has always been political. Even during discussions of economic issues, the political perspective took precedence. The Turkish government's consecutive raisons d'état were achieving political independence by means of attaining economic self-sufficiency. On the other hand, American advisors were concerned that the economic assistance programs might fall victim to domestic problems rather than being used for what they perceived as being the "American mission" (Ekbladh, 2011, p. 154). They wanted to guide Turkey in its endeavor to become like its Western counterparts. This mission was also a hegemonic project wherein the dominance of the capitalist model was presented to members of the Third World. While the power of this system was stressed with the military bases and assistance, the vision for a modernized economy and society was supposed to pave the way for the acceptance of the capitalist system.

Knowing this predicament, Turkey used its strategic importance as leverage to gain more foreign aid to finance its trade and budget deficit. Throughout the 1950s, Turkey requested that its share of allocations from the Mutual Security funds be increased. In 1954 and 1955, Turkish officials made several visits to the United States and made requests for a loan of 300 million dollars (Wendelin, 1955). In contrast to previous foreign assistance programs like the ERP and Exim Bank credits, Turkey requested a cash loan without being tied to a specific project, in order to finance its import program. The US administration rejected this demand because they were "not convinced that the remedy proposed by the Turkish Government is the one which will achieve the desired results" ("Turkish Loan Request," 1955). During the negotiations, Turkish Foreign Minister Zorlu, when reminded of the inflationary pressure in the Turkish economy, said that Turkey might reduce its army's size and therefore its defense spending, but that "Turkey was more concerned about an invasion rather than inflation" ("Turkish Economic Problem," 1955).

Lack of planning, coupled with trade liberalization and uncontrolled import flow, led to an accumulation of commercial arrears equal to almost half a billion dollars in 1958. Without any assistance, Turkey's insolvency could have transformed into a default. After the general elections in 1957, the Turkish government was ready to swallow the bitter pill. In July of 1958, after several months of negotiations, the Turkish government reached an agreement with the Organization for European Economic Cooperation (OEEC) and the International Monetary Fund (IMF) missions for a stabilization program (Moore, 1958). In August 1958, the negotiations resulted in plans for the program: Turkey was to receive 359 million dollars, of which 234 million was to come from the United States, 100 million from the members of the OEEC and European Payments Union, and 25 million from the IMF. As part of the program, Turkey devalued the Turkish lira and lifted import restrictions that were imposed after 1953 due to excessive commercial arrears. Again, the stabilization program could not be a remedy for the Turkish economy. Imported goods began to flow into the Turkish market and increased the current account deficit even more. In one decade, Turkey managed to implement a great land extension program but failed to increase agricultural production, which had always been prone to weather conditions. Foreign debts had accumulated in the form of both aid and commercial arrears. Structural investments were confined to transportation and export of agricultural goods and raw materials.

Conclusion

The United States saw Turkey as an important ally in the region. Ensuring the security and development of the republic was in the interest of the United

States. The US decision makers envisioned Turkey as a model for the newly emerging countries of the postcolonial period. Turkey already had a strong anti-communist inclination, as perceived by CIA reports (Central Intelligence Agency, 1949), and it accepted the security umbrella proposed by the United States willingly after the Soviet demands. It is still unclear how far the Turkish armed forces were aware of the Griddle Plan and whether they considered the ramifications of defending a possible Soviet attack on Turkish soil.[4] The end result would have been the invasion of the Eastern Anatolia by Soviet armies and bombing of US bases in Turkey and the cities that hosted them. The cost of accepting these conditions was too high, yet the Turkish government preferred that to a position of nonalignment.

As it is argued, US foreign policy toward Turkey was not limited to a security and strategic perspective. Turkey was one of the first laboratories of the American modernization project throughout the early Cold War. The US foreign aid programs that were implemented in Turkey later provided a backbone story for the theoreticians of modernization theory in the 1960s. The postwar US advisors wanted to guide Turkey in its endeavor to become like its Western counterparts. This was also part of a hegemonic project where the dominance of the capitalist model was presented to the members of the Third World as a success story. While the hard power of this system was supported with military bases and assistance, the vision for a modernized economy and society was supposed to provide for the acceptance of the capitalist system.

Initially, Turkey proved to be a success story for this alternative narrative against communist ideals. The economic side of this story was shattered when Turkey had to accept an IMF stabilization program in 1958 to close its debts, while the political side began to be questioned after the surfacing of the Johnson Letter. Whether its outcomes were positive or negative, postwar US foreign policy had a huge impact on Turkey's foreign and domestic policies in the decades that followed. The reflections of the ties that bound the two countries in this period can still be seen in contemporary US-Turkey relations.

Notes

1 For a more detailed analysis of the postwar aid agreements between the United States and Turkey, see: Gökçay, G. (2015). İkinci Dünya Savaşının Ardından Türkiye'de Amerikan Yardımları [US aid in Turkey during the postwar period]. *Kebikeç, İnsan Bilimleri İçin Kaynak Araştırmaları Dergisi, 39*, 315–341.
2 In fact, the architect of the containment policy, Kennan, objected to Turkish military aid because "Russia's challenge was political" (Offner, 2002, p. 200).
3 The IBRD had made significant contribution in the establishment of the Turkish Industrial Development Bank and provided a loan of 9 million dollars in 1950 (Kuniholm, 1950).
4 The Turkish side of the story cannot be verified due to a lack of documents from the Ministry of Foreign Affairs of the Republic of Turkey.

References

Aid to Turkey. (1946, November 16). Memorandum of conversation. Subject: Aid to Turkey; Subject File: Turkey, 1947–50. Records of the Office of Greek, Turkish and Iranian Affairs, 1947–1950; General Records of the Department of State, *Record Group 59*. College Park, MD: National Archives.

Central Intelligence Agency. (1949, January 4). Opposition to ECA in participating countries. CIA Electronic Reading Room, National Intelligence Council (NIC) Collection, Document Number (FOIA) /ESDN (CREST): 0000258571. Retrieved from https://www.cia.gov/library/readingroom/document/0000258571.

Chenery, H.B. (Ed.). (1953). *Turkish investment and economic development*. Ankara: United States of America Operations Mission to Turkey, Foreign Operations Administration.

Chuev, F.I. (2007). *Molotov Anlatıyor*. Istanbul: Yordam Kitap.

Cohen, M.J. (1997). *Fighting World War Three from the Middle East: Allied contingency plans, 1945–1954*. London: Frank Cass.

Dorr, R.H. (1950, January 14). Review of 1950/1951 Turkish program. Submitted by Special Mission to Turkey; Records of U.S. Foreign Assistance Agencies, 1942–1963, U.S. Operations, Mission to Turkey, Office of the Chief of Mission, Administrative Records, 1948–1956, *Record Group 469*. College Park, MD: National Archives.

Economic and Financial Review. (1954, May 19). Economic and financial review, Turkey – January–March 1954. Department of State; Central File: *Decimal File 882.00*, Internal Economic, Industrial and Social Affairs, Turkey, Economic Matters, Conditions, (General), January 5, 1950–July 14, 1954, 882.00/5–1954; Records of the Department of State relating to Internal Affairs: Turkey, U.S. National Archives. Archives Unbound.

Economic Cooperation Administration. (1949). *Turkey, country study, European Recovery Program*. Washington, DC: U.S. Government Printing Office.

Ekbladh, D. (2011). *The Great American mission: Modernization and the construction of an American world order*. Princeton, NJ: Princeton University Press.

Keith, G. (1951, March 23). Confidential letter on agricultural equipment project agreement. Letter from Gerald Keith of American Embassy, Ankara to Robert Moore, Office of Greek, Turkish and Iranian Affairs, Department of State; Central File: *Decimal File 782.13*, Internal Political and National Defense Affairs, Executive Branch of Government, Turkey, Cabinet, Ministry, March 7, 1950–December 30, 1954, 782.13/3–2351; Records of the Department of State relating to Internal Affairs: Turkey, U.S. National Archives. Archives Unbound.

Kuniholm, B. (1950, September 28). Events of the week September 21–27, 1950 (No. 197). Department of State; Central File: *Decimal File 782.00*, Internal Political and National Defense Affairs, Turkey, Political Affairs and Conditions, January 5, 1950–June 28, 1951, 782.00/9–2850; Records of the Department of State relating to Internal Affairs: Turkey, U.S. National Archives. Archives Unbound.

Leffler, M.P. (1985). Strategy, diplomacy, and the Cold War: The United States, Turkey, and NATO, 1945–1952. *Journal of American History*, 71(4), 807–825.

Leffler, M.P. (2005). National security and US foreign policy. In M.P. Leffler and D.S. Painter (Eds.), *Origins of the Cold War: An international history* (2nd ed.) (pp. 15–41). New York: Routledge.

Loan for Turkey. (1945, October 4). Subject: Loan for Turkey from Export–Import Bank, Memorandum of Conversation with the Ambassador Baydur (National

Archives Microfilm Publication M1292, Roll 14), Records of the Department of State, Relating to Internal Affairs of Turkey 1945–1949, *Decimal File 867*, 867.51/10–1845.

Maier, C.S. (1977). The politics of productivity: Foundations of American international economic policy after World War II. *International Organization*, 31(4), 607–633.

Mark, E. (2005). The Turkish war scare of 1946. In M.P. Leffler and D.S. Painter (Eds.), *Origins of the Cold War: An international history* (2nd ed.) (pp. 112–133). New York: Routledge.

Moore, C.R. (1958, July 18). Weekly economic review–No. 29. Department of State; Central File: *Decimal File 882.00*, Internal Economic, Industrial and Social Affairs, Turkey, Economic Matters, Conditions (General), May 1, 1958–February 19, 1959, 882.00/7–1858; Records of the Department of State relating to Internal Affairs: Turkey, U.S. National Archives. Archives Unbound.

Munson, H.A. (2012). *The joint American military mission to aid Turkey: Implementing the Truman Doctrine and transforming U.S. foreign policy, 1947–1954.* Unpublished Ph.D. thesis, Washington State University, Pullman, WA.

Offner, A.A. (2002). *Another such victory: President Truman and the Cold War, 1945–1953.* Stanford, CA: Stanford University Press.

Robinson, R. (1948). *American aid to Turkey.* Washington, DC: Institute of Current World Affairs.

Robinson, R. (1951). *A new farm program in Turkey.* Washington, DC: Institute of Current World Affairs.

Secondé, R.L. (1951, February 14). The association of Turkey with N.A.T.O. and Middle Eastern planning. The National Archives of the UK (TNA), *Foreign Office (FO)* 371/96539.

Turkish Economic Problem. (1955, May 20). Memorandum of conversation. Subject: Turkish Economic Problem; Department of State; Central File: Decimal File 882.00, Internal Economic, Industrial and Social Affairs, Turkey, Economic Matters, Conditions (General), March 15, 1955–December 7, 1955, 882.00/5–2155; Records of the Department of State relating to Internal Affairs: Turkey, U.S. National Archives. Archives Unbound.

Turkish Loan Request. (1955, May 21). Memorandum of conversation. Subject: Turkish Loan Request; Department of State; Central File: *Decimal File 882.00*, Internal Economic, Industrial and Social Affairs, Turkey, Economic Matters, Conditions (General), March 15, 1955–December 7, 1955, 882.00/5–2155; Records of the Department of State relating to Internal Affairs: Turkey, U.S. National Archives. Archives Unbound.

U.S. Agency for International Development. (2005). *U.S. overseas loans and grants.* Washington, DC: U.S. Agency for International Development. Retrieved from http://purl.access.gpo.gov/GPO/LPS74907.

U.S. Department of State. (1964). *Foreign relations of the United States, diplomatic papers, 1943, The Near East and Africa* (Vol. 4). Washington, DC: U.S. Government Printing Office.

U.S. Department of State. (1971). *Foreign relations of the United States, 1947, The Near East and Africa* (Vol. V). Washington, DC: U.S. Government Printing Office.

U.S. Department of State. (1974). *Foreign relations of the United States, 1949, The Near East, South Asia, and Africa* (Vol. VI). Washington, DC: U.S. Government Printing Office.

U.S. Department of State. (1979). *Foreign relations of the United States, 1951, The Near East and Africa* (Vol. V). Washington, DC: U.S. Government Printing Office.

Wendelin, E. (1955, June 23). Turkish reaction on question of loan from U.S. Records of U.S. Foreign Assistance Agencies, 1942–1963, U.S. Operations, Mission to Turkey, Office of the Chief of Mission, Administrative Records, 1948–1956, *Record Group 469*. College Park, MD: National Archives.

Wood, R.E. (1986). *From Marshall Plan to debt crisis: Foreign aid and development choices in the world economy.* Berkeley, CA: University of California Press.

5 American atomic policy and Hashemite Iraq, 1954–1958

Elizabeth Bishop[1]

Baghdad Pact as legal basis

A consensus among historians has emerged that the Baghdad Pact appeared to negate some of the anti-colonial effects of both world wars in that it brought an independent Iraq into alliance with Turkey and Pakistan. According to Thomas Hörber, the proposed Middle East Defense Organization (MEDO) was comparable with the North Atlantic Treaty Organization (NATO), especially since it was meant to contain the expansion of communism, stabilize the region, and serve as a constructive stage of transition from colonial rule towards independence (Hörber, 2007, p. 285). The pact built on two recent developments: the fact that Turkey joined NATO in 1952 (Biçer, 2016) and an unpublished diplomatic agreement between the United States and Great Britain in 1954 (Freiberger, 2007).

That said, there is also widespread acknowledgement that what came to be known as the "Baghdad Pact" was never entirely set in stone. Historian Steven Freiberger has acknowledged that consensus has proved elusive with regard to the agreement's origins, asking,

> did [an] initial suggestion come from Secretary of State Dulles, who then used Turkey as a vehicle for its implementation? Or did the proposal originate with Foreign Secretary Eden, who sought collusion between Turkey and Iraq in order to maintain London's role as a Middle East power?
>
> (Freiberger, 2007, p. 83)

As far as Behçet Kemal Yeşilbursa was concerned, the Baghdad Pact represented the continuation of a joint Anglo-American project to establish a MEDO; when Egypt's leaders told the United States that their country would not participate in any such "defense organization" until Britain evacuated the Suez Canal Zone, Dulles was compelled to look to the "Northern Tier" of countries (Yeşilbursa, 2005, p. 16). While the accession of regional allies to the original Iraq-Turkey bilateral agreement appears to have been a carefully sequenced set of events, the failure of the United States to sign the pact's central instrument left other nations' place in this strategic vision unfixed.

The fact remains that Turkey was a NATO member and Pakistan was a member of the Commonwealth of Nations. To assess Iraq's membership in the Baghdad Pact (as well as to understand the implications of membership for Hashemite Iraq's place in UK/US atomic policy), we must acknowledge that the word "politics," as commonly used, has a number of different meanings. A premise of *visibility* wends its way through all; such definitions vary from "the activities associated with the governance of a country or other area" (oxford dictionaries.com); to the sum total of government activities, extended to characterize relations between countries. "Politics" can also mean the various activities within a given organization, particularly when these are aimed at improving an individual's status or position; a particular set of beliefs or principles; or the assumptions or principles relating to or inherent in particular relations.

In his description of dependency theory, Patrick Wolfe emphasized "a hierarchically replicated cyclopean structure whereby a metropolis (also known as 'center,' 'core,' etc.) dominated a number of (usually surrounding) satellites (the periphery)"; what is particularly helpful in Wolfe's description is the fact that any given metropolis "was itself satellite to a higher-order metropolis further up the chain of dependency" (1997, p. 396). Writing on "neo-colonialism," Kwame Nkrumah noted that among "methods used by neo-colonialists to slip past our guard" were the departing colonialists' retention of various kinds of privileges that "infringe on sovereignty: that of setting up military bases or stationing troops in former colonies and the supplying of 'advisers' of one sort or another" (1965, p. 246). Finally, Achille Mbembe started his discussion of necropolitics from the position that "modernity was at the origin of multiple concepts of sovereignty", a process which included such conflicting elements as self-limitation and self-institution (2003, p. 13).

In the following, I argue that – after the war – Great Britain introduced the United States to its between-the-wars regime of unequal treaties. The Baghdad Pact paralleled those treaties that permitted Great Britain to renew its privileged relationship with Iraq as sole provider of Iraq's military materiel, creating a "land bridge" between different multilateral jurisdictions. Second, to appreciate the pact's significance, we must also acknowledge the role biophysics played in bringing Iraq into this agreement. In this, it can be helpful to acknowledge certain characteristics of UK/US atomic policies during World War II and the immediate postwar era. The wartime atomic research program – carried out in the strictest secrecy – was global in its scale. As Niels Bohr observed, in order to yield sufficient plutonium to create a nuclear bomb, the Manhattan Project required turning America into "a factory" (Masco, 2006, p. 18); and under the legal terms of wartime alliance, the common research project exceeded the borders of the United States. The process Bohr described is helpful in understanding the availability of facilities at Chalk River, Canada, for UK staff, where they collaborated on aspects of plutonium separation (Hurst and Critoph, 1997, p. 6).

"Technopolitical regimes"

Having acknowledged that, some of Gabrielle Hecht's assertions regarding the atomic research community in 1950s France are helpful as well. Hecht found sets of individuals, engineering and industrial practices, and institutional ideologies within the French state's nuclear research program to have been linked. Her innovative work introduced the concept of "technopolitical regimes," particularly with regard to its premise of visibility (Hecht, 2009). While the analytical contribution of Hecht's work is clear, it is not exhaustive; a necessary area of analysis for this particular thesis is the global dimensions.

The notion of technopolitical regimes has two aspects. On the one hand, it refers to "linked sets of individuals, engineering and industrial practices, technological artifacts, political programs, and institutional ideologies acting together to govern technological development" (p. 56) On the other hand, Hecht's use of the term "regime" reflects her informants' widespread belief in a "necessary interweaving of technology and politics" (p. 56). Hecht's conceptual vocabulary invokes Timothy Mitchell's work on "techno-politics." It addresses the powers of global capitalism, seeking to account for technical sciences while avoiding the trap of reproducing their views of the world. For Mitchell,

> techno-politics is always a technical body, an alloy that must emerge from a process of manufacture whose ingredients are both human and nonhuman, both intentional and not, and in which the intentional or human is always somewhat overrun by the unintended.
>
> (Mitchell, 2002, p. 42)

Hecht's concept of technopolitical regimes is followed here in order to trace state and meta-state controls on the international trade in uranium during and after World War II. While Iraq was neutral during the conflict, I argue that the Allies' wartime alignments remained in place after hostilities ended, with the result that while Iraq was never an Ally, the Allies' wartime policies came to govern postwar Iraq. It is in this way that Hecht's reliance on "linked sets of individuals, engineering and industrial practices, technological artifacts, political programs, and institutional ideologies acting together to govern technological development" as well as her use of the term "regime" to address legal and administrative controls over circulation of radioactive materials – as she refers to it, a "necessary interweaving of technology and politics" (Hecht. 2009, p. 56) – informs this history of the Cold War in the Middle East. Others have written about NATO's nuclear policy (Johnston, 2005; Scheinman, 2015); I note administrative measures put in place in order to implement these policies, measures which attempted to bring Iraq into wartime technopolitical regimes. Here, the atomic geography of the Cold War slowly grew, linking the United States with Great Britain, and NATO with the Commonwealth of Nations, in contingent, specific, and unique ways.

Commonwealth of Nations

Hecht's concern for "linked sets of individuals, engineering and industrial practices, technological artifacts, and institutional ideologies" (2009, p. 56) is useful in assessing the Commonwealth of Nations' integration into the atomic era. Tracing transnational developments, contemporary journalism can be useful. While the *Christian Science Monitor*'s Washington bureau chief wrote that "Strict constructionists would sometimes discount the Commonwealth because it has no closely written constitution, no set meeting place, no busily functioning central secretariat" (Strout, 1999, p. xv), this journalist (who had studied law and was knowledgeable regarding British politics) also noted that

> the thin red line of empire, in new and modern garb, still traces its pulsating way around the globe, a force for peace, an impetus to world trade, a compulsion for international law observance, an example of the adaptability of Anglo-Saxon institutions.
>
> (Stringer, 1953, p. 25)

Without a constitution, set meeting place, or central secretariat, the "thin red line of empire" traced its way around the globe via the "modern garb" of the raw materials necessary for atomic warfare.

Stringer's reference to the "pulsating way" of the "thin red line of empire" serves as reference to international trade in uranium and fissionable materials. During World War II, atomic research (most famously, the Manhattan Project) developed from unequal treaties and legal exceptionalism, by which Europe's 19th-century relations with Africa, the Americas, and Oceania, continued into the twentieth century. During the 1930s, uranium ores (pitchblende and carnotite) were available for exploitation in Austria, the Belgian Congo, Madagascar, Portugal, and the Soviet Union. They were also found in the United States and various Commonwealth nations including Australia, England, Canada, and South Africa (Anonymous, 1945, August 9). The Commonwealth developed raw materials in support of the Allies' war effort. Production of uranium oxide ('yellow cake') in Canada was minimal until – as a wartime measure – the Canadian government purchased the Eldorado Mining Company from its shareholders in 1944 (General Agreement on Trade and Tariffs, 1966, June 2). At approximately the same time, Winston Churchill asked Australian Prime Minister John Curtin "for all the uranium it could produce for atomic bombs" (Anonymous, 1945, August 8). A system of rewards for discovery of radioactive materials was in place at that time, administered by Australia's national Bureau of Mineral Resources (Anonymous, 1948, April 3). Agreements between the governments of the Commonwealth of Australia and of South Australia with the joint Anglo-American purchasing agency for uranium (Hansard, 1954, February 1) ensured that raw ore from Australia's sole exploited field, Rum Jungle, was shipped for refinery (into uranium oxide) elsewhere in the Commonwealth (Anonymous, 1953, September 30).

As Neils Bohr recognized, the United States had a specific role to play in this project. A British Technical and Scientific Mission (the Tizard mission, after its initiator, Sir Henry Tizard) was a six-member scientific delegation that visited the United States at the very beginning of World War II to arrange the industrial resources to realize plans developed in preparation for the war, that Britain itself could not exploit immediately. With the approval of Prime Minister Winston Churchill, members of the delegation gathered technical documentation of potential military value, including a memorandum describing the feasibility of an atomic bomb. At the end of August, Tizard travelled to Washington, DC to make preliminary arrangements; other members of the mission followed by ship. The classified documents which accompanied them were secured in a lockable metal deed box. With physicist John Cockcroft as its deputy head, the delegation assembled in Washington, DC on September 12, 1940. Technically, the US was a peacetime nation.

The Tizard mission succeeded in establishing a multinational research program that – as Bohr attested – flourished during wartime. Once the war ended, national authorities reasserted temporary control over key components of the wartime programs. Uranium serves as an illustrative example. In the United States, President Harry S. Truman issued an executive order withdrawing public lands bearing radioactive ores from general sale, reserving them instead for Federal use (Anonymous, 1945, September 16). A new Atomic Energy Commission (AEC) was "authorized to acquire at a fair price, by purchase or by condemnation, any minerals or other materials from which the sources of atomic energy can be derived" (Anonymous, 1945, October 4). The AEC served as Congress' measure to gain control over atomic research carried out in the United States, preventing international circulation of American ores and US-produced radioisotopes as well as atomic expertise.

Hecht described France's research program as an attribute of that nation's glory, and in jurisdictions around the world, local political interests were successful in limiting the powers of global markets to command natural resources. For the United States, such controls extended beyond the 50 states to occupied territories, as when General Douglas MacArthur banned Japanese nationals from carrying out research "involving uranium or radioactive unstable elements" (Anonymous, 1945, September 24). Parallel developments characterized independent jurisdictions, as President Truman's executive order gave rise to a new market among American consumers and would-be prospectors for uranium, including the "instrument makers and device vendors" of new atomic research-centered industries (Anonymous, 1945, November 23). In Australia, while the government announced "a scheme to encourage private persons or companies to prospect for and mine uranium," it promised to buy all uranium produced during the next decade. In effect, serving as contractors to the US Atomic Energy Commission, local authorities permitted the AEC to supervise all work (Anonymous, 1953, March 21). The new atomic powers' desires for resources during the 1950s had a contradictory effect of *strengthening* local authorities' controls.

After the war ended, the US Congress forbade sharing atomic secrets with wartime allies. The US agreement with Australia subjected local prospecting to "the full security precautions laid down in the Atomic Energy Bill," which included heavy penalties for unsecured circulation of information (Anonymous, 1953, March 21). This led to a "long dry spell" in the UK's development of atomic technologies and nuclear strategies (Hayward, 1956, June 15). Minister of Supply Duncan Sandys warned the House of Commons of restrictions on freedom of movement that scientists with nuclear knowledge should expect (Anonymous, 1957, January 18). During this "dry spell," Commonwealth members sought to take ownership of all radioactive substances in these jurisdictions (Anonymous, 1946, July 13), initiating an intergovernmental system to govern access to raw materials (Anonymous, 1954, September 18). Over the course of the dry spell, the *Iraq Times* was sprinkled with nuclear news from the former Allies. While an advisory committee of industrial and scientific leaders told the US Department of Defense that there was no safe response to an attack with nuclear weapons (Anonymous, 1953, June 9), readers of the *Times* learned that Britain was preparing for a successful nuclear defense by scattering telephone exchanges and water mains throughout the suburbs of the capital city (Bertin, 1953, July 5).

Communications within the former Allied nations were complemented by communications between *les métropoles* and their settler colonies, as leaders of Australia, Canada, India, New Zealand, Pakistan, Rhodesia, South Africa, and Sri Lanka met to discuss the reduction of their budgets for conventional weapons and increased trade between their nations (Hayward, 1956, June 26). Member nation-states of the Commonwealth were already carrying out military training together at UK Staff College Camberley, under the code name "For'ard On." Over three days of maneuvers, British and Commonwealth armed forces practiced integrating new nuclear weapons into conventional warfare under the direction of officers representing Britain's Imperial Defense College, the ministries of Defense and Supply, the Royal Air Force, and the Royal Navy (Anonymous, 1953, August 5). Iraq's military was also in something of a dry spell. While readers in Iraq were aware that both Canada and New Zealand's general chiefs of staff had taken part in these multinational military exercises and that the commanders-in-chief of the Indian and Pakistani armies were also present (Anonymous, 1953, August 27), their nation's armed forces were outside this atomic circle.

Even so, the atomic-enabled military force that the Commonwealth was denying independent Iraq might be provided by the United States. Foreign observers of Iraq's conventional military forces noted "shortages in motor transport, radar, standardized ammo, anti-tank mines, replacement parts, etc." (Claussen, Lee and Raether, 1986). During that year's celebration of Army Day in Baghdad, the chief of the Hashemite monarchy's military staff acknowledged his forces' shortcomings, pledging to "make every effort and seize every opportunity to arm our forces and supply them with modern equipment in order to prepare an army ready to reply to the country's call when danger threatens" (Anonymous, 1953, Nur al-Din Urges Army Preparedness). Toward this effort, Iraq's military leaders drew closer to the United States. Photographs of President Dwight D. Eisenhower's inaugural ceremony in January 1953 depict Iraqi Minister Abdullah Ibrahim Bakr sitting four rows back from and directly behind the new head of state (see the front cover of *Life Magazine* from February 2, 1953). Later that month in Baghdad, the Crown Prince declared, "the Government is attentive to the enlargement of the Army and its supply with the most modern arms, and equipment, and the adoption of current procedures of modern armies" (Anonymous, 1953, Regent Delivers Speech From Throne).

United Kingdom

Historians agree about the Baghdad Pact's implications for Britain's "informal empire" after the war. As P. Preston indicated, "the informal empire territories related both to oil interests around the Arabian Gulf ... and to the Canal Zone in Egypt, nominally an independent country, again part of the informal empire" (Preston, 2014, p. 29). As historian John Kent pointed out, "radical cutbacks were altering military strategy in operational terms and favouring a shift from Cold War priorities and sizeable bases to emphasizing the nuclear deterrent as the number one requirement for global strategy" (Kent, 2007, p. 64). During the first postwar decade, when Iraq's dinar was fixed to the UK pound, "the economic situation of the sterling area" suffered from the fact that British payments for wartime leases (along with other capital exports to Sri Lanka, Egypt, India, and Pakistan – as well as Iraq) totaled $3 billion (Chamberlin, 1953, June 8).

With that said – no Iraqi representative was present at 10 Downing Street when Commonwealth prime ministers exchanged views on the development of "nuclear energy for peaceful purposes" within the context of a larger Cold War where "America's eagerness to lend a hand would be vastly increased the moment the Commonwealth can effectively join forces with the mother country" (Polyzoides, 1956, June 29). In the course of these mid-summer meetings, the heads of state of the Commonwealth nations further expressed their "hope to have an opportunity for an exchange of views about the economic situation of the sterling area and the development of nuclear energy for peaceful purposes" (Press Notice, 1956). No representative of was Iraq present either when the UK Atomic Energy Establishment initiated cooperation with Commonwealth nations. Historians Guy Hartcup and T. E. Allibone noted that the mid-1950s witnessed collaboration between Indian nuclear physicist Homi Bhabha and British Nobel laureate Sir John Cockcroft (then serving as director of the Atomic Energy Research Establishment at Harwell, Cockcroft had previously served as deputy head of the Tizard mission). Hartcup and Allibone noted that at the first Geneva conference, Bhabha's vague reference to the possibility of fusion gave rise to proposals that thermonuclear research be made openly available within the community of Commonwealth member nations (Hartcup and Allibone, 1984).

In London, the Board of Trade attempted to close a twentieth-century trade gap by exporting nineteenth-century manufactures to Commonwealth nations, as well as beyond them. British manufacturers had already exhibited hospital furnishings, laboratory equipment, and machine tools at the Canadian International trade fair in order to "capture the Canadian market and reorient it toward British industrial practice" (Anonymous, 1950, January 23). Advertisements in the *Iraq Times* depicted the British luxury goods (from biscuits to silver plate) available for sale in Baghdad at the time; nonetheless, Iraq was different from Commonwealth nations, as the Board of Trade acknowledged. In its internal documentation, the Board concluded that demand for industrial goods was more elastic than for such household luxuries as biscuits and tableware:

> in consumer goods the demand for better class goods is growing slowly ... there will be an increasing demand for all classes of ... electrical plants and equipment for generation, transmission, and distribution, for industrial and domestic use, will be in demand.
>
> (Board of Trade, 1953, p. 87)

With passenger cars and woven cotton fabrics making strong contributions, steel "made 1954 a record year for British exports" (Anonymous, 1955, January 21). Export of hospital furnishings, laboratory equipment, and machine tools could contribute more to the recovery of Britain's economy than crackers and silver-plated trays.

A shift in the export profile from consumer goods to capital items would further assist in the UK's economic recovery. Metropolitan-Vickers' X-ray department had taken over the business of a subsidiary, Newton Victor, during 1946. Newton Victor then acquired a division responsible for medical and industrial X-ray apparatus, the Victor X-Ray Corporation, from the General Electric X-Ray Corporation of America and built a new factory in Motherwell, near Glasgow. New-style treatments spread throughout the Commonwealth, supporting the equipment manufactures at the center. The Brisbane General Hospital installed a 4-million-volt treatment unit that "resembles a radial arm drill. One of the features of it is that it can be focussed on the patient not that the patient has to be adjusted to the machine" (Queensland, 1955, p. 11). The British Medical Association sent a representative to Baghdad as well in order to communicate with the Iraqi Medical Society, the Ministry of Health, and the Ministry of the Interior (Anonymous, 1954, March 17).

A scientific research center in Iraq would help tip the balance of trade in the UK's favor in complementary ways. First, it would open a new export market for British-manufactured laboratory equipment to a nation enjoying its first significant petroleum wealth (Louis, 1984). Second, since the United States was beginning to provide mutual security funds "to help friendly countries initiate or develop nuclear energy programs," London could count on Washington, DC to fund at least this aspect of its postwar reconstruction

(Vance, 1959, p. 821). While the UK Board of Trade mission to Iraq emphasized capital over consumer goods, the Ministry of Health's *Bulletin of Endemic Diseases* indicated the extent of this project's success. Advertisers in the January 1957 issue included local agents for Parke, Davis & Co.'s Middlesex division, and Burroughs Wellcome & Co. of London.

United States

As far as historian Peter L. Hahn is concerned, Presidents Truman and Eisenhower laid the foundations of a US Middle East policy "that endured for decades" (Hahn, 2006, p. 3). Other scholars, however, have drawn attention to a gap between the policies of successive administrations. Isaac Alteras noted, "in contrast to the Truman presidency, the new administration would exhibit in private as well as in public a very close cooperation and coordination between the president and the secretary of state" (Alteras, 1993, p. 21). Salim Yaqub pointed out that Truman "never saw Middle Eastern affairs as a priority in foreign policy, preoccupied as he was with the revival of Western Europe and the containment of Soviet communism" (Yaqub, 2004, p. 24). In short, according to Roby Barrett, "the Truman administration left no blueprint" for its successor (Barrett, 2007, p. 4).

As President and as NATO leader, Eisenhower drew on his wartime experiences of being Supreme Allied Commander. Andrew Polsky observed that "during World War II, Ike had worked closely with the CIA's predecessor, the Office of Strategic Services (OSS), which ran clandestine operations behind enemy lines" (Polsky, 2015, p. 120). Hugh Wilford referred to a group of Middle East-born OSS officers who, during the 1940s, worked secretly to head off the partition of Palestine; the British imperial legacy and the American missionary tradition split the CIA of the early Cold War (Wilford, 2013, p. xxi).

Alongside the United States, Great Britain agreed to forestall any Middle East command until after Turkey was admitted to NATO and "until after a satisfactory command arrangement under The Supreme Allied Commander Europe (SACEUR) had been worked out" (Anonymous, 1986 – negotiating paper January 4, 1952). Around the same time as the Commonwealth premiers' meeting, Australians began to mine their own uranium ore, having technical assistance from the US Atomic Energy Commission and a loan from that country's Export–Import Bank; this new source evaded Congressional controls to supply *both* the United Kingdom and the United States "with today's most precious metal" (Norman, 1952, September 10). By the time Congress permitted President Eisenhower to sign bilateral agreements for sharing "secret information on peaceful uses of the atom," such "research bilaterals" also permitted the sale of up to 500 kilograms of uranium, enriched up to 20 percent, as nuclear fuel for research "piles" and power reactors (Anonymous, 1956, June 21).

A fateful decision by the US Atomic Energy Agency opened new possibilities, reaching around the controls established by national legislatures and returning to the kind of transnational cooperation exemplified by the Tizard mission during wartime. A "disposition of rights between the US, UK, and Canada in inventions in the atomic energy field" introduced a new concept of the "cross assignment of rights on industry." This concept would permit individual nation-states to license home manufacture without requiring equivalent permissions from the national legislatures of other members. In addition, the "disposition" clarified that when exporting to either of the other two member nation-states, "exporting firms would be subject only to the royalty terms imposed upon nationals of the importing country" (RG 326, Records of the Atomic Energy Commission, Office of the Secretary, General Correspondence, 1951–1958; AEC 874/2; June 14, 1956. File: "legal 3, foreign"; box 31, NN3–326–93–010 HM 1993; United States National Archives and Records Administration). In other words, the legal terms of the "importing country" were granted precedent over the legal terms of other, ostensibly sovereign, states.

During August 1955, the United Nations conducted a first International Conference on Peaceful Uses of Atomic Energy, held in Geneva, Switzerland. This conference, called for as part of President Eisenhower's Atoms for Peace program, aimed at fostering international cooperation in transitioning atomic knowledge from military to peaceful uses, found its legal basis in General Assembly resolution 810 (IX) of December, 1954 (Peaceful Uses of Atomic Energy, 1955, December 5). During the two-week conference, more than 62,000 people queued to see the blue glow of a 'swimming pool'-type reactor, designed and built at the Oak Ridge National Laboratory (which had been built hurriedly during 1943 as a pilot project to enrich uranium for the Manhattan Project). Commonwealth member Australia was one of the first nations to sign a "research bilateral" with the United States.

K. E. Halnan's textbook for the Atoms for Peace series, *Atomic Energy in Medicine*, followed the entire production cycle of radioactive isotopes: from production at Harwell to "air dispatch to hospitals overseas," whether in Australia or Iraq, and finally to the patient. As the preface informed administrators,

> the radiation emitted by the "ash," or waste products, produced in the nuclear reactor furnaces of nuclear power stations and in the reactors for nuclear energy research and those used for the production of the plutonium used in the manufacture of atomic bombs, is also being increasingly used in medical therapy to combat cancers and other growths.
>
> (Halnan, 1957, p. vii)

Among plates included in Halnan's book were "A 4-million volt X-ray treatment unit" and "A large radioactive cobalt treatment unit," taking into account both the capital and consumer aspects of this technopolitical regime that would join *les métropoles* and neo-colonies in new ways.

A new Research Center was established under the pact's Economic Committee, and its tasks and functions were organized at several closed meetings held by pact member nation-states between January 6 and January 11, 1956. At the Committee's initial meeting, plans were carefully drawn to proceed along several lines of economic activity, with one of these being the development of 'atomic energy.' Toward this end, a resolution was drafted calling upon the UK to: (1) provide facilities for training and (2) aid in the development of a Joint Atomic Energy Training Center (Records of the Atomic Energy Commission, Office of the Secretary, General Correspondence, 1951–1958; RG 326, Research and Development I, box 128, NN3-326-93-010 HM 1993; Folder: "research and development; Baghdad pact," Report to the General Manager by the Director of the Division of International Affairs). Establishment of an atomic research center under the Baghdad Pact would, eventually, permit Iraq to sign another such agreement (Records as President, White House Central Files; Iraq Case File, OF 108-F-2 Atoms for Peace, Agreements between Foreign Governments and the US re: peaceful uses of atomic energy (5), box 454, Official Files, Eisenhower, Dwight D.; Dwight D. Eisenhower Presidential Library and Museum).[2]

The International Cooperation Administration (ICA) was a US government agency established on June 30, 1955, that was responsible for foreign assistance and "nonmilitary security" programs (Sunaga, 2006). As historian Michael D. Gambone pointed out, the ICA had a liaison function between the Departments of State and Defense. According to Gambone, "the State Department [controlled] assistance through the new International Cooperation Administration after July 1955, using its resources as a supplement to diplomatic activity. The Defense Department in turn would retain complete control of military aid" with the goal of decreasing overlap and increasing efficiency, resulting in a foreign-assistance policy accomplishing more with less (Gambone, 1997, p. 28).

Iraq appropriated nearly $3 million for studies regarding atomic energy; "the funds [were] to be used for research and development on processes and products for the adaptation of atomic energy to uses in Iraq" (Thompson, 1957, September 11). While the United States distributed raw atomic materials by means of bilateral agreements, British diplomats were pursuing their distinct vision of a multilateral agreement to permit wider sharing of nuclear expertise. Sir Arthur Douglas Dodds-Parker testified before Parliament regarding technical assistance to the Baghdad Pact countries, explaining that "The Economic Secretary to the Treasury announced at the Tehran meeting of the Baghdad Pact Economic Committee that Her Majesty's Government were [sic] willing to contribute a sum of £250,000" for technical assistance to approved projects, designed to increase the economic well-being of the Baghdad Pact area (Hansard, 1956, May 31).

As Mr Vance later testified before US Congress, "Since 1955, the United States has been prepared to contribute up to one-half of the cost of a research reactor project, with the stipulation that the grant cannot be in excess of $350,000" (Vance, 1959, pp. 821–822). Eventually, the United States signed 24 bilateral agreements with foreign governments, enabling new partners to acquire

Atoms for Peace technologies (Krige, 2010, p. 156). Indeed, the decision to set up a nuclear research center had been made during the Tehran meeting (United States National Archives and Records Administration, RG 59, box 500, folder 21.48 country file "Iraq," item: "Baghdad Pact Economic Committee Working Paper, item 3 of the proposed agenda, progress report on Atomic Energy Training Center").

Classified documents from the conference seem to contradict Dodds-Parker's statement before parliament. While all government representatives present at the Tehran summit had agreed to make available 1,400 Iraqi dinars each (as a one-fifth share of the fund of 7,000 dinars for the center's running expenses for the year 1956–1957) to the "Baghdad nuclear center" account, which had been opened by the secretariat at the Ottoman Bank in Baghdad, the government of the United States demurred from participation in the operation of the center as well as its financing (United States National Archives and Records Administration, RG 59, box 500, folder 21.48 country file "Iraq: General 1952, 1955–1959, and 1961," item: Baghdad Pact, Secretary General, Memorandum: "Atomic Energy Training Center," January 19, 1957).

The £250,000 in funds that Dodds-Parker was referring to was to be made available over a five-year period; the Treasury would disburse, on average, £50,000 per year. Later in his statement, he clarified,

> Her Majesty's Government have [sic] also undertaken to contribute equipment and provide a director and other staff for [the] proposed Atomic Training Center at Baghdad, and to give initial training in the United Kingdom for teachers from the Center, at an estimated total cost of £30,000.

In other words, 60 percent of the budgeted funds would be spent on equipment sourced in the UK, administrative staff seconded from public and private UK institutions, and the costs of training foreign specialists in the UK. Such "technical assistance" served as a boon to the nation's balance of trade. Sir John Cockcroft was seconded to serve as chairman of the Baghdad Pact's scientific consul (Cockcroft, 1957). Seeking a technical director for the center, Cockcroft wrote W. J. Whitehouse at Harwell's Nuclear Physics Division: "The Nuclear Training Center proposed in connection with Baghdad Pact agreements is considered to be of national importance" (AB 6, 1956).

Dodds-Parker's speech followed a meeting the Foreign Office had convened in order to facilitate inter-agency communications. On May 4, 1956, the Treasury, Atomic Energy Office, Atomic Energy Authority, and Board of Trade were all represented, as well as Harwell (a familiar designation, for the Atomic Energy Authority), to discuss atomic training programs under the Baghdad Pact. At this meeting, all participants agreed that

> the students of the Centre would be working exclusively on British equipment, and when they returned to their own countries, would be

likely to order apparatus with which they were already familiar, thus offering an important opening for sales to local universities, technical institutions, and industry; Mr. Putman offered to back up the Board of Trade's efforts with personal explanations to manufacturers, should they require further conviction.

(AB 6, 1956)

Thus, while the legal forms differed, the program goals of the United States and the United Kingdom were, for the most part, parallel, and under such terms, the UK's strategic planners seemed to consider a steadily growing pool of experts to be equally important to a steady supply of uranium.

In 1950s Baghdad, the United States Operations Mission in Iraq (USOM/Iraq) became a secondary center of efforts to establish atomic studies locally, donating most of the AEC's unclassified reports as well as some innocuous nuclear detection equipment. True to the spirit of the bilateral agreement, USOM staff coordinated closely with the Government of Iraq. Later, the USOM director, Dr. Henry Wiens, noted that

under the direction of the Iraq Development Board (an agency of the Iraqi Government), three kinds of aid were provided: United States technicians advised or worked with the government of Iraq; supplies and equipment were provided for demonstration purposes; and Iraqi personnel were sent to the United States or third countries for observation or training programs.

(Wiens, 1959, p. 140)

A decision to establish a Baghdad Pact Nuclear Training Center, located in Baghdad, was made in April 1956 (Records of the Atomic Energy Commission, Office of the Secretary, General Correspondence, 1951–1958; RG 326, Research and Development I, Box 128, NN3-326-93-010 HM 1993; Folder: "research and development; Baghdad pact," Report to the General Manager by the Director of the Division of International Affairs). The UK Ambassador in Baghdad had already urged the Board of Trade to pool "experience and information between member countries on development programs," as well as to urge other pact members to consider "projects which two or more members may undertake jointly" (Board of Trade, 1955). Iraq had already joined the Baghdad Pact Economic Committee, and its participation in the Atomic Energy Center for nuclear studies (Harris, 1958, p. 242), and an Atomic Library and Exhibition had already become a prominent part of Baghdad's "development week" (Birdwood, 1959, p. 247).

While Gabrielle Hecht acknowledged the individual political positions of senior French nuclear scientists, Wiens' career provides an opportunity to internationalize William Whyte's observation that postwar Americans had become convinced that organizations and groups could make better decisions than individuals (Whyte, 1956). Born in India, naturalized during 1919, and having found a new home in Fresno, California (Anonymous, 1968, July 2), Wiens graduated from Fresno State Teachers College during 1933. He pursued a master's degree at the University of California, Berkeley, where his 1936 thesis was titled "The Career of Franklin K. Lane in California Politics" (Anonymous, 1954, January 15). Four years later, in 1940, Wiens submitted a dissertation entitled "Nazi racial theory and legislation and the German Jew" for a PhD from Northwestern University (OCLC #25945656). Like Tom Rath, protagonist of Sloan Wilson's bestselling 1955 novel *The Man in the Gray Flannel Suit*, Wiens followed his wartime service with a job in a non-governmental organization. Working as a relief worker in Lyon, France, Wiens served as a financial advisor to Iran's government and then as a financial expert in Greece (Anonymous, 1968, July 2) before moving to Baghdad.

Among the State Department's published documentation, Wiens' signature has been identified on one document, a Cooperative Program of Community Welfare ("Subsidiary Agreement Between the Government of the United States of America and the Government of Iraq for a Cooperative Program of Community Welfare," 1955, March 2). In USOM documentation, it appeared that a sister laboratory to Oak Ridge, Argonne National Laboratory, and its training program "in the operation of reactors and research in the basic science" (USOM, 1955, July 11) would become a model for the new Baghdad Pact nuclear research center.

Yet, among the voluminous published records of atomic America, documentation pertaining to Wiens and the Baghdad Pact's nuclear research center is scant. For that reason, we must address some of the less visible aspects of the April 1955 pact by looking closely at circulation of information regarding the Atoms for Peace program. The "symbolic importance of ... nuclear achievement" is a semantic field, which in Iraq extended into the health professions. Readers of the *Iraq Times* were familiar with some health treatments that came from peaceful uses of atomic energy – for instance, it was proposed that while surgery or poison "destroy" cancer cells, new therapies would "'help' them live faster and thus by a process of acceleration of the life cycle of the cell let the cancer tumor burn itself out" (Anonymous, 1953, August 4).

Meeting minutes suggest that the USOM's high-profile atomic materials were exchanged under the innocuous title of "development aid." As Wiens credited the local government with "attempting to move forward in this field" and noted that "at the present time the question of training if [sic] of primary concern," he pressed individual civil servants within that government to use all technical means at their disposal to advance the atomic research program. The Baghdad USOM's internal documents emphasized the importance of training Iraqi nationals, "particularly at the sub-professional (foreman-mechanic-equipment operator) level," which Weins considered to "be a key governing factor in the implementation of the development program" (USOM, 1956, July 5).

While Wiens later claimed that "Iraqi personnel were sent to the United States … for observation and training programs," and while a special committee of Iraqi cabinet ministers, representing Agriculture, Economics, Education, and Health, were appointed "to select nominees for the study of atomic uses" (USOM, 1955, July 11), documentation suggests a variety of ways by which the atomic research program's reach was extended. As the USOM noted, the Argonne National Laboratory offered a course "in the operation of reactors and research in the basic science." The nature of this research is barely indicated by the observation that

> Dean Arif of the Abu Ghraib Agricultural College, who is now in the US, requesting that he meet with people in this field and have them explain what is being done in other areas; with regard to atomic energy uses as applied to agricultural experiment in relation to dairy products, the matter will be discussed with Mr. McLeroy upon his return from the field.

Russell's return from the United States was expected, and it was noted that the "application of atomic uses might be applied to soils" (USOM, 1955, July 11). The substantive content of this basic science research – the application of atomic energy to dairy products – remains obscure.

Conclusion

As Prime Minister Nuri al-Said formally inaugurated the USIS (United States Information Service) Atoms for Peace exhibition, jointly sponsored by the governments of the United States and Iraq, Baghdad saw the advent of the atomic age (Foreign Service Journal, 1956). As a follow-up to the exhibition, USOM held an internal seminar to brief technicians on acceptable peacetime uses for atomic energy (USOM, 1956, July 5), and the United States gave an "extensive library of nuclear information" (Wendt, 1955, p. 110). While the French physicists who Gabrielle Hecht interviewed craved publicity, many of the individuals who worked to make the Baghdad Pact's nuclear research center possible were unknown – their doctrine one of self-obscurement; the engineering and industrial practices they followed covert; their technological artifacts concealed.

Wiens reported plans to the Minister of Health to visit the United States, adding that "at some point, all medical trainees should learn something of atomic uses when on leader grants in the States" (USOM, 1955, July 11). At a February 1957 USOM staff meeting in Baghdad, controller Sidney Knight reported that "the Government of Iraq had decided to send two Iraqi officials to the States for training in atomic energy" (USOM, 1957, February 12). At the University of Birmingham,

> the Medical Research Council's findings on the dangers of nuclear radiation were only partially reassuring. They gave a grim warning of the

genetic hazards attending any increase in the rate of test explosions. Such an increase may well occur if the present senseless race between the three nuclear nations continues, each contestant reluctant to stop unless its own explosion is the last and places it in the lead.

(Anonymous, 1956, July 24)

By the end of the year, Wiens was promoted to head of USOM's Near East division, sharing a Washington, DC office with a staff of two (U.S. National Archives database, "U.S. and Iraqi Relations: U.S. Technical Aid, 1950–1958," U.S. Operations Mission, Baghdad, Minutes of Meeting, August 6, 1956).

As the UK Ministry of Foreign Affairs, under Selwyn Lloyd, was in the process of relinquishing its responsibility for nuclear research for peaceful purposes to the UK Atomic Energy Authority, the five states represented on the Baghdad Pact secretariat held a second council meeting, choosing to gather in the building designated for the research center. They welcomed the UK representative's statement that his government was prepared to use their country's experience in the field of atomic energy to assist others with their own atomic energy projects (United States Department of State, *Foreign Relations of the United States, 1955–1957. Near East; Iran; Iraq (1955–1957)*, Washington, "Review of Long-Range US Policy Toward the Near East" [September 5, 1957], enclosure 2, summary of publicly announced United States policy on Near East questions, p. 582). The Baghdad Pact nations delegated questions regarding atomic capabilities to what was called, somewhat euphemistically, the "economic committee"; participation in this caucus was open to states-parties that had not signed the military agreement (such as the United States). The economic committee became responsible for practical applications of nuclear policies.

Preliminary plans placed a nuclear research center close to the University of Baghdad's new campus (United States National Archives and Records Administration, RG 59, box 500, folder 21.48, country file "Iraq," item: Dr. William Kerr/University of Michigan, "Visit to Iraq," October 1957). The director of the International Cooperation Administration requested multiple copies of the American Institute of Chemical Engineers' brochure *College Programs in Nuclear Engineering* (USOM, 1957, July 13). The ICA reported that one "independently financed participant" departed for atomic energy training in the United States, concluding, "there are 34 participants now in the United States and one in Beirut" (USOM, 1958, November). In the atomic center building, the delegation decided that the short courses be extended to seven weeks "to enable [students] to carry out special experiments in using radioactive isotopes and training with them"; Harwell was asked to send out information concerning the "special physical properties of liquids" and that the member countries send students with appropriate qualifications for the study of electronics. Finally, the council "welcomed establishment of a radioactive isotopes department in the Royal Hospital" (Anonymous, 1957).

An noted earlier, describing dependency theory, scholar Patrick Wolfe traced "a hierarchically replicated cyclopean structure whereby a metropolis (also known as 'center,' 'core,' etc.) [which] dominated a number of (usually surrounding) satellites (the periphery)"; what is particularly helpful in Wolfe's description is the fact that any given metropolis "was itself satellite to a higher-order metropolis further up the chain of dependency" (1997, p. 396). Kwame Nkrumah noted a variety of means by which neo-colonialists managed to evade suspicion; among these were "retention ... of various kinds of privileges" which included "the supplying of 'advisers' of one sort or another" (1965, p. 246). Finally, Achille Mbembe started his discussion of necropolitics from the position that "modernity was at the origin of multiple concepts of sovereignty," a process which included such conflicting elements as self-limitation and self-institution (2003, p. 13).

During World War II, Niels Bohr noted that – to meet the requirements established by the Tizard mission – the United States would be turned into "a factory" as part of a global network of supply that culminated in the Manhattan Project (Masco, 2006, p. 18). After the war ended, national legislatures managed to impose controls on components of this transnational project; US President Dwight David Eisenhower's Atoms for Peace program succeeded in liberating the programs which grew from the Manhattan Project from the control of national legislatures. While Iraq (which was not a Commonwealth nation and was neutral during World War II) was initially outside this dynamic, the Baghdad Pact provided the country's rulers a legal mechanism to join in alliance with Commonwealth member Pakistan, as well as NATO member Turkey.

Notes

1 The author would like to thank Nick Spencer, Gökser Gökçay, and unidentified external readers. All remaining errors are, of course, my own.
2 I'm grateful to Christopher Abraham for drawing this document to my attention.

References

AB 6 (1956). UK Atomic Energy Authority; Cockcroft to Whitehouse, May 3, 1956; 1653; United Kingdom National Archives.
Alteras, I. (1993). *Eisenhower and Israel: US-Israeli Relations, 1953–1960*. Gainesville, FL: University Press of Florida.
Anonymous. (1945, August 8). Uranium Flown from Australia. *Christian Science Monitor*, p. 9.
Anonymous. (1945, August 9). Atom Rivals Petain in French Interest. *The New York Times*, p. 6.
Anonymous. (1945, September 16). Uranium for Bombs. *The New York Times*, p. E2.
Anonymous. (1945, September 24). MacArthur Bans A-Bomb Research: Jap Wage, Price, and Rationing Controls Ordered Immediately: A-Bomb Study Denied to Japs. *Los Angeles Times*, p. 1.

Anonymous. (1945, October 4). Atom-Energy Sources Prove Widely Known: Thorium Included Other Sources. *Christian Science Monitor*, p. 11.

Anonymous. (1945, November 23). Don't Prospect for Uranium. *Austin Statesman*, p. 9.

Anonymous. (1946, July 13). Australia Gets Atomic Bill. *New York Times*, p. 6.

Anonymous. (1948, April 3). Not Covered by Rewards. *Burnie Advocate*, p. 6.

Anonymous. (1950, January 23). British to Open Drive for Tool Sales in Canada. *Chicago Daily Tribune*, p. 6.

Anonymous. (1953). Nur al-Din Urges Army Preparedness. Daily Report. Foreign Radio Broadcasts, FBIS-FRB-53–005 on 1953-01-08.

Anonymous. (1953). Regent Delivers Speech From Throne. Daily Report. Foreign Radio Broadcasts, FBIS-FRB-53–016 on 1953-01-26.

Anonymous. (1953, March 21). New Plan on Uranium. *Sydney Morning Herald*, p. 5.

Anonymous. (1953, June 9). US Vulnerable to Atomic Attack. *Iraq Times*, p. 4.

Anonymous. (1953, August 4). New British Atomic Trials. *Iraq Times*, p. 9.

Anonymous. (1953, August 5). Use of Atomic Weapons; US Developments. *London Times*, p. 5.

Anonymous. (1953, August 27). Staff College Exercises. *Iraq Times*, p. 6.

Anonymous. (1953, September 30). Move to Open Up More Uranium Fields Here. *Sydney Morning Herald*, p. 1.

Anonymous. (1954, January 15). Iraq's Wisdom and Vision in Planning its Development Praised. *Iraq Times*, p. 2.

Anonymous. (1954, March 17). A Baghdad Diary. *Iraq Times*.

Anonymous. (1954, September 18). Australia Opens Plant to Crush Uranium Ore for US and Britain; Menzies Sees a Contribution to Defense of Free World in Atomic Project. *New York Times*, p. 3.

Anonymous. (1955, January 21). Britain's Exports Headed by Steel. *New York Times*, p. 31.

Anonymous. (1956, June 21). US to Give Secret A-Data to Australia. *Washington Post*, p. 13.

Anonymous. (1956, July 24). Nuclear Tests. *Birmingham Post*. AP4/2/9, University of Birmingham, Special Collections.

Anonymous. (1957). Pact Group Discusses Atomic Affairs. Baghdad, Iraqi home service. Daily Report. Foreign Radio Broadcasts, FBIS-FRB-57–233 on 1957-12-03.

Anonymous. (1957, January 18). Scientists' Tongues Cut to Prevent Divulging Secrets. *Iraq Times*, p. 16.

Anonymous. (1968, July 2). Henry Wiens Dies; Economist for US. *Washington Post*, p. B6.

Anonymous. (1986). General US Policies in the Near and Middle East; Military and Economic Policies with Respect to the Near and Middle East. Negotiating paper prepared in the Department of State. January 4, 1952. In *Foreign Relations of the United States, 1952–1954, The Near and Middle East, Vol. IX, Part 1*, p. 186. Washington, DC: Government Printing Office.

Barrett, R.C. (2007). *The Greater Middle East and the Cold War: US Foreign Policy Under Eisenhower and Kennedy*. London: IB Tauris.

Bertin, L. (1953, July 5). Britain Prepares Against Atomic Bombs. *Iraq Times*, p. 5.

Biçer, S. (2016). Turkey and NATO: What is Required? In Sertif Demir, ed., *Turkey's Foreign Policy and Security Perspectives in the 21st Century* (pp. 77–96), Boca Raton, FL: Brown Walker Press.

Birdwood, L. (1959). *Nuri as-Said*. London: Cassell.

Board of Trade. (1953). *Mission to Iraq*. London: Her Majesty's Stationary Office, p. 87.

Board of Trade. (1955). 11/5378, p. 40. Sir Michael Wright. United Kingdom National Archives.

Chamberlin, W.H. (1953, June 8). European Recovery: Western Nations are Not Out of the Economic Woods. *Wall Street Journal*, p. 6.

Claussen, P., Lee, J.M. and Raether, C.N. (eds.) (1986). *Foreign Relations of the United States, 1952–1954, Volume IX, Part 2, The Near and Middle East*. Washington, DC: Government Printing Office. Document 1378.

Cockcroft, John. (1957, May 11). The Baghdad Pact Nuclear Training Center. *Nature*, 179(4567), 936.

Foreign Service Journal. (1956, September). News from the Field: Baghdad. *Foreign Service Journal*, 33(9), 36, 57. Retrieved from www.afsa.org/foreign-service-journal-september-1956.

Freiberger, S.Z. (2007). *Dawn over Suez: The Rise of American Power in the Middle East, 1953–1957*. Lanham, MD: Rowman & Littlefield.

Gambone, M.D. (1997). *Eisenhower, Somoza, and the Cold War in Nicaragua*. Westport, CT: Praeger Publishers.

State-Trading Enterprises. (1966). General Agreement on Trade and Tariffs, L/2593/Add. 9, June 2, 1.

Hahn, P.L. (2006). *Caught in the Middle East*. Chapel Hill, NC: University of North Carolina Press.

Halnan, K.E. (1957) *Atomic Energy in Medicine*. Atoms for Peace. New York: Philosophical Library.

Hansard. (1954, February 1). House of Commons Debate, vol. 523, cc12–13W.

Hansard. (1956, May 31). House of Commons Debate, vol. 553, col. 25W.

Harris, G.L. (1958). *Iraq: Its People, Its Society, Its Culture*. New Haven, CT: HRAF Press.

Hartcup, G. and Allibone, T.E. (1984). *Cockcroft and the Atom*. Bristol: Adam Hilger.

Hayward, H.S. (1956, June 15). US-British A-Pool Hailed "Ultimate Deterrent". *Christian Science Monitor*, p. 1.

Hayward, H.S. (1956, June 26). Soviet Tack Studied by Commonwealth; Arms Cuts Weighed. *Christian Science Monitor*, p. 14.

Hecht, G. (2009). *The Radiance of France*. Cambridge, MA: The MIT Press.

Hörber, T. (2007). *The Foundations of Europe: European Integration Ideas in France*. Berlin: Springer Science & Business Media.

Hurst, D.G. and Critoph, E. (eds.) (1997). *Canada Enters the Nuclear Age. A Technical History of Atomic Energy of Canada Limited as Seen from Its Research Laboratories*. Montreal: McGill-Queen's University Press.

Johnston, A. (2005). *Hegemony and Culture in the Origins of NATO Nuclear First Use, 1945 –1955*. Berlin: Springer.

Kent, J. (2007). The Foreign Office and Defense of the Empire. In Greg Kennedy, ed. *Imperial Defence: The Old World Order, 1856–1956* (pp. 50–70), Abingdon: Routledge.

Krige, J. (2010). Techno-Utopian Dreams, Techno-Political Realities. In Michael D. Gordin, Helen Tilley and Gyan Prakash, eds. *Utopia/Dystopia* (pp. 151–175), Princeton, NJ: Princeton University Press.

Louis, W.R. (1984). *The British Empire in the Middle East*. Oxford: Oxford University Press.

Masco, J. (2006). *Nuclear Borderlands.* Princeton, NJ: Princeton University Press.

Mbembe, A. (2003). Necropolitics. *Public Culture,* 15(1), 11–40.

Mitchell, T. (2002). *Rule of Experts: Egypt, Techno-Politics, Modernity.* Berkeley, CA: University of California Press.

Nkrumah, K. (1965). *Neo-Colonialism, The Last Stage of Imperialism.* London: Thomas Nelson & Sons, Ltd. Retrieved from https://www.marxists.org/subject/afric a/nkrumah/neo-colonialism/.

Norman, A.E. (1952, September 10). Fourth Uranium-Bearing Field in Australia Called "Promising". *Christian Science Monitor,* p. 5.

Polsky, A.J. (2015). *The Eisenhower Presidency: Lessons for the Twenty-First Century.* Lanham, MD: Lexington Books.

Polyzoides. (1956, June 29). British Seek Way to Deal With Russia. *Los Angeles Times,* p. 12.

Press Notice (1956). AP 13/3/50E; 29.6.56, no. 12. Special Collections, University of Birmingham.

Preston, P. (2014). *Britain After Empire: Constructing a Post-War Political-Cultural Project.* Berlin: Springer.

Queensland. (1955). Parliamentary Debates. Legislative Assembly. August 9. Retrieved from https://www.parliament.qld.gov.au/documents/hansard/1955/1955_08_09_A.pdf.

Scheinman, L. (2015). *Atomic Energy Policy in France Under the Fourth Republic.* Princeton, NJ: Princeton University Press.

Stringer, W.H. (1953, May 9). Commmonwealth Picks Up Gauntlet Thrown Down By Communism. *Christian Science Monitor,* p. 25.

Strout, L.N. (1999). *Covering McCarthyism: How the Christian Science Monitor Handled Joseph R. McCarthy, 1950–1954.* Westport, CT: Praeger Publishers.

Sunaga, K. (2006). L'essence du mouvement de productivité – une étude à partir des sources américaines. *Histoire, Économie et Société,* 25(2), 261–279.

Thompson, H.L. (1957, September 11). Review of Industrial Program for Iraq. 13. folder 10, Box 194, Series 1, Development and Resource Corporation Records, Mudd Library, Princeton University.

United Nations General Assembly (1955). Peaceful Uses of Atomic Energy. 912 (X), United Nations General Assembly, tenth session, A/PV.550, December 5, p. 4.

United Nations Treaty (1955). Subsidiary Agreement Between the Government of the United States of America and the Government of Iraq for a Cooperative Program of Community Welfare. New York, March 2, United Nations Treaty Series, vol. 250, no. 3526.

USOM. (1955, July 11). USOM staff meeting, p. 188. Meetings, Staff, 1955–1958, US Operations Mission in Iraq, 1950–1954, United States National Archives and Records Administration.

USOM. (1956, July 5). Monthly summary report. ICATO Circular NA-119, Report, Monthly Director, 1956–1958; United States National Archives and Records Administration.

USOM. (1957, July 13), p. 16. Brown, Ben H., Jr., Director, ICA. 1950–1954, Training.

USOM. (1957, February 12). USOM staff meeting, p. 2. Meetings-Staff, 1955–1958, US Operations Missions in Iraq, 1950–1954, United States National Archives and Records Administration, p. 101.

USOM. (1958, November). Monthly summary report. ICATO Circular NA-119, Report, Monthly, Director, 1956–1958; US Operations Missions in Iraq, 1950–1954: United States National Archives and Records Administration.

Vance, H.S. (1959). Statement of Hon. Harold S. Vance, Commissioner, US Atomic Energy Commission. *Mutual Security Act. Hearings Before the Committee on Foreign Affairs, House of Representatives, 86th Cong., part 4*. Washington, DC: US Government Printing Office.

Wendt, G. (1955). *The Prospects of Nuclear Power and Technology*. New York: David Van Nostrand.

Whyte, W. (1956). *The Organization Man*. New York: Simon & Schuster.

Wiens, H. (1959, May). The United States Operations Mission in Iraq. *Annals of the American Academy of Political and Social Science*, 323, 140.

Wilford, H. (2013). *Playing Both Sides: America's Great Game*. New York: Basic Books.

Wolfe, P. (1997). History and Imperialism: A Century of Theory, From Marx to Postcolonialism. *The American Historical Review*, 102(2), 388–420.

Yaqub, S. (2004). *Containing Arab Nationalism: The Eisenhower Doctrine and the Middle East*. Chapel Hill, NC: University of North Carolina Press.

Yeşilbursa, B.K. (2005). *The Baghdad Pact: Anglo-American Defence Policies in the Middle East, 1950–1959*. Abingdon: Routledge.

Part III
Balancing Regional Alliances

6 Understanding the US-Israeli alliance

Jeremy Pressman[1]

The United States and Israel are close allies. It is one of the few US alliances often characterized as a special relationship, with top leaders on both sides regularly praising the strength, importance, and durability of the alliance.[2] The relations, President Bill Clinton (1998) said, are "not just an alliance but a profound friendship." President George W. Bush (2004) explained, "The United States is strongly committed, and I am strongly committed, to the security of Israel as a vibrant Jewish state." For President Barack Obama (2011): the "[US] commitment to Israel's security is unshakeable." President Donald J. Trump (2017) referred to ties to Israel as "our unbreakable bond with our cherished ally, Israel." On the Israeli side, Prime Minister Ariel Sharon (2001) called the United States "our great friend and ally." Standing next to President Trump, Prime Minister Benjamin Netanyahu called it a "remarkable alliance" (Trump, 2017).

What explains the origins and maintenance of this relationship? Why does Israel want a close alliance with the United States? Why does the United States want a close alliance with Israel? What one finds is an important difference between the two countries. Israel has little choice in its great power partner; there have only been one or two great powers at a time since 1948. In contrast, the United States may choose from many different potential regional partners in the Middle East. Israel is one option, but the United States also has or has had close alliance ties with Egypt, Iran, Jordan, and Saudi Arabia, to name a few examples. The US alliance with Israel is usually explained according to one of three ideas: Israel is a strategic asset; domestic interest groups in the United States pressure the US government to have the alliance; or the two countries share values (e.g. democratic values, biblical values). That said, each explanation faces certain shortcomings. In 2017, US policy on many issues is undergoing significant change under President Donald Trump, but the US-Israeli reliance remains important to both parties and thus does not appear subject to reconsideration.

Israeli national security

Israel is a small country with a small population of 8.7 million, that sits in the midst of a contentious region.[3] Three of Israel's neighbors have had civil wars – Jordan (1970–1971), Lebanon (1975–1990), and Syria (2011 to present) – and external powers like the United States and the Soviet Union or Russia have been deeply involved militarily in the region. While Israel has the most powerful armed forces in the region and the only cache of nuclear weapons, other countries like Egypt, Iran, Iraq, and Saudi Arabia have aspired to regional leadership at different times since World War II.

Israel's primary national security problem has been its conflict with the Palestinians and the Arab states. Since independence in 1948, the State of Israel fought inter-state wars in 1948, 1956, 1967, 1969–1970, 1973, 1982, and 2006. It faced two Palestinian uprisings (1987–1993 and 2000–2005), terrorist attacks, and major military confrontations with Hamas (the Palestinian Islamists) in Gaza in 2008–2009, 2012, and 2014. The Israeli occupation since 1967 of millions of Palestinians who live in the West Bank (2.7 million Palestinians) and Gaza Strip (1.8 million) creates tremendous security problems, compounded by Israel's settlement project in the West Bank.[4]

In this difficult region and as party to a long-running internal and external conflict, Israel has long sought external allies and patrons. A patron could provide arms and aid; it could give access to military intelligence and advanced military technology; it could balance against the patron of Israel's Arab enemies, the Soviet Union; and it could provide diplomatic protection by blunting Soviet pressure or providing cover at the UN Security Council and in other international settings.

Two countries in particular have played the largest role. First, Israel had a strong security partnership with France, including crucial cooperation for Israel's nuclear weapons program (Cohen, 1999). Second, starting in the 1960s and intensifying after 1967 when the Israeli-French relationship broke down, Israel partnered with the United States.[5]

In the 1960s, Israel did not have many options for its great power ally. France and the United Kingdom were faded empires. The Soviet Union, one of the world's only two superpowers, had allied itself with Israel's Arab rivals in Egypt, Iraq, and Syria. The only other great power was the United States, so the development of the US-Israeli link was as good as things could have gone for Israel. In sum, Israel needed a great power ally; it did not have many choices (really only one if it wanted a genuine superpower); and it worked out with a now decades-long alliance with the United States. Let me now turn to the other side of the ledger, US alliance needs.

US national security

During the Cold War, the United States had three fundamental national interests in the Middle East.[6] In the strategic realm, it sought to prevent Soviet penetration of the region. Once the Soviets had allies, the United States sought to limit the Soviet ability to benefit from those allies and keep US allies stronger. The Middle East was like much of the rest of the world; it became an arena for US-Soviet competition.

One of the great US triumphs in this regard was bringing Egypt into the US orbit in the 1970s. Egypt saw itself as the leader of the Arab world and felt its economic and strategic position would benefit from allying with Washington instead of Moscow. Through warming Egyptian-US ties and through the Egyptian-Israeli peace process of the late 1970s, the United States was able to cement Egypt's shifting alliance.

The second US national interest was maintaining the flow of energy resources – oil and natural gas – from the Middle East at a reasonable price. These energy resources were vital to the functioning of the US-led global capitalist economy. Even when US dependence on Middle East, and especially Persian Gulf, oil declined in recent decades, US economic partners and military allies in Western Europe and Japan remained deeply dependent upon the smooth flow of these energy resources.

The third national interest, developing in the 1960s and fully formed by the 1970s, was the US commitment to Israel's survival. The United States would not let Israel be destroyed by Arab armies. This was not only a theoretical commitment but led to specific US actions. In 1967, when Israel feared Arab militaries might attack, the United States first tried to resolve the situation with US-led action, an international regatta to reopen the Straits of Tiran. But when that failed, the United States did not stop Israel from taking matters into its own hands and launching a conventional first strike against its Arab neighbors (Pressman, 2008). In 1973, when Egypt and Syria's surprise military attack had Israel burning through its stocks of arms, the United States authorized and implemented an emergency military resupply even before the war had ended (Quandt, 2001).[7] As President Clinton (1998) phrased the point, "Let us in the United States say that we will stand by Israel, always foursquare for its security." A "secure Israel," Obama (2011) said, must be one basis of resolving the Israeli-Palestinian conflict.

Two events in the 1970s demonstrated some of the benefits and shortcomings of a US alliance with Israel. To put it another way, they showed how US national interests in the Middle East might be compatible or might be in conflict. These two events also act as a useful transition into the question of whether the Israeli-US alliance is based on positive strategic gains for Washington.

On the one hand, in September 1970, Israel, at the request of the United States, deterred Syria, a Soviet client, from invading Jordan and possibly toppling the Hashemite regime, a monarchy favored by the United States. According to Yitzhak Rabin, at the time Israeli ambassador to the United States and later prime minister, "a US Navy plane carrying squadron leaders from the Sixth Fleet flew to Tel Aviv to coordinate military plans with the Israelis"; Israel and the United States knew that the Soviet Union would detect the flight and other maneuvers and thereby "hear" the deterrent signal the United States and Israel were trying to send (Washington Institute for Near East Policy, 1986, p. 1). The US government first asked Israel to fly a reconnaissance mission to get a better sense of the Syrian moves. The government of Israel saw intervening on Jordan's behalf as a chance to better Israeli ties with the United States (Rubinovitz, 2010). Israel and the United States agreed that Israel could launch ground and aerial strikes to dislodge Syria from Irbid, Jordan. But Quandt (2001, p. 82) wrote that Jordan, knowing it was now backed by Israel and the United States, attacked Syrian forces; Syria began to withdraw. The need for Israeli military intervention ended. That the 1970 episode came on the heels of the 1967 war when Israel had demonstrated its regional military prowess added to the argument that Israel could provide significant strategic benefits to the United States.

On the other hand, just a few years later, the oil crisis of 1973–1974 suggested that the flow of resources was not guaranteed and could be endangered, as it was in that case by Arab-Israeli conflict. As a result of US support for Israel during the 1973 Arab-Israeli war, Arab oil-exporting countries cut oil production and cut oil exports to the United States and a few other countries. The cuts had a negative impact on the US economy. The US commitment to Israel's security and the capitalist system's massive thirst for oil might not go hand in hand. After the war, the Nixon administration launched Arab-Israeli peace talks, in part to address this tension between major US interests. The negotiations helped bring an end to the oil embargo in March 1974.[8]

With the end of the Cold War in the late 1980s and the collapse of the Soviet Union in 1991, the US interest in undermining Soviet policy disappeared. Within a decade, that strategic interest had been replaced by the battle with al-Qaeda and later the Islamic State. The new US strategic interest in the Middle East was defeating al-Qaeda and other violent, anti-US Islamist organizations with regional and global aspirations.

In the context of these US national interests, why has the alliance lasted as long as it has? Scholars have traditionally resorted to three categories of explanation for the origins and maintenance of the alliance: strategic, domestic, and ideational. The answer could be a combination of factors, and the driver could change over time.

The first explanation is that Israel is a *strategic asset* for the United States.[9] The two countries share intelligence and counterterrorism tactics. During the Cold War, the United States learned how its weapons would perform against Soviet and other East bloc weapons wielded by Arab states in wars with Israel. Israel battled, and usually defeated, Soviet client states, a victory by proxy for the United States. In a region with many states hostile toward the United States, as well as many unstable states that cannot be relied upon, Israel is a bastion of stability and strategic commitment. In the aftermath of September 11, 2001, some Israeli leaders have also emphasized that the two countries share a common anti-terrorism agenda. As President George W. Bush (2004) stated, "Our nation is stronger and safer because we have a true and dependable ally in Israel." Once allied with the United States, Israel has not wavered.

That said, the strategic argument for explaining the origins of the alliance raises a number of questions, all of which derive from Israel's conflict with the

Arab side. Many Arab parties will not act in concert with Israel for ideological reasons: Israel's occupation of Arab land broadly construed (Israel's existence since 1948) or more narrowly construed (Israel's occupation of the West Bank, Gaza, and the Golan since 1967) and the absence of a State of Palestine. While Israel has sought open relations and normal ties, the Arab world, with some notable exceptions, has not, instead seeing normalcy as something that should result from an Arab-Israeli resolution. Israel's very pursuit of normalcy has probably fueled the common Arab rejection of normalcy.

In practice, for example, this ideological divide complicates the fact that the US commitment to Israel's survival exists side by side with US energy interests, another vital US national interest. In other words, the US-Israeli alliance and need for US-Arab ties for energy, at a minimum, complicate those energy relations. Arab states are uncomfortable to hostile about US support for Israel, sometimes making for unsettled economic relations. The classic example is the 1973–1974 oil crisis already mentioned.

Furthermore, Israel, unlike other close US allies such as Australia or the United Kingdom, is often limited in what it can contribute to US military operations and, ultimately, in its ability to suffer casualties in tandem with US forces. Ben-Ephraim (2017) noted that Israel did not help the Carter administration achieve the Carter Doctrine.[10] Similarly, under George H. W. Bush, Israel could not contribute arms or personnel to the 1991 US-led Gulf War to reverse the Iraqi invasion and occupation of Kuwait. Iraq, aware of Israel's dual status as Arab adversary and US ally, fired missiles at Israel in order to try to peel Arab allies of the United States away from the anti-Iraq military coalition by forcing the Israel issue to the fore. The United States would not allow Israel to go after Iraq's missile launchers, again fearing Israeli aerial involvement would upset its Arab military partners like Saudi Arabia and Syria (Pressman, 2008, pp. 109–114). It was not the result of a limit in Israel's capabilities but, rather, ideological constraints based on the Arab-Israeli conflict.

In recent years, the question of Palestine has also obstructed what otherwise might be natural security cooperation between Israel and some Arab states such as Saudi Arabia. Why is it hard for Israel and Saudi Arabia to naturally balance against their mutual enemy Iran in the 2010s? Most Arab states do not want normalization with Israel, including on military matters, until the Palestinian national movement is satisfied. In 2016–2017, the Netanyahu government in Israel talked about the possibility of a regional pact that would subsume security issues and lead to a resolution of the Palestinian problem, but it is highly doubtful Saudi Arabia would dramatically and publicly increase cooperation toward Israel before the emergence of an independent State of Palestine (see Gause, 2015). Ideological tension obstructs strategic necessity.

Israel and the United States have also disagreed over US arms sales to Arab countries. Under the Reagan administration, for example, Israel strongly objected to US AWACS sales to Saudi Arabia (Bard, 1988). But Reagan prevailed and the sale went through.

A final strategic problem is that US support for Israel may stoke support for al Qaeda and other radical, violent Islamists. Whether US support has this effect has been a long-running debate inside the US political and national security establishment, with prominent figures on both sides. For example, General David Petraeus, then head of US Central Command, publicly warned of "a certain spillover effect" from the Arab-Israeli conflict to other issues in the region. While his language was cautious, he noted that the continued Israeli-Palestinian conflict "does make situations more challenging, particularly for moderate [Arab] leaders" in the Middle East (Duss, 2010).

These tensions explain much of the appeal to the United States of the Arab-Israeli peace process. If Israel and the Palestinian national movement could settle their differences, along with Israel and Syria, these contradictions would fade away. The ideological barrier to cooperation or normalization would disappear. Israel could work militarily with the United States and Washington's Arab military allies in public fashion. The quiet nature of current cooperation, which likely limits the nature and extent of that cooperation, would no longer be necessary.

The second explanation is that certain US *domestic interest groups* pushed for the US alliance with Israel. This explanation is based on the general idea that US foreign policy is not simply a rational, unitary response to fixed national interests. Instead, US foreign policy is an amalgamation of pressures from constituents and organizations in the United States. The US government does not formulate policy based on what is best for the United States as a whole but, rather, on the desires and demands of certain organized and vocal groups or subsets of the population (Mearsheimer and Walt, 2007). To illustrate with similar examples from domestic policy, the National Rifle Association (NRA) causes deviations in gun control policy that bend toward NRA demands, and the American Association of Retired Persons (AARP) does the same for, say, retiree medical care and the Social Security program.

In the case of US-Israeli ties, the interest group supporting strong relations is usually described as the Jewish Lobby or the Israel Lobby. The best-known organization is the American Israeli Public Affairs Committee (AIPAC), but other lobbying and policy organizations include the Israel Policy Forum, J Street, the Zionist Organization of America, and Christians United for Israel. What these organizations share is being part of the American body politic and supporting the idea of the State of Israel and its continued existence. In some cases, like AIPAC, they also almost always support the policies of the Israeli government.

The argument is that the Israel lobby shapes US policy. According to critics of US policy, despite negative strategic impacts from allying with Israel, the two countries have a special relationship. Despite the Israeli occupation of Palestinian land, the expansion of the Israeli settlement project, and Israeli rejection of many concessions that would be necessary for a two-state solution – if not a wholesale rejection of the idea of a Palestinian state alongside Israel – the United States allies with Israel because of successful interest group pressure. Mearsheimer and Walt (2007) go further, arguing that the Israeli lobby drives much of US policy not only in the Arab-Israeli arena but also in the wider Middle East such as the US-led invasion of Iraq in 2003.

The domestic argument for explaining the origins of the US-Israeli alliance faces a number of challenges as well (Mead, 2007). The United States has always been and remains far stronger than Israel. When US administrations want to squeeze Israel and go against Israeli policy and domestic interest groups acting for Israel, they do so. Presidents Gerald Ford (reassessment), Ronald Reagan (arms sales to Saudi Arabia), George H. W. Bush (Madrid peace conference), and Barack Obama (Iran nuclear agreement) all had prominent moments when they went against Israel and supportive US-based interest groups and prevailed.[11] The lobby has limited options in the face of a major presidential policy push.

To put it another way, who really makes US foreign policy? Is it outside interest groups or is it the executive branch of the US government? Critics of this domestic explanation for the alliance would suggest the latter much more than the former. And for the sake of argument, let's say interest groups do drive US foreign policy. In that case, one would need to take account of other lobbies as well, including those funded by the oil industry or by Arab states. They might counteract the Israel lobby. Also, defining this lobby is difficult. Is it a certain list of organizations? Is it American Jews only, or does it include all American supporters of Israeli policy? (See Waxman, 2010.)

It is worth noting that interest groups supportive of Israel will utilize the first and third explanations to justify the alliance. Because they do not want the alliance to be seen as based primarily on lobbying, and possibly contrary to general US interests and values, the interest groups will often argue that Israel is a strategic asset for the United States, and Israel and the United States have shared values. Under the "US & Israel" tab on the AIPAC website, visitors have seven options including "Fighting Terrorism," "Military Partnership," "Shared Values," and "Strong Allies."[12]

The third explanation, then, is that the alliance between Israel and the United States is based on *shared values*.[13] Exactly what values are shared varies depending on the argument. In some cases, the emphasis is on shared political values and, in particular, the fact that both countries are democracies (Barnett, 1996, p. 434, 436). A different emphasis is on the shared religious tradition of the bible, sometimes referred to as the Judeo-Christian tradition. President George W. Bush (2004) told an AIPAC gathering, "We have both built vibrant democracies, built on the rule of law and market economies. And we're both countries founded on certain basic beliefs: that God watches over the affairs of men, and values every life." Obama (2011) explained, "our friendship is rooted deeply in a shared history and shared values." Trump (2017) argued that "The partnership between our two countries built on our shared values has advanced the cause of human freedom, dignity, and peace. These are the building blocks of democracy." AIPAC's website agreed: "The two countries have developed a resilient friendship, based in large part on an unshakable dedication to common values. Commitment to democracy, the rule of law, freedom of religion and speech and human rights are all core values shared between the United States and Israel."[14]

On the political side, the notion that the United States picks allies based solely on regime type is not supported by the empirical record. The United States has had alliances with both democracies and dictatorships. Washington has been perfectly willing to ally with countries that are monarchies, military regimes, or other forms of authoritarian systems, including in Egypt, Jordan, and Saudi Arabia or, pre-1979, in the Shah's Iran.

The shared religious heritage reason seems questionable as a key driver of the military alliance. Much is made of the Judeo-Christian tradition and the two religions do share a holy book, the Torah or Old Testament. However, the theology and practices of the two religions also embody many differences. While I would not discount the rhetorical flourish of politicians citing this tradition, private evidence from internal government deliberations of how said factors affect US policy decisions would be useful. Also, the Judeo-Christian tradition predates the establishment of the State of Israel in 1948; the argument would predict a special relationship from Israel's founding, and that did not happen. The argument may have some background impact, but it is hard to sustain the claim that it is the (or a) primary factor driving the close alliance ties.

Policy disagreement

Despite the special relationship, points of US-Israeli policy contention are common (Quandt, 2001; Reich, 2007; Spiegel, 1985; Pressman, 2008, pp. 78–119). Going back to the formation of the alliance in the 1960s, every US administration has had differences with Israeli governments. Sometimes, as was clearly the case with Obama and Netanyahu, there are personality differences. But Israeli and US chief executives who get along well also have some core differences on important Middle East and Arab-Israeli policies even as the underlying alliance relationship and billions in US aid since the 1970s has stayed tight.[15]

The peace process is the central sticking point as the United States has often, though not always, wanted Israel to make concessions to bring about peaceful relations.[16] Whether on Israeli policy in Jerusalem, settlements (Neff, 1994), or other issues, the United States and Israel have often disagreed. Carter pressed Israeli Prime Minister Begin for a settlement freeze, and interpreting their agreement on the matter led to a near crisis after the Camp David Accords of 1978. In his peace plan, Reagan (1982) spoke out strongly against settlements:

> Indeed, the immediate adoption of a settlement freeze by Israel, more than any other action, could create the confidence needed for wider participation in these talks. Further settlement activity is in no way necessary

for the security of Israel and only diminishes the confidence of the Arabs that a final outcome can be freely and fairly negotiated.

George W. Bush (2002) said, "Israeli settlement activity in the occupied territories must stop." Obama sought a settlement freeze in his first term.

The obvious point is that if the United States is going to act as the primary mediator in the Arab-Israeli conflict, it is going to need to secure concessions from all the different parties involved, including Israel. In 2002, the George W. Bush administration adopted the Israeli government's favored approach at the time. Unlike in the Rabin era, terrorism had to stop before negotiations could commence. In other words, the sequencing put the onus on the Palestinians. But if/when this happened, Bush (2002) still expected Israel to: withdraw military forces to pre-intifada II positions; stop Israeli settlement activity; help the Palestinian economy; restore Palestinian freedom of movement; and release frozen Palestinian revenue. Ultimately, he said, the Israeli occupation would have to end. By the time of the Annapolis process in 2007–2008, Bush officials were also facilitating Israeli-Palestinian negotiations about the core issues like land, settlements, and Jerusalem.

While the United States usually defends the Israeli position at the UN Security Council, every US administration has occasionally either supported or abstained – and thereby not exercised its veto power – on resolutions the Israelis disliked. Even at the time of President Nixon, the United States had voted with the majority to censure Israel over its moves in occupied Jerusalem. Similar US votes have occurred periodically across administrations (Friedman, 2016).[17]

Lastly, the United States and Israel do not always have similar estimates about threats or, to put it another way, who the enemy is and what should be done about it. In 1981, the United States criticized Israel's bombing of an Iraqi nuclear facility at Osiraq. The Israel government thought preventive action was necessary, and it acted (see Feldman, 1982). In 2015, the government of Israel, and some supportive interest groups, vociferously criticized the Obama administration for its diplomatic agreement to curtail the Iranian nuclear program. Both saw the Iranian program as dangerous but differed deeply about the best approach for controlling it (Xu and Rees, 2016, pp. 9–10).

Conclusion

Could the alliance weaken in the next few years? In the short term, it seems unlikely.[18] Although President Trump has expressed some general isolationist sentiments, he has spoken strongly in favor of this alliance. The US Congress remains strongly in favor of the alliance. Polls suggest the US public remains decidedly more sympathetic to Israel than to the Palestinian cause (Pew Research Center, 2016). Israeli-US military and intelligence cooperation, including US aid and arms sales, seems likely to continue, especially given the $38 billion/ten-year agreement signed late in the Obama presidency. There does not appear to be growing support for arguments that Israel is a strategic liability to the United States.

Israel is a much wealthier country than when the alliance started. It has less need for US military aid because it generates more wealth and technology on its own. But access to advanced US military technology and US diplomatic cover cannot be replaced by anyone else at this time. Israel has been able to maintain different policy stances than the United States on some important issues while protecting the underlying alliance.

Both the United States and Israel are in rough spots with regard to their commitment to liberal democratic values. The occupation undermines Israel's democratic claims, as do illiberal statements and legislation from Israel's government. Trump's harsh attacks on the press, the judiciary, and his political opponents strike at pillars of the US system. If shared democratic values were the sole basis of the alliance, it might at least be time to ask some questions. Yet with both countries moving in the same political direction, any impact on the alliance will be minimal.

Notes

1 Many thanks to Brent Sasley and Mira Sucharov for helpful feedback. Any errors are my own.
2 Earlier works on the alliance include Bar Siman Tov (1998); Chomsky (1999); Druks (2001); Lewis (1999); and Reich (2007).
3 To learn more about Israel itself, see Sasley and Waller (2017). The figure of 8.7 million does not include Palestinians who live in Gaza and the West Bank, with the exception of Palestinians who live in East Jerusalem.
4 Israel contends the Gaza Strip is no longer occupied since the withdrawal of Israeli settlers in 2005.
5 For details on the development of the US-Israeli alliance in the 1960s and thereafter, see Pressman (2008, pp. 81–87).
6 For a review of policy toward Israel in each US administration, see Reich (2007), Spiegel (1985), and Quandt (2001).
7 This tripartite depiction of US interests in the region leaves some possibilities out. Contrast my argument with this statement by President Barack H. Obama (2011):

> For decades, the United States has pursued a set of core interests in the region: countering terrorism and stopping the spread of nuclear weapons; securing the free flow of commerce and safe-guarding the security of the region; standing up for Israel's security and pursuing Arab-Israeli peace.

Others might emphasize the spread of democracy, human rights, or liberalism; for example, Bush (2004) said: "And so across that vital region, America is standing for the expansion of human liberty."
8 Office of the Historian, "Oil Embargo, 1973–1974," https://history.state.gov/miles tones/1969-1976/oil-embargo.
9 For example, see Oren (2011). Interestingly, prominent critics of the US-Israeli alliance, like Chomsky (see Wells, 2010), also argue that strategic factors, including US hegemonic aspirations and the need for oil, drive the relationship. Of course, such critics use a different tone when talking about Israel's strategic utility to the United States.

10 Carter (1980) stated:

> An attempt by any outside force to gain control of the Persian Gulf region will be regarded as an assault on the vital interests of the United States of America, and such an assault will be repelled by any means necessary, including military force.

11 In 1975, the Ford administration re-evaluated relations with Israel after US dissatisfaction with Israeli policies in political negotiations with Egypt. The Israeli government opposed US arms sales to Saudi Arabia in the early 1980s. Later, the Bush (41) administration had to press a reluctant Israeli government to attend the 1991 Arab-Israeli peace conference at Madrid. And most recently, the Israeli government opposed the 2015 Joint Comprehensive Plan of Action – negotiated by the Obama administration and others – meant to control Iran's nuclear program.

12 "US & Israel" was under the top-line tab "LEARN": www.aipac.org/ (accessed on September 1, 2017).

13 For example, see Oren (2011).

14 "Shared Values": www.aipac.org/learn/us-and-israel/shared-values (accessed on September 1, 2017).

15 On the history and amounts of US aid, see Sharp (2016).

16 For a study of the success and failure of the US negotiating efforts, see Pressman (2014). See also Eisenberg and Caplan (1998), Kurtzer et al. (2013), and Kurtzer and Lasensky (2008).

17 Friedman (2016) was published before the Obama administration abstained on a UN Security Council resolution addressing Israeli settlements in December 2016.

18 For the contrary argument that the alliance could experience more turbulence in the coming years, see Allin and Simon (2016) and Waxman (2016).

References

Allin, D.H. and Simon, S.N. (2016). *Our Separate Ways: The Struggle for the Future of the US-Israel Alliance.* New York: PublicAffairs.

Bar Siman Tov, Y. (1998). The United States and Israel Since 1948: A Special Relationship? *Diplomatic History*, 22(2), 231–262.

Bard, M. (1988). Interest Groups, the President, and Foreign Policy: How Reagan Snatched Victory from the Jaws of Defeat on AWACS. *Presidential Studies Quarterly*, 18(3), 583–600.

Barnett, M.N. (1996). Identity and Alliances in the Middle East. In Peter J. Katzenstein, (ed.) *The Culture of National Security.* New York: Columbia University Press, pp. 400–447.

Ben-Ephraim, S. (2017). *Can We Settle This: The Settlements in the Occupied Territories and US – Israel Relations, 1967–1981.* PhD Dissertation, University of Calgary.

Bush, G.W. (2002, June 24). President Bush Calls for New Palestinian leadership. Retrieved from https://georgewbush-whitehouse.archives.gov/news/releases/2002/06/20020624–3.html.

Bush, G.W. (2004, May 18). President Speaks to the American Israel Public Affairs Committee. Retrieved from https://georgewbush-whitehouse.archives.gov/news/releases/2004/05/20040518–1.html.

Carter, J. (1980, January 23). The State of the Union Address Delivered Before a Joint Session of the Congress. Retrieved from www.presidency.ucsb.edu/ws/?pid=33079.

Chomsky, N. (1999). *Fateful Triangle: The United States, Israel, and the Palestinians.* Cambridge, MA: South End Press.

Clinton, W.J. (1998, April 27). Remarks at a Reception Celebrating Israel's 50th Anniversary. Retrieved from www.presidency.ucsb.edu/ws/index.php?pid=55859.

Cohen, A. (1999). *Israel and the Bomb.* New York: Columbia University Press.

Druks, H. (2001). *The Uncertain Alliance: The US and Israel from Kennedy to the Peace Process.* Westport, CT: Greenwood Press.

Duss, M. (2010, March 25). Petraeus Explains The Reality Of Middle East 'Linkage'. Retrieved from https://thinkprogress.org/petraeus-explains-the-reality-of-middle-east -linkage-6e122397d168/.

Eisenberg, L.Z. and Caplan, N. (1998). *Negotiating Arab-Israeli Peace: Patterns, Problems, Possibilities.* Bloomington, IN: Indiana University Press.

Feldman, S. (1982). The Bombings of Osiraq – Revisited. *International Security*, 7(2), 114–142.

Friedman, L. (2016, April 10). Israel's Unsung Protector: Obama. *The New York Times.* Retrieved from https://www.nytimes.com/2016/04/12/opinion/international/isr aels-unsung-protector-obama.html?.

Gause, F.G. (2015). Ideologies, Alliances and Underbalancing in the New Middle East Cold War. Retrieved from http://pomeps.org/2015/08/26/ideologies-alliances-and-un derbalancing-in-the-new-middle-east-cold-war/.

Kurtzer, D.C. and Lasensky, S.B. (2008). *Negotiating Arab-Israeli Peace: American Leadership in the Middle East.* Washington, DC: United States Institute of Peace.

Kurtzer, D.C., Lasensky, S.B., Quandt, W.B., Spiegel, S.L. and Telhami, S.Z. (2013). *The Peace Puzzle: America's Quest for Arab-Israeli Peace, 1989–2011.* Ithaca, NY: Cornell University Press.

Lewis, S.W. (1999). The United States and Israel: Evolution of an Unwritten Alliance. *Middle East Journal*, 53(3), 364–378.

Mead, W.R. (2007). Jerusalem Syndrome: Decoding The Israel Lobby. *Foreign Affairs*, 86(6), 160–168.

Mearsheimer, J.J. and Walt, S.M. (2007). *The Israel Lobby and US Foreign Policy.* New York: Farrar, Straus and Giroux.

Neff, D. (1994). Settlements in US Policy. *Journal of Palestine Studies*, 23(3), 53–69.

Obama, B.H. (2011, May 19). Remarks by the President on the Middle East and North Africa. Retrieved from https://obamawhitehouse.archives.gov/the-press-office/ 2011/05/19/remarks-president-middle-east-and-north-africa.

Oren, M. (2011, April 25). The Ultimate Ally. *Foreign Policy.* Retrieved from http://fo reignpolicy.com/2011/04/25/the-ultimate-ally-2/.

Pew Research Center. (2016). Views of Israel and Palestinians. Retrieved from www. people-press.org/2016/05/05/5-views-of-israel-and-palestinians/.

Pressman, J. (2008). *Warring Friends: Alliance Restraint in International Politics.* Ithaca, NY: Cornell University Press.

Pressman, J. (2014). American Engagement and the Pathways to Arab-Israeli Peace, *Cooperation & Conflict*, 49(4), 536–553.

Quandt, W.B. (2001). *Peace Process: American Diplomacy and the Arab-Israeli Conflict Since 1967.* Revised edition. Berkeley CA: The University of California Press.

Reagan, R. (1982, September 1). Address to the Nation on United States Policy for Peace in the Middle East. Retrieved from https://www.reaganlibrary.archives.gov/a rchives/speeches/1982/90182d.htm.

Reich, B. (2007). The United States and Israel: The Nature of a Special Relationship. In David W. Lesch, (ed.), *The Middle East and the United States: A Historical and Political Reassessment.* 4th Edition. Boulder, CO: Westview Press, pp. 205–225.

Rubinovitz, Z. (2010). Blue and White 'Black September': Israel's Role in the Jordan Crisis of 1970. *The International History Review*, 32(4), 687–706.

Sasley, B.E. and Waller, H.M. (2017). *Politics in Israel: Governing a Complex Society.* New York: Oxford University Press.

Sharon, A. (2001, March 7). Inauguration Speech of Prime Minister Ariel Sharon in the Knesset. Retrieved from http://mfa.gov.il/MFA/PressRoom/2001/Pages/Inauguration%20Speech%20of%20Prime%20Minister%20Ariel%20Sharon.aspx.

Sharp, J.M. (2016, December 22). US Foreign Aid to Israel. Congressional Research Service, RL 33222. Retrieved from https://fas.org/sgp/crs/mideast/RL33222.pdf.

Spiegel, S.L. (1985). *The Other Arab-Israeli Conflict: Making America's Middle East Policy, from Truman to Reagan.* Chicago: University of Chicago Press.

Trump, D.J. (2017, February 15). Remarks by President Trump and Prime Minister Netanyahu of Israel in Joint Press Conference. Retrieved from https://www.whitehouse.gov/the-press-office/2017/02/15/remarks-president-trump-and-prime-minister-netanyahu-israel-joint-press.

Washington Institute for Near East Policy. (1986, September 1). US-Israel Strategic Cooperation. *Policy Focus*, Issue 3, p. 1.

Waxman, D. (2010). The Israel Lobbies: A Survey of the Pro-Israel Community in the United States. *Israel Studies Review*, 32(1), 5–28.

Waxman, D. (2016). *Trouble in the Tribe: The American Jewish Conflict Over Israel.* Princeton, NJ: Princeton University Press.

Wells, K. (2010, August 16). Noam Chomsky: The Real Reasons the US Enables Israeli Crimes and Atrocities. *Alternet*. Retrieved from www.alternet.org/story/147865/noam_chomsky%3A_the_real_reasons_the_u.s._enables_israeli_crimes_and_atrocities.

Xu, R. and Rees, W. (2016). Comparing the Anglo-American and Israeli-American Special Relationships in the Obama Era: An Alliance Persistence Perspective. *Journal of Strategic Studies.* doi:10.1080/01402390.2016.1184147.

7 The United States' strategic relationship with Iran and Turkey

Implications for Cold War and post-Cold War order

Suleyman Elik

The role of first and second image in the making of foreign policy is an important tool in explaining the foreign policy behavior of modern states. But it is perhaps the systemic (international) level of analysis or third image that provides the most pertinent and wide-ranging scope to exemplify middle power and great power relations. Here, an international level of analysis is used to assist in understanding the cases of US relations with Iran and Turkey from the Cold War to the present. During the Cold War, both Iran and Turkey were located in what was referred to as the "Northern Tier," which extended from Turkey to Pakistan (Ramazani, 1966). Iran and Turkey were key allies in the Baghdad Pact and the Periphery Pact and served to uphold American regional strategic interests. In addition, the economic instrument of this partnership in the form of the Regional Cooperation for Development (RCD) and the Economic Cooperation Organization emphasized the importance of this regional partnership.

This chapter explores the significance and importance of the Iran–Turkey security and economic engagement with the United States, especially during the early decades of the Cold War and pre-1979 period. Furthermore, while Turkey became the main ally of the United States against Russian aggression in the North Atlantic Treaty Organization (NATO), Iran also played an essential proxy role for the United States throughout the 1970s. But after Iran's 1979 Islamic Revolution, the geopolitical importance of Iran was identified as a negative balancer, in Kenneth Waltz's (1959, 2008) terms, in the security belt of the Middle East. The strategic positioning of Iran has continued to this day under the Islamic Republic of Iran. And since the Arab Spring, the rise of Iran's proxy engagement in Syria, Yemen, Iraq, and Bahrain has challenged the status quo of regional security.

The changing dynamics of the international system enforce regional countries' relations with the United States, which have been both competitive and hostile. This chapter helps explain how great power security interests affect regional middle power relations through the cases of Iran and Turkey. From a US-centric perspective, Turkey is frequently classified as a client state while Iran was a proxy power of the United States until Khomeini's Islamic Revolution in 1979. In defining client and proxy state relations between Iran and

Turkey, this chapter emphasizes the interaction capacities of both regional middle powers and explains their competitive capacity to gain leverage in establishing alliance relations with great powers such as the United States. This chapter lays an emphasis on the systemic level in order to explain the "patron-proxy," "patron-client," and "proxy-client" state security relations.

US strategic engagement with Iran, 1945–1979

The pivotal years from 1930 to 1945 witnessed a transition of power whereby the British Empire lost its global preeminence and left its control over the Middle East to the United States. The December 1943 meeting of Franklin Roosevelt, Winston Churchill, and Josef Stalin regarding Nazi Germany and Imperial Japan was a turning point for US–Iran relations. On the eve of the Second World War, the United States and Great Britain revisited the strategic importance of Iran in the Northern Tier concept for Western security interests, encapsulated by the "Pentagon Talk" in October 1947. In order to contain Soviet expansionist policy and provide protection for Iran's oil reserves, Britain and the United States agreed that the independence of Iran, Turkey, Greece, and Italy would have to be preserved to protect vital US and British security interests in the eastern Mediterranean (McKercher, 1999).

During the Second World War, Muhammed Reza Shah maintained Iran's national unity by defeating the Kurdish and Azerbaijani nationalist uprisings in the 1940s, though this presented him with new leadership challenges. Due to rising Iranian nationalism and his weak leadership, he could not stop the rise of elected Prime Minister Musaddiq's political power in Iranian domestic politics. The Prime Minister's foreign policy agenda was completely different from that of Muhammed Reza Shah. His policy agenda included the nationalization of oil and a new geopolitical definition of Iran, which put Iran at the center as a sovereign power. He successfully contextualized the concept of "negative equilibrium" whereby Iranian liberal nationalism had been implemented by enforcing the nationalization of Iranian oil fields on March 15, 1951 (Zabih, 1982a). However, in 1953 a CIA-supported military coup d'état named Operation Ajax ousted the elected Iranian Prime Minister Musaddiq from his post to reinstall the power of Muhammad Reza Shah Pahlavi (Zabih, 1982b). The special relationship between the Pahlavi dynasty and the US government became more strategic, which changed assessment of the region for the US. The Shah was effectively reliant on his relationship with the US government. This engagement between Tehran and Washington served to protect US interests under the proxy leadership of Iran in the Persian Gulf.

However, during the consolidation of Pahlavi's power, the Turkish government's fear of a communist takeover in Iran pushed its policy openly in favor of Britain and the West. Turkish political elites felt that the political influence of Soviet Russia in Iran could be construed as an eternal threat to Turkey's national security. Therefore, during this critical time in Iran, one can describe the relationships between the two neighbors as fragile with Turkey and untrusting of the Musaddiq government (Gasiorowski and Byrne, 2004).

The "peaceful transition of power" from Britain to the United States occurred when Britain announced the termination of its protectorate position over the Gulf in 1968. The rise of US supremacy necessitated a new settlement over boundary disputes, especially in offshore areas where there had been exploration of the new Southern Pars gas and oil fields. On the one hand, Iran's position as the "gendarme" of the Persian Gulf was enhanced with the support of US political and military support. Muhammad Reza Shah implemented more of a revisionist policy towards the Persian Gulf to expand its maritime border and support Iraqi Kurds against Baghdad. The special relationship between the US government and the Shah provided Iran with leverage to gain "a proxy role" for the security of energy supplies in the Persian Gulf. Leaving behind the Ottoman legacy and British primacy, the US government found an opportunity to establish a special relationship that lasted until the revolution of 1979. Khomeini's revolutionary movement against Pahlavi's constitutional monarchy resulted in the cutting of all security ties with the US government, including cancellation of collective regional and security cooperation especially within the context of the Central Treaty Organization (CENTO) and RCD. The Islamic Revolution in Iran caused a strategic rupture with the US. Due to the loss of Iran, the US government not only engaged more with Turkey but also deployed its strategic forces to the Persian Gulf.

US strategic engagement with Turkey, 1945–1979

The Soviet threat to the national security of both Iran and Turkey and their sovereignty pushed their capitals into the Western camp. This phenomenon was demonstrated when Turkey received demands from the Kremlin to relinquish the provinces of Kars and Ardahan and allow Soviet forces to establish a naval base in the Dardanelles. This aspect of the Cold War system pushed Turkey into making strategic changes to its national security doctrine and internal political settings. For instance, during the Menderes government (1950–1960) in Turkey, the Turkish state joined NATO after troops were sent to Korea in 1952. Ankara received a substantial amount of economic aid from the Marshall Plan, which also secured Turkey's democratic transition from a one-party to a multiparty system. In turn, Turkey's positioning was secured and guaranteed by the Western alliance, and Russia recognized Turkey's territorial legacy in 1953. Turkey's role is identified within the framework of offshore balancing by Christopher Layne (2009). In addition, US strategists and diplomats such as George Kennan and Henry Kissinger presumed that deployment of a strategic arm in foreign territories was less expensive than the full deployment of strategic forces. During the Cold War, Turkey was considered geopolitically critical for Western security interests as it offered a "second strike" option for the United States against Soviet Russia.

There were three military engagements between Turkey and the Western security apparatus: the deployment of US strategic weapons systems in Turkish territory, the storage of B-61 nuclear bombs, and the setup of military installations across Turkish territory. US military aid to the Turkish army was essential for Turkey's strategic engagement with the Western security apparatus. For instance, between 1950 and 1974, the average military aid to Turkey was $165 million per annum.

As mentioned, nuclear and missile systems played an essential role for Turkey's national security and strengthened its role in the collective defense umbrella under NATO. The UHF radar system in eastern Turkey also played a crucial role in the establishment of communications with other key US intelligence networks. Long-range radar systems in the city of Diyarbakır, which became operational in June 1957, monitored Soviet Russia's military activities, nuclear weapons, and missile testing (Zabetakis and Peterson, 1964). In addition to this, an electronic listening post was located along the Black Sea coast at army sites in the cities of Sinop and Trabzon. During the Cold War, Turkey's hosting of US forces and military installations in Adana, Balikesir, Konya, and Izmir provided an opportunity to monitor Soviet Russia's regional activities. According to Duke (1989), the presence of US combat forces in the city of Muş, which is only 500 miles away from Tehran and 700 miles away from Abadan, was not considered as a threat to Pahlavi's Iran. The Turkish army's full integration with alliance countries strengthened its position in the collective defense system.

A Turkish–American security engagement that materialized with the strategic weapons system was the Jupiter missile program that started in 1955. Due to reservations over its deployment, the US government installed this system in Italy and in Turkey. The installation of the Jupiter missiles in July–August 1962 on the Çiğli base near Izmir was the result of an agreement concluded with Turkey in October 1959, but it soon proved obsolete due to lack of mobility. During the Cuban missile crisis, American President John F. Kennedy decided to dismantle these weapons without warning or consultation with the Turks, and they were removed from Turkish territory in April 1963 (Holloway, 1960).

The controversy over Turkey's nuclear capability, along with its position as a host country, was reviewed in a Natural Resources Defense Council report in February 2005 (Kristensen, 2005). It should be noted that Turkey is a signatory to both the Non-Proliferation Treaty (NPT) and the Comprehensive Test Ban Treaty. Turkey's strategic nuclear capabilities are operated under the supervision of NATO and the International Atomic Energy Agency (IAEA). For instance, 90 B-61 nuclear gravity bombs were deployed by the United States at Incirlik Air Base during the Cold War. In 1996, President Clinton's government transferred these strategic weapons from Akinci Air Base (near Balikesir city) to Incirlik Air Base (near Adana city), where they continue to be earmarked for delivery by the Turkish Air Force. According to Kristensen's 2005 report, the number of nuclear bombs was reduced to 70 B-61s

(Kristensen and McKinzie, 2012). Turkey's ballistic cruise missiles and delivery systems can be classified as tactical (Cirincione, 2005).

The Incirlik base is located in southern Turkey near the Syrian border. There are 58 Protective Aircraft Shelters on the base, 25 of which are equipped with WS3 Vaults for nuclear weapons storage. The vaults, which have a maximum capacity of 100 weapons, were completed in 1998. The base stores 90 B-61 nuclear bombs, 50 of which are for delivery by US F-16C/Ds from the 39th Fighter Wing, with 40 of them earmarked for delivery by the Turkish F-16 fighters of the 4th Wing at Akinci and the 9th Wing at Balikesir (Kristensen, 2005). Turkey's strategic fighter and ground attack aircraft include 121 F-16Cs, 24 F-16Ds, 93 F-4Es (65 in service with planned upgrades to the F-4E Phantom 2000), 54 F-4E Phantom 2000s, 63 F-5A/Bs, 44 NF-5A/Bs, and cooperation in the F-35 JSF project.

The Islamic Revolution in 1979 altered the regional security setting, which allowed the US government to position US military forces into the Gulf and enforce a Turkish–US rapprochement to enhance security relations during the 1980s. Following the revolution, Iran's isolation from the international system, along with a series of economic sanctions, limited Iran's revolutionary activities in the region. Due to a worsening relationship with Iran, the Turkish and US governments found an opportunity to rehabilitate uneasy relations that had been severely damaged by the US arms embargo stemming from the 1974 Turkish military operations.

Iran–Turkey relations and the US strategy in the Northern Tier

In the framework of the Northern Tier, the regional security engagement of Turkey and Iran, as demonstrated by the Baghdad Pact, Periphery Pact, and CENTO, was established under the rubric of a quasi-regional security arrangement.

Due to this important engagement with the US, both Turkey and Iran also developed relationships with Israel. In so doing, Turkey and Israel agreed to a secret "Periphery Pact" designed to link Israel, Turkey, Iran, and Ethiopia in 1958. Turkey distanced itself from the historical claims of the Ottoman Empire and consequently further preferred to isolate itself from the region by positioning itself with Tel Aviv against the rise of pan-Arab nationalism. The successive events of the Suez crisis between Egypt and England/France in 1956 buoyed Gamal Abd al-Nasir's pan-Arab nationalist movement in addition to further alienating Arab countries from Iran and Turkey. Therefore, together with Tehran, Ankara pursued a pro-Western and pro-Israeli policy during the Arab–Israeli War in the 1950s. For the United States, securing this region necessitated encouragement for Iran and Turkey to establish better relations with Israel.

The concept of the Northern Tier on the southern periphery aimed to create a "collective security system" against the Soviet threat for both Turkey and Iran. The Baghdad Pact was established for this purpose between 1954 and 1955 by Britain, Iraq, Iran, Pakistan, and Turkey (Kemal Yesilbursa, 2005). But due to the Ba'athist revolution in Iraq and the developments that followed in Iraqi politics, Iraq left the pact as the first loss of the Northern Tier in 1959. Ramazani (1966) found it unfortunate that the loss of Iraq in the Northern Tier bloc weakened the position of the pact in the region, making it no longer viable (Dawisha, 2003).

Despite Iraq's departure, the Northern Tier countries still banded together with the establishment of an organization for economic, technical, and cultural cooperation called the Regional Cooperation for Development in July 1964. The effort was launched by Turkey, Iran, and Pakistan in the Northern Tier security belt. In creating this new institutional body, the three states emphasized the security aspect of CENTO (Ersoy, 1994). These developments further substantiated the image in Arab eyes of Iran and Turkey as "puppets" of Western imperialism within the Northern Tier. Turkey had previously benefited from its pro-Western policies; with the signing of the Ankara Agreement in 1962, for example, Turkey signaled its strategic vision of being considered a European nation.

But Turkey's strategic engagement with the US was soon and quickly re-examined after a series of unfortunate incidents that occurred between Turkey and the United States. These included the Jupiter Missile crisis for Turkey in 1963, the correspondence between Johnson and Inonu about the Cyprus question in the 1960s, and the arms embargo of 1975 following Turkey's military intervention in Cyprus in 1974. Due to a US arms embargo, the Turkish government announced that the 1969 Defence Cooperation Agreement (DECA) and all other agreements with the United States had lost their legal validity. The Turkish government demanded that alliance member states halt NATO's operations at the Belbaşı, Diyarbakır, Karamürsel, and Sinop military bases, which were to be placed under the full control and custody of Turkish armed forces. However, this uneasy relationship between Turkey and the alliance states could not fully stop Turkey's strategic engagement with NATO. For instance, there was a drop in US military aid $165 million to $130 million per year during the arms embargo period (Duke, 1989), but the US government had found an opportunity to maintain its initiatives with the Turkish army even at this critical time with Turkey.

Turkey's other opening in foreign policy strategy had occurred when relations with the US government weakened. Due to Turkey's pro-Western policies, Arab nationalists advanced their anti-Turkish stance in international organizations. For instance, during the United Nations vote over the Cyprus crisis, most of the Arab countries were against the Turkish proposal. Instead, they supported Greek Cyprus' proposal in the United Nations. In order to gain a new position in Arab society, Turkey also revised its relationship with its Arab brethren. Hence, Turkey remained neutral during the Arab–Israeli War in 1967 (Laqueur, 1967) and also joined the Organization of Islamic Countries in 1969. As part of improving relations with the Arab world, Turkey recognized the Palestine Liberation Organization (PLO) in 1976 and allowed the PLO authority to open an office in Ankara in 1979.

Similar to Turkey's diversification of its foreign policy strategy, Iran also adopted a more multidimensional and diversified foreign policy approach when it improved relations with Moscow after September 1962 (Ramazani, 1975). This aside, and in contrast to Turkey's uneven relations with the United States at the time, the relations between the United States and Iran improved during the Nixon administration. In February 1971, for example, President Nixon's broad agreement with Iran to sell sophisticated weapons systems set the stage for Iran's current military buildup. Iran was engaged in an unprecedented buying spree of defense equipment worth billions of dollars, which would enhance its claim to be the gendarme of the Gulf.

While Iran became the rising power in the region, Turkey was faced with internal terror and an economic crisis during the 1970s. Turkey was not impressed by the Shah's ambition to make Iran a regional power in the Middle East while strengthening ties with the West. The Shah tried to strengthen his power domestically through land reform and the so-called "White Revolution," which was aimed at reducing the authority of the religious structure in Iran (Pahlavi, 1967). Despite certain success in domestic politics, the reformation program saw the emergence of a new class of elites. Iran started to play a role in the regional balance of power in the Middle East after Britain withdrew from the Gulf in 1971. The United States, along with Germany, France, and other European states, helped with a new policy direction for Iran. The presence of about 60,000 US personnel and 40,000 European entrepreneurs made Iran a Western capital in the late 1970s (Kinzer, 2003). For US President Jimmy Carter's relationship with Muhammad Reza Pahlavi meant that the United States could use Iranian territory to gather intelligence and monitor Soviet missile testing.

Iran's territorial nationalism displayed its power by seizing three small islands from the Gulf Sheikdoms (Abu Musa and the greater and lesser Tunbs) on the eve of the formation of the United Arab Emirates (UAE). After achieving success, the Shah turned his ambitions toward Iraq. Iran and Iraq's Shatt-al Arab waterway dispute was another cause of regional conflict, which ultimately served as a rationale for the eight-year Iran–Iraq War of the 1980s. Despite the institutional connection with Western security systems, engagement by both Iran and Turkey remained limited in the systemic context, but the process can be identified as a competitive relationship, exposing new client states for Turkey and proxy powers for Iran. They were also trying to win superpower backing from the United States.

Thus, while Turkey's relations with the United States weakened in the 1970s, Iran was considered akin to a Western country. Washington proclaimed Iran as its "stable island" in the region, a location in which the US military buildup had the potential to instill a regional equilibrium less vulnerable to disturbance from outside powers, particularly the USSR. This was the case because Iran's military buildup was constructed with US arms supplies such as F-4 aircrafts, a major factor in America's ability to react quickly in the region because of the compatibility between the US military equipment and that of Iran.

Despite the systemic engagement of two neighbors, Muhammad Reza Shah continued his revisionist policies to weaken Turkey's regional position. For instance, the Shah started to use the Alevi communities in Turkey. He considered the Alevi community as an affiliated branch of Shi'a Islam, which was considered one pillar of Pahlavi's Persianate strategic culture. The Shah used the religious card and Shi'a nationalism in Iran and Iraq to divert a potential religious uprising in Iran. The Shah brought Alevi students from Eastern Anatolia and provided them with an Iranian type of Shi'a education in the city of Qom. Turkish authorities saw the rise of an Iranian influence in Anatolia and perceived this as a policy of penetration into the domestic affairs of Turkey. In fact, the Shah's sectarian foreign policies did not receive any political success. In negating the Shah's regional influence, Turkey began to use the Iranian–Azeri political card, which resulted in a diplomatic crisis in late 1970. The incident occurred when the Turkish ambassador commented that "While driving from the Turkish border into Tehran, I had felt as if I was in my own country" (as cited in Boruvali, 1989, pp. 90–91). That statement was interpreted by the Shah as an obvious reference to the prevalence of Azeris in Iranian Azerbaijan. Tehran viewed Ankara's promotion of Turkish Azeri nationalism as a method of withstanding the Soviet threat. This dynamic increased the tension between the two countries and created a diplomatic crisis, resulting in the recall of ambassadors from both capitals.

The other thematic issue at hand in the regional competition between Turkey and Iran was that of Kurdish and Azeri ethnic nationalism, which undermined opportunities for cooperative Turkish–Iranian relations in the 1970s. Iran gained leverage over Kurdish issues against Iraq, which in turn affected Turkey's internal issues. This was especially evident with regard to the Kurdish problem between the three countries when the Shah and the US government provided support for Iraqi Kurdish guerrillas (the Patriotic Union of Kurdistan and the Kurdistan Democratic Party), who fought for an autonomous Iraqi Kurdistan during the 1970s (McDowall, 2004). Iran previously had strong ties with Iraqi Kurds since it had hosted Iraqi Kurdish refugees who had escaped from the Ba'ath regime's brutal oppression of Kurds. Hence, it can easily be said that the connection between Iraqi Kurds and Iranian Kurds was stronger than that with Turkey's Kurds. Moreover, Turkish authorities closely watched the Shah's regional power activities involving the Iraqi Kurds. Iranian sympathy and shelter for the Kurds provided Iran with the opportunity to use Kurdish ethnicity to weaken the Ba'ath regime during the internal Kurdish–Arab war of the 1970s. Iran's intervention in Iraqi internal affairs further heightened tensions over the Shatt al-Arab waterway between Baghdad and Tehran, but these tensions temporarily abated when Iraq accepted the division of the Shatt al-Arab. For the United States, the Kurdish question remained a key element that needed to be resolved. That said, through Henry Kissinger's shuttle diplomacy in the Middle East, the US was able to push a peace settlement with the signing of the Algiers Accord in 1975. In turn, the Shah was pushed to stop his support for the Iraqi Kurds.

These dynamics aside, the US still believed in the relative importance of Iran and Turkey to assist in containing any further Soviet expansion toward Eurasia's rimland. The US government was not interested in the democratization of either Iran or Turkey. The main goal of US strategic interests was to keep both countries in the Western hemisphere. However, the systemic engagement of Iran and Turkey with the US government did not impede their regional competition in the framework of the proxy role for Iran and client role for Turkey during the first phases of the Cold War. While there has been an alliance relationship between Turkey and the United States within the collective security system, Iran would soon identify itself as neutral using Khomeini's motto: "Neither East nor West" (Abrahamian, 1982).

The emergence of a negative balancer

Some political analysts argue that due to Iran's rise as a regional power, the US government did not prevent the fall of Muhammed Reza Shah. Iran's globalized vision under the Shah's regime ended with Khomeini's Islamic Revolution. Instead, the Islamic Republic of Iran (IRI) launched a more independent foreign policy pursuing "Neither East nor West," which contributed significantly to the survival of the Islamic Republic's regime. Its defense doctrine was inspired by the disastrous experience of Iraq's invasion of Iran in 1980. This disruption was followed by instability, which remained as a long-term threat to all internal and external players. It also attracted foreign forces to the region to maintain their interests in the Middle East.

The emergence of the IRI was not welcomed by Soviet Russia and the US government. Both superpowers found that it disturbed their influence in the Middle East. The new republic, with its commitment to political Islam and its revolutionary rhetoric, was also perceived as a threat to its Arab neighbors. This threat was particularly evident in the Persian Gulf region, especially since it meant that the preservation of interests for the extra-regional powers would be much greater. The major goals of Iranian decision makers have been effective in terms of developing Iran's "mixed strategy of defense," which can be categorized as a military strategy, military development, a deterrence policy, forward defense, energy/economic leverage, domestic unity, and the spread of an Islamic ideology. It can be argued that there has been both continuity and change in Iran's political culture and defense policy. Similar to the Musaddiq government, the IRI has designed its defense doctrine based on its "negative balance" policy in the Middle East. Iran has identified its regional policy strategy as being a resistance bloc against US primacy in the Middle East, including strategic alignments with Syria, North Korea, and a handful of Latin American countries. Part of Iran's frontline resistance bloc has always been Hamas and Hezbollah, which have served Iran's forward defense strategy in the Levant. This is basically aimed at keeping war as far away as possible from its own land by developing military capabilities to operate outside its territory and, by extension, to contain its enemies in those regions.

Iran's security environment was complex during the second phases of the Cold War (1980–1991), with the deployment of US forces into the Middle East. The US military presence posed a constant threat to Iran's borders, which caused Iran to pursue relations with other regional states based on geopolitical factors. The insecurity surrounding Iran forced the country to build strategic coalitions in order to assure its own national security. Tehran pursued a policy of forward defense due to their lack of success in building a regional coalition, especially in the Persian Gulf.

Since the Islamic Revolution, subsequent regimes have addressed the United States and Israel as the "Great Satan" and the "eternal enemy of Iran." In 1979, Iranian militants overran the US Embassy in Tehran and seized 51 diplomatic hostages, holding them for 444 days. As part of the hostage release in 1981, the US government negotiated with Iranian officials in Algiers and jointly issued an agreement in January. The agreement called for the lifting of US sanctions against Iran, returning seized Iranian government property being held by the United States, and prohibiting the hostages from suing Iran for damages. In addition, the US government pledged not to intervene directly or indirectly, politically or militarily, in Iranian internal affairs. The US government has not truly honored this agreement; however, the agreement remains a judicially recognized international settlement.

In addition to the upheaval in Iran, Turkey also took its own actions against the US with Ankara rejecting Washington's request to use the Incirlik Air Base for military operations, as well as denying the international economic sanctions against Iran (Carkoglu, Eder, and Krisci, 1999). Moreover, Turkey preferred to follow more of a neutrality policy, especially when it came to the outbreak of the first Gulf War (Berresiye, 1983). As a result, Tehran and Baghdad considered Ankara a reliable supplier of goods and a crucial transit point for imports from Europe. As such, Turkey welcomed an expansion of export and revenues. This expansion was derived from the transportation of goods, which provided Turkey with a formidable degree of foreign exchange to assist in the development of a liberal, open market economy.

Deployment of US military forces in the Gulf

One of the weightier arguments of this research is that the United States deployed its military forces to the Gulf region in response to the Iranian Islamic Revolution. The emergence of American supremacy in the region was especially seen in offshore areas where oil-field exploration occurred in the Persian Gulf. The Persian Gulf's rectangular-shaped continental shelf places Iranian territory on the northern side of most Arab states. This transition of power left behind two complicated border issues between Iran and Saudi Arabia in 1968, and a border settlement between Iran and Sharjah over Abu Musa in 1971. As mentioned above, the special relationship between the US government and the Shah provided Iran leverage to gain a proxy role for the security of its energy policy in the Persian Gulf. According to a Memorandum of Understanding from November 30, 1971, Iran occupied Abu Musa and the greater and lesser Tunb islands, which are also claimed by Ras al-Khaimah. Tension also arose later on the same topic between the UAE and Iran during the 13th Summit of the Gulf Cooperation Council in 1992 wherein they called on Iran to terminate its occupation of the Tunb islands.

To balance growing Gulf tensions, the US military grew its regional presence. Beginning in the 1970s, Bahrain served as the primary base for the US Fifth Fleet, which is tasked with protecting the Persian Gulf and Strait of Hormuz. However, the proliferation of land-based anti-ship missiles and small attack craft made the Gulf an increasingly dangerous place to base large ships. Oman soon became one of the safer host countries willing to sign a formal agreement granting access rights to the US military. Two of the United States' closer Arab allies, Egypt and Saudi Arabia, refused to sign a similar accord during this period. Putting the fleet at a location right outside the Gulf, such as the Omani port of Muscat, allowed the navy to control access to the area with less danger to its ships. During the Gulf War in 1991, more than 3,000 US troops were stationed at Omani air bases, including Masirah Island, Thumrait, and Seeb International Airport near Muscat. And Saudi Arabia did allow US troops basing access throughout the Kingdom due to the threat posed by Saddam Hussein during the first Gulf War. But after the US-led invasion of Iraq in 2003, Saudi Arabia asked the US to vacate its forward operating bases on Saudi territory. As a result, the US government strengthened its ties with Qatar, one of the smallest Gulf monarchies. Since then, it has hosted an estimated 11,000 US troops and F-16 fighter jets in order to operate military warfare in Afghanistan and Iraq (Lendon, 2017).

The Iranian regime believes that the US military presence and its encirclement from Central Asia to the Arabian Peninsula has produced greater national insecurity for Iran. It is understandable that Iran's self-sufficiency strategy and the establishment of a resistance bloc against US supremacy is a necessity for Iran's future national security and regime preservation. In addition, the rehabilitation of American–Turkish relations, especially during the mid-2000s, further increased Tehran's aggressive policies towards the region.

Restoration of American–Turkish strategic relations

On the eve of Iran's Islamic Revolution, the troubled alliance between the Turkish and American governments moved in a new, positive direction. The alliance between Turkey and the US government transformed military and economic relations for each country. Ultimately, the Carter administration managed to lift the US arms embargo against Turkey by signing a new

DECA agreement in 1978. The agreement came into force on December 18, 1980. It became the main document guaranteeing the presence of US military forces in Turkey until 1990. The Transit Terminal Agreement between the two countries allowed US aircraft to use Incirlik Air Base for supporting the UN Multinational Force in Lebanon in 1984. The supplementary agreements also permitted the United States to participate in joint defense measures at 12 locations and authorized the US administration to support organizations and activities outside of these installations. Turkey received $868 million between 1985 and 1986, $590 million of which was in the form of military and economic aid (Bölme, 2012).

The agreement between George Shultz and Turkish Foreign Minister Vahit Halefoğlu renewed the same aid program on March 16, 1987. Under this agreement, the Pentagon trained Turkish officers under the aegis of the International Military Education and Training programs and provided over $3 million of training assistance annually to the Turkish army staff.

After the collapse of the Soviet Union, Turkey needed to reshape its military and geopolitical positioning in the region. One negative development for Turkey was the 40 percent reduction of military assistance from the US Congress, cut from a prior proposed amount of $913.5 million. This also resulted in a reduction of US military personnel in Turkey from 20,000 to 5,000 (Duke, 1989, pp. 280–281). Following this reduction, another important turning point in Turkish–American relations came with the signing of the Turkish–Israeli military training agreement in 1996. Despite the reductions cited above, Turkey's engagement with the Western security system became more concrete after the economic and military training agreement with Israel (Bengio, 2004, p. 80). In addition, the presence of US military installations in Turkish territory remained the main component of Turkey's engagement with the Western security system.

Since the onset of the post-Cold War era, the United States and Turkey have shared a high degree of interest in NATO's southern region, particularly over issues of stability in Bosnia and the Balkans. During the mid-1990s, Turkey readily contributed troops to peacekeeping efforts in the region, having sent more than 2,000 troops to Operation Joint Endeavour and approximately 1,400 to support the Stabilization Force in Bosnia. Additionally, Turkey deployed nearly 800 armed forces personnel to peace operations in Albania and shared responsibility for keeping the Tirana airport open at the time (Müftüler-Bac, 1998). Turkey's later role in the NATO-led International Security Assistance Forces and Lebanon were also essential for the systemic setting of Turkey.

The instrument of US foreign policy towards Iran: Economic sanctions

The US government has imposed economic sanctions on Iran since the 1979 hostage crisis, and it banned the import of Iranian goods entirely in 1987. In addition, President Bill Clinton issued several executive orders preventing US companies from investing in Iranian oil and gas and trading with Iran. The US Congress also passed the Iran–Libya Sanctions Act in 1996, one of the requirments of which was that the US government impose sanctions on foreign firms investing more than $20 million a year in Iran's energy sector. However, the US government terminated the applicability of the Iran–Libya Sanctions Act to Libya in 2004.

During the early 2000s, Iran's clandestine nuclear program served to further deteriorate US–Iran relations. The US government believed at the time that Iran was attempting to develop the capability to produce both plutonium and highly enriched uranium and that it was actively pursuing the acquisition of fissile material along with the expertise and technology necessary to form it into nuclear weapons. In President George W. Bush's "Axis of Evil" speech, his first State of the Union address on January 29, 2002, he claimed that "Iran aggressively pursues" weapons of mass destruction. Similarly, President Barack Obama, in his first State of the Union address on January 27, 2010, claimed that Iran was "violating international agreements in pursuit of nuclear weapons." Hence, the US government launched a series of economic and political pressures to force Iran into abandoning its pursuit of acquiring nuclear weapons (Katzman, 2017).

Throughout the 2000s and at the start of the 2010s, the US government, the European Union (EU), and the United Nations imposed increasingly severe sanctions against Iran to force the Iranian government to live up to its obligations under the NPT, IAEA safeguards agreements, and UN Security Council resolutions. The EU, for example, imposed visa bans on senior officials such as the leader of the Revolutionary Guards, Mohammad Ali Jafari, Defense Minister Mostafa Mohammad Najjar, and former atomic energy chief Gholamreza Aghazadeh, as well as nuclear and ballistic experts. On June 18, 2013, the British government declared that Iranian assets, which totaled £976 million ($1.59 billion), had been frozen. In addition, Britain announced on October 12 that it was freezing business ties with Bank Mellat and the Islamic Republic of Iran Shipping Lines, both of which have previously faced sanctions from the United States (Rennack, 2016).

One of the more important sanctions imposed in 2010 targeted Iran's ability to sell crude oil on the world market and import refined petroleum products, making it more difficult for Iran's Central Bank and other financial institutions to engage in transactions abroad. These sanctions have caused significant damage to Iran's economy, particularly in Iranian oil exports, which dropped from 2.5 million barrels per day in 2011 to about 1 million barrels per day in 2013. As a result, Iran's revenue from oil exports has declined an estimated 55 percent from its peak in 2011 (Khabbazan and Farzanegan, 2016, pp. 215–217).

Iran–US nuclear negotiations

The nuclear program of Iran is considered a necessity for the self-help approach of the country's military strategy. Iran had left its nuclear program at the beginning of the Islamic Revolution. However, a new post-Cold War order has compelled Iran to establish a deterrence strategy for regime survival in the international system. The first step in its nuclear program was made by Parliament Speaker Hashemi Rafsanjani in 1989. He made diplomatic visits to both China and Russia to discuss foreign support and the construction of a uranium enrichment facility and to negotiate the completion of the Bushehr nuclear power plant. Despite being a signatory to the NPT, Iran successfully hid its nuclear program from the IAEA. However, the situation changed with the revelation of Iran's nuclear program in 2003, a year after Iran's opposition group Mujahidin-e Khalq Organization (MKO) signaled the existence of the secret program (Johnson, 2005).

Hassan Rouhani took over the nuclear portfolio as the chief nuclear diplomacy negotiator under Iran's Supreme National Security Council. During Rouhani's tenure as a nuclear negotiator from 2003 to 2005, Tehran appeared more cooperative with the West. However, during the government of hardliners under President Ahmedinejad (2005–2013), the tense relationship between the United States and the Iranian government led to increased regional friction, especially with Iran and Israel. By the end of the Ahmedinejad era and with Hassan Rouhani's coming to power in 2013, the transition of power brought new hope for opening the door to engagement with Western powers, including a revitalized hope for diplomatic progress over Iran's clandestine nuclear issue. This new approach was similar to an effort made by those in the Clinton administration in 1997 after President Khatami came to power.

Iran's pursuit of a nuclear weapons capability over the past 24 years has challenged American supremacy in the wider region. This pursuit is now set to enter a critical phase. In considering the recent government shift in Iranian politics, one can further appreciate Rouhani's thinking on the subject when examining his memoir, *National Security and Nuclear Diplomacy*. Rouhani does not explain the reasons why Iran wants a robust nuclear program, but he instead describes a "far-reaching effort to obtain a broad range of nuclear technology from foreign sources" (Clawson, 2013, para. 4).

On the one hand, Israel is concerned about Iran–US rapprochement due to Iran's challenge of Israel's regional ambitions in the Middle East. For instance, Israeli Prime Minister Benjamin Netanyahu compared Iran–US negotiations to Neville Chamberlain's meeting with Adolf Hitler in 1938 and Reagan's meeting with Mikhail Gorbachev in 1985 (Wheatcroft, 2013).

During the six-month phase of US–Iran nuclear negotiations, oil sanctions, which caused $25 billion in lost revenues to Iran, or over $4 billion a month, remained in place. The vast majority of Iran's approximately $100 billion in foreign exchange holdings was inaccessible or in some way restricted. On November 24, the P5+1 interim agreement marked the conclusion of the sanctions relief program, which provided $6–7 billion dollars for Iran. Over the next six months, the P5+1 agreed to pause efforts to further reduce Iran's crude oil sales, enabling Iran's customers to purchase their current average amounts of crude oil. The sanctions relief program freed up $4.2 billion by giving Iran access to oil revenue frozen in foreign banks and an additional $1.8–2.8 billion by temporarily pausing other sanctions measures. The P5+1 also agreed to give Iran access to $1.5 billion in revenue from trade in gold and precious metals and to suspend some sanctions on Iran's auto sector as well as its petrochemical exports. Additionally, Iran gained license for the supply and installation of spare parts for the Iranian civil aviation industry. The agreement also granted Iran access to oil revenues held in foreign bank accounts provided that those funds were used to pay the UN, for tuition fees for Iranian students studying abroad, or to facilitate humanitarian trade in food and medicine for the Iranian people (Elik, 2013).

With Iranian President Rouhani's successful diplomacy, the Iran–US nuclear deal was achieved in July 2015, ending Iran's further isolation from the international system, not to mention lifting the economic sanctions against Iran. Together with the rehabilitation of its relations with the great powers, Iran increased its regional role and began to engage in proxy wars in Bahrain, Lebanon, Iraq, Syria, and Yemen. That said, the rise of a negative balance of power not only challenged Turkey's geopolitical positioning, but also threatened US alliances with Gulf allies.

Proxy war in the Middle East

In addition to the nuclear dilemma associated with Iran, the United States and other regional actors have had to contend with the rise in proxy warfare. Beginning in the early 2000s, Iran's two regional enemies, the Taliban in Afghanistan and Saddam Hussain in Iraq, were ousted from power following the tragedy of 9/11. Initially, reformist Iranian President Khatami wanted to establish a cooperative relationship with the United States. However, the George W. Bush administration ignored Iran's positive response to the US global war on terror strategy. President Bush at the time proclaimed Iran to be part of a larger "axis of evil" in world politics. The relations remained hostile throughout Bush's administration and its global war on terror. This aside, the removal of Saddam Hussein, as well as the Taliban, provided Iran with an opportunity to fill power vacuums in the region. And more recently with the outbreak of Arab revolts against many of the region's authoritarian regimes, Iran has been more visibly active, especially in Shi'a-dominated regions. Indeed, Iran has extended its sphere of influence, spreading from Syria, Iraq, Lebanon, Bahrain, and Yemen. In so doing, Iran has continued to promote sectarian elements of its soft power and proxy hard power via Lebanon's Hezbollah in Syria and the Houthi in Yemen. As a result, there has been an increase in geopolitical competition and tension between Iran and Turkey, among other actors. But the main proxy war has been in Syria since the onset of the Arab Spring, especially with the growing power of Hezbollah.

With the growing sectarian tensions and geopolitical competition in recent years, one Iranian MP openly declared, "Four Arab capitals (Beirut, Damascus, Baghdad, and Sana'a) have already fallen into Iran's hands and belong to the

Iranian Islamic Revolution" (Segall, 2014). Iran's major aim has been to instigate regime change in Bahrain and to establish greater control over the Persian Gulf, especially if they are successful in further weakening's Bahrain's government. Certainly, after the Iranian nuclear negotiations, Iran is sitting in a greater position of power regionally and in the international arena. Some scholars expect that this re-emergence of Iran will reshuffle the regional security system and give Iran a stronger standing in international society.

As for Turkey's role in the region's proxy war dynamics, Turkish–Syrian relations have experienced both friendliness and enmity since the AK Party came to power in Turkey. During the early 2000s, Syrian President Bashar Asad provided positive responses toward increased bilateral cooperation in various sectors with the Turkish government. The relationship between Damascus and Ankara peaked in 2004 with Asad's visit to Turkey, even though it marked the first time a Syrian political leader had stepped foot in the capital for 57 years. During this visit, Asad announced the international legal framework for acceptance of the Turkish borders (Morinson, 2016). But the positive trip was also stifled due to protests against the Asad regime.

Certainly, Iran considered Syria to belong to the resistance bloc in addition to being a major Russian ally against the West's hegemonic ambitions in the Middle East. Iran also initially saw Turkey on the opposite side of the US when the Syrian opposition challenged Asad's regime. The honeymoon between the Turkish and Syrian governments, however, quickly ended, and it has since turned into a very fraught and contentious relationship due to Turkey's support of Syrian opposition groups, in addition to demands for regime change in Syria. In contrast to Turkey, Iran, Russia, Iraq, and Lebanese Hezbollah have supported the Asad regime. Although Syria has become one of Turkey's national security concerns, both countries have pursued policies to maintain distance between them, including any direct conflict in the region. Turkey, for example, has pursued open-door policies towards Syrian refugees in this attempt at avoiding direct conflict with the Syrian regime. That said, there have still been mounting civilian casualties, and a series of accidents have been experienced between Turkey and Syria. Incidents such as Syria's shooting down of Turkey's military plane in 2012 and the firing of cross-border cannon shots from Syria as Syrian forces and Free Syrian Army fighters clashed have increased tensions between the Asad government and Turkey. Consequences of the civil war between Asad's oligarchy and opposition movements include over 500,000 dead, 9.5 million internally displaced persons in Syria, and over 3.5 million refugees relocated to neighboring countries. According to the AFAD statistics, total refugees in Turkey reached 2 million, which cost over $5.5 billion (AFAD, 2014).

If the Asad regime falls, Iran may lose its regional alliance, which would dramatically reduce Iranian influence in the region. Some believe that the exclusion of Iran from the Geneva I and Geneva II talks is a poor strategy for the great powers to embrace. Therefore, neither initiative has led to positive results for the Syrian crisis. For Iran and Turkey, the Syrian crisis is the most important question testing the reliability of Iranian–Turkish relations.

Another dynamic to be considered is the transnational Kurdish question. The Syrian civil war ended counterterrorism cooperation between Iran, Syria, and Turkey. This development isolated Turkey in its fight against the Kurdistan Workers' Party (PKK) and the PKK-affiliated Democratic Union Party (PYD) when it took over large swaths of northern Syria as a result of the Syrian revolution. The isolation of Turkey from the region was revealed when Turkey's strategy of dealing with the Kurds was contested by the US government. The US supported Syrian Kurdish groups since they were viewed by the US as an important surrogate alliance to fight the Islamic State in Syria. Turkey tried to introduce and propose its no-fly secure zone in northern Syria on several occasions. However, the proposal did not receive a positive response from the international community. Consequently, the rise of the Islamic State of Iraq and Syria (ISIS) and various violent nonstate actors only pushed Turkey to seek out a guarantee for its own national security, especially along its border. In 2015, for example, Turkey launched Operation Euphrates Shield to further secure the border with Syria. Turkey's contention is that the US prefers to act together with the PKK-affiliated PYD against ISIS terrorism. Moving forward, Turkey has no clear policy strategy if the great powers such as Russia and the US allow the establishment of a Kurdish enclave in Syria.

Conclusion

There have been six major characteristics of the US strategy towards Turkey and Iran since the Cold War. First, the structural change in the international system from a multipolar to a bipolar system allows us to apply a systemic level of analysis, which also provides the necessary evidence to contextualize the features of security relations between Iran and Turkey. Turkey is seen more as part of a patron-client relationship, while Iran was identified in terms of a proxy state power competition under the rubric of superpower protection during the first period of the Cold War. Turkish–Iranian security treaties such as the Baghdad Pact and CENTO introduced systemic security mechanisms between the two neighboring states in the interest of great power settlement. During the second period of the Cold War (1980–1989), Iranian–Turkish security relations were reduced to low-level affairs due in large part to the Iran–Iraq War of the 1980s and Turkey's shift toward a more neutral foreign policy.

Second, the transformations in both of these countries' domestic politics also related to the systemic demand of the US government. Even though Turkey experienced four military coups, the development of Turkey's democracy has been tied in part to US policies toward Turkey. Similarly, the US government supported land reforms and the promotion of civil society in Iran during the 1960s and 1970s, maintaining similar demands even today.

Third, though a Pahlavi Iran did not join the systemic security engagement with the United States, there was "a special relationship" between Washington and Tehran. Iran gained a globalized vision by developing its engagement with the international community in various sectors during the Shah's rule.

Fourth, following the Islamic Revolution, the US government deployed its military forces into the Middle East, especially the Persian Gulf. Amidst the hostage crisis, small-scale Cold War tensions between Tehran and Washington developed as a result of changes in the systemic and regional setting. Iran successfully exercised its "negative" balance of power strategy in the region by using different political cards.

Fifth, a revolutionary expansionist policy on the part of the Arab Middle East was blocked by the US government. As a result, successive Iranian governments have similarly not been able to achieve any measure of great success in the Persian Gulf.

And finally, sixth, since the emergence of Iran's nuclear program, Iran has always been seen as a threat to the Arab countries and Israel. Moreover, Turkey is similarly not pleased with the ongoing Iranian–US Cold War between Iran and a US-led coalition.

References

Abrahamian, E. (1982). *Iran between two revolutions*. Princeton, NJ: Princeton University Press.

AFAD (Disaster and Emergency Management Authority). (2014). *Population influx from Syria to Turkey: Life in Turkey as Syrian guests*. Ankara: AFAD. Retrieved from https://www.afad.gov.tr/upload/Node/3905/xfiles/population_influx.pdf.

Bengio, O. (2004). *The Turkish-Israeli relationship: Changing ties of Middle Eastern outsiders*. New York, NY: Palgrave Macmillan.

Berresiye, T. (1983). *Ektesadiye Kesver Baad Az Enghlab* (Iran's economy after the revolution). Tehran, Iran: Iran Central Bank, Centre for Economic and Financial Studies Publishing.

Bölme, S. (2012). *İncirlik Üssü: ABD'nin Üs Politikası ve Türkiye*. Istanbul: İletişim Yayınları.

Boruvali, F. (1989). Iran and Turkey: Permanent revolution or Islamism in one country? In M. Rezun, (ed.), *Iran at the crossroads: Global relations in a turbulent decade* (pp. 81–93). Boulder, CO: Westview Press.

Carkoglu, A., Eder, M. and Krisci, K. (1999). *The political economy of regional cooperation in the Middle East*. London: Routledge.

Cirincione, J. (2005). *The declining ballistic missile threat, 2005*. Policy Outlook. Washington, DC: Carnegie Endowment for International Peace. Retrieved from http://research.policyarchive.org/6600.pdf.

Clawson, P. (2013). *Rouhani's nuclear views: An open book?* Washington, DC: Washington Institute. Retrieved from www.washingtoninstitute.org/policy-analysis/view/rouhanis-nuclear-views-an-open-book.

Dawisha, A. (2003). *Arab nationalism in the twentieth century: From triumph to despair*. Princeton, NJ: Princeton University Press.

Duke, S. (1989). *United States military forces and installation in Europe*. London: Oxford University Press.

Elik, S. (2013, December 20). Iran-Turkey relations at Hasan Rouhani era: A special reference to Iran-US nuclear negotiations. BILGESAM Analysis/Middle East, No. 1108. Retrieved from www.bilgesam.org/Images/Dokumanlar/0-75-2014030920 1108.pdf

Ersoy, H. (1994). *Turkey's involvement in Western defence initiatives in the Middle East in the 1950s.* Unpublished doctoral dissertation, University of Durham, Durham, England.

Gasiorowski, M.J., and Byrne, M. (2004). *Mohammad Mosaddeq and the 1953 coup in Iran.* Syracuse, NY: Syracuse University Press.

Holloway, T. (1960). *The Jupiter Missile mystery.* New York, NY: Thomas Bouregy.

Johnson, Z.K. (2005, May). Iran – going nuclear: Background to a crisis. *PBS Frontline.* Retrieved from www.pbs.org/frontlineworld/stories/iran403/background.html.

Katzman, K. (2017, April 14). *Iran sanctions.* Washington, DC: Congressional Research Service. Retrieved from https://fas.org/sgp/crs/mideast/RS20871.pdf.

Kemal Yesilbursa, B. (2005) *The Baghdad Pact: Anglo-American defence policies in the Middle East 1950–1959.* London: Frank Cass.

Khabbazan, M.M. and Farzanegan, M.R. (2016). Household welfare in Iran under banking sanctions: From open economy toward autarchy. In M.R. Farzanegan and P. Alaedini, (eds.), *Economic welfare and inequality in Iran: Developments since revolution* (pp. 213–232). New York: Palgrave Macmillan.

Kinzer, S. (2003). *All the Shah's men: The hidden story of the CIA's coup in Iran.* New York: Wiley.

Kristensen, H.M. (2005). *US nuclear weapons in Europe: A review of post-Cold War policy, force levels, and war planning.* Washington, DC: National Resources Defense Council. Retrieved from www.nrdc.org/nuclear/euro/euro.pdf.

Kristensen, H.M., and McKinzie, M. (2012). *Reducing alert rates of nuclear weapons.* Geneva: United Nations Institute for Disarmament Research.

Laqueur, W. (1967). *The road to Jerusalem: The origins of the Arab-Israeli conflict.* New York: Macmillan.

Layne, C. (2009). The waning of US hegemony – Myth or reality? A review essay. *International Security,* 34(1), 147–172. doi:10.1162/isec.2009.34.1.147.

Lendon, B. (2017, June 6). Qatar hosts largest US military base in MidEast. *CNN.* Retrieved from www.cnn.com/2017/06/05/middleeast/qatar-us-largest-base-in-mideast/index.html.

McDowall, D. (2004). *A modern history of the Kurds.* London: I.B. Tauris.

McKercher, B.J.C. (1999). *Transition of power: Britain's loss of global pre-eminence to the United States, 1930–1945.* Cambridge: Cambridge University Press.

Morinson, A. (2006). The strategic depth doctrine of Turkish foreign policy. *Middle Eastern Studies,* 42(6), 945–964.

Müftüler-Bac, M. (1998). *Turkey and Israel: An evolving partnership.* Tel Aviv, Israel: Ariel Center for Policy Research.

Pahlavi, M.R. (1967). *The white revolution.* Tehran: Imperial Pahlavi Library.

Ramazani, R. (1966). *The Northern tier: Afghanistan, Iran and Turkey.* Princeton, NJ: Van Nostrand.

Ramazani, R.K. (1975). *Iran's foreign policy 1941–1974: A study of foreign policy in modernizing nations.* Charlottesville, VA: University Press of Virginia.

Rennack, D.E. (2016, January 22). *Iran: US economic sanctions and the authority to lift restrictions.* Washington, DC: Congressional Research Service. Retrieved from https://fas.org/sgp/crs/mideast/R43311.pdf.

Segall, M. (2014). How Iran views the fall of Sana'a, Yemen: "The fourth Arab capital in our hands". *Institute for Contemporary Affairs*, 14(36). Retrieved from http://jcpa. org/article/iran-sanaa-yemen/.

Waltz, K.N. (1959). *Man, the state and war: A theoretical analysis.* New York: Columbia University Press.

Waltz, K.N. (2008). *Realism and international politics.* New York: Routledge.

Wheatcroft, G. (2013, December 4). On the use and abuse of Munich. *New Republic.* Retrieved from https://newrepublic.com/article/115803/munich-analogies-are-inaccur ate-cliched-and-dangerous.

Zabetakis, S.G. and Peterson, J.F. (1964). The Diyarbakir radar. *Studies in Intelligence*, 8(3), 41–47.

Zabih, S. (1982a). *Iran since the revolution.* Baltimore, MD: Johns Hopkins University Press.

Zabih, S. (1982b). *The Mossadegh era: Roots of the Iranian revolution.* Chicago, IL: Lake View Press.

8 American-Qatari partnership in the post-Gulf War era

A mutually beneficial relationship

Fatma Aslı Kelkitli

Qatar, the tiny state that lies on the northeastern coast of the Arabian Peninsula surrounded by the Persian Gulf and Saudi Arabia, is a relative latecomer to the international scene. It became independent in September 1971 after Britain, which had become its official protector with a treaty signed in November 1916, decided to relinquish its protector role as part of a general withdrawal east of the Suez Canal beginning in 1968. By doing so, it aimed at mitigating its many financial pressures at home. Qatar, with a meager territory, small population, and limited military capability, sought to survive in a competitive environment where more assertive and regionally powerful actors were vying for influence.

Iran's Islamic Revolution in 1979 came as further unsettling news to the region. The revolution was a popular uprising, resulting in the overthrow of a neighboring monarchy that had the potential to spread over in some manner to Qatar. Moreover, the revolution precipitated an attack in September 1980 from Iraq, which was aspiring to raise its profile in the Persian Gulf region against Iran. Baghdad tried to exploit the political instability and social turmoil in Iran to its benefit by occupying the country's oil-rich Khuzestan province, which possessed a significant ethnic Arab population. As a result and under mounting pressure, Qatar felt compelled to align itself with Saudi Arabia, which was regarded as a lesser evil compared to revolutionary Iran or an ambitious Iraq.

The Saudi-Qatari cooperation kicked off in May 1981 under the aegis of the Gulf Cooperation Council (GCC). This regional, intergovernmental, political, and economic organization came into existence under the leadership of Saudi Arabia, and Qatar became one of the founding members along with Bahrain, Kuwait, Oman, and the United Arab Emirates. Following a failed coup attempt in Bahrain that was allegedly backed by Iran, Qatar also concluded a bilateral defense agreement with Saudi Arabia in 1982 (Roberts, 2016).[1] Moreover, Doha started to participate in the military exercises of the Peninsula Shield Force of the GCC alongside Riyadh in October 1983. These exercises had been established in November 1982 with the objective of deterring military aggression against GCC member states (Lea, 2001).

Iraq's 1990 invasion of Kuwait and the subsequent failures of both the GCC and the Saudi army to cope with the assault served to discredit Riyadh as a dependable patron in the eyes of Qatari officials. As a result, Qatar began the search for a more competent ally that would ensure its survival in the event of a similar crisis. The United States came out as the most suitable candidate after demonstrating adroit leadership and superior military capabilities against the Iraqi forces during Operations Desert Shield and Desert Storm. However, Washington's engagement with Doha was limited at the time. The two states had established diplomatic relations in 1972, but the United States did not send a resident ambassador to Doha until 1974 (Wright, 2011). As such, there was little interaction between the two countries in security, economic, or cultural domains. A stronger American-Qatari alliance required a change of policy in Washington vis-à-vis the Persian Gulf, which would take place shortly after the Gulf War.

In August 1991, six months after the Gulf War's conclusion and the expulsion of belligerent Iraqi forces from Kuwaiti territory by a coalition of states led by Washington, the White House published the US National Security Strategy. The document underscored the significance of security and stability in the Gulf region for American interests, owing to the fact that it contained two-thirds of the world's proven oil resources. Washington also declared its intention of adopting measures to ensure a continued US presence in the Gulf in line with the needs and desires of its regional allies (The White House, 1991). Accordingly, the United States began to hammer out defense cooperation agreements with the Gulf countries, starting with Kuwait in September 1991, one month after the publication of its national security blueprint. Qatar quickly followed suit and signed a security agreement with the United States in June 1992. This move initiated a rewarding association between the two states, which encompassed various collaborative attempts in political, economic, and educational fields.

The post-Gulf War American-Qatari partnership could be described as an alliance between a great power and a small state. The United States exerted substantial influence throughout the international system (Keohane, 1969) and had worldwide interests reaching beyond its immediate borders (Paterson, 1969). Therefore, Washington entered into security engagements with regional states in the areas that were deemed significant for American interests. The Persian Gulf, with its rich oil and natural gas resources along with its strategic location, was appraised as one of these vital areas that should be kept under constant surveillance. Qatar, on the other hand, was a small state which had limited impact on the international system (Keohane, 1969) and had to rely primarily on external aid to obtain security (Liska, 1968; Rothstein, 1968). Qatar thus formed an alliance with the United States to avert more powerful regional actors such as Iraq, Iran, and Saudi Arabia from dominating the Persian Gulf region (Domingo, 2014) and endangering its existence as a sovereign state.

The defense agreement with the United States came as a relief to Qatar, particularly in its long-lasting but occasionally turbulent relationship with its southern neighbor, Saudi Arabia. Border disputes between the two countries occasionally triggered minor clashes, but the disagreement was ultimately settled in the early 2000s (Peterson, 2006). After Riyadh's attempts in the mid-1990s to instigate a counter-coup to reinstate Khalifa bin Hamad as the ruler of Qatar came to naught, it was forced to accept the fact that it would not be able to impose its will on its smaller neighbor as easily as it had in the past (Roberts, 2016).

The asymmetric relationship between the United States and Qatar enabled the latter to enhance its security in the face of encroachments from more assertive regional actors by sacrificing its own autonomy (Morrow, 1991). The long-term endurance of this arrangement demonstrates that it adequately served the interests of both parties. This chapter aims to trace the details of this burgeoning and vibrant relationship between Washington and Doha by examining its military, political, economic, and educational dimensions.

Following an outline of the Gulf security framework designed by the United States in the post-Gulf War period, the first part of the chapter focuses on Qatar's role in this defense scheme. The second part focuses on the political aspects of the relationship, paying special attention to Qatar's provision of good offices and mediation in the Middle East, as per the request of the United States. Washington benefited from Qatar while conveying its political messages to countries such as Iraq and Libya with which it did not have stable diplomatic relations. Qatari help was also significant for the American officials in reaching out to the parties that had qualms about their intervention, as was the case in the Israeli-Hamas ceasefire agreement. Qatari mediation was also instrumental when the United States did not want to get into any direct contact with the other side, such as with the Taliban and al-Nusra Front, because of political concerns and legal constraints. The third section sheds light on the commercial side of the association, while the final section examines the educational and cultural ties between the two states, which have taken their most explicit form in American assistance to Qatar in bolstering its higher education system.

Although the United States is the dominant party in all these dimensions of the bilateral relationship, Qatar also derives considerable benefits from this association in security, diplomacy, commerce, and science realms. This chapter aims to reveal the underpinning of this multidimensionality in American-Qatari ties, which is a significant feature of the relationship.

The Persian Gulf security structure in the post-Gulf War period

The declaration of the Nixon Doctrine by US President Richard Nixon in July 1969 and its spin-off, the Twin Pillars Policy, had led the United States to pursue a policy of delegation concerning the Persian Gulf, which included protection of Western economic and security interests in the region by two regional actors, Iran and Saudi Arabia, under its guidance and supervision.[2] This strategy changed in 1979 when the Shah of Iran, a longtime ally of

Washington, was overthrown and replaced by a new cadre of politicians who designated the United States as their number one enemy. The policy of delegation unraveled further in 1990 when Iraq, the new American proxy in the Persian Gulf, annexed Kuwait, another oil-rich American ally in the region.

This precarious situation in the Persian Gulf envisaged closer American-Qatari military ties, which had been strained for several years due to the imposition of a US arms embargo on Qatar. This embargo was implemented in response to Qatar's refusing inspection of US-made Stinger missiles displayed in a military parade in March 1988 (Crystal, 1995). The relationship got back on track after Qatar permitted the deployment of coalition forces on its territory during the Gulf War. It also sent some of its own forces to assist in staving off an Iraqi attack on the Saudi town of Kafji in January 1991. The Qatari tanks proved to be helpful in driving the Iraqi forces from the town (Murphy and Gugliotta, 1991). After the end of the Gulf War and in accordance with the new National Security Strategy of August 1991, Washington and Doha signed a defense cooperation agreement on June 23, 1992 which provided for US access to Qatari military bases, joint military exercises, and pre-positioning of the US military equipment on Qatari soil.[3]

The Clinton administration that came to power in the United States in January 1993 announced a new policy of dual containment in May of that year, which aimed at countering both Iraq and Iran simultaneously rather than playing them off against each other (Indyk, 1993). This new foreign policy outlook necessitated a renewed military commitment to Gulf security on behalf of the United States which encapsulated attempts at encouraging collective security arrangements, strengthening local defense capabilities, and improving deployment capabilities via bilateral defense cooperation schemes (Kraig, 2004; The White House, 1994).

Assaults directed against the American military installations and personnel in Saudi Arabia started from the mid-1990s and continued into the 2000s, especially following the 9/11 attacks on the US soil carried out by Saudi nationals. As the United States invaded Afghanistan in 2001, Saudi Arabia's refusal to permit jets stationed in Prince Sultan Air Base to launch air strikes on Afghanistan led the United States to transfer its main operating bases and staff in the Kingdom to neighboring Gulf countries (Crystal, 2009). Indeed, Qatar benefited directly from this new security arrangement when in 2003 the United States decided to move the Combat Air Operations Center for the Middle East from Prince Sultan Air Base to the Al Udeid Air Base in Doha. The United States started using this facility as a logistical hub for operations in Afghanistan and Iraq. Additionally, and beginning in 2000, Qatar hosted the Camp As-Sayliyah, which serves as the largest American pre-positioning base abroad (Crystal, 2009).

US-Qatari military cooperation has surpassed arms sales, joint military exercises, and military education programs in recent years and has extended into collaboration in counterterrorism activities and military campaigns. Qatar took part in NATO's military campaign of March 2011 in Libya with six Mirage fighter jets and two C-17 transport airplanes (McShane, 2011). They, along with the French aircraft, helped to enforce the no-fly zone over Libya. Moreover, Qatar provided anti-tank missiles and assault rifles to the rebel forces in Libya (Roberts, 2011). It set up training camps in Benghazi and western Tripoli and hosted some of the rebel fighters in Doha as well for special exercises (Beydoun and Baum, 2012). In addition to the Libyan operation, Qatar's air force also contributed to the coalition military operations against ISIS targets in Syria in September 2014.

However, bilateral cooperation in limiting the financial backing of international terrorist groups has run into problems. Since 2004, Qatar has passed several laws to monitor and control domestic and international charitable activities. The February 2004 Law on Combating Terrorism listed the felonies considered terrorist crimes, stated specific punishments for them, and provided measures against terrorist financing or fundraising activities (Qatar Financial Centre Regulatory Authority, 2014). In March 2004 a new law established the Qatar Authority for Charitable Works, which was held responsible for monitoring overseas charitable, developmental, and humanitarian projects and for reporting annually to concerned ministries on the status of all projects (US Department of State, Office of the Coordinator for Counterterrorism, 2005). Another law, passed in 2006, expanded charitable oversight and equipped the Ministry of Civil Service and Housing Affairs with additional authority (Levitt, 2014). Finally, in 2010 Qatar enacted legislation to freeze funds of UN-designated terrorist organizations (Boghardt, 2014).

Yet, from the American point of view, enacting legislation did not make sense unless the laws were implemented and enforced. For example, in March 2014, David Cohen, then Under Secretary for Terrorism and Financial Intelligence, expressed American dissatisfaction regarding lax Qatari oversight of terrorist financing, claiming that Qatar was soliciting donations to fund extremist insurgents in Iraq and Syria (US Department of the Treasury, 2014). Six months later, in order to ward off international criticism, Qatar announced the formation of a regulatory body to oversee domestic charities, which would make it more difficult for them to move money outside of the country (Kovessy, 2014).

The US-Qatari partnership that started in the security sphere a quarter-century ago has since expanded and diversified into other domains, as laid out below. While the security cooperation continues to be the most important aspect of the relationship, collaboration in political, commercial, and educational dimensions plays a significant role as well in ensuring overall stability of the bilateral association.

Qatar's mediating role in the Middle East

Mediation became the major tool of Qatari foreign policy, aligned with the proclamation of its constitution in 2003. Article seven of the constitution stated that Qatar would help to maintain international peace and security by encouraging the settlement of international disputes by peaceful means (Constitute Project, 2016). Commensurate with this policy, Doha has engaged in various conflict mediation efforts across the Middle East since the mid-2000s, in an attempt to extend and increase Qatari influence in the region, especially as a small state. Washington wasted no time in turning this new Qatari foreign policy activism to its advantage. Qatar proved to be a valuable intermediary in cases when the United States had to transmit messages to countries such as Iraq and Libya with which it had troubled political relations, when the disputing sides discountenanced American intervention efforts as was the case in the Israeli-Hamas ceasefire deal, or when the United States did not want to enter into direct contact with the other parties such as the Taliban and al-Nusra Front due to political concerns and legal limitations.

American officials began using Qatari mediation in early 2003, when Qatar helped broker an agreement with the United States, the United Kingdom, and Libya which secured the dismantling of Libya's nuclear program (Shah, 2015). In the same year, Washington sent then Qatari Foreign Minister Hamad bin Jassim to Baghdad in order to convey the seriousness of the United States' war intentions to Iraqi President Saddam Hussein (Fromherz, 2012). In July 2014, US Secretary of State John Kerry requested assistance from Qatar and Turkey in hammering out a ceasefire deal between Hamas and Israel. Their help was solicited because Egypt, the previous mediator, now classified Hamas as a terrorist organization (Akpınar, 2015). However, this mediation effort was stifled in the wake of the Israeli opposition, and in the end, Egypt assumed responsibility to broker a deal.

Qatar had greater success in hostage mediation, thanks largely in part to Qatar's ample financial resources and much-criticized ties with non-state actors and radical Islamist groups (Lister, 2016). Doha has also arranged meetings between the Taliban and American authorities since 2010, and in 2013, the Taliban was permitted to open an office in Doha to use as a platform for further indirect talks (Boyce, 2013). In May 2014, Qatar negotiated the release of five Taliban leaders from the Guantanamo Bay detention camp in exchange for the release of US Army Sergeant Bowe Bergdahl (Kaussler, 2015).

In August 2014 Qatar again played a major role in the release of American journalist Theo Padnos, who had been held in Syria by the al-Nusra Front since 2012 (Bakr, 2014). There have been allegations that Qatar facilitated a ransom payment to ensure Padnos' release (Weinberg, 2015). The killings and kidnappings of American journalists and human rights activists in Iraq and Syria, coupled with Doha's connections with radical Islamic groups in these countries, may raise doubts regarding Qatar's resolve in the fight against terrorism. Qatar may simply have wanted to demonstrate its usefulness to US authorities by carrying out the Padnos rescue operation.

The mediatory role played by Qatar in the Middle East as per the request of the United States attested to the fact that although Qatar was the minor partner in the bilateral relationship, it might be of considerable help to Washington in some regional political matters. Doha succeeded in reaching out to states and non-state actors with which Washington either had serious issues or did not have any connections. This situation, as well as raising Qatar's regional profile, enhanced its importance in the eyes of American foreign policy makers.

Potential for growth: American-Qatari commercial ties

US-Qatari economic relations have experienced an upsurge in the last decade, notwithstanding modest bilateral trade figures and investment concentration in a few sectors. The commercial association was institutionalized via the Trade and Investment Framework Agreement that was signed in April 2004 (US Department of State, 2015). Bilateral trade came in at nearly $7 billion in 2014, a 7.8 percent increase from the previous year (US Department of State, Office of the Spokesperson, 2015). The value of American exports to Qatar was $5.2 billion, including aircraft, machinery, vehicles, optical and medical instruments, and agricultural products, whereas Qatari exports to the United States amounted to $1.7 billion and were comprised of Liquefied Natural Gas (LNG), aluminum, fertilizers, and sulphur (US Department of State, Bureau of Near Eastern Affairs, 2014).

The United States, with approximately $11 billion worth of foreign direct investment, is the largest foreign investor in Qatar (Office of the US Trade Representative, 2014). More than 120 American firms operate in Qatar, and in 2010 the American Chamber of Commerce became the first legally established foreign trade association in the country (US Chamber of Commerce, 2015). The American investments in Qatar are concentrated in sectors such as energy, defense, and construction.

Leading American energy companies, specifically ExxonMobil, ConocoPhillips, and Occidental Petroleum, have taken part in many oil and gas projects in Qatar. ExxonMobil, working as a joint venture with Qatar's state oil company Qatar Petroleum, is developing the North Field, the largest non-associated gas field in the world (ExxonMobil Qatar, 2016a). It has also participated in many LNG projects in the country through joint ventures with state-owned LNG firms; namely, Qatargas and RasGas. ExxonMobil is the sole foreign participant in two domestic gas development projects in Qatar, the Al Khaleej and Barzan. It also retains a 10 percent stake in the Laffan refinery through its affiliate ExxonMobil Qatar Refinery (ExxonMobil Qatar, 2016b). Furthermore, ExxonMobil, in cooperation with Qatar Petroleum, is constructing an LNG export terminal at Golden Pass in Texas (Fattouh, Rogers, and Stewart, 2015). ConocoPhillips, with a 30 percent stake in a joint venture with Qatar Petroleum, has been working on a large-scale LNG project in Ras Laffan Industrial City since 2003 (ConocoPhillips Qatar, 2016). Occidental Petroleum operates the Idd El Shargi North Dome, Idd El Shargi South Dome, and Al Rayyan offshore oil fields in Qatar (Occidental Petroleum Qatar, 2016). Moreover, the company also has a 24.5 percent stake in the Dolphin Gas Project, which aims to transfer natural gas from offshore wells in Qatar to customers in the United Arab Emirates and Oman through an underwater pipeline.

Another area of cooperation between the United States and Qatar is the United States' provision of military equipment and education services to the Qatari Armed Forces through American defense firms operating in Qatar. In October 2014 Lockheed Martin forged a deal with the government of Qatar to sell PAC-3 missiles (Lockheed Martin, 2014). The PAC-3 missiles were accepted as effective defensive mechanisms against tactical ballistic missiles, cruise missiles, and aircraft. They remained the only combat-proven hit-to-kill interceptor in the world, which meant they destroyed threats through kinetic energy in body-to-body contact (Lockheed Martin, 2016). Lockheed Martin will also provide basic wings and advanced pilot training for the Qatari Emir Air Force (US Chamber of Commerce, 2015). The Raytheon Company, another American defense contractor, clinched a deal in December 2014 to sell ten Patriot missile defense systems to Qatar (Shalal, 2014). Since 2009, Qatar has been purchasing air defense systems and transport aircraft from Boeing, the prominent American defense and aerospace company, which it utilizes in humanitarian airlift missions (Cortes, 2009). It was also announced in March 2014 that Qatar would purchase 24 AH-64E Apache attack helicopters and three 737 airborne early warning and control aircraft from Boeing (Menon, 2014). Doha's granting of basing rights to the US army, along with its weapon and military equipment purchases from the American defense firms, enhanced the asymmetric nature of the bilateral relationship by deepening Washington's leverage on the country in the security realm.

Another promising sector for American investments in Qatar appears to be the construction and infrastructure industry. The Qatari government has allocated a significant portion of its budget, about $200 billion, to build stadiums, hotels, and complete infrastructure work in anticipation for the 2022 FIFA World Cup (Smith, 2015). Accordingly, many American construction and engineering firms such as Global Building Solutions (Booth and Withers, 2013), CH2M, Aspire Logistics, Bechtel, Fluor, AECOM, Parsons, and KBR have engaged in various construction and infrastructure projects in Qatar (US Department of State, Office of the Spokesperson, 2015). AECOM (2017) has been awarded the Al Wakrah Stadium project, while Parsons has been building the Lusail Stadium. CH2M, Aspire Logistics, Bechtel, Fluor, and KBR have engaged in infrastructure projects, and Global Building Solutions (2017) has been constructing the Worker's Village.

Qatar has roughly $7 billion worth of investments on American soil, primarily in real estate, recreation, media, and banking industries. Qatar is the smaller partner in the relationship and, hence, not only struggles to enhance its visibility and impact in the vast American market, but also may try to create interdependence with American corporations in order to leverage them in times of crisis or disagreement with the US administration.

In 2010, through its real estate investment arm, Qatari Diar, Qatar became the majority owner in the CityCentreDC project in Washington, DC. This encompassed the development of condominiums, apartments, offices, public spaces, hotels, restaurants, and shops in a ten-acre lot (Fisher, 2013). Qatari Al Faisal Group bought the Radisson Blu Aqua hotel in Chicago in May 2012 (McGinley, 2012), and its international hospitality subsidiary, Al Rayyan Tourism Investment Company, purchased the St. Regis Bal Harbor Resort in South Florida in January 2014 (Salacanin, 2014). In January 2013 Qatar bought the Current Television cable channel, established by former US Vice President Al Gore, to use it as a platform to launch Al Jazeera America, a US-based news channel ("Al Jazeera buys," 2013). In October 2013 Qatar Holding acquired a stake worth $1 billion in Bank of America, the second-largest bank by assets in the United States (Hall, 2013).

In September 2015 Qatar Investment Authority, Qatar's sovereign wealth fund, decided to open up an office in New York in order to speed up its operations in North America after suffering serious losses in various Asian and European ventures. The company set its sights on expanding the current investments in the United States more than fivefold (The Economist Intelligence Unit, 2015). Concomitant to this purpose, the fund acquired a 40 percent share in Brookfield's Manhattan West real estate project (Levitt, 2015) and made an agreement with Douglas Emmett, a real investment trust, to purchase an office portfolio in West Los Angeles ("Qatari Fund JV acquires," 2016). The bulk of Qatari investments in the United States has been made in the real estate sector. This might be attributable to the important potential of the industry to generate billions of dollars in revenue on an annual basis. The Qatari entrepreneurs might have realized that there existed plenty of opportunities for themselves to get good return on their investments.

Growing economic bonds between the United States and Qatar have acted as a contributing factor to the strengthening of the bilateral association throughout the years. Yet, because of the fact that mutual investments are concentrated in a few sectors such as energy, defense, construction, and real estate, there is still room for development. Qatar, being the smaller partner in the economic interaction, has increased its investments in the United States in recent years in order to create interdependence and lessen the negative impact of its overdependence on the United States in the defense realm.

American-Qatari collaboration in the educational sphere

Aside from economic cooperation, higher education has been an important soft power tool employed by the United States since the first part of the 19th century. The first American higher education institutions in the Middle East were set up in the form of Protestant missionary organizations in what were then territories of the Ottoman Empire. Over time, these organizations gradually transformed into secular institutions, especially after the First World War and following the breakup of the Ottoman Empire. The most prominent examples of these higher education institutions are the Lebanese American

University founded in 1835 in Lebanon (Lebanese American University, 2016), Boğaziçi University established in 1863 in Turkey (Boğaziçi University, 2016), American University of Beirut opened in Lebanon in 1866 (American University of Beirut, 2016), and the American University in Cairo founded in Egypt in 1919 (American University in Cairo, 2016).

The US administration provided material and moral support to these tertiary education institutions as they had proved instrumental in espousing and disseminating American norms, values, mindset, and language across the Middle East. The structured and versatile curriculum, the presence of qualified and experienced faculty members, and the usage of English as medium of instruction attracted many promising and successful young people from all over the region to study at these universities. Many Middle Eastern local and regional graduates of these institutions assumed leadership positions in politics, bureaucracy, and business in their respective home countries. While these people generally disagreed with the United States' Middle Eastern policies, they nevertheless appreciated the academic quality and intellectual freedom they enjoyed in these universities and maintained their connections with American society (Bertelsen, 2012).

Beginning in the mid-1990s and accelerating after the events of 9/11, American higher education institutions explored new avenues for extending their reach into the Middle East by establishing satellite/branch campuses throughout the Persian Gulf. These institutions loomed large in exposing Gulf students to the English language, thus strengthening channels of communication between the United States and their countries. The knowledge and skills transmitted by these universities to the citizens of the Gulf, which would assist them in competing successfully in a tough business environment, equipped the United States with new tools to penetrate the region. Furthermore, these branch campuses proved to be useful in averting risk of reduced international student enrollments at home campuses in the cases of political and economic crises (Wilkins, 2011).

Qatar is home to the largest enclave of American universities abroad, operating under the Qatar Foundation, which was established with the objective of supporting programs in education, science and research, and community development (Qatar Foundation, 2016). The Foundation hosts a total of seven colleges/universities, including Carnegie Mellon University (Carnegie Mellon University Qatar, 2016), Georgetown University, Northwestern University (Northwestern University in Qatar, 2016), Texas A&M University (Texas A&M University at Qatar, 2016), Virginia Commonwealth University (Virginia Commonwealth University Qatar, 2016), Cornell University, and Houston Community College (Houston Community College in Qatar, 2016), which offer programs in medicine, engineering, business administration, international relations, journalism, and fashion.

The Qatar Foundation shoulders the construction and operating costs of these universities, including the salaries of administrative and academic personnel. Furthermore, a generous amount of management fees is allocated to each university on an annual basis to operate in Qatar (Vora, 2015). Virginia Commonwealth University, for example, disclosed that it had received a management fee of more than $3.6 million in 2013 (Anderson, 2015). The country pledged to undertake this financial burden because local university graduates have generally lacked the required intellectual, technical, and managerial skills to compete with their peers coming from East Asia and other developing nations (Coffman, 2015).

Qatar is cognizant of the fact that its tremendous wealth depends primarily on exploitation of energy resources which may deplete in the future. In order to cope effectively with such a situation, the country will need to find alternative means of revenue generation. This can only be achieved with the help of a well-educated, creative, and competent workforce that has the ability to muddle through in an increasingly competitive international environment. The American tertiary education institutions in Qatar come into play within this context. They emphasize a learning culture which nurtures critical thinking and problem-solving. They also stress individual accomplishment and multiculturalism. These qualities are expected to nurture the emergence of a new Qatari labor force which will be more attuned to market needs and, over time, will decrease the nation's reliance on expatriates, who currently make up nearly 85 percent of the total Qatari workforce (Ministry of Development Planning and Statistics, 2016).

There were also practical considerations that played a role in bringing American universities to Qatar. Under the new US Citizenship and Immigration Services regulations introduced after 9/11, Qatari nationals began to encounter difficulties obtaining student visas in the United States (Davis, 2010). Having American universities in Qatari territory eliminated this kind of a problem. The Qatari students who want to study at higher education institutions in the United States may face additional hurdles in the coming days if American President Donald Trump extends the executive order that has suspended the entry of nationals of some Muslim countries from entering the United States (The White House, 2017) to Qatar. The American universities in Qatar have also increased women's access to higher education as Qatari women are not allowed to attend overseas universities without a chaperone. At American universities in Qatar, however, they are educated in gender-integrated classrooms and receive the same treatment as their male counterparts (Khodr, 2011).

US-Qatari cooperation in the education field is a novel phenomenon, and has developed rapidly in the last two decades. Each year approximately 2,000 (Qatar Foundation, 2015) Qatari students enroll in American educational institutions of higher learning in Qatar to acquire the necessary knowledge and skills to compete in a rapidly changing and interconnected world. The presence of these universities is a valuable asset for both Doha and Washington as they ensure continuous intellectual interaction as well as cultural connection between the two countries.

Conclusion

The enhanced ties between the United States and Qatar are relatively recent. The two countries commenced diplomatic relations in 1972 after Qatar declared independence from the United Kingdom. However, there was little interaction between Washington and Doha during the Cold War years, since Washington relied more upon influential regional states such as Iran until 1980 and then Saudi Arabia and Iraq, rather than the small emirate, to safeguard Western economic and security interests in the Persian Gulf area. Iran's Islamic Revolution, followed by the hostage crisis of November 1979, during which 52 Americans were held hostage in the US embassy in Tehran by a group of Iranian students, led to the two countries breaking off diplomatic relations in 1980. One decade later, in August 1990, Iraq, the new American proxy in the Gulf, invaded Kuwait, another American ally in the region. These two incidents served as an impetus for a revised Gulf strategy on behalf of American foreign policy makers, due to the rapidly changing regional power dynamics ushered in by the increased rivalries.

The new American strategy towards the Persian Gulf region foresaw a substantial military role for Qatar, and the content and scope of this role have expanded continuously, especially in recent years. Cooperation in the security sphere ultimately led to enhanced collaboration in diplomatic, economic, and educational fronts. Washington made use of Doha's mediation capabilities in order to reach out to countries or groups that were either estranged from the United States because of its policies in the Middle East, such as Iraq, Libya, and Hamas, or were off limits to the United States due to legal restrictions, such as the Taliban and al-Nusra Front. The reciprocal investments and collaboration in the realm of higher education further consolidated these bilateral ties.

US-Qatari relations seem to rest on a solid foundation with the potential to grow and diversify into other areas of cooperation in the future. This continuity and stability stems from the asymmetrical power configuration in the relationship, which favors the United States as it dominates the military, economic, and educational facets of the bilateral interaction. The mediatory role played by Qatar to the benefit of the United States, on the other hand, equips Doha with some leverage on Washington in this unequal association. Yet, if US President Donald J. Trump abandons indirect political contacts with the non-state actors with which the United States has complex relations and instead adopts a hard-line approach to them that does not rule out the utilization of military options. Moreover, Qatar will be devoid of an important bargaining chip in the bilateral relationship. Even so, the Qatari side will still enjoy close bonds with the United States. This is especially true in trying to strike a balance between Iran and Saudi Arabia, the Persian Gulf's most assertive, compelling, and competitive powers.

Notes

1 Saudi Arabia signed similar bilateral defense agreements with Bahrain, Oman, and the United Arab Emirates as well.

2 The Nixon Doctrine called on the allies of the United States to take more responsibility for their own defense while continuing to receive economic and military assistance from Washington.
3 This agreement was renewed on December 10, 2013 at the time of US Secretary of Defense Chuck Hagel's visit to Qatar.

References

AECOM. (2017). Al Wakrah Stadium and precinct. Retrieved from www.aecom.com/projects/al-wakrah-stadium/?ql%5B0%5D=212&qp=1&qt=12.

Akpınar, P. (2015). Mediation as a foreign policy tool in the Arab Spring: Turkey, Qatar and Iran. *Journal of Balkan and Near Eastern Studies*, 17(3), 252–268. doi:10.1080/19448953.2015.1063270.

Al Jazeera (2013, January 3). Al Jazeera buys US channel Current TV. Retrieved from www.aljazeera.com/news/americas/2013/01/2013132255769130.html.

American University in Cairo. (2016). History. Retrieved from www.aucegypt.edu/about/about-auc/history.

American University of Beirut. (2016). History. Retrieved from www.aub.edu.lb/main/about/Pages/history.aspx.

Anderson, N. (2015, December 6). In Qatar's Education City, US colleges are building an academic oasis. *The Washington Post*. Retrieved from https://www.washingtonpost.com/local/education/in-qatars-education-city-us-colleges-are-building-an-academic-oasis/2015/12/06/6b538702-8e01-11e5-ae1f-af46b7df8483_story.html?utm_term=.22b0da42945f.

Bakr, A. (2014, August 27). Qatar seeks to free more US hostages in Syria. *Reuters*. Retrieved from www.reuters.com/article/us-syria-crisis-qatar-usa-idUSKBN0GQ0JW20140826.

Bertelsen, R.G. (2012). Private foreign-affiliated universities, the state, and soft power: The American University of Beirut and the American University in Cairo. *Foreign Policy Analysis*, 8(3), 293–311. doi:10.1111/j.1743-8594.2011.00163.x.

Beydoun, N.M. and Baum, J. (2012). *The glass palace: Illusions of freedom and democracy in Qatar*. New York: Algora.

Boğaziçi University. (2016). History. Retrieved from www.boun.edu.tr/en-US/Content/About_BU/History.

Boghardt, L.P. (2014, May 2). The terrorist funding disconnect with Qatar and Kuwait. *The Washington Institute*. Retrieved from www.washingtoninstitute.org/policy-analysis/view/the-terrorist-funding-disconnect-with-qatar-and-kuwait.

Booth, R. and Withers, I. (2013, November 21). British firm plans "humane" housing for Qatar World Cup migrant labourers. *The Guardian*. Retrieved from https://www.theguardian.com/world/2013/nov/21/qatar-world-cup-british-humane-housing-migrant-labourers.

Boyce, G. (2013). Qatar's foreign policy. *Asian Affairs*, 44(3), 365–377. doi:10.1080/03068374.2013.826003.

Carnegie Mellon University Qatar. (2016). About. Retrieved from https://www.qatar.cmu.edu/about-us/.

Coffman, J. (2015). Higher education in the Gulf: Privatization and Americanization. *International Higher Education*, 33, 17–19. Retrieved from http://ejournals.bc.edu/ojs/index.php/ihe/article/view/7393/6590.

ConocoPhillips Qatar. (2016). Our projects. Retrieved from www.conocophillips.qa/wh o-we-are/Pages/our-projects.aspx.

Constitute Project. (2016). Qatar's constitution of 2003. Retrieved from https://www. constituteproject.org/constitution/Qatar_2003.pdf?lang=en.

Cortes, L. (2009, September). First C-17 delivery builds ties with Qatar. *Boeing Frontiers*, p.10. Retrieved from www.boeing.com/news/frontiers/archive/2009/septem ber/i_nan.pdf.

Crystal, J. (1995). *Oil and politics in the Gulf: Rulers and merchants in Kuwait and Qatar.* New York: Cambridge University Press.

Crystal, J. (2009). US Relations with Qatar. In R.E. Looney (Ed.), *Handbook of US-Middle East relations: Formative factors and regional perspectives* (pp. 391–402). London: Routledge.

Davis, C.J. (2010). *American higher education in the Arabian Gulf: A force for liberalization.* Master's thesis, Naval Postgraduate School, Monterey, CA. Retrieved from http://calhoun.nps.edu/bitstream/handle/10945/5351/10Jun_Davis_Christian.pdf?seq uence=1&isAllowed=y.

Domingo, F. (2014). The RMA theory and small states. *Military and Strategic Affairs*, 6(3), 43–58. Retrieved from www.inss.org.il/uploadImages/systemFiles/03_Domingo.pdf.

The Economist Intelligence Unit. (2015, September 30). Qatar Investment Authority seeks new role as its holdings take a buffeting. Retrieved from http://country.eiu. com/article.aspx?articleid=1723549756&Country=Qatar&topic=Economy_1.

ExxonMobil Qatar. (2016a). About us. Retrieved from www.exxonmobil.com.qa/Qata r-English/PA/about.aspx.

ExxonMobil Qatar. (2016b). Liquefied natural gas. Retrieved from www.exxonmobil. com.qa/Qatar-English/PA/about_what_partnerships.aspx.

Fattouh, B., Rogers, H. V. and Stewart, P. (2015). *The US shale gas revolution and its impact on Qatar's position in gas markets.* New York: Columbia University Center on Global Energy Policy. Retrieved from http://energypolicy.columbia.edu/sites/defa ult/files/energy/The%20US%20Shale%20Gas%20Revolution%20and%20Its%20Imp act%20on%20Qatar's%20Position%20in%20Gas%20Markets_March%202015.pdf.

Fisher, M. (2013, December 17). Qatar is suddenly investing heavily in the US, bank-rolling D.C.'s City Center, other projects. *The Washington Post.* Retrieved from https:// www.washingtonpost.com/local/qatar-is-suddenly-investing-heavily-in-the-us-bankrolli ng-dcs-city-center-other-projects/2013/12/17/1ffaceca-5c6a-11e3-95c2-13623eb2b0e1_st ry.html.

Fromherz, A.J. (2012). *Qatar: A modern history.* London: I. B. Tauris.

Global Building Solutions. (2017). Worker's village-Qatar. Retrieved from https://www. gbsdevelopment.com/projects-under-development.html.

Hall, C. (2013, October 30). Qatar fund quietly builds $1bn Bank of America stake. *Financial Times.* Retrieved from www.ft.com/topics/organisations/Qatar_Holding_LLC.

Houston Community College in Qatar. (2016). About. Retrieved from http://sites.hccs. edu/qatar/about/.

Indyk, M. (1993). The Clinton administration's approach to the Middle East. *The Washington Institute for Near East Policy.* Retrieved from www.washingtoninstitute. org/policy-analysis/view/the-clinton-administrations-approach-to-the-middle-east.

Kaussler, B. (2015). *Tracing Qatar's foreign policy and its impact on regional security.* Doha, Qatar: Arab Center for Research and Policy Studies. Retrieved from http:// english.dohainstitute.org/file/get/d31b5ea7-be0b-4a01-b37a-e0df9dc663a9.pdf.

Keohane, R.O. (1969). Lilliputians' dilemmas: Small states in international politics. *International Organization*, 23(2), 291–310. doi:10.1017/S002081830003160X.

Khodr, H. (2011). The dynamics of international education in Qatar: Exploring the policy drivers behind the development of Education City. *Journal of Emerging Trends in Educational Research and Policy Studies*, 2(6), 514–525. Retrieved from http://jeteraps.scholarlinkresearch.com/articles/The%20Dynamics%20of%20Internat ional%20Education%20in%20Qatar.pdf.

Kovessy, P. (2014, September 20). Qatar clamps down on charities that send funds abroad. *Doha News*. Retrieved from http://dohanews.co/qatar-clamps-charities-send-funds-abroad/.

Kraig, M. (2004). Assessing alternative security frameworks for the Persian Gulf. *Middle East Policy*, 11(3), 139–156. doi:10.1111/j.1061-1924.2004.00172.x.

Lea, D. (Ed.). (2001). *A political chronology of the Middle East*. London: Europa.

Lebanese American University. (2016). History. Retrieved from www.lau.edu.lb/about/history/.

Levitt, D.M. (2015, October 28). Qatar joins Brookefield's $8.6 billion Manhattan West Project. *Bloomberg*. Retrieved from www.bloomberg.com/news/articles/2015-1 0-28/brookfield-joins-with-qatar-for-8-6-billion-manhattan-project.

Levitt, M. (2014, September 24). Qatar's not-so-charitable record on terror finance. *The Washington Institute*. Retrieved from www.washingtoninstitute.org/policy-analy sis/view/qatars-not-so-charitable-record-on-terror-finance.

Liska, G. (1968). *Alliances and the third world*. Baltimore, MD: The Johns Hopkins University Press.

Lister, C. (2016). Profiling Jabhat al-Nusra. *The Brookings Project on US Relations with the Islamic World Analysis*: Paper No. 24. Washington, DC: Brookings Insti-tution. Retrieved from https://www.brookings.edu/wp-content/uploads/2016/07/iwr_ 20160728_profiling_nusra.pdf.

Lockheed Martin. (2014, October 15). Qatar becomes 8th international customer for Lockheed Martin's PAC-3 missile. Retrieved from www.lockheedmartin.com/us/new s/press-releases/2014/october/mfc-101514-qatar-becomes-8th-international-customer--lockheed-martin-pac-3-missile.html.

Lockheed Martin. (2016, September 21). PAC-3 destroys tactical ballistic missile target. Retrieved from www.lockheedmartin.com/us/news/press-releases/2016/septem ber/mfc-092116-pac-3-destroys-tactical-ballistic-missile-target.html.

McGinley, S. (2012, May 21). Qatar's Al Faisal acquires Chicago Radisson Blu Hotel. *Arabian Business*. Retrieved from www.arabianbusiness.com/qatar-s-al-faisal-acquir es-chicago-radisson-blu-hotel-458610.html#.V9h5NfmLTrc.

McShane, L. (2011, March 25). Qatar fighter jet flies mission over Libya, first Arab nation to join no-fly zone against Khadafy. *New York Daily News*. Retrieved from www.nydailynews.com/news/world/qatar-fighter-jet-flies-mission-libya-arab-nation-jo in-no-fly-zone-khadafy-article-1.119546.

Menon, P. (2014, March 27). Qatar buys helicopters, missiles in $23 billion defense deals. *Reuters*. Retrieved from www.reuters.com/article/us-qatar-defence-idUSBREA 2Q1KI20140327.

Ministry of Development Planning and Statistics. (2016). Labor force survey-the third quarter (July-September 2016) [Statistical release]. Retrieved from www.mdp s.gov.qa/en/statistics/Statistical%20Releases/Social/LaborForce/2016/Q3/LF_Q3_201 6_AE.pdf.

Morrow, J.D. (1991). Alliances and asymmetry: An alternative to the capability aggregation model of alliances. *American Journal of Political Science*, 35(4), 904–933. doi:10.2307/2111499.

Murphy, C. and Gugliotta, G. (1991, February 1). Saudi town reclaimed. *Washington Post Foreign Service*. Retrieved from www.washingtonpost.com/wp-srv/inatl/longter m/fogofwar/archive/post013191_2.htm.

Northwestern University in Qatar. (2016). Academics. Retrieved from www.qatar.nort hwestern.edu/education/index.html.

Occidental Petroleum Qatar. (2016). Our businesses. Retrieved from www.oxy.com/Ou rBusinesses/OilandGas/MiddleEast/Pages/Qatar.aspx.

Office of the US Trade Representative. (2014, May 6). US-Qatar trade facts. Retrieved from https://ustr.gov/countries-regions/europe-middle-east/middle-east/nor th-africa/qatar.

Paterson, W.E. (1969). Small states in international politics. *Cooperation and Conflict*, 4, 119–123. doi:10.1177/001083676900400107.

Peterson, J.E. (2006). Qatar and the world: Branding for a micro-state. *The Middle East Journal*, 60(4) 732–748. doi:10.3751.60.4.15.

Qatar Financial Centre Regulatory Authority. (2014). Law no (3) of 2004 on combating terrorism. Retrieved from www.qfcra.com/en-us/legislation/Laws/Law%20No% 20(3)%20of%202004%20on%20Combating%20Terrorism.pdf.

Qatar Foundation. (2015). *Annual Report 2013–2014*. Doha, Qatar: Author. Retrieved from www.qf.org.qa/qf-annual-report-archive.

Qatar Foundation. (2016). Mission. Retrieved from https://www.qf.org.qa/about/about.

Trade Arabia. (2016, March 3). Qatari fund JV acquires $1.34 billion US office portfolio. Retrieved from www.tradearabia.com/news/CONS_302071.html.

Roberts, D. (2011, September 28). Behind Qatar's intervention in Libya: Why was Doha such a strong supporter of the rebels? *Foreign Affairs*. Retrieved from https:// www.foreignaffairs.com/articles/libya/2011-09-28/behind-qatars-intervention-libya.

Roberts, D.B. (2016). The four eras of Qatar's foreign policy. *Comillas Journal of International Relations*, 2(5), 1–17. doi:10.14422/cir.i05.y2016.001.

Rothstein, R.L. (1968). *Alliances and small powers*. New York: Columbia University Press.

Salacanin, S. (2014, February 13). Qatari expansion in USA. *Business in Qatar and Beyond Magazine*. Retrieved from www.bq-magazine.com/economy/2014/02/qatari-expansion-in-usa.

Shah, A. (2015, October 19). Qatar cultivates a new global image: Analysis. *Eurasia Review*. Retrieved from www.eurasiareview.com/19102015-qatar-cultivates-a-new-gl obal-image-analysis/.

Shalal, A. (2014, December 19). Raytheon wins $2.4 billion contract for Qatar patriot system. *Reuters*. Retrieved from www.reuters.com/article/us-raytheon-qatar-idUSKB N0JX2FO20141220.

Smith, D.S. (2015, Spring). US-Qatar relations: Realizing the full potential of a growing strategic partnership. *The Ambassadors Review*, 20–23. Retrieved from https:// www.ciaonet.org/attachments/27652/uploads.

Texas A&M University at Qatar. (2016). Undergraduate degrees. Retrieved from www. qatar.tamu.edu/academics/undergraduate-degrees/.

US Chamber of Commerce. (2015). *US business outlook in Qatar 2015*. Washington, DC. Retrieved from https://www.uschamber.com/sites/default/files/documents/files/ US_business_outlook_in_qatar_report.pdf.

US Department of State. (2015). Qatar investment climate statement. Retrieved from www.state.gov/documents/organization/241921.pdf.

US Department of State, Bureau of Near Eastern Affairs. (2014, August 26). *US relations with Qatar* [Fact sheet]. Washington, DC. Retrieved from www.state.gov/r/pa/ei/bgn/5437.htm.

US Department of State, Office of the Coordinator for Counterterrorism. (2005). *Country reports on terrorism 2004*. Washington, DC: US Government Printing Office.

US Department of State, Office of the Spokesperson. (2015, October 26). US-Qatar economic and investment dialogue. Retrieved from www.state.gov/r/pa/prs/ps/2015/10/248734.htm.

US Department of the Treasury. (2014, March 4). Remarks of Under Secretary for Terrorism and Financial Intelligence David Cohen before the Center for a New American Security on "Confronting new threats in terrorist financing". Washington, DC. Retrieved from https://www.treasury.gov/press-center/press-releases/Pages/jl2308.aspx.

Virginia Commonwealth University Qatar. (2016). Academics. Retrieved from www.qatar.vcu.edu/.

Vora, N. (2015). Is the university universal? Mobile (re) constitutions of American academia in the Gulf Arab States. *Anthropology & Education Quarterly*, 46(1), 19–36. doi:10.1111/aeq.12085.

Weinberg, D.A. (2015). *Terrorist financing: Kidnapping, antiquities trafficking, and private donations*. Washington, DC: Foundation for Defense of Democracies. Retrieved from www.defenddemocracy.org/content/uploads/documents/Terrorist_Financing_Kidnapping_Antiquities_and_Private_Donations.pdf.

The White House. (1991). *National security strategy of the United States*. Washington, DC: Author. Retrieved from http://nssarchive.us/NSSR/1991.pdf.

The White House. (1994). *A national security strategy of engagement and enlargement*. Washington, DC: US Government Printing Office.

The White House. (2017, January 27). *Executive order: Protecting the nation from foreign terrorist entry into the United States*. Washington, DC: Author. Retrieved from https://www.whitehouse.gov/the-press-office/2017/01/27/executive-order-protecting-nation-foreign-terrorist-entry-united-states.

Wilkins, S. (2011). Who benefits from foreign universities in the Arab Gulf States? *Australian Universities' Review*, 53(1), 73–83. Retrieved from http://opus.bath.ac.uk/22814/1/Who_benefits_from_foreign_universities_in_the_Arab_Gulf_States.pdf.

Wright, S. (2011). Foreign policies with international reach: The case of Qatar. In D. Held and K. Ulrichsen (Eds.), *The transformation of the Gulf: Politics, economics and the global order* (pp. 296–312). London: Routledge.

9 US-Gulf Cooperation Council Relations in the age of the Obama Doctrine

Michael McCall

The Gulf has long been considered a bastion of US hegemony, with no contenders in waiting to assume the role. Since the withdrawal of British forces in the 1970s, the Gulf has been militarily dominated by the United States, with what would eventually become the Gulf Cooperation Council (GCC)[1] firmly within the US sphere of influence. The region's geostrategic position combined with the largest proven energy reserves in the world (Fasano and Iqbal, 2003) all but assures that the region will maintain a unique significance to US foreign policy. The articulation of the Carter Doctrine in January 1980 cemented the role of the United States as the primary guarantor of security in the Gulf (Kuniholm, 1986). Though regional events over many decades have generated a great deal of turbulence, there has been no divorce.

Despite massive differences in political structures and social culture between the United States and the GCC, the former being a liberal democracy while the latter are conservative monarchies, their relationship is cemented in a set of long-term and crucial shared interests and, more important, the United States' commitment to the bloc's security (Al-Shayji, 2014). However, it is no secret that the partnership is between two parties immensely unequal in military strength and international clout. This type of partnership is often characterized by an inherent concern that the stronger party will not prioritize the weaker party's interests (Snyder, 1984). Though the GCC countries are dependent on the military umbrella of the United States, the United States does not have a similarly dependent relationship with the GCC countries. As this is a structural facet of the relationship, little can be done to remedy the discrepancy.

Compared to previous administrations, the Obama administration adopted a distinct foreign policy strategy towards the Middle East. Tacit support for regional uprisings, mending ties with Iran, and an aversion to engaging in the Syrian Civil War have been signature aspects of this approach, and these policies alienated many of the United States' historic GCC allies. The Bush administration applied the neoconservative strategy of high-profile military engagement as a means of securing US interests (Klare, 2006), while the Obama administration preferred a strategy closer to offshore balancing (Allin and Jones, 2012). In the context of analyzing the divergence in policies between the two countries towards crises in Bahrain and Iraq, Abdulaziz bin Sager, chair of the Gulf Research Center in Jeddah, summed up the current perspective of GCC countries thusly: "It is not clear whether the GCC states can continue to rely on US policy to not only protect the region, but to move it towards a more stable future" (2013, para. 8). Based on this type of sentiment emerging from the GCC, it can be unequivocally stated that GCC-US relations are at a turning point.

US interests will ultimately take priority over the concerns of GCC states. This is the case due to a number of systemic and domestic factors that influence US policy in a manner that GCC states are unable to counter. The changing balance of power in the Middle East regional system, especially in regards to a rising Iran, led to the Obama administration altering US foreign policy priorities from those of previous administrations. Where interests remain aligned, particularly in the realm of Gulf security from external threats and in combating global terrorism, cooperation will still be possible. This chapter aims to reveal the effects of the Obama administration's "retrenchment" foreign policy towards the Middle East by examining the GCC-US partnership that has defined the regional power structure since the 1970s.

From this perspective, the chapter argues that the nature of the partnership is undergoing a slow but fundamental shift towards less direct dependence as the United States changes its regional posture. The military element of the partnership remains the strongest and most static aspect of the relationship, but the economic and diplomatic elements have become increasingly strained under the Obama administration. The first section will provide the context of the existing relationship by analyzing the current status of strategic interests and postures on both sides. This will be followed by an analysis of exactly how the relationship changed as a result of the Obama administration's foreign policy towards the Middle East.

Changing factors influencing a new US foreign policy strategy

Though second-tier states, such as the People's Republic of China, have begun to challenge US primacy, from a realist perspective, the current nature of the international system remains distinctively unipolar. The United States lacks any external elements restricting the unilateral implementation of hard power as it desires; counterbalancing US influence, particularly in the Gulf, is beyond the reach of any state. Although unipolarity remains the dominant paradigm, the decline in relative power wielded by the United States globally and the growth of emerging powers' influence are the defining aspects of the modern international system. No fundamental upset in the state system has yet occurred, but Randall Schweller (2010) claims that the initial stages of power deconcentration are beginning to be visible as military and economic crises have substantially affected US capabilities.

Richard Haass emphasizes how the growing disparity between US and global GDP underlines an absolute decline in US influence, despite the fact that the United States remains the single largest power center. Additionally, raw military power is becoming unlinked from diplomatic influence (Haass, 2008). Thus, US military supremacy should not be considered synonymous with system leadership. For the moment, however, no single contender has emerged with the capability or the will to take on the responsibility of providing security in the same manner as the United States. While it is indisputable that the United States will retain its position as the unipole for the foreseeable future, its ability to exercise primacy in far-flung regions is becoming increasingly untenable (Flournoy and Davidson, 2012; Shu Xianlin, 2013).

Furthermore, perceived failures in the exercise of hegemonic power have generated substantial negative political externalities that have impacted US interests. The most potent example of these effects is the Iraq War, which damaged regional perceptions of the United States and provided evidence of US military failure (Layne, 2007). These negative externalities, on the domestic front, have shifted US public opinion against extensive involvement in affairs overseas (Kohut, 2013; Parent and MacDonald, 2011). High-profile, expensive military conflicts such as the Iraq War eventually resulted in a backlash from the domestic electorate. The Obama administration was elected on a platform of reducing US involvement in costly, high-profile military interventions abroad. The doctrine that bears his name, advocating for limiting the use of military force when the United States is not itself threatened (Schmierer, Jeffrey, Nader, and Nazer, 2016), has essentially functioned as a practical observation of these limits resulting from power deconcentration while, simultaneously, catering to the political demands of the US electorate.

The "Obama Doctrine" can be better described as a combination of "containment and offshore balancing instead of primacy" (Stepak and Whitlark, 2012, p. 52). Both of these constituent strategies imply less reliance on direct military action. In the case of the GCC, the offshore balancing element of the Obama Doctrine is clearly more applicable than containment. Like primacy, offshore balancing is similarly derived from the realist school of international relations. Compared to other strategies, offshore balancing presents a low-cost, small-footprint mechanism for securing national interests. Rather than seeking to maintain the dominant military posture of the United States globally, such a strategy accepts that new powerful actors will arise and should be accommodated (Layne, 1997). Generally, the strategy seeks to limit the use of hard power when it is unnecessary, but it is distinct from an isolationist foreign policy in that it is by no means apathetic to developments elsewhere. National interests worth expending resources outside the borders of the state do exist, though the United States is not always the only force willing and able to defend them.

Offshore balancing alone has been criticized as an insufficient framework for analyzing the Obama Doctrine's impact on Gulf policy. This criticism stems from the fact that the United States actively remains committed to combating non-hegemonic actors onshore. Therefore, strategic retrenchment better describes the exact phenomenon under analysis as the key question facing the United States is how to renegotiate the terms of onshore engagement (Simón, 2016). The implications of this retrenchment in the GCC as dictated by the Obama Doctrine represented a deviation from previous US administrations, which actively participated in regional geopolitics and refrained from devolution. Additionally, the "pivot to Asia" recognized that the Middle East was not as significant as the growing challenges to historical US hegemony in the Asia-Pacific region. In the context of this fluid international environment, relations between the United States and the GCC underwent their own transformation.

Why the GCC (still) matters to the United States in an age of retrenchment

Alongside Europe and East Asia, security of the Gulf represents the most critical class of geostrategic concern for the United States (Mearsheimer and Walt, 2016). These regions are among few worthy of dedicated military assets under a strategy of offshore balancing. The unrivaled importance of the Gulf region, due to its role as the fulcrum of the global economy, has continually placed it at the center of US foreign policy interests (Layne, 1997). The United States' key policy, maintained through successive administrations, has been to balance competing powers and prevent the rise of a hegemon in the region that could be capable of harming US economic interests through the manipulation of the largest proven oil reserves on earth (Layne, 2009). The GCC countries, all being littoral to the Gulf, are thus key allies to retain in order to exercise effective control over the region as well as to balance any state with hegemonic intentions.

The significance of maintaining security in the Gulf is difficult to overstate, as the Strait of Hormuz is an irreplaceable oil transit route. For the United States, the stability of world energy markets is a serious economic security interest. GCC oil exports comprise 20 percent of the international oil trade, 90 percent of which is exported from the GCC through the Strait. As such, the global economy would be unable to withstand any interruption to the flow of oil through this vital waterway. Aside from energy, the free flow of traffic permits the United States to move essential military assets in the region (Al-Barasneh, 2015). This makes the transportation route equally important for both its economic and strategic military value.

It is important to note, however, that the United States is not itself substantially dependent on GCC energy exports directly. Changes in the nature of US energy consumption have led to the United States becoming largely independent of energy imports from GCC member states. In 2015, the United States imported approximately 1.51 million barrels of oil per day, or 16 percent of total US oil imports, from Persian Gulf OPEC[2] countries (EIA). East Asia is the biggest consumer of GCC oil, with the International Energy Agency predicting that up to 90 percent of GCC oil exports will be destined for these markets in the future (Sartori, 2014). This means that the United States will be, at most, a minor consumer of the most strategic GCC export. Additionally, the steadily increasing capabilities of the United States in terms of exploiting unconventional energy sources, such as the advances in exploiting shale oil, can potentially render the United States energy self-sufficient by 2035 (Neff and Coleman, 2014).

This changing pattern of energy consumption has enabled the retrenchment posture seen under the Obama administration by providing the United States with a freer hand in terms of dealing with Middle East affairs, as the United States is now far more detached from direct economic consequences resulting from regional political turmoil. The 2011 "leading from behind" approach adopted in Libya, the relative lack of US involvement in Syria, and the improvement of relations with Iran all stem from the growing autonomy of the United States as a result of its decreased energy dependence (Sartori, 2014). Arab regimes are worried that this reduction of US energy dependence will fundamentally alter the nature of relations between the United States and the region, fostering retrenchment by the United States (Yergin, 2014). A drop in direct energy imports, however, does not undermine the core interest of maintaining the security of Gulf energy routes as a public good for the sake of the global economy. In a 2013 address to the United Nations, President Obama assured that the United States will guarantee the "free flow of energy from the region to the world"; this is despite the fact that the United States itself has reduced its dependence on energy imports from the region (Obama, 2013, n.p.).

Beyond the immediate security environment of the Gulf, GCC countries are important partners in the pursuit of US policies in the larger Middle East realm. The GCC countries themselves wield substantial political influence throughout the region and have proven themselves capable of manipulating events through the use of financial inducements, soft power assets, and their own military forces. While it is commonplace to refer to the GCC states as a monolith, the exercise of foreign policy outside the Gulf region often represents an important point of contention between them; for example, Saudi Arabia and Qatar have pursued conflicting agendas regarding their respective policies in Egypt (L. Khatib, 2013). However, it is undeniable that the GCC states play an outsized role in regional affairs, considering their small sizes and populations. They have, therefore, the potential to play a major role in regional dispute mediation. The United States has utilized the diplomatic position of Qatar, for example, to pursue its peace agenda in Afghanistan (Karzai, 2013).

Finally, since the September 11 attacks and the declaration of the "War on Terror," counterterrorism cooperation between the United States and GCC states has become a major strategic interest. GCC states are in a unique position on this issue; they hold immense potential in regards to counter-terrorism cooperation and have engaged in such cooperation extensively. However, GCC countries are viewed in some quarters of the United States as culpable for generating the conditions that have originally spawned many terrorist threats (Eisenstadt, McInnis, Weinberg, and Katzman, 2015;

Goldberg, 2016). Because of their pivotal position in this respect, they represent an indispensable partner.

Why the GCC (still) needs the United States

In terms of competition within the Gulf regional subsystem, GCC countries have always found themselves vulnerable to larger, more powerful neighbors: Iraq and Iran. The importance of regional defense and the US role in maintaining the security of the bloc were both demonstrated during the First Gulf War. The existence of the Gulf Deterrent Force provided little genuine "deterrent" to these competing regional hegemonic contenders, and as a result, GCC countries have accepted the reality that a foreign power is necessary to ensure their security. In the wake of the conflict, the United States implemented bilateral defense arrangements with all GCC member countries (Lefebvre, 2003). These arrangements continue to this day, making the United States the ultimate guarantor of security for all states in the bloc. With the effective elimination of Iraq as a potential regional hegemon, the biggest current security threat for GCC states emanates from Iran (Balzán, 2014), which is directly competing for hegemony with Saudi Arabia in proxy conflicts in Yemen, Syria, and Bahrain. Unless circumstances drastically change, such as a collapse of the Iranian regime or a large-scale military conflict between Iran and the United States, without the presence of the United States, there would be a clear regional imbalance in Iran's favor over the GCC countries.

One of the main reasons that the GCC remains vulnerable is that collective autonomous military defense, one of the purposes of the establishment of the GCC as an organization, remains an elusive goal (Legrenzi, 2011). Due to their inability to develop an independent security apparatus capable of taking on the substantial security challenges present in the region, all GCC states remain dependent on external actors to guarantee their defense (Al-Motairy, 2011). In filling this gap, the United States has effectively attained a hegemonic status over the region. With the presence of the US Central Command and large-scale military installations in Kuwait, Bahrain, Oman, the UAE, and Qatar (Committee on Foreign Relations, 2012), the United States is still deeply committed to the region militarily.

In terms of economic security, GCC economies are dangerously dependent on energy exports for their continued functioning. Despite extensive efforts by many GCC countries to diversify their economies into new sectors, their economic security remains at the mercy of prices dictated by global energy markets and potential impediments to trade from hostile regional actors. While diversification efforts remain underway, there is a consistent inflow of foreign capital from oil exports, averaging 79 percent of government revenue for GCC countries (Losman, 2010). This has generated requisite conditions for the adoption of the rentier state model, which demands the continual inflow of capital for its maintenance. From a regime perspective, the nature of this state model makes economic security as fundamentally important as military security since failing to continue lavish social spending undermines the basis of the established social contract (Ulrichsen, 2009).

These structural disadvantages afflicting the GCC states have historically been ameliorated through close military cooperation with the United States, as there is simply no other actor that is capable of guaranteeing the multi-dimensional aspects of security necessary for their survival. Even the current major importers of GCC energy, such as China, are effectively free riders equally dependent on the public good of regional security provided by the United States. Therefore, despite any differences GCC regimes may have with US foreign policy, they are structurally mandated to maintain close links with the United States for the present time.

What "retrenchment" has meant in practice towards the GCC

With these significant systemic structural features at play, retrenchment naturally marks a major change in policy. Though begun by the Obama administration, this trend of retrenchment from the Middle East is likely to continue for the foreseeable future and through the next administration due to both external factors and domestic sentiment. Barack Obama was elected promising a policy of reducing US military engagement in the region, though in practice the systemic elements of deconcentration have propelled the adoption of this policy as well. Unlike other areas of the Middle East where the Obama administration has been resolute in its effort to remain as aloof as possible, GCC countries are fundamentally different due to their role in the overall US Gulf security strategy. This means that disengagement cannot take place on the same scale as the withdrawal of military assets from other Middle East countries, such as Iraq, which are more peripheral to US interests. The United States clearly seeks to be unburdened from the intimate involvement it has historically held, but in a manner that does not compromise its interests or upset the existing balance of power.

Once the Obama administration took office in 2008, the size of US military bases within the GCC shrunk substantially (Degang, 2010), particularly due to the withdrawal from Iraq. By 2014, the total US troop numbers in the GCC states was in the range of 35,000, based on numbers available from open-source material (Burns, 2014), compared to the substantially higher figures during the Iraq War (Heritage Foundation, 2015). The politically sensitive nature of the bases makes exact figures difficult to obtain, but the trend of the Obama administration was one of stagnation and decline, though with a slight uptick beginning in 2013 in an effort to counter ISIS. There are no plans to substantially expand the military footprint of the United States in GCC states, and President Obama stated in 2015 that the current force levels are considered sufficient to handle any foreseeable situation (Obama, 2015). The main assets that are likely to endure are the Navy's Fifth Fleet in Bahrain and the al-Udeid Air Base in Qatar, as well as the bases in Kuwait and Oman; they represent the main mechanisms for power projection to the greater region, a necessity for reducing regional military assets elsewhere. Therefore, while the total regional military presence has lessened, the necessity of remaining "onshore" in this regard, even in a more limited capacity, will continue to be a crucial aspect of US strategy and will not be eliminated entirely (Simón, 2016). Considering these elements, the Obama administration has shown a clear preference for a lighter footprint.

The enormity of strategic interests means that the United States will remain committed to the maintenance of security of the GCC states even if the quantity of military assets dedicated on the ground is reduced in size. Previous military actions taken by the United States have proven the seriousness of its commitment to protecting its interests in the region, and the integrity of GCC states is effectively implied in protecting US regional interests. Decreasing levels of military commitment on paper should not be perceived as an indication of declining US interest. However, these relationships will, in all likelihood, stay at the level of strategic partnerships, lacking explicit articulation in a treaty arrangement. This is partially due to the inconvenient treaty process in US domestic politics and partially because the level of cooperation desired by the United States does not demand a formal treaty. Again, as history has proven, the current partnership arrangement has more than sufficed to weather regional conflicts and challenges.

The most important aspect in regards to developing a win-win retrenchment strategy towards the Gulf is for GCC countries to shoulder more of the costs associated with their own defense and the pursuit of security in their region. The Obama administration pushed for increased burden-sharing, asking GCC countries to contribute additional resources in joint regional endeavors (Liptak, 2016) while simultaneously upgrading their military capacities. In this manner, the United States can offset the costs of maintaining regional stability onto the pertinent actors without sacrificing the integrity of GCC security. CENTCOM's current regional security strategy relies heavily upon "Building Partner Capacity" as a mechanism of reducing dependence on US military assets (Lloyd, 2016, sec. Senate Armed Services Committee 38).

In order to foster a genuinely "regional" defense apparatus to reduce dependence on the current bilateral security arrangement status quo, the United States has advocated for a bloc-based approach to security through the GCC Peninsula Shield Force, the joint military force of the GCC states. The United States has sought to augment the coherence of this force by facilitating sales of arms to the GCC as a whole rather than the previous series of bilateral arms arrangements (Khan, 2014). US-provided security to the Gulf region as a whole has been prone to free riders, and this should at least partially alleviate this issue in the short term. Looking towards the future, with a more militarily cohesive collective GCC force, a greater level of military disengagement on the United States' part could become a feasible reality if the GCC manages to develop an effective military force capable of credibly deterring a potential hegemon. The United States can only do so much with these policies aimed at fostering security cooperation; the GCC has to complete the process of integration themselves. Whether they are capable of overcoming their internal divisions concerning their vision for regional security remains to be seen.

Points of contention as a result of retrenchment

The Obama administration's foreign policy approach to the Middle East generated a greater rift between the United States and GCC states, as some of these developments were perceived by GCC regimes as a decreasing level of commitment by the United States to their regional strategic interests. Obama administration officials, however, continued to tout their unwavering commitment to the security of GCC states through security guarantees and provision of weapons, such as a ballistic missile defense system (Burns, 2014). It is virtually inconceivable that the United States would abandon GCC states to their inferior position in the Gulf regional subsystem, considering the weight of US strategic interest in the security of Gulf oil transport routes and the role the GCC has in maintaining the status quo.

From the GCC perspective, however, the retrenchment of the Obama Doctrine made the United States appear as a fickle ally – while US policy on the Arabian Peninsula has remained static relative to its shifting policies on other regions of the world, the foreign policy of the Obama administration changed US policies in a manner deemed detrimental to GCC interests. Mohammed bin Salman opined in an interview with *The Economist* that "The United States must realize that they are the number one in the world and they have to act like it" (2016, n.p.). Based on systemic factors, however, and despite the altered posture of the United States in the Middle East under the Obama Doctrine, the Gulf region will remain a high priority for the United States. GCC countries are attempting to improve relations with alternative powers, such as China, as a mechanism to avoid putting all their eggs in one basket. Beyond the growing levels of bilateral Chinese-GCC trade, one example of diversification is the increasing arms sales from China to GCC countries (Gresh, 2016), a traditionally Western-dominated market. It is this potential for their interests to be sidelined, inherently stemming from the imbalanced and dependent relationship with the United States, that has generated an interest in developing closer ties with other major powers as a counterbalance to historical US hegemony in the region. While growing economic ties with alternative partners in this regard have flourished, no other power is willing to provide a replacement for the bloc's external security; indeed, no other power is capable.

Considering the scale of the commitment from the United States in this regard, concerns voiced by GCC leaders are less associated with direct security issues, revolving instead around growing differences in foreign policy approaches in the region. GCC regimes perceive many current US policies, ranging from warming relations with Iran to the administration's failure to act in Syria, as harmful to their interests. Even the perception of what constitutes a threat differs between the two sides: the primary approach of the United States to the security of the Gulf is through the prism of traditional military challenges, whereas GCC leaders perceive ideational challenges from rival political forces as a greater threat to their stability (Ulrichsen, 2009). These competing visions of what constitutes security make it difficult to reconcile the two sides.

Although it is clear that the United States remains the sole actor capable of guaranteeing the security of GCC countries and that it will continue to do so, there is a growing perception among the GCC monarchies that their interests and the interests of the United States are becoming increasingly misaligned. While it would be impossible for GCC states to emerge from underneath the US security umbrella in the present context, they would like to establish as much autonomy as possible within the existing security framework. GCC states increasingly seek to assert a foreign policy independent to that of Washington; indeed, in some cases, it appears to be in direct contradiction to the policies advocated by the US administration. The two parties' respective Iran policies represent a case in point: while the GCC states fear an ascendant Iran and have adopted confrontational rhetoric, the Obama administration actively pushed for rapprochement (Al-Shayji, 2014).

Where Iran represents a challenge in GCC-US relations

The current defrosting of bilateral relations between the United States and Iran is inextricably linked with GCC-US relations. Iran represents the only potentially viable hegemon in the Gulf region today, where it competes directly with the GCC countries. Regions, as opposed to inter-state competition on the systemic level, have a partially independent structure from both the systemic power structure and domestic political affairs (Lobell, 2009). Therefore, the influence of the United States plays a substantial role in such regional competition. Many regimes in the GCC consider an unconstrained Iran as an existential threat (Al-Shayji, 2014) and are hence predisposed to view the United States' relations with Iran and the GCC as a zero-sum game. Saudi leaders, in particular, are concerned that improved relations will eventually result in the United States recognizing Iran's dominant role in the Gulf (Mattair, 2007). In response to such criticism, Obama bluntly stated that GCC countries need to "share the neighborhood" with an ascendant Iran (Goldberg, 2016, n.p.).

The Iranian nuclear negotiations represented another visible application of the Obama Doctrine to the Gulf realm. Rather than engaging militarily, the Obama administration decided an offshore balancing technique, a dual-track strategy of engaging diplomatically while maintaining a credible threat of deterrence, was most prudent for handling the Iranian negotiations, with diplomacy being the preferred option (Layne, 2009). This appears to have paid off successfully in terms of achieving the aims vis-à-vis offshore balancing; that is, securing national interest objectives at the expense of fewer military resources. A secure regional framework involving the major regional parties would naturally require the least amount of investment by the United States.

However, as mentioned previously, the United States' key interest in the Gulf is to avoid the emergence of a regional hegemon. Going forward, even in the event of total normalization of bilateral Iran-US relations, the GCC would still act as the major counterbalance against Iran gaining hegemony in the Gulf. They remain collectively the most suitable candidate for the job. The GCC will continue to be an indispensable strategic partner for the United States regardless of any developments in the Iran-US relationship; therefore, relations with the United States are not necessarily a zero-sum game between the GCC and Iran, despite the fact that the GCC perceives it as such.

Even so, the GCC regimes continue to have deep-rooted beliefs that Iran is pursuing an agenda designed to establish its own hegemony over the entirety of the Gulf, which extends far beyond the nuclear issue. Indeed, they consider the United States' role in bringing Iran back into the international fold as nothing less than enabling Iranian regional expansion (Schmierer et al., 2016). Most GCC regimes have common political features that inherently foster hostilities towards the Islamic Republic on the opposite side of the Gulf, and the Iranian regime holds these same sentiments towards GCC regimes. Even though direct military threats from Iran towards the GCC are therefore a secondary concern, the nuclear program was the only aspect upon which the United States focused in the negotiations with Iran.

As a supporter of militant groups and opposition parties throughout the Arab world, Iran is perceived as a threat due to its efforts to prop up domestic opposition among GCC Shi'a minority populations (Shabaneh, 2015). The Bahraini uprising of 2011 was described as such by the Bahraini state. Additionally, Iran is actively engaged in proxy wars throughout the region from Syria to Yemen, with GCC regimes as their primary opposition proxy sponsors on the other side. Because of this, the United States, under the Obama administration, and GCC countries were working from substantially different scripts in how they perceived the nature of the Iranian threat, so cooperation in this regard was difficult. Finding an arrangement where the GCC would feel secure, despite an Iran-US rapprochement, would require going further than merely committing additional military forces. From a purely military perspective, the current balance of power should be more than acceptable to GCC countries; Iran is nowhere close to being an overwhelmingly dominant force in the Gulf (Cordesman, 2015). Despite the rhetoric coming from the Trump administration, GCC countries are hesitant to roll back the Iranian nuclear deal given the potential regional instability it would cause. Therefore, the respective Iran policies of the two parties remain allied, yet distinct.

The Trump administration has displayed a marked adherence to the GCC perspective regarding Iran, as particularly expressed in his 2017 speech to the Arab American Islamic Summit in Riyadh (Trump, 2017). The new administration's policy towards the nuclear deal itself has initially appeared negative, though there does not appear to be any immediate momentum towards annulling it. The multilateral nature of the deal itself, however, makes it impossible for the United States to unilaterally reinstate the status quo ante;

the other involved global powers, such as the EU, Russia, and China, will undoubtedly continue their development of bilateral relations. For the time being, however, the United States has come more into alignment with the zero-sum perspective of the GCC countries and abandoned the pragmatism of the Obama Doctrine.

US policy regarding regime security

The nature of the GCC regimes has fused the concepts of regime security and state security (Ulrichsen, 2009). One of the GCC states' key priorities is the continuity of the existing political power structures. Development and reform, even limited political reform, is recognized as an eventual necessity by GCC regimes, but only without threatening the political structure currently in place (Pollack, 2003). Suppressing any existential threats to the existing regime structure is considered a shared responsibility among the GCC states themselves; the Bahraini uprising of 2011 and the subsequent intervention of the GCC Peninsula Shield Force demonstrated the concern that a threat to the political stability of one member nation was a threat to the political stability of all.

The United States feels the need to offer supportive rhetoric to democratically inclined movements within GCC countries, but consistently maintains significant reservations. Domestic pressures within the country demand that the United States, at the very least, publicly praises liberal reform movements in the Middle East, though the actual interests of the United States may not be served by them (Committee on Foreign Relations, 2012). Regardless, GCC states, particularly Saudi Arabia, have come to the conclusion that the United States cannot always be considered a stalwart supporter of the status quo (Kamrava, 2012). This perceived threat, and the relatively muted US response, engendered a great deal of anxiety for GCC monarchies in similar positions; if they were to be faced with similar situations, how would the United States respond? The United States' abandonment of other Arab regimes, such as the Mubarak regime in Egypt, only further reinforced this perception. Generally, however, the United States is distinctly in support of the political structures currently in place. In the case of the current Yemeni conflict, for example, the United States has quietly permitted the Saudi intervention in order to support the internationally recognized government, despite the human toll. While the United States has concerns regarding the nature of monarchies in the GCC, sudden regime change, similar to the case of the Iranian Revolution, would be disastrous to the US position in the region. Such regime change would likely bring into power forces that are distinctly antipathetic towards the United States and, thus, would be a significant blow to US interests (Pollack, 2003). Given the continuing antipathy against the Iranian regime, momentarily tempered by the Obama administration but revitalized by the Trump administration, this perception has not changed. As such, the United States did not and does not view wholesale political liberalization towards democracy within GCC countries as inherently positive.

While it is a tangential aspect of the overall nature of the relationship, an interesting point worth noting is that GCC states have attempted to utilize their economic clout to influence US policy through lobbying operations, with mixed results. It is difficult to speak of a "GCC lobby" or even an "Arab lobby," because their actions have been largely sporadic, uncoordinated, and lacking in any grand strategy (D. K. Khatib, 2016). Lobbying from GCC countries tends to be conducted in a bilateral fashion rather than on behalf of the GCC as a whole. Substantial sums have been invested into lobbying operations in efforts to shift US foreign policy. The UAE, for example, ranked first in terms of overall spending on lobbying operations by foreign countries in 2014, and Saudi Arabia ranked fourth (Itkowitz, 2014). They have histori-cally been successful in achieving short-term tactical gains (for example, the acquisition of advanced weapons systems such as the F-15 fighter jet and AWACS), but in terms of fostering a major shift in the nature of US foreign policy towards a more sympathetic posture, these efforts have been ineffective (Koleilat, 2014).

However, in essence, the lack of an active Arab voting bloc within the United States on the same level as other politically active domestic con-stituencies, such as the American Armenian or the American Jewish popula-tions, generates obstacles in any attempt to seriously alter the course of US policy (Koleilat, 2014). Additionally, political-cultural differences make the process of lobbying in the United States rather incomprehensible to GCC regimes, who are more inclined to spend lavishly on big-name lobbying firms rather than working to develop a grassroots apparatus within the United States. Due to the general lack of efficacy of such lobbying operations, evident with the passage of the 2016 bill permitting legal action against Saudi Arabia in response to the September 11 attacks (Slack and Tumulty, 2016), GCC lobbying does not present a major factor in the formulation of US policy towards the region.

Conclusion

The Gulf remains dominated by the United States and relations are still cordial, but the changing nature of the US global posture brought about by the Obama Doctrine has had a substantial impact on the GCC-US dynamic. Retrenchment in the Middle East was one of this policy's cornerstones, and the Obama administration explicitly stated the United States' intent was to partially disengage from the Middle East in its "pivot to Asia." Viewing the recent US conflicts in the Middle East as damaging failures, there is little appetite left in the United States for expanding the American presence in the region. Though the Trump administration has offered little clarity regarding its own Gulf policy, apart from an antipathy towards the Iranian regime, this path of reducing US involvement in Middle Eastern affairs may have become an irreversible trend, as the unilateral use of US hard power in the Middle East no longer appears beneficial.

Even if the United States retreats from its commitments in more peripheral areas of the Middle East, structural factors mandate that the United States and GCC retain close cooperation; the Gulf region is one of the United States' top priorities due to the ongoing conflicts in Syria and Yemen and its continued support to such allies as Israel and Jordan. Moreover, the importance of the GCC to global energy markets, and therefore the entire global economy, cannot be overtaken by any other bloc. Unless a massive systemic shift in the dynamics of energy consumption takes place on a global scale, the GCC will retain this role and thus its importance in US grand strategy. Additionally, the GCC is the only viable counterweight against an Iran with hegemonic ambitions and therefore will continue to play a crucial role in US regional policy.

For the GCC, the United States is the only actor capable of fulfilling its external security needs. GCC countries remain wholly reliant on external security guarantees in a complex security environment. Even with declining US interest and a desire for increased policy autonomy on the part of GCC countries, they remain unable to achieve any real measure of security independence. Each GCC state will have to rely upon their own bilateral security arrangements with the United States, as their military capabilities remain ill-equipped to handle the challenges they face. A successful US retrenchment would augment existing capabilities, and there is a clear indication that the United States is attempting to do so. Considering these elements, the long-standing shared interests between the US and the GCC cannot be denied, and these factors will continue to justify the relatively close relationships between the United States and GCC countries. However, relations confronted a turning point towards the end of the Obama administration and could face further decline under the Trump administration as well.

Notes

1 The Gulf Cooperation Council, formed in 1981, is currently composed of Bahrain, Kuwait, Oman, Qatar, Saudi Arabia, and the United Arab Emirates.
2 The term "Persian Gulf OPEC" countries as used by the EIA are all GCC members as well (Saudi Arabia, Kuwait, UAE, and Qatar) with the exception of Iraq, which is also included in this calculation.

References

Al-Barasneh, A.S. (2015, November 18). *United States foreign policy towards the Gulf Cooperation Council Countries (GCC) 2001–2008: Searching for stable security framework*. PhD Thesis, University of Leicester, Leicester, England. Retrieved from https://lra.le.ac.uk/handle/2381/35931.

Allin, D.H. and Jones, E. (2012). Barack Obama and the limits of superpower. *Adelphi Series*, 52(430–431), 71–110. doi:10.1080/19445571.2012.701969.

Al-Motairy, S.F. (2011). *The Gulf Cooperation Council and the challenges of establishing an integrated capability for upholding security*. Master's thesis, Naval Postgraduate School. DTIC Document.

Al-Shayji, A. (2014). The GCC-US relationship: A GCC perspective. *Middle East Policy*, 21(3), 60–70. doi:10.1111/mepo.12082.

Balzán, C. (2014, April 10). *Security cooperation in the GCC: Challenges and opportunities. Capstone Working Paper*, Florida International University. Retrieved from http://maga.fiu.edu/program/capstone-project/2014-capstone-working-papers/dia-fin al_gcc_balzan_edited_dawndavies.pdf.

Burns, W. (2014). A renewed agenda for US-Gulf partnership. Presented at the Manama Dialogue, Bahrain, February 19. Retrieved from www.state.gov/s/d/form er/burns/remarks/2014/221809.htm.

Committee on Foreign Relations. (2012). *The Gulf Security architecture: The partnership with the Gulf Cooperation Council*. Washington, DC: United States Congress.

Cordesman, A.H. (2015). *The Arab-US strategic partnership and the changing security balance in the Gulf: Joint and asymmetric warfare, missiles and missile defense, civil war and non-state actors, and outside powers*. Lanham, MD: Rowman and Littlefield. Retrieved from https://csis-prod.s3.amazonaws.com/s3fs-public/legacy_files/files/public ation/151014_Cordesman_ArabUSStrategicPartnership_Web.pdf.

Degang, S. (2010). The US military bases in the Gulf Cooperation Council states: Dynamic of readjustment. *Journal of Middle Eastern and Islamic Studies (in Asia)*, 4(4), 44–63.

The Economist. (2016, January 6). Transcript: Interview with Muhammad bin Salman. Retrieved from www.economist.com/saudi_interview.

Eisenstadt, M., McInnis, J. M., Weinberg, A. and Katzman, K. (2015, July 9). *The Gulf Cooperation Council Camp David Summit: Any results? § Foreign Affairs*. Washington, DC: US Government Publishing Office. Retrieved from https://foreign affairs.house.gov/hearing/subcommittee-hearing-the-gulf-cooperation-council-camp-david-summit-any-results/.

Fasano, U. and Iqbal, Z. (2003). *GCC countries: From oil dependence to diversification*. Washington, DC: International Monetary Fund.

Flournoy, M. and Davidson, J. (2012). Obama's new global posture: The logic of US foreign deployments. *Foreign Affairs*, 91(4), 54–63.

Goldberg, J. (2016, April). The Obama Doctrine. *The Atlantic*. Retrieved from www.th eatlantic.com/magazine/archive/2016/04/the-obama-doctrine/471525/?utm_source=S FTwitter.

Gresh, G.F. (2016). The Gulf looks East. *Sociology of Islam*, 4(1–2), 149–165. doi:10.1 163/22131418-00402003.

Haass, R.N. (2008). The age of nonpolarity: What will follow US dominance. *Foreign Affairs*, 87(3), 44–56.

Heritage Foundation. (2015). *2015 Index of US Military Strength*. Washington, DC. Retrieved from http://index.heritage.org/military/2015/chapter/op-environment/midd le-east/.

Itkowitz, C. (2014, May 14). Which foreign countries spent the most to influence US politics? *Washington Post*. Retrieved from https://www.washingtonpost.com/blogs/ in-the-loop/wp/2014/05/14/which-foreign-countries-spent-the-most-to-influence-u-s-p olitics/.

Kamrava, M. (2012). The Arab Spring and the Saudi-led counterrevolution. *Orbis*, 56 (1), 96–104. doi:10.1016/j.orbis.2011.10.011.

Karzai, H. (2013, December 12). Transcript of interview by President Karzai with French Daily Le Monde Newspaper. Retrieved from http://president.gov.af/en/news/ transcript-of-interview-by-president-karzai-with-french-daily-le-monde-newspaper.

Khan, T. (2014, May 14). Hagel in Saudi to push for more GCC security cooperation. *The National*. Retrieved from www.thenational.ae/world/hagel-in-saudi-to-push-for-more-gcc-security-cooperation.

Khatib, D.K. (2016). Arab Gulf lobbying in the United States: What makes them win and what makes them lose and why? *Contemporary Arab Affairs*, 9(1), 68–81. doi:10.1080/17550912.2015.1121647.

Khatib, L. (2013). Qatar's foreign policy: The limits of pragmatism. *International Affairs*, 89(2), 417–431. doi:10.1111/1468-2346.12025.

Klare, M.T. (2006). Oil, Iraq, and American foreign policy: The continuing salience of the Carter Doctrine. *International Journal*, 62(1), 31–42. doi:10.2307/40204243.

Kohut, A. (2013, July 11). *American international engagement on the rocks*. Washington, DC: Pew Research Center. Retrieved from www.pewglobal.org/2013/07/11/american-international-engagement-on-the-rocks/.

Koleilat, D.N.K. (2014, March 24). *Aspects of Arab lobbying: Factors for winning and factors for losing*. Doctoral thesis, Exeter University, Exeter, England. Retrieved from https://ore.exeter.ac.uk/repository/handle/10871/15658.

Kuniholm, B.R. (1986). The Carter Doctrine, the Reagan Corollary, and prospects for United States policy in Southwest Asia. *International Journal*, 41(2), 342–361. doi:10.2307/40202373.

Layne, C. (1997). From preponderance to offshore balancing: America's future grand strategy. *International Security*, 22(1), 86–124. doi:10.2307/2539331.

Layne, C. (2007). Who lost Iraq and why it matters: The case for offshore balancing. *World Policy Journal*, 24(3), 38–52. doi:10.1162/wopj.2007.24.3.38.

Layne, C. (2009). America's Middle East grand strategy after Iraq: The moment for offshore balancing has arrived. *Review of International Studies*, 35(1), 5–25. doi:10.1017/S0260210509008304.

Lefebvre, J.A. (2003). US military hegemony in the Arabian/Persian Gulf: How long can it last? *International Studies Perspectives*, 4(2), 186–190. doi:10.1111/1528-3577.402007.

Legrenzi, M. (2011). The GCC in light of international relations theory. In *The GCC and the international relations of the Gulf: Diplomacy, security and economic coordination in a changing Middle East* (pp. 41–56). London: I.B. Tauris.

Liptak, K. (2016, April 21). Obama looks for Gulf leaders to step up. *CNN*. Retrieved from www.cnn.com/2016/04/21/politics/obama-saudi-visit/index.html.

Lloyd, A. (2016, March 8). The posture of US Central Command § Senate Armed Services Committee. Retrieved from www.armed-services.senate.gov/imo/media/doc/Austin_03-08-16.pdf.

Lobell, S.E. (2009). Threat assessment, the state, and foreign policy: A neoclassical realist model. In S.E. Lobell, N.M. Ripsman, and J.W. Taliaferro (Eds.), *Neoclassical realism, the state, and foreign policy* (pp. 42–74). Cambridge: Cambridge University Press.

Losman, D.L. (2010). The rentier state and national oil companies: An economic and political perspective. *The Middle East Journal*, 64(3), 427–445. doi:10.3751/64.3.15.

Mattair, T.R. (2007). Mutual threat perceptions in the Arab/Persian Gulf: GCC perceptions. *Middle East Policy*, 14(2), 133–140. doi:10.1111/j.1475-4967.2007.00304.x.

Mearsheimer, J.J. and Walt, S.M. (2016). The case for offshore balancing: A superior US grand strategy. *Foreign Affairs*, 95(4), 70–83.

Neff, S. and Coleman, M. (2014). EIA outlook: Reversal in US oil import dependency. *Energy Strategy Reviews*, 5, 6–13. doi:10.1016/j.esr.2014.10.007.

Obama, B. (2013, September). Remarks by President Obama in address to the United Nations General Assembly. Retrieved from https://www.whitehouse.gov/the-press-office/2013/09/24/remarks-president-obama-address-united-nations-general-assembly.

Obama, B. (2015, May 15). US President Barack Obama in an exclusive interview with Al Arabiya. *Al Arabiya Network*. Retrieved from http://ara.tv/83wb9.

Parent, J.M. and MacDonald, P.K. (2011). The wisdom of retrenchment: America must cut back to move forward. *Foreign Affairs*, 90(6), 32–47.

Pollack, K.M. (2003). Securing the Gulf. *Foreign Affairs*, 82(4), 2–16.

Sager, A. (2013, March 29). Whither GCC-US relations? *Arab News*. Retrieved from www.arabnews.com/news/446395.

Sartori, N. (2014). Geopolitical implications of the US unconventional energy revolution. *The International Spectator*, 49(2), 66–82. doi:10.1080/03932729.2014.906955.

Schmierer, R.J., Jeffrey, J.F., Nader, A. and Nazer, F. (2016). The Saudi-Iranian rivalry and the Obama Doctrine. *Middle East Policy*, 23(2), 5–30. doi:10.1111/mepo.12192.

Schweller, R.L. (2010). Entropy and the trajectory of world politics: Why polarity has become less meaningful. *Cambridge Review of International Affairs*, 23(1), 145–163. doi:10.1080/09557570903456374.

Shabaneh, G. (2015). *The implications of a nuclear deal with Iran on the GCC, China, and Russia*. Doha, Qatar: Al Jazeera Center for Studies. Retrieved from http://studies.aljazeera.net/mritems/Documents/2015/6/14/20156148505316734Iran.pdf.

Simón, L. (2016). Seapower and US forward presence in the Middle East: Retrenchment in perspective. *Geopolitics*, 21(1), 115–147. doi:10.1080/14650045.2015.1085382.

Slack, D. and Tumulty, B.J. (2016, September 28). Congress rejects Obama veto of 9/11 bill; first override of his presidency. *USA Today*. Retrieved from https://www.usatoday.com/story/news/politics/2016/09/28/senate-poised-override-obama-veto-911-bill-allowing-saudi-suits/91184976/.

Snyder, G.H. (1984). The security dilemma in alliance politics. *World Politics*, 36(4), 461–495. doi:10.2307/2010183.

Stepak, A. and Whitlark, R. (2012). The battle over America's foreign policy doctrine. *Survival*, 54(5), 45–66. doi:10.1080/00396338.2012.728344.

Trump, D. (2017, May). Full transcript: Trump's speech to the Arab Islamic American Summit, Riyadh. Retrieved from http://politi.co/2pZwiRN.

Ulrichsen, K.C. (2009). *Gulf security: Changing internal and external dynamics*. London, England: Center for the Study of Global Governance. Retrieved from https://www.lse.ac.uk/collections/LSEKP/documents/Ulrichsen%20report%2012.5.09.pdf.

Xianlin, Shu. (2013). The United States' strategy toward the Middle East oil and China's energy security. In Yang Guang (Ed.), Liu Maomin and Michelle Wan (Trans.), *China-Middle East relations: Review and analysis* (Vol. 1, pp. 38–50). Reading: Paths International Ltd.

Yergin, D. (2014, January 8). The global impact of US shale. *Project Syndicate*. Retrieved from https://www.project-syndicate.org/commentary/daniel-yergin-traces-the-effects-of-america-s-shale-energy-revolution-on-the-balance-of-global-economic-and-political-power.

Part IV
Rapid Political Change and the Spread of Regional Instability

10 When partisanship displaced strategy
American foreign policy and war in Iraq

Russell A. Burgos

> Iraq has for such a long time taken its political direction from one man. His elimination from the political scene in one form or another might create a vacuum which could be exploited by extremist forces.
>
> *Political Instability in Iraq*, Department of State, Bureau of Intelligence Research, Report 5782.1 (April 1952)

> Once you've got Baghdad, it's not clear what you do with it.
>
> Dick Cheney, Secretary of Defense (April 1991)

Reviewing the draft Middle East policy of the new John F. Kennedy administration, Robert B. Elwood of the State Department's Bureau of Intelligence and Research (INR) revised language in the section on military strategy for the region: "In the event of disturbances threatening a Communist takeover in Iraq," he suggested, the United States must "be prepared in concert with UK or with anti-Communist Arab element, or if necessary unilaterally, etc." (Elwood, 1961). The "etc." referred to language about military intervention for regime change in Baghdad. Having accepted the notion that Iraq was a key member of the so-called "Northern Tier" – front-line states along the southern border of the Soviet Union – for most of the decade, policymakers and strategists in Washington were caught off guard by Iraq's July 1958 revolution. Because they had long feared that local Communist "fifth columns" would undermine Western-oriented regimes in the Gulf region, from the moment reports of the revolution arrived in Washington, many assumed the coup d'état signaled the creation of a "Cairo-Damascus-Baghdad-Moscow axis" ("Relations with Iraq," 1958). As had been the case with other nominally pro-American regimes (like Batista's in Havana and Somoza's in Managua), officials in Washington tended to assume that Iraqi political stability would be an inevitable consequence of a "pro-Western" orientation – despite the fact that within the living memories of those officials there had already been three violent coups in Iraq and over fourty changes of prime minister alone in the three decades since independence.

As was the case throughout the developing world, American policymakers of this era tended to view the Middle East and Gulf region through the lens of the Cold War. What mattered to Washington generally had less to do with the internal dynamics of Arab governance than it did with what those dynamics might mean for the strategic position of the United States. In the case of Iraq, it was an article of faith in Washington that the Soviet Union had strategic designs on the Gulf. In 1956, one of the country's early "Sovietologists," Herbert J. Ellison, warned darkly that there could be no doubt "Soviet Russia is making a bid to take Britain's place as protector of the Middle East," offering as proof passages in a transcript from negotiations between the Nazi and Soviet foreign ministries that seemed to suggest Berlin would accept what were vaguely defined as "Soviet aspirations" in the "general direction of the Persian Gulf" (Ellison, 1956; Sontag and Beddie, 1994). Though no one really knew what "aspirations" or "general direction" actually meant in context to either the Nazi or Soviet officials involved (or whether, in fact, either the Germans or the Soviets took the Tripartite Pact seriously), given the period, it seemed the safest course of action was to assume the worst – something American officials from both political parties were more than willing to do.

Within hours of the coup, American officials were trying to fit coup leader Brigadier 'Abd al-Karim Qásim into a familiar mold: was he "another Nasser" or simply a Communist stooge? There were voices for moderation both outside and inside the government; for example, *The New York Times* opined that the United States need not treat a nationalist coup as being, by definition, a Communist threat, and the Central Intelligence Agency argued that the goals of even "radical" Arab nationalists did not have to be thought of as being inevitably "in conflict with US interests" ("Relations in Iraq," 1958; Central Intelligence Agency, 1993). Yet instead of analyzing the 1958 revolution on its own merits and approaching the Qásim regime accordingly, American officials defaulted to the most malign interpretation possible of the implications of his rule and fell back on a familiar policy response – ousting a foreign head of state (Burgos, 2005). Little wonder, then, that the United States started assessing prospects for regime change in Iraq: if the "problem" was the leader, then the "solution" was perforce removing the leader (Wolfe-Hunnicutt, 2015). Iraq's July revolution was a "problem" only to the extent that it (allegedly) involved the Soviets – the details of how Iraqi politics were brought to the brink of revolution, and then carried over it, were of little consequence. From the administration's point of view, what was important about the July revolution was its implications for America – little attention was paid to its implications for Iraq itself. This has been a pattern in American foreign relations with Iraq almost from the moment they began in the late nineteenth century when Mesopotamia was still part of the Ottoman Empire. Rather than engage with Iraqi issues on their own merits, American diplomats and, later, American strategists have tried to "fit" Iraq into some wider context that generally had little to do with Iraq itself. For most of the twentieth century, that wider context reflected the contours of the Cold War. However, at the end of the Cold War, Iraq policy increasingly became a partisan issue rather than a strategic one.

The politics of foreign policy

In this chapter I argue that Iraq policy is an example of an accelerating – and pernicious – trend in American foreign policy in which American interests are increasingly defined in narrowly partisan terms for narrowly partisan gains. In other words, the "meaning" of the Iraq problem (and many others in foreign policy) is increasingly defined in terms of party politics and not in terms of divergent understandings of appropriate uses of American power. All else equal, one expects partisan debate over foreign policy in a democracy; what has changed is the substance of those debates. Indeed, there is a great deal of literature on the domestic determinants of foreign policy (Gourevitch, 2002). What is changing is the partisan quality associated with domestic influences on foreign policy. In effect, foreign policy has been transformed into domestic policy. Not only does politics not "stop at the water's edge," but there is no edge: at home or abroad, policy is subjected to a partisan litmus test. Here I look only at two periods in American policy towards Iraq: 1998 and 2002–2004. I argue that American foreign policy towards Iraq was co-opted by partisan politics and that Bush administration policies in Iraq were shaped as much by the "facts on the ground" in American electoral politics as they were by the military "facts on the ground" in Iraq. I further contend that when the partisan facts of the war proved more troubling to the Bush administration than the strategic-military ones, Iraq policy was subordinated to partisan and not strategic needs. In essence, the entire trajectory of the Iraq War can be defined in partisan terms, from the politics of getting into the war (2002–2004) to the politics of managing the war (2004–2007) to the politics of getting out of the war (2008–2011). In each phase, the "national interest" was essentially defined in terms synonymous with the president's narrow partisan interests.

The "national interest" has long been a contested term in International Relations, and there is general agreement in the literature that it has always been less a matter of objective evaluation than structural theories would have one believe (Burchill, 2005). My focus here is on the *way* in which national interests are defined. While I accept the Realist premise that strategists and central decision-makers act in accordance with what they take to be American national interests, I am also sympathetic to the Constructivist premise that the *substance* of those interests – the meanings and significance that are attached to them – will vary depending upon who those central decision-makers are. Unlike political psychology scholars interested in the cognitive processes and idiosyncrasies of specific policymakers (Larson, 1989, 2000; Renshon, 2003), I am interested in the partisan political context in which interests are defined. In other words, I believe that policymakers act on endogenous, subjectively defined "interests" *as if* they were exogenous and objectively defined. Moreover, I believe that specific policy choices do not necessarily follow from specific "interests" – what matters is how the interest is defined and by whom. For example, Democrats and Republicans alike agree that national survival is an "interest," but the substance of ensuring that survival can vary greatly depending upon both the distribution of power in the international system and the specific configuration of government at the time.

Even during the period of the so-called "Cold War consensus," politics influenced American national security and foreign policy, often to the frustration of policymakers themselves. As President Harry S. Truman put it in 1948, "foreign policy should be the policy of the whole nation and not the policy of one party or other – partisanship should stop at water's edge" (quoted in Smith, 1999, p. 1). Were it not for the fact that partisanship did not stop at water's edge, of course, Truman would not have found it necessary to say so. For example, Robert F. Kennedy's actions during the Cuban Missile Crisis – especially his rejection of the preemptive air strike proposed by Air Force Chief of Staff Curtis LeMay – was surely influenced by concern for the political fortunes of his brother (Allison and Zelikow, 1999). President Harry S. Truman's Korea policies – particularly his firing of General Douglas A. MacArthur – met with partisan rancor, and Congressional activism at the end of the war in Vietnam constrained President Gerald Ford's ability to respond to events in South Vietnam and Cambodia. There is a growing literature on the "politicization" of foreign policy both in the United States and internationally. Much of this literature emphasizes the institutional determinants of foreign policy, the domestic impact of international policies on domestic politics, and the impact of public opinion on foreign policy choices (Holsti, 2011; McCright and Dunlap, 2011; Rixen and Zangl, 2013; Hurst and Wroe, 2016).

However, the mythology of the water's edge persists. In 2012, for example, The Chicago Council on Global Affairs claimed that the foreign policy preferences of "Democrats and Republicans are very similar" (p. 41), and political scientists Joshua Busby, Jonathan Monten, and William Inboden (2012) claimed that "American foreign policy is already post-partisan" and that differences between Democrats and Republicans are exaggerated. Peter Gries (2014) rejected the "water's edge" hypothesis and, using survey data, argued that "liberals and conservatives maintain consistent – if consistently different – international attitudes and foreign policy preferences" (p. 265). Similarly, Verlan Lewis (2017) has argued elites' views about military intervention flip depending upon whether or not their co-partisans control the White House. Thomas Alan Schwartz (2009) argued persuasively that "domestic partisan politics, the struggle for power at home, has played ... a substantial role in the making and direction of American foreign policy" (p. 173). However, even that literature tends to focus on ideological influences on foreign policy preferences, such as disagreements over climate change policy (McCright and Dunlap, 2011). My argument here is that partisanship directly influences the execution of foreign policy. Where the United States confronts ambiguous or ill-defined strategic challenges, ambiguity creates a space for ever more idiosyncratic (that is, ever more partisan) definitions of American national interests and, therefore, idiosyncratic preferences in policy responses. For much of the US-Iraqi foreign relationship, this has taken the form of an inchoate set of reactions guided by political necessity rather than strategic desirability.

Over the course of the twentieth century, the "Iraq problem" gradually moved from the periphery to the core of America's strategic agenda. With little for the United States to draw upon in the way of preexisting consensus about what Iraq "meant," foreign policy towards Iraq was either reactionary or hijacked by narrower partisan considerations. In the Gulf region as a whole, American foreign policy has been characterized by a lack of "self-awareness" (Bacevich, 2016) and a conspicuous "absence of grand strategy" (Yetiv, 2008). Like much of its Middle East policy, America's foreign relationship with Iraq has involved a series of short-term, triage policies intended to fix *a* problem today rather than address *the* problem for tomorrow. In other words, there has not been an overarching framework for US-Iraqi foreign relations. For instance, if we consider the Reagan administration's short-lived "tilt" towards Iraq or the Clinton administration's policy of "dual containment" (Jentleson, 1994; Haley, 2006), in both cases, the policies were intended to address a problem "now," rather than to set the scope and boundary conditions for a strategic interaction over time. As Yetiv (2008) put it, American strategy towards Iraq has been one of "reactive engagement" that has not been "governed by ... interests" so much as it has been "driven by events" (pp. 193–194). Due in part to the fragmentation of the media-information market in American politics and the ever-accelerating news and information cycle, day-to-day "events" increasingly overdetermine policy responses. In effect, Iraq-as-security-problem gave way to Iraq-as-political-problem. As a result, long-term strategic policymaking takes a back seat to short-term partisan needs.

Decisions about Iraq during both the George W. Bush and Barack Obama presidencies were dominated by a political (that is, partisan) need to achieve something "now." There is ample evidence that both presidents were aware of the complexities of domestic Iraqi politics as well as Iraq's position within the Gulf regional balance of power; National Security Adviser Condoleezza Rice, for example, hoped to use the issue of the Mujahadin e-Khalk (MEK), an anti-Iranian terrorist organization, as leverage to get the Islamic Republic of Iran to interdict al-Qaeda fighters (Gordon and Trainor, 2013, p. 45). Nevertheless, there is comparatively little evidence available to date that suggests strategic issues were not subordinated to partisan ones. Rather than define a grand strategy or even what Terry Deibel (2007) has called a "foreign affairs strategy" for the US relationship with Iraq, American policymakers backed their way into a series of short-term reactions in the hope of partisan, rather than strategic, payoffs. Deibel defined foreign affairs strategy as "an intellectual activity that takes place in the minds of people who are determined to influence ... the direction of the nation's foreign relations" (p. 24). It should involve "the conscious coordination, orchestration, and control of all the instruments of statecraft" given a clearly defined understanding of the strategic problem (p. 24). Yet outside of the framework of military-to-military relations, there is still little evidence that either the Bush or Obama administrations conceived of the long-term US-Iraqi strategic interaction in terms more specific than lists of general desiderata. Even now, it remains unclear how (or if) the Trump administration has defined Iraq's place within the wider contours of near- and mid-term American foreign policy. In the absence of such clarity, Iraq policy becomes a domain of political contest – as Deibel (2007) put it, "a seemingly endless struggle" among political actors to make their preferences "determine the statements and actions – the policies – of the government" (pp. 10–11).

There is a vast literature on the Iraq War. In his 2011 book, *Vortex of Conflict*, Pepperdine University Professor Dan Caldwell included in an appendix a select bibliography of Iraq War literature that ran for 27 pages, excluding publications after 2009. On the American experience alone, the literature comprises every form of writing imaginable – from poetry and fiction to the memoirs of politicians, military leaders, aid workers, and rank-and-file troops; from polemics and partisan critiques (Gardner and Young, 2007; Bacevich, 2016) to intensely detailed insider and day-by-day "tick-tock" accounts of the White House, the Coalition Provisional Authority, and almost every level of military organization from corps down to squad (Woodward, 2004, 2011; Chandrasekaran, 2007; Gordon and Trainor, 2007, 2013; Dobbins, Jones, Runkle, and Mohandas, 2009) to official military histories and fine-grained security studies (Cordesman, 2003; Keegan, 2005; Fontenot, Degen, and Tohn, 2004; Wright and Reese, 2008) and a growing scholarly literature on the politics of the war (Burgos, 2008; Caldwell, 2011; Holsti, 2011; Hooker and Collins, 2015; Mintz and Wayne, 2016).

My goal here is a modest one: to show that Iraq policymaking was politicized (that is, made partisan) and that partisan considerations drove key points in the decision-making for the war – indeed, that even at the operational level, the war was conceived of in partisan terms, especially where reconstruction was concerned. Given the limitations of space, I focus on two periods and two presidents: President William J. Clinton during 1998 over the signing of the Iraq Liberation Act; and President George W. Bush from the invasion of Iraq to the transfer of sovereignty in 2004. I center my discussions on the way the Iraq problem was defined in 1998, 2002–2003, and 2004, and show how the framing of the problem was partisan rather than strategic. In the next section, I briefly review the scope of US-Iraqi foreign relations prior to the Persian Gulf wars. I then discuss the partisan politics of the Iraq Liberation Act, the road to war in 2002–2003, and the invasion and first year of occupation. The chapter then concludes with suggestions for further research.

The United States and Iraq before the Persian Gulf wars

Scholarship in the past twenty years has refined understanding of pre-World War II American policy in the then Near East, contradicting earlier studies that posited limited or no systematic contact between the United States and the region; in fact, there have been Arab-American relations since the founding of the republic (Lenczowski, 1968; Badeau, 1968; Field, 1969; Baram, 1978; Oren, 2008). It is more accurate to describe the United States as having no significant *military-strategic interests* in the Middle East prior to the Cold War. Prior to the end of World War II, America's regional engagement was commercial, cultural, and philanthropic (Tejirian and Simon, 2012). To the extent that there was a Near East foreign policy, it was derivative of the broader American interest in the Open Door and was almost exclusively the purview of the State Department; with few exceptions, events in the Middle East seldom rose to the level of presidential politics (Baram, 1978; Samuel, 2014).

The Open Door dispute over Iraqi oil is well documented in the literature (Earle, 1924; DeNovo, 1956; Stivers, 1981), though it is important to note that the oil itself was largely incidental to the policy dispute; because the Iraqi oil industry was in its infancy and the United States was a net exporter, America's grievance with Britain over the Red Line Agreement centered less on oil than it did on the perception that Britain was engaged in unfair commercial practices. The Department of State insisted upon defending the principle that the United States would be treated according to a most favored nation status, even within a British sphere of influence, in recognition of its new status as a great power. Indeed, there were other economic disputes during the 1920s and 1930s, all of which shared the same basic issues; by virtue of its special relationship with Britain, Iraqi markets treated American entrepreneurs as having what was, from the US point of view, second-class status. Whether it was energy or rail concessions or trade in Singer sewing machines, the State Department insisted upon fair – that is, equal – treatment for American business (Earle, 1924; Martin, 1925). However, in aggregate, the overall level of US-Iraqi trade was comparatively low, though the United States ran a trade deficit with Iraq until 1940 because Iraq imported comparatively few finished American goods while the United States imported comparatively large amounts of raw agricultural goods – specifically dates, licorice, and casings (sheep's intestines for the making of sausage). It is important to note even at this early stage in US-Iraqi relations, policy controversies were not about Iraq per se – they were about Great Britain and the changing global balance of power occasioned by America's emergence as a great power.

Just as World War II changed the institutional structure of American foreign policymaking, it also pulled Iraq from the periphery to the core of US strategic concerns. The brief Anglo-Iraqi War of 1941 called attention to the threat hostile powers (in that case, Nazi Germany and a putatively sympathetic Iraqi regime) posed to Britain's regional position in the Gulf (Lyman, 2006). Though it was the second Iraqi military coup d'état, the 1941 coup was the first to highlight the strategic dangers posed by "radical" regimes to regional stability and to the stability of the British oil supply from Iran. Likewise, the Anglo-American occupation of southern Iraq and Anglo-American-Soviet occupation of Iran during World War II, when the American-led Persian Gulf Command transferred Lend-Lease supplies to the Soviet southern border, called strategists' attention to the usefulness of Gulf bases for reaching the oil-producing and industrial regions of the Soviet Union, most of which were in the south (Motter, 1952). If one could supply the USSR from the south, one could also attack it from the south.

World War II taught American policymakers and strategists a decisive lesson: in modern warfare, perhaps no single commodity is more important than oil. For example, in the Pacific theater of operations, a single B-29 Superfortress consumed 10,000 gallons of fuel on a single mission to Japan, and as many as 1,000 B-29s could be dispatched on a mission (Frey and Ide, 1946, p. 7). US military aircraft consumed almost 10 billion gallons of fuel during the war – around 600 million barrels of oil – nearly half during 1944 alone (USAAF, 1945). On average, General George S. Patton's Third Army burned 350,000 gallons of gasoline per day between August 1944 and May 1945 (Grassi, 1993). Indeed, the armed forces used over 500 different kinds of petroleum-based products during the war, and the United States supplied 6 billion barrels of oil for its own use and that of the Allied nations; nearly 90 percent of the oil consumed by the Allies came from the Western Hemisphere (Frey and Ide, 1946, pp. 1–2). In 1944, the Foreign Operations Committee of the Petroleum Administration for War concluded that "the center of gravity of world oil production is shifting ... to the Persian Gulf area and is likely to continue to shift until it is firmly established in that area" (Frey and Ide, 1946, p. 277).

World War II marked the point at which the Gulf region became an area of American strategic concern. In the first general war plans produced by the Joint Chiefs of Staff after the war, securing – and if necessary, destroying – Iraq's oil fields to deny them to the Soviets would be among the first American military offensives of the notional World War III (Ross, 1996). Based on the experience of World War II, strategists concluded that Iran and Iraq were especially vulnerable to the Soviets – which helps explain the determination of both Britain and the United States to maintain the two countries' respective monarchies, including embedding them in the Northern Tier. A November 1946 Joint War Planning Committee strategic study of the region called "Caldron" concluded that "the importance of [Gulf] oil in a world war within the next three years cannot be over emphasized [and] these Middle East oil resources would be vital to the successful prosecution of the war by the Soviets" (Ross and Rosenberg, 1989). In 1950, E. A. Speiser, an archaeologist and specialist in Assyria who directed the Near East section of the Office of Strategic Services during World War II, noted a key lesson of the war for Iraq and the Gulf states was that they "cannot expect much [privacy] in the future" since the region had the "full complement of geostrategic require-ments: central strategic location; convergence of land, water, and air routes; and vital natural resources" (Speiser, 1950, p. 133, 165). Taken together, these facts helped transform Iraq from a commercial problem to a strategic one – though again we see that Iraq was important given some other inter-est. Iraqi oil was not vital to the United States, but would be vital to the Soviet Union; denying Moscow access to Iraq's oil fields, therefore, was an American national interest.

The fear of Soviet penetration of Baghdad that led Elwood to add his "etc." to the Kennedy administration's draft Middle East policy was firmly situated in the strategic context of the period. For a comparatively brief period, there was, then, a strategic rationale to US-Iraqi relations. From 1946 to 1958, American strategists and policymakers dealt with Iraq in terms of its geopolitical significance: it was both an important source of oil (for both sides of the Cold War) and a possible land bridge for the Soviets to use to threaten and capture the Suez Canal. During the years between the 1958 revolution and the 1967 war, US-Iraqi relations were correct, if cool, and the United States dealt with Gulf security issues at arm's length, at least until the British withdrawal from east of Suez. After the severing of diplomatic relations between the Six-Day War and the Iran-Iraq War, there were essentially no bilateral relations to speak of; Iraq was merely one part of a multi-nation portfolio of peripheral Arab states for a State Department desk officer, of occasional interest primarily as an avatar of the so-called "radical Arab front" and in the context of the Shah of Iran's quest for modern arms. For sixty years, between 1921 and 1981, the overall pattern in US-Iraqi relations was set: brief periods of intense interest (the oil dispute of the 1920s, the logistics operations of the 1940s, and the early Cold War) that alternated with comparatively longer periods of policy neglect. Nevertheless, the American approach to Iraq was largely driven by strategic concerns as Realist theories of International Relations would expect. In the wake of Operation Desert Storm (1990–1991), however, the strategic began to give way to the partisan.

The politics of regime change: The Iraq Liberation Act

On September 22, 1980, Saddam Hussein invaded Iran in what he originally intended to be a short-duration military campaign with the goal of absorbing Iranian lands near the Iraqi border and resolving long-standing territorial disputes with Tehran. Eight years later, the war ended with the status quo ante. On August 2, 1990, Saddam invaded Kuwait in what he intended to be a short-duration military campaign with the nominal goal of "recovering" a "lost" Iraqi province (Kuwait) stolen by the British – a claim first promulgated by King Feisal I – but the practical goal was actually to channel his army's energies away from potential conspiracies at home. Eight months later the war ended with the Iraqi armed forces in tatters, the economy broken, citizens subject to punishing international sanctions, and Iraqi sovereignty truncated, with the international community claiming de facto suzerainty over much of Iraq's airspace.

The Iraq policies of both the Reagan and George H. W. Bush administrations followed previous patterns: Iraq was periphery and then core, but in both instances America's interests were driven primarily by traditional, strategic concerns. As Bruce Jentleson (1994) has shown, the Reagan administration's "tilt" towards Saddam – a policy of providing intelligence and material support to the Ba'athist regime during the Iran-Iraq War – was ultimately intended to ensure that the Gulf status quo was preserved; the United States had an interest in neither Iraqi nor Iranian victory and was content to see both countries fight each other to a stalemate (Karsh, 2002; Razoux, 2015; Malovany, 2017), though there was a second-order domestic politics issue that also played a role in the "tilt." The 1979 Soviet grain embargo imposed by President Jimmy Carter in retaliation for the invasion of Afghanistan harmed American farmers; it is unsurprising then that Farm Belt representatives like Senator Bob Dole of Kansas were strong supporters of the Reagan administration's Iraq policy, since farm goods were one of the biggest forms of assistance the United States provided Iraq during the war (Jentleson, 1994, p. 55).

The brief US-Iraqi honeymoon afforded by the Iran-Iraq War paid few long-term dividends, however, and came to an abrupt end with Iraq's invasion of Kuwait in August 1990. Though Iraq was rhetorically transformed in short order from being the "eastern flank of the Arab world" to the principal threat to regional stability, it is nevertheless the case that Operation Desert Storm was intended to restore the status quo ante. Though a few voices outside of government called for regime change, the Bush administration recognized there was little to be gained from ousting Saddam; as the Central Intelligence Agency noted as early as 1952, Iraqi governance was strongman governance, and the strategic uncertainties associated with the vacuum of power resulting from toppling that strongman greatly outweighed whatever benefits might theoretically be associated with regime change. As Secretary of State James A. Baker III noted, there was "no sentiment at senior levels of the US government for occupying even part of Iraq" (Baker, with DeFrank, 1995, p. 438).

However, within the year the strategic environment changed in ways all but unimaginable: the Soviet Union ended, not with a bang but with a whimper, as the hammer-and-sickle flag was pulled down from atop the Kremlin on December 25, 1991. The balance-of-power rationale that governed US foreign policy for 45 years was suddenly less pressing, and in the heady early days of the so-called "unipolar moment," think-tank scholars, pundits, and even some in government began to suggest the United States should press its newfound advantage (Krauthammer, 1990/91; Mastanduno, 1997; Brands, 2016). Merely maintaining the balance of power was no longer necessary nor sufficient; the unipolar moment was an opportunity to remake the international system. It was in that context that the Bush administration's 1991 decision to leave Saddam Hussein in power began to be criticized, but it was the politics of the post-1994 Congressional elections that transformed Iraq from a strategic problem into a partisan one.

The 1992 presidential election was the first post-Cold War election, and, symbolically, it reflected the transformation of the international system, with President George H. W. Bush representing the Cold War era and Democratic Party challenger William J. Clinton representing the possibilities of the nascent post-Cold War era. As many presidents do, Clinton came into office determined to focus on domestic politics "like a laser beam" (Kaufman, 2010, p. 125), but the administration's attention was focused instead on military interventions in Bosnia, Haiti, and Somalia. The use of armed forces for "nation-building" was controversial during the Clinton years, and the president himself seemed unable to commit to a specific security policy; in the case of Bosnia, for example, Kaufman described Clinton as having a "bifurcated policy," one split between "an overwhelming desire not to get involved" and an "impulse to jump in and take a leadership role" (p. 130).

Apart from a lack of consensus within the Democratic Party on what American leadership meant in the post-Cold War era, the Clinton administration's ability to craft a foreign affairs strategy was made manifestly more difficult by the 1994 "Republican revolution" in which control of both the House of Representatives and Senate passed to the Republican Party. Here too the change from Cold War to post-Cold War is important: the bipartisan consensus on foreign policy, which had frayed during the Vietnam War, finally broke apart (Wittkopf and McCormick, 1998; Morris, 2001). The new 104th Congress intended to aggressively challenge the Clinton administration, yet despite two years of controversies (real and imagined), witch-hunts, and increasingly hostile rhetoric, the president was re-elected in 1996 by a greater margin of victory than in 1992 (defeating another Republican avatar of the Cold War, Kansas Senator Robert Dole). For House and Senate Republicans, however, the only clear "victory" was preventing the administration from reforming healthcare, and that was clearly insufficient to shift the balance of power from the White House to the Capitol.

Republican partisans in Congress and in the media, therefore, shifted their attention to foreign affairs – an area where presidents typically have greater latitude. Indeed, observers noted that one thing that contributed most to Republican Party unity in the 1990s was the "disdain the Republicans harbored for Clinton and his foreign policy" (Tarr, 2002, p. 173). Beginning with critiques of his policy in Bosnia, Republicans in Congress shopped for an issue on which to challenge the White House. The issue that "stuck" was Iraq. Since Desert Storm there had been conservative ideologues outside of government advocating for Saddam's ouster. For example, Angelo Codevilla, a mid-ranking Reagan administration official, and economist Mancur Olson demanded in the *Wall Street Journal* that the United States "get rid of Saddam now" (Codevilla and Olson, 1991); Richard Perle (1990) called diplomatic resolution to the Iraqi invasion of Kuwait a "chilling prospect"; *Washington Post* columnist Jim Hoagland (1991) declared the only "proper" policy was "taking the war to Saddam" instead of liberating Kuwait; pundit Charles Krauthammer (1991) accused the Bush administration of "an astonishing misreading of our interests." Even the famous deterrence strategist Albert Wohlstetter (1991) joined in the call for Saddam's ouster: in an era of unchallenged American primacy, he argued, a status quo that tolerated illiberal regimes was indefensible.

One thing the proponents of regime change in Iraq shared – and there were many of them – was that they were out of government. They were in the Washington, DC wilderness, writing op-eds and white papers and holding seminars and conferences. More importantly, they were aggrieved by the Clinton administration's continuation of the Bush era status quo – Saddam could not be "kept in a box," per the period phrase. *The Washington Post's* Jim Hoagland, for example, praised Clinton's nomination of Wisconsin Representative Les Aspin to be Secretary of Defense, because Aspin was an early supporter of the use of force against Iraq in 1990 (Hoagland, 1992); but within a year Hoagland regularly denounced the administration, calling for a "strategy that will bury Saddam Hussein" (Hoagland, 1993). Clinton clearly intended to sustain the post-Desert Storm containment status quo. Apart from continuing to pen scathing editorials, the regime change hawks were powerless. However, Republicans in Congress were not powerless, and they were on the hunt for a new stick with which to bludgeon the president politically. They found that stick in Iraq.

While much has been made about the influence of the so-called "neocons" in the George W. Bush administration, to the extent they had influence over Iraq policy this was an artifact of the Republican Congress during the Clinton administration (Burgos, 2008). During the Clinton years, Saddam Hussein frequently tested the limits of his strategic "box," moving forces in and out of the no-fly/no-drive zones, targeting American aircraft with surface-to-air missile radar systems, and playing an ultimately fatal game of cat and mouse with U.N. weapons inspectors. There was in other words a steady drumbeat of Iraq "crises" in the news, and with each iteration the American response was the same: hostile rhetoric, retaliatory air or missile strikes, and a return to the status quo. The frequency of Republican criticism directed at Clinton increased every year during his presidency, and Republicans were able to legitimize their critiques by drawing upon the ideologues and intellectuals who had called for Saddam's ouster since 1991. Congressional Republicans weaponized the editorial pages and politicized Iraq policy; but unlike editorial writers, the Republicans' goal was partisan, not strategic. Iraq policy was useful as a means of attacking Clinton and limiting his power. Though regime change hawks like Richard Perle and Paul Wolfowitz focused on Saddam, the Republicans who adopted their proposals focused on Clinton (Burgos, 2008). Iraq policy was partisan, not strategic.

In 1998, House and Senate Republicans held a series of hearings attacking Clinton's Iraq policy while there was a robust media debate over regime change. On February 23, Pennsylvania Senator Arlen Specter introduced Senate Resolution 179 calling for "the removal of Saddam Hussein"; in a *CBS/New York Times* survey, 54 percent of respondents said they approved of US military intervention to oust Saddam (Burgos, 2008). By November 1998, 70 percent of respondents would approve. Interest groups such as the Project for a New American Century and the Committee for Peace and Security in the Gulf – cut-outs for hawkish think tanks like the American Enterprise Institute – published open letters to the president demanding a "comprehensive political and military strategy for bringing down Saddam and his regime" (Lippman, 1998). In April, three Republicans introduced House Resolution

3599, which attempted to coerce the International Monetary Fund to deny Iraq access to aid and programs; in June, House Joint Resolution 125 declared Iraq to be in "material breach" of UN Security Council Resolution 687 (which set the terms for the cessation of hostilities in 1991). Congressional hearings were dominated by witnesses who supported regime change; for example, on October 8 the House Committee on International Relations convened hearings on "The Foreign Policy of the Clinton Administration" in which only conservatives were called to testify – including L. Paul Bremer III, who would head the Coalition Provisional Authority in Iraq just five years later. In September 1998, House Republicans introduced the Iraq Liberation Act, which declared "it should be the policy of the United States to support efforts to remove the regime headed by Saddam Hussein from power" (An Act to Establish a Program to Support a Transition to Democracy in Iraq, 1998).

President Clinton, then mired in impeachment proceedings over a sexual affair, was also attacked on Iraq by the liberal wing of the Democratic Party, which demanded an end to the UN sanctions regime in the wake of reports of extreme humanitarian suffering in Iraqi civil society. Of course, the possibility that Clinton would respond and lift sanctions merely added urgency to the conservative claim that Saddam was "winning," especially given the fact the UN weapons inspectors upon whom the logic of containment depended had been expelled from Iraq and could no longer verify termination of Saddam's proscribed weapons programs. In short, Clinton's Iraq policy was beyond salvaging, and he signed the Iraq Liberation Act on October 31, 1998. While none of the various Republican legislative gambits was decisive – indeed, as defense analyst Anthony Cordesman put it, the Iraq Liberation Act was "absurd tokenism," a tiny commitment "to show Saddam we don't like him" (Loeb, 1998) – taken together they illustrate the way foreign policy towards Iraq had been transformed from one focused in 1991 on national interests and strategic stability to one in 1998 being debated in partisan terms like any piece of domestic politics legislation. The politics of Iraq foreign policy were party politics.

From inauguration to occupation

With respect to Iraq, regime change was the foreign policy status quo for both parties in the 2000 presidential election, though there was a clear split in the way both parties viewed the issue. The Democratic Party tried to thread a needle by simultaneously endorsing regime change and the containment status quo that prevailed from 1991: "we are committed to working with our international partners to keep Saddam Hussein boxed in, and we will work to see him out of power. ... As President, Al Gore will not hesitate to use America's military might against Iraq when and where it is necessary" (Democratic Party, 2000). By contrast, the Republican Party platform reflected partisan anger at the Clinton administration's slow-walking of the Iraq

Liberation Act; Republicans declared they "support the full implementation of the Iraq Liberation Act, *which should be regarded as a starting point* in a comprehensive plan for the removal of Saddam Hussein" (Republican Party, 2000, italics added). Campaign advisor and future National Security Advisor and Secretary of State Condoleezza Rice told party convention delegates that Bush would replace containment with a "regime removal strategy" for Iraq (Wolfe, 2002, p. 10).

Much has been said in both popular and scholarly discourses about the many controversies attendant to the invasion of Iraq, including the ways in which intelligence information was used (and abused) to rationalize the case for invasion, but what cannot be disputed is that in January 2001 the Bush team came into office having made plain its endorsement of ousting Saddam Hussein – militarily and unilaterally if need be. In their accounts, as counter-terrorism czar Richard Clarke has noted, there existed plans for the invasion of Iraq "since the beginning of the administration, indeed well before" (Clarke, 2004, p. 7), and Treasury Secretary Paul O'Neill reported that Iraq was the subject of the Bush administration's first two National Security Meetings (Suskind, 2004). This should surprise no one. The question in 2001 was not *would* the United States overthrow Saddam Hussein, but *how* would the United States overthrow him. That the regime had to be done away with was by 2001 the Iraq policy orthodoxy in Washington. Again, what is important is that the policy was defined to meet the needs of political partisans and not on the basis of a systematic review of Iraq policy and strategy. Instead of a strategic orthodoxy, it was a partisan one – but, importantly, it was a partisan orthodoxy that had been endorsed at least superficially by the Democratic Party as well, so proponents of regime change could plausibly claim during political debates over the invasion that regime change had "bipartisan support," invoking the mythology of the Cold War consensus.

Indeed, this is perhaps the most puzzling aspect of the Bush administration's handling of the 2002–2003 period: given the preexisting consensus on regime change and public support for ousting Saddam (as Holsti [2011] noted, support ran from 52 to 74 percent), the administration did not need to construct a narrative about Weapons of Mass Destruction (WMD). As Holsti put it, "the American public [was already] predisposed to believe the worst about the Saddam Hussein regime" and, more importantly, the "administration received a virtually blank check from the media" after 9/11 (p. 133). The Bush administration's decision to hang its case for invasion on the chimera of WMD fatally undermined the support it might otherwise have had during the first year of the occupation.

Lamb and Franco (2015) also showed how internal government politics complicated the process of making and implementing Iraq strategy; inter-agency rivalries and political differences led to a "persistent inability to generate the full range of capabilities for success" (pp. 167–168). This is especially problematic for a decision-making process that can be "idiosyncratic at best," as expressed by retired US Army General George W. Casey Jr., who commanded

Multi-National Forces-Iraq from June 2004 to February 2007 (cited in Lamb and Franco, 2015, p. 168). I would submit that the more "idiosyncratic" the decision-making process at the highest levels of national strategy, the greater the probability that partisan political influences will reshape – and misshape – foreign policy in unpredictable but consequential ways. Moreover, idiosyncrasies in decision-making are likely to reflect idiosyncrasies in the things over which decisions are being made – including the "national interest." As I suggested above, the national interest is seldom objective and readily definable; as Terry Deibel (2007) argued, "the national interest rests on nothing more substantial than value judgments" (p. 134), and value judgments in a democracy will inevitably reflect the partisan biases of those making them. Gordon and Trainor (2007) have shown that at the level of military strategy, the planning and execution of the invasion of Iraq was competent and professional, though it did not take place without interference from the White House – which, all else equal, one would expect in a democracy. Unfortunately, partisan considerations shaped, and often misshaped, the execution of the military plan and, far more importantly, the early months of the occupation in pernicious ways. Military strategy was subordinated to political narrative.

One well-known example is Secretary of Defense Donald Rumsfeld's insistence that military planners reduce the size of the invasion force. In a 2001 meeting at the Pentagon, Rumsfeld grew "exasperated" during a briefing on Operation Plan 1003–98, the contingency plan for the invasion of Iraq that had been drafted by US Central Command (CENTCOM) planners, because it called for a half-million troops. According to Rumsfeld, the invasion should not have required more than 125,000 troops "and even that was probably too many" (Gordon and Trainor, 2007, pp. 4–5). Throughout the 2002 planning process for the invasion, Rumsfeld constantly prodded Army General Tommy Franks, CENTCOM commander, to reduce his troop estimates. The ease with which the United States toppled the Taliban regime in Afghanistan may have overly influenced Rumsfeld's belief in the value of the "transformation" paradigm he had brought to the Pentagon. The fact that there were strategically and operationally significant differences between the comparatively young Taliban regime and the long-standing government of Saddam Hussein seems not to have troubled him. The military's plan, Rumsfeld declared, was "old think" and failed to reflect the impact of innovations he had spearheaded (Caldwell, 2011, p. 116). It was politically important to the administration that invading Iraq and defeating the regime not appear to require a Desert Storm-like commitment of forces.

Appearing before the Senate Armed Services Committee on February 25, 2003, Army Chief of Staff Eric Shinseki was asked how many troops it would take to manage Iraq after toppling Saddam; based on his experience in Bosnia, Shinseki replied "several hundred thousand" (Gordon and Trainor, 2007). Where Rumsfeld's interference with Franks' planning was an example of institutional politics, Shinseki's almost offhand observation – one based on experience – created a domestic politics crisis. Two days after Shinseki's appearance on the Hill, Paul Wolfowitz was scheduled to testify before the House Budget Committee, but "his main purpose that day was to douse a potential fire" (Isikoff and Corn, 2006, p. 193) – one that threatened to undermine the Bush administration's narrative. Shinseki's estimate, Wolfowitz declared, was "wildly off the mark" (Isikoff and Corn, 2006, p. 194). To reinforce the narrative, the administration dispatched other partisans to reinforce the notion that invading Iraq would be comparatively easy, much as toppling the Taliban had been. Andrew Natsios, the US Agency for International Development (USAID) administrator (and an Army Reserve Civil Affairs officer and former NGO director with broad experience in humanitarian relief) was scheduled to appear on ABC News' *Nightline* program on April 23, where he informed an incredulous Ted Koppel that postwar economic assistance would cost only $1.7 billion; indeed, based on this, the Bush administration's initial request for Iraq reconstruction was only $2.4 billion (Dobbins et al., 2009, p. 109).

Throughout 2002 and 2003, the Bush administration deliberately constructed a best-case narrative for the invasion of Iraq. To do so, they enlisted Iraqi expatriates and conservative intellectuals to validate assumptions the administration had already used to rationalize the invasion. As the war dragged on, the administration enlisted retired military officers in an especially pernicious example of partisan narrative construction; the armed forces are the most trusted institution of government in the United States, even then after 16 years of warfare. In a 2016 Gallup poll, for example, 73 percent of respondents stated they trusted the military "a great deal" or "quite a lot," double the support they expressed for the next most trusted institution of federal governance (Gallup, 2016). The administration capitalized upon Americans' dependence upon the media as a watchdog on government and deliberately preyed upon their trust in the armed forces by dispatching retired senior officers with a pre-approved set of talking points to reinforce the administration's position on the invasion, the occupation, and the insurgency (Barstow, 2008, November 29). While the electorate might assume White House spokespersons would be likely to put a positive gloss on things, they are equally likely to trust the allegedly "independent" professional judgment of those who have served at the highest levels of the most trusted institution of the state. That the administration would stoop to such a level illustrates just how important partisan narrative construction was during the Bush years. Indeed, as much of the literature shows, the invasion of Iraq was all but a foregone conclusion by early 2002. As Isikoff and Corn (2006, pp. 9–11) showed, for example, Central Intelligence Agency officers were already operating in northern Iraq by April 2002 to coordinate with Kurdish partners, and in his forays to the Agency's Langley, Virginia, headquarters, Vice President Dick Cheney – who had been chary of occupying Baghdad in 1991 – continually pushed intelligence analysts to produce information justifying what was clearly a foregone conclusion. "Cheney was not posing the sorts of questions a policy would need answered in order to determine whether Iraq posed a threat," they noted, but was instead asking questions "pegged to the assumption that Iraq would be invaded" (Isikoff and Corn, 2006, p. 11).

Partisan considerations continued to complicate policy during the year of occupation. Debates over the transfer of sovereignty, the substance of Iraqi sovereignty, troop rotations, and of course the lack of a WMD "smoking gun" put the Bush administration on the political defensive – with presidential elections approaching, the Iraq problem was increasingly defined in partisan (e.g., electoral) terms. As a result, throughout 2003–2004 there was a "yawning disconnect" between Iraqi reality "and the Bush administration's political strategy" (Gordon and Trainor, 2013, p. 66). In effect, the Bush administration was trying to fit events in Iraq into a frame more conducive to American politics. National Security Advisor Condoleezza Rice, for example, was enamored of inapplicable historical analogies, often comparing the American occupation of Iraq to the Allied occupation of Germany after World War II without taking into account a key difference: even during the occupation, domestic politics within Iraq were robust and highly contested – something that had not troubled the military governors of post-World War II Germany. Rice also tended to apply familiar partisan frames to Iraqi governance; at one point, for example, she proposed helping the Iraqis draft a "100-day plan," which Gordon and Trainor (2013) characterized as a "telling example of the [administration's] tendency to interpret" Iraqi politics "in American terms" (p. 135). Instead of asking what would be the nature of U.S.-Iraqi relations after the transfer of sovereignty in 2004, the administration "turned its attention to messaging" – an especially important consideration given that 2004 was a presidential election year (p. 74). As White House aide Harriet Miers put it, "how good we do is limited by how well we can communicate our success" (cited in Gordon and Trainor, 2013, p. 75). The substance of Iraqi sovereignty was less important than the fact of it for American electoral purposes. Indeed, by 2004 it was not only the case that strategy had been subjected to partisan litmus tests, but partisan objectives were also becoming a focus of military strategy: Army Lieutenant General Thomas Metz, for example, "suggested in a classified memo that the [Army's campaign] plan explicitly treat the support of the American public as a 'center of gravity'" (Gordon and Trainor, 2013, p. 98).

Even staffing and policy decisions for the Coalition Provisional Authority (CPA) were driven by partisan considerations. As Rajiv Chandrasekaran (2007) showed, subject matter expertise took a back seat to party loyalty in CPA staffing decisions. In late 2002 and early 2003, the Defense Department was given lead in postwar policymaking, and one of the Department's key considerations in managing that policy was the political reliability of those assigned to duties in Iraq. This had the effect of alienating Secretary of State Colin Powell and many at the State Department – so much so, in fact, that American failure was not necessarily thought of as a bad thing by aggrieved State Department staffers. Political scientist and democratization expert Larry Diamond, who had been personally approached by Rice to serve in the CPA, observed that Rumsfeld was "zealously opposed to any role for career State Department experts" in Iraq's reconstruction (Diamond, 2007, p. 31). Rumsfeld dismissed the findings of the Future of Iraq Project because they were too "negative" – that is, they would have called the Bush administration's projections into question. One senior State Department official, Tom Warrick, was rejected by Rumsfeld because Warrick disliked Ahmad Chalabi, a favored Iraqi exile within the Bush administration (Chandrasekaran, 2007, p. 37). Michael Fleischer, brother of the White House press secretary, was put in charge of Iraqi economic privatization policy. A 24-year-old real estate agent and loyal Republican was tasked with overseeing the reconstruction of Iraq's stock exchange (pp. 94–97). Six young Heritage Foundation interns, who became known as the "Brat Pack," were put in charge of managing Iraq's $13 billion budget though none had any experience in financial management (p. 94). Even the day-to-day minutiae of the occupation could be subject to partisan litmus tests; Rumsfeld dismissed Diamond's concerns about nonpayment of wages for Iraqi civil servants in 2003–2004, because what "mattered" was the fact that "the American taxpayer wouldn't stand for the United States paying Iraqi civil servants" – a reflection both of traditional conservative orthodoxy about the "wastefulness" of paying government workers and of Americans' widely shared dislike of foreign aid (Diamond, 2007, p. 31). In their generally sympathetic treatment of the CPA, even scholars from the RAND Corporation observed that Authority staffers' "enthusiasm ... greatly exceeded their other qualifications" (Dobbins et al., 2009, p. 29). In almost every case, CPA staffing was subject to partisan litmus tests. Contemporary observers on military bases often remarked on the ubiquity of *Fox News* – and the absence of other, allegedly "liberal," news channels – in conference rooms and dining facilities. As Chandresekaran observed, the social etiquette of the occupation was based upon the expectation that one would say only positive things about "the mission."

Conclusion

As Iraq moved from the periphery to the center of the US strategic agenda in the Middle East, domestic political considerations increasingly informed the definition of each administration's approach to the "Iraq problem." This is not to say there were no legitimately strategic considerations in American policy towards Iraq, nor am I criticizing the idea that there will be domestic politics influences in foreign policymaking. Even well-known Realists like John Mearsheimer and Stephen Walt recognize that domestic politics influences foreign policy (though they are critical of it). However, in the second US-Iraqi War, the strategic often seems to have been subordinated to the domestic. It is not much of an exaggeration to suggest that at the strategic level from 2003 until, perhaps, the surge in 2007, the Bush administration ran the war in Iraq in very much the same way it ran its political campaign.

Messaging, for example, was a paramount consideration for the Bush administration, especially as the insurgency took hold. For example, during my yearlong deployment as an Army Reserve officer in Iraq, the enemy was renamed multiple times, with the Bush administration trying desperately to avoid using terms like "insurgency" or "guerillas," as if by naming the enemy properly, one would arrive at the proper strategy for dealing with him. As Michael Keane (2005), then a professor at the University of Southern California, observed in a *Los Angeles Times* essay, during the first year of the war, coalition forces were fighting "dead-enders," then "Baathist holdouts," then "former regime loyalists," then (as Keane observed, "when it was pointed out that 'loyalty' generally has a positive connotation,") "former regime elements," and, finally, by the time I was rotated back to the United States, "anti-Iraq forces" – as if the insurgents were opposed to the very notion of Iraq itself.

Indeed, among the early political controversies sparked by Bush administration policy was the revelation that a cadre of retired flag officers (generals and admirals) retained by news networks as presumptively objective subject matter experts were systematically parroting talking points provided to them by the Bush administration through the Assistant Secretary of Defense Victoria Clarke (Barstow, 2008, April 20; see also Mitchell, 2008). An exposé in *The New York Times* showed that the so-called "key influentials" were given privileged access to decision-makers and classified information they would then use to bolster their allegedly independent analysis. To critics, this was an especially pernicious form of messaging by the Bush administration because it capitalized upon the fact that in survey after survey, the armed forces are reported to be the most trusted institution of governance in the United States; given the comparatively small percentage of the American population that has served in the armed forces, civil society is critically dependent upon those with expertise in military strategy. Those two factors – trust in the military and an inability to independently verify or confirm the expertise of retired generals – was seen by the Bush administration as an opportunity to promote a specific (and favorable) strategic narrative that capitalized upon what Gary J. Miller (2005) called "Weber's asymmetry" – the fact that in many principal-agent relationships, while the principal (in this case, the American people) is the source of a president's legitimacy, the agent (the administration) has an information advantage that can be used to deceive or otherwise manipulate the public.

The importance of narrative construction was even reflected in the Coalition Provisional Authority's abortive attempt to redesign the Iraqi flag. In 2004, Bremer (who also directed that Iraq have a new national anthem) commissioned a new flag to respond to Kurdish sensitivities to what was called the "Saddam flag" – the redesigned flag of the Iraqi republic that Saddam adopted during the first US-Iraqi War on which "Allahu Akbar" appeared in his handwriting. The new design was roundly rejected owing to its resemblance to the Israeli flag (Raphaeli, 2006), and a modified version of the then current Iraqi flag was adopted with Saddam's handwriting replaced by traditional Kufi script. (In 2008 the flag was again redesigned with the three stars from the era of the post-Qásim era removed, and in 2012 the Government of Iraq again proposed redesigning the flag.)

One of the lessons of this case, then, is the close relationship of domestic political considerations – both material and ideational – in foreign policymaking, even during times of war. One material consideration that underpinned the Reagan administration's "tilt towards Saddam," for example, was the need for a market for Midwest farm commodities: grain farmers lost their Soviet market after the invasion of Afghanistan and so the Reagan administration found them a substitute in Iraq. However, that material consideration was closely linked to a strategic goal – maintaining the status quo in the Gulf by ensuring neither Iran nor Iraq prevailed in their war. By taking on the task of feeding Iraq, in essence, the Reagan administration made it possible for Saddam Hussein to continue purchasing armaments and, as a result, helped ensure Iran could not prevail and upset the Gulf balance of power. In the early years of the second American war with Iraq, however, ideational considerations exercised strong influence over strategic policymaking – but the ideational concerns were strictly partisan. It was as if one strategic goal of Operation Iraqi Freedom was simply to make the Bush administration look good. One area of future research, then, is the salience of partisan politics in strategic policymaking over time. For example, one could hypothesize that as partisan polarization increases – as research shows it is doing at a significant rate – then all else being equal, foreign policymaking will be increasingly subject to partisan litmus tests.

A related area of research might explore what David Mayhew famously called "the electoral connection" at the presidential level in foreign policymaking towards the Middle East; with respect to Iraq, for example, if constructing some kind of "win" was viewed by the Bush team in 2004 as a necessary part of the president's re-election campaign, then withdrawing from Iraq appears to have been viewed by the Obama administration as a nonnegotiable electoral promise, regardless of the strategic implications. Whereas Mayhew argued that for Congress, the provision of goods to home districts was the optimal strategy for re-election, since presidents are unable to deliver material rewards in the same way members of the House and Senate can, scholars might explore how electorally relevant (and partisan) ideational factors influence an administration's strategies in foreign policy. This could be an especially productive area of research given the increasingly fragmented information markets and a tendency within civil society to self-select into ideologically friendly narratives – conditions that call into question the ability of any administration to construct a dominant (let alone accurate) strategic narrative.

Finally, the Iraq case from 2003 to the present day illustrates the growing complexities of Gulf regional politics and, by extension, the growing need for specific area expertise in policy planning and execution. Yet in American domestic politics, there is an increasing suspicion of expertise – indeed, some scholars and analysts suggest that the Obama era ushered in an affirmative *rejection* of expertise by electorally significant groups within civil society. The so-called "Tea Party" movement, for example, built part of its appeal on the rejection of "elites" – that is, individuals with substantive experience in governance (Parker and Barreto, 2014) – and with respect to Middle East policy, there has long been suspicion of the so-called "Arabists" among Republican Party and conservative ideologues, the very people who have subject matter expertise relevant to strategic policymaking. For example, in a May 2012 debate with Jeremy Ben-Ami of the J Street organization at New York's B'nai Jeshurun synagogue, the influential neoconservative ideologue and media figure William Kristol was reported to have celebrated the three-decade-long purging of so-called "Arabists" from the Republican Party, a process that took on greater urgency in the mid-1990s – at precisely the same time that the insurgent Newt Gingrich-led House of Representatives was challenging Clinton administration policy on Iran and Iraq (Kaplan, 1995). As many accounts of the 2002–2003 period show, subject matter experts on Iraq from the State Department were systematically sidelined by the Bush administration, largely on the grounds that they failed partisan purity tests. This too is a fruitful area of further research.

Lurking beneath the surface of this chapter is a counterfactual thought experiment: the idea that there can be such a thing as strategic policymaking in the United States that is not influenced by domestic political considerations. What we might call the "Realist Ideal" would posit that wartime decision-making would be focused exclusively on wartime demands; that the national interest would be well defined; that a clear statement of strategy would drive war planning and war execution at all levels from the tactical to the strategic; and that strategies and decisions would be aimed at enhancing the power and position of the nation-state as opposed to the party in control of the White House. Given a Realist Ideal hypothesis, then, one might ask if the Bush administration's policies towards Iraq were an exception to the rule. My research suggests they were not. As I have argued in this chapter, the national interest is an almost infinitely elastic term, and whether one is talking about the Kennedy administration's "etc." or the Trump administration's shifting alliances with various rebel groups in the counter-ISIS campaign, there is an implicit (and often explicit) partisan litmus test that any president's foreign policy must meet; and as partisan polarization continues to grow in the United States, this chapter suggests that such litmus tests will become more, rather than less, frequent and rigid in coming years.

Disclaimer

The views expressed here are those of the author and are not an official policy or position of the National Defence University, the Department of Defence, or the US Government.

References

Allison, G. and Zelikow, P. (1999). *Essence of decision: Explaining the Cuban missile crisis* (2nd ed.). New York: Longman.

Bacevich, A.J. (2016). *America's war for the greater Middle East: A military history.* New York: Random House.

Badeau, J.S. (1968). *The American approach to the Arab world.* New York: Harper & Row.

Baker, J.A. (with DeFrank, T.M.). (1995). *The politics of diplomacy: Revolution, war and peace, 1989–1992.* New York: G. P. Putnam's Sons.

Baram, P.J. (1978). *The Department of State in the Middle East, 1919–1945.* Philadelphia, PA: University of Pennsylvania Press.

Barstow, D. (2008, April 20). Behind TV analysts, Pentagon's hidden hand. *The New York Times,* p. A1.

Barstow, D. (2008, November 29). One man's military-industrial-media complex. *The New York Times,* p. A1.

Brands, H. (2016). *Making the unipolar moment: U.S. foreign policy and the rise of the post-Cold War order.* Ithaca, NY: Cornell University Press.

Burchill, S. (2005). *The national interest in international relations theory.* New York: Palgrave MacMillan.

Burgos, R.A. (2005). *Teaching them to elect good men: Ideological determinants of coercive regime change.* Unpublished doctoral dissertation, University of California, Los Angeles.

Burgos, R.A. (2008). Origins of regime change: Ideapolitik on the long road to Baghdad. *Security Studies,* 17(2), 221–256.

Busby, J.W., Monten, J. and Inboden, W. (2012, May 30). American foreign policy is already post-partisan: Why politics does stop at the water's edge. *Foreign Affairs.* Retrieved from www.foreignaffairs.com/articles/united-states/2012-05-30/american-foreign -policy-already-post-partisan.

Caldwell, D. (2011). *Vortex of conflict: U.S. policy toward Afghanistan, Pakistan, and Iraq.* Palo Alto, CA: Stanford University Press.

Central Intelligence Agency. (1993). Arab nationalism as a factor in the Middle East situation [August 12, 1958, SNIE 30–3–58]. In *Foreign relations of the United States, 1958–1960. Vol. 12: Near East region; Iraq, Iran, Arabian peninsula.* Washington, DC: Government Printing Office.

Chandrasekaran, R. (2007). *Imperial life in the emerald city: Inside Iraq's green zone.* New York, NY: Vintage.

The Chicago Council on Global Affairs. (2012). *Foreign policy in the new millennium: Results of the 2012 Chicago Council survey of American public opinion and U.S. foreign policy.* Chicago, IL: The Chicago Council on Global Affairs.

Clarke, R.A. (2004). *Against all enemies: Inside America's war on terror.* New York: Free Press.

Codevilla, A. and Olson, M. (1991, February 25). Get rid of Saddam Hussein now. *The Wall Street Journal,* p. A8.

Cordesman, A.H. (2003). *The Iraq war: Strategies, tactics, and military lessons.* Santa Barbara, CA: Praeger.

Deibel, T.L. (2007). *Foreign affairs strategy: Logic for American statecraft.* New York: Cambridge University Press.

Democratic Party. (2000, August 14). Democratic Party Platform. Retrieved from www.presidency.ucsb.edu/ws/?pid=29612.

DeNovo, J. (1956). The movement for an aggressive American oil policy abroad, 1918–1920. *American Historical Review,* 61(4), 854–878.

Diamond, L. (2007). *Squandered victory: The American occupation and the bungled effort to bring democracy to Iraq.* New York: Times Books.

Dobbins, J., Jones, S.G., Runkle, B. and Mohandas, S. (2009). *Occupying Iraq: A history of the Coalition Provisional Authority.* Santa Monica, CA: RAND Corporation.

Earle, E.M. (1924). The Turkish Petroleum Company: A study in oleaginous diplomacy. *Political Science Quarterly*, 39(2), 265–279.

Ellison, H. (1956, April 15). Russia's Middle East drive follows 1940 goal. *Washington Post and Times Herald*, p. E1.

Elwood, R.B. (1961, June 28). Comments on guideline of U.S. policy toward the Near East. *NARA* (RG 59, Box 7).

Field, J.A., Jr. (1969). *America and the mediterranean world, 1776–1882.* Princeton, NJ: Princeton University Press.

Fontenot, G., Degen, E.J. and Tohn, D. (2004). *On point: The United States Army in Operation Iraqi Freedom.* Leavenworth, KS: Combat Studies Institute.

Frey, J.W. and Ide, H.C. (Eds.). (1946). *A history of the Petroleum Administration for War 1941–1945.* Washington, DC: Government Printing Office.

Gallup. (2016). *Confidence in institutions* [Results of the Gallup poll of June 1–5, 2016]. Retrieved from www.gallup.com/poll/1597/confidence-institutions.aspx

Gardner, L.C. and Young, M.B. (2007). *Iraq and the lessons of Vietnam: Or, how not to learn from the past.* New York: The New Press.

Gordon, M.R. and Trainor, B.E. (2007). *Cobra II: The inside story of the invasion and occupation of Iraq.* New York: Vintage.

Gordon, M.R. and Trainor, B.E. (2013). *The endgame: The inside story of the struggle for Iraq, from George W. Bush to Barack Obama.* New York: Pantheon.

Gourevitch, P. (2002). Domestic politics and international relations. In W. Carlsnaes, T. Risse and B.A. Simmons (Eds.), *Handbook of international relations* (pp. 309–328). Thousand Oaks, CA: Sage Publications.

Grassi, D.G. (1993, Summer). Refuel on the move: Resupplying Patton's Third Army. *Quartermaster Professional Bulletin*, 4–7.

Gries, P.H. (2014). *The politics of American foreign policy: How ideology divides liberals and conservatives over foreign affairs.* Palo Alto, CA: Stanford University Press.

Haley, P.E. (2006). *Strategies of dominance: The misdirection of U.S. foreign policy.* Baltimore, MD: Johns Hopkins University Press.

Hoagland, J. (1991, April 2). Too cautious on Iraq. *The Washington Post*, p. A21.

Hoagland, J. (1992, December 28). Clinton's flair for synthesis. *The Washington Post*, p. A15.

Hoagland, J. (1993, January 21). Crank up to bury Saddam. *The Washington Post*, p. A23.

Holsti, O.R. (2011). *American public opinion on the Iraq war.* Ann Arbor, MI: University of Michigan Press.

Hooker, R.D., Jr and Collins, J.J. (Eds.). (2015). *Lessons encountered: Learning from the long war.* Washington, DC: National Defense University Press.

House of Representatives (1998, September 29)An Act to Establish a Program to Support a Transition to Democracy in Iraq, H.R. 4655, 105th Cong., 2nd sess.

Hurst, S. and Wroe, A. (2016). Partisan polarization and US foreign policy: Is the centre dead or holding? *International Politics*, 53(5), 666–682.

Isikoff, M. and Corn, D. (2006). *Hubris: The inside story of spin, scandal, and the selling of the Iraq War.* New York: Three Rivers Press.

Jentleson, B.W. (1994). *With friends like these: Reagan, Bush, and Saddam, 1982–1990*. New York: W. W. Norton.

Kaplan, R.D. (1995). *The Arabists: The romance of an American elite*. New York: The Free Press.

Karsh, E. (2002). *The Iran–Iraq war, 1980–1988*. New York: Osprey Publishing.

Kaufman, J.P. (2010). *A concise history of U.S. foreign policy* (2nd ed.). Lanham, MD: Rowman & Littlefield.

Keane, M. (2005, January 18). Our tortured language of war. *Los Angeles Times*.

Keegan, J. (2005). *The Iraq war: The military offensive, from victory in 21 days to the insurgent aftermath*. New York: Vintage.

Krauthammer, C. (1990/91). The unipolar moment. *Foreign Affairs*, 70(1), 23–33.

Krauthammer, C. (1991, April 19). Good morning, Vietnam: The syndrome returns, courtesy of George Bush. *The Washington Post*, p. A23.

Lamb, C.J. (with Franco, M.) (2015). National-level coordination and implementation: How system attributes trumped leadership. In R.D. Hooker Jr, and J.J. Collins (Eds.), *Lessons encountered: Learning from the long war* (pp. 165–276). Washington, DC: National Defense University Press.

Larson, D.W. (1989). *Origins of containment: A psychological explanation*. Princeton, NJ: Princeton University Press.

Larson, D.W. (2000). *Anatomy of mistrust: U.S.–Soviet relations during the Cold War*. New York: Cornell University Press.

Lenczowksi, G. (Ed.). (1968). *United States interests in the Middle East*. Washington, DC: American Enterprise Institute for Public Policy Research.

Lewis, V. (2017, March). The president and parties' ideologies: Party ideas about foreign policy since 1900. *Presidential Studies Quarterly*, 47(1), 27–61.

Lippman, T.W. (1998, February 5). In U.S., calls grow louder for Hussein's removal. *The Washington Post*, p. A1.

Loeb, V. (1998, October 20). Congress stokes visions of war to oust Saddam. *The Washington Post*, p. A1.

Lyman, R. (2006). *Iraq 1941: The battles for Basra, Habbaniya, Fallujah, and Baghad*. Tenterton, UK: Osprey Publishing.

McCright, A.M. and Dunlap, R.E. (2011, Spring). The politicization of climate change and polarization in the American public's views of global warming, 2001–2010. *Sociological Quarterly*, 52(2), 155–194.

Malovany, P. (2017). *Wars of modern Babylon: A history of the Iraqi army from 1921 to 2003* (R. Engelsberg, Trans.). Lexington, KY: University Press of Kentucky.

Martin, L. (1925). The Iraq dispute. *Foreign Affairs*, 3(4), 687–688.

Mastanduno, M. (1997, Spring). Preserving the unipolar moment: Realist theories and U.S. grand strategy after the Cold War. *International Security*, 21(4), 49–88.

Miller, G.J. (2005). The political evolution of principal-agent models. *Annual Review of Political Science*, 8, 203–225.

Mintz, A. and Wayne, C. (2016). *The Polythink Syndrome: U.S. foreign policy decisions on 9/11, Afghanistan, Iraq, Iran, Syria, and ISIS*. Stanford, CA: Stanford University Press.

Mitchell, G. (2008). *So wrong for so long*. New York: Union Square Press.

Morris, J.S. (2001, February). Reexamining the politics of talk: Partisan rhetoric in the 104th House. *Legislative Studies Quarterly*, 26(1), 101–121.

Motter, T.H.V. (1952). *The Persian corridor and aid to Russia*. Washington, DC: US Army Center for Military History.

The New York Times. (1958, July 29). Relations with Iraq, p. 22.

Oren, M.B. (2008). *Power, faith, and fantasy: The United States in the Middle East 1776–present.* New York: W. W. Norton, Inc.

Parker, C.S. and Barreto, M.A. (2014). *Change they can't believe in: The Tea Party and reactionary politics in America.* Princeton, NJ: Princeton University Press.

Perle, R. (1990, September 23). In the Gulf, the danger of a diplomatic solution. *The New York Times,* sec. 4, p. 21.

Raphaeli, N. (2006, September 19). *Mini-crisis in Iraq: Which Iraqi flag?MEMRI Inquiry and Analysis Series,* No. 293. Retrieved from https://www.memri.org/reports/m ini-crisis-iraq-which-iraqi-flag.

Razoux, P. (2015). *The Iran–Iraq war* (N. Elliott, Trans.). Cambridge, MA: Harvard University Press.

Renshon, S.A. (2003). Psychological sources of good judgment in political leaders: A framework for analysis. In S.A. Renshon and D.W. Larson (Eds.), *Good judgment in foreign policy: Theory and application* (pp. 25–57). Lanham, MD: Rowman and Littlefield.

Republican Party. (2000, July 31). Republican Party Platform. Retrieved from www.pr esidency.ucsb.edu/ws/?pid=25849.

Rixen, T. and Zangl, B. (2013, September). The politicization of international economic institutions in US public debates. *Review of International Organizations,* 8(3), 363–387.

Ross, S.T. (1996). *American war plans, 1945–1950.* Portland, OR: Frank Cass.

Ross, S.T. and Rosenberg, D.A. (Eds.). (1989). *America's plans for war against the Soviet Union, 1945–1950, Vol. 3: Pincher: Campaign plans, Part 1.* New York: Garland Publishing, Inc.

Samuel, A.T. (2014). The open door and U.S. policy in Iraq between the world wars. *Diplomatic History,* 38(5), 926–952.

Schwartz, T.A. (2009). "Henry, … winning an election is terribly important": Partisan politics in the history of U.S. foreign relations. *Diplomatic History,* 33(2), 173–190.

Smith, E.T. (1999). *Opposition beyond water's edge: Liberal internationalists, pacifists, and containment, 1945–1953.* Westport, CT: Greenwood Press.

Sontag, R.J. and Beddie, J.S. (1948). *Nazi-Soviet relations 1939–1941: Documents from the archives of the German Foreign Office.* Washington, DC: Government Printing Office.

Speiser, E.A. (1950). *The United States and the Near East.* Cambridge, MA: Harvard University Press.

Stivers, W. (1981). International politics and Iraqi oil. *Business History Review,* 55(4), 517–540.

Suskind, R. (2004). *The price of loyalty: George W. Bush, the White House, and the education of Paul O'Neill.* New York: Simon & Schuster.

Tarr, D.R. (Ed.). (2002). *Congress and the nation, vol. X: 1997–2001.* Washington, DC: Congressional Quarterly Press.

Tejirian, E.H. and Simon, R.S. (2012). *Conflict, conquest, and conversion: Two thousand years of Christian missions in the Middle East.* New York: Columbia University Press.

USAAF (United States Army Air Forces). (1945). *Army Air Forces statistical digest of World War II.* Washington, DC: USAAF.

Wittkopf, E.R. and McCormick, J.M. (1998, August). Congress, the president, and the end of the Cold War: Has anything changed? *Journal of Conflict Resolution,* 42(4), 440–466.

Wohlstetter, A. (1991, April 24). Iraq: Dictatorship is the problem. *The Washington Post*, p. A21.

Wolfe, R. (2000, August 2). Bush plans to undermine "rogue" states. *Financial Times (London)*, p. 10.

Wolfe-Hunnicutt, B. (2015). Embracing regime change in Iraq: American foreign policy and the 1963 coup d'etat in Baghdad. *Diplomatic History*, 39(1), 98–125.

Woodward, B. (2004). *Plan of attack: The definitive account of the decision to invade Iraq.* New York: Simon & Schuster.

Woodward, B. (2011). *Obama's wars.* New York: Simon & Schuster.

Wright, D.P. and Reese, T.R. (2008). *On Point II: Transition to the new campaign; The United States Army in Operation Iraqi Freedom, May 2003–January 2005.* Leavenworth, KS: Combat Studies Institute.

Yetiv, S.A. (2008). *The absence of grand strategy: The United States in the Persian Gulf, 1972–2005.* Baltimore, MD: Johns Hopkins University Press.

11 The United States and Political Islam

Dealing with the Egyptian Muslim Brothers in the Arab revolutions

Mohamed-Ali Adraoui

The purpose of this chapter is to shed light on the Islamic policy of the United States. As a great power, the United States attaches a crucial importance to the actors who have the ambition to shape the political landscape in the Muslim world, particularly in the Middle East, a region where they have interests. This is especially true since this region is in turmoil due to the upheavals and revolutionary dynamics that have enabled the representatives of political Islam to come to power in several countries. The United States also has to address the violence emanating from some groups that target them, as well as with the upheavals of recent years, which have put an end to the status quo in the region (Fawcett, 2013).[1]

Islamism is now a relatively old school of thought; it appeared almost a century ago, specifically structured around the legacy of the Association of the Muslim Brothers. Islamism was founded by Hassan al-Banna in 1927. It was among the actors that benefited from the new realities initiated in 2010, at least until political circumstances (i.e., elections in Tunisia, coup d'état in Egypt) took it away from the spheres of power in several countries. Egypt is one of the most striking illustrations. This makes the study of the relations between the United States and the Muslim Brothers in Egypt even more interesting. From the beginning of the Arab Spring, Egypt aroused a great deal of attention from US authorities. It is a key country for the defense of US interests and its allies, Israel being in first place. Additionally, Egypt is historically the cradle of political Islam; that is, an ideological movement oriented to coming to power at the head of the predominantly Muslim societies and with the aim of establishing a state governed by a fundamentalist vision of the religious norm.

The links between US officials and members of the Muslim Brothers are not new. In fact, they date back at least to the beginning of the Cold War and even to the colonial era.[2] Yet, for the first time in history, for more than a year, the leading world power was dealing with the main contemporary face of Islamism in the largest Arab country. Laid out next are the three characteristics of the Islamist policy of the United States.

The first characteristic concerns the interaction between a traditional state seeking to defend its interests and a religious-political actor propelling itself at the Muslim-world scale (or even beyond). Thus, the study of this relationship is a part of global studies, which today constitutes one of the privileged paradigms in reviewing the history and sociology of international relations.

The second characteristic concerns the relationship between a dominant state of the international system and a movement whose political ethics overtly aim to reverse the structures of this international system. Indeed, the international system's structures are perceived as supportive of the "arrogance" of the actors (especially the Western states) who have Islam in their sight. This is why the revisionist agenda (Tammen et al., 2000) of the Muslim Brothers in diplomacy is clearly displayed as one of the priorities of the renewal policy they want to initiate. In this respect, when we study the speeches and pronouncements of theorists, cadres, and activists of political Islam in the field of international relations, American foreign policy is clearly labeled as "unjust" toward Muslims (Mohamed-Ali, in press).

Finally, despite its status as a transnational movement, Islamism and its followers, especially the Egyptian Muslim Brothers, seek to exercise power by taking position in a given state. The Islamists' goal is to build a society that is faithful to the precepts of Islam and then to consider a reunification of all their coreligionists around the world, which is a prelude to the restoration of the Caliphate. Therefore, the Islamist policy of the United States must take into account the dual nature of political Islam. Because it is a current of thought aimed at overcoming the state, political Islam also seeks to preside over public affairs in every country where actors from this ideology are present. As such, the Egyptian Muslim Brothers receive particular attention from US think tanks. Indeed, for many years they have been seen as one of the forces that have the most to gain from questioning the political structures that existed until the Arab revolutions. The debates on how to exercise power once having come into power represent a major antiphon characterizing the production of academic circles, think tanks, and politicians involved in American strategic thinking. Having for several years appeared as wannabe leaders, Islamists have nurtured an academic and political thought that the contemporary changes in the Arab world came to interrogate.

In conducting a study of the American vision of Egyptian Islamism inspired by the Brothers, it is interesting to focus on official statements from US officials. Egyptian Islamism is embodied on the domestic political scene by its partisan element, the Freedom and Justice Party. According to a constructivist analysis, the interests of an agent are determined by intersubjective representations and discourses in which s/he is featured centrally, as represented in speeches and public statements. Although it is not the only one, this framework is well-suited to understand the interpretation of political Islam by American officials – starting with those of the Obama administration in power at the time of the Arab revolutions – and for the definition of the best policy to conduct. This is why we are primarily interested in public statements of the president, the secretary of state, and the senior US diplomats dealing specifically with the Egyptian Muslim Brothers. Since all these actors are linked by a common line defined at the highest level of political power, it should be possible to see the rationales, outlines, and developments of American Islamist policy.

Thinking about political Islam in the American debate: Between suspicion and opportunities for cooperation

Opened by the dynamics of protest, the period did not produce a change in the nature of US diplomacy vis-à-vis the Muslim Brothers. Indeed, the academic and political debate about the nature of the movement and its future practices if it were to come to power has existed for some time. US officials – those stationed in Egypt and executives of the Bureau of Near Eastern Affairs – have been in contact with representatives of the Muslim Brothers for a long time (Hamid, 2014a), although to different degrees depending on the period. US officials are also involved in public diplomacy, the aim of which is to establish channels of contact and dialogue with non-democratic societies, where opposition actors oscillate between being bullied and punished. Drawing to a large extent on contacts made with the opponents of regimes seen as having been conciliatory or even allies of the Soviet Union during the Cold War, American diplomacy has, at least since that time, tried to understand and to work with actors, groups, and movements from the Brothers' matrix. This also applies to non-Sunni Islamists, whose importance is evident in Middle Eastern politics (Gerges, 1999; Pinto, 1999). The conscience of the fundamentalist character of the Islamist offer is surely the characteristic feature perceived by the United States. However, the different administrations in contemporary times have swung between two positions (more theoretical than practical) as to the Islamist question. Thus, in 2006 when President George W. Bush was questioned about political participation of the Lebanese Hezbollah in his country, he replied:

> I like the idea of people running for office. There's a positive effect. Maybe some will run for office and say, "Vote for me. I look forward to blowing up America." But I don't think so. I think people who generally run for office say, "Vote for me. I'm looking forward to fixing your potholes."
>
> (Hamid, 2014a, p. 39)

Before his election as president, Barack Obama publicly said that he was suspicious regarding the father movement of political Islam – namely, the Muslim Brothers – describing them as "untrustworthy," "harbor[ing] anti-American views," and probably "not honoring the Camp David Peace Treaty with Israel" (Gerges, 2013b). Although political, this debate has undeniably deep ramifications for the intellectual and academic field. In fact, the think tanks, generally considered "centrist," have in recent years distinguished themselves from the positions expressed by US presidents Barack Obama and George W. Bush. While emphasizing the radical nature of Islamist ideology, those think tanks have not denied opportunities for development – in particular, the possibility of a more democratic political game in which the different political forces would be able to express their opinions. This is especially true of many reports from the Carnegie Endowment for International Peace and the Brookings Institution (Hamid, 2014b), while other institutions, such as the RAND Corporation, are characterized by a higher degree of mistrust vis-à-vis the Muslim Brothers.[3]

The difficulty of committing to a conscious Islamist policy lies in oscillation between an assumed reality principle[4] and the search for the most suitable strategy to deal with the potential, contained in the Islamic ethic, to disrupt the status quo. This recent debate echoes great fractures in academia caused by the Orientalist tradition that came from Europe in the 20th century, which created multiple discrepancies regarding the interpretation of the Islamist fact. This happened at a time when the United States was taking over the traditional powers from the other side of the Atlantic, and as the Islamist fact was becoming a major focus of analysis of the contemporary Muslim world. Understanding the political Islam phenomenon is therefore subject to different explanations. At different times its religious nature is either highlighted or minimized by the producers of academic knowledge. In fact, this same questioning can be observed regarding the reactive dimension of Islamism in an era of domination of Muslim societies (Marzouki, 2013),[5] because religious exegesis is not, for some, the main lens by which Islamism should be addressed. Influencing policy makers, these various approaches of radical Islam have been convened to justify certain military and diplomatic strategies in the Middle East.[6]

Integrating the Muslim Brothers into the political game: Applying the democratic push to Islamists

Representing a dual political force, the Muslim Brothers have been the target of a commitment policy tinged with mistrust (Gerges, 2013a). Indeed, while some argue that they are likely to be integrated into the political game, others underline that they seek to harm US interests in a region that is key for their safety. Until the revolution, the policy which prevailed was that of opposition to Hosni Mubarak's regime. Indeed, it appears that the last years of the regime then in place in Egypt have generated much debate over its sustainability and, therefore, also much debate regarding the position to be taken vis-à-vis the actors likely to challenge that power. This must be situated in the wider thinking about the necessary democratization of the states in the region known as the Great Middle East. Hence, the Bush years were characterized by the establishment of a democratic push (Hamid, 2014a) that also included the Islamist forces[7] in the countries where diplomacy was chosen over military intervention.

The theory of an Islamist movement untied from its "absolutist" roots seems to prevail. We can say that the potential of political moderation that was noted by the liberal think tanks such as Brookings, Carnegie, and the Wilson Center played a role. For many years, these think tanks have highlighted the possibility of moderation in the case of democratization in Egypt. According to US officials, the renunciation of violence (which has been the official position of the leaders of the Brothers since the 1970s) is the discriminating factor that could justify talking with representatives of political Islam, then in opposition.

President Obama pursued a substantially similar strategy. For Obama, the time had come to question the foundations on which American foreign policy in the region was built. Thus, even before the beginning of the Arab Spring, the highest US authorities had begun to consider a redefinition of the links between the United States and undemocratic states, even while perpetuating the structures of the alliance with Egypt. Supporting the sovereign right of the people to choose the political elites in the Arab world, in his speech in Cairo on June 4, 2009, President Obama further pursued this thinking in August 2010 with a five-page note addressed to his highest advisers. Entitled "Political Reform in the Middle East and North Africa" (Gerges, 2013a), the central argument of Obama's note was the need to stop believing that stability in this region comes from the support of autocratic regimes and that American interests benefit from the absence of representative government. Meanwhile, in 2009, Margaret Scobey, the US ambassador in Cairo at the time, said that "despite incessant whispered discussions, no one in Egypt has any certainty about who will eventually succeed Mubarak nor under what circumstances" (Kirkpatrick & Myers, 2012, n.p.).

At the time of the revolutions: Gradually open the door to the Muslim Brothers

The months of January and February 2011 saw the power of Mubarak falter; before this time,[8] he had finally left the power to a board of directors composed of soldiers. In the wake of the Tunisian revolution, many Egyptians expressed their desire to see the *Rais* leave. In the early days of the protest movement, which was physically crystallized by hundreds of thousands of people converging on Tahrir Square, US officials were primarily concerned about the president's situation. Yet, the question of the Muslim Brothers quickly became central as the need for Mubarak's departure became vested. It is in this context that Secretary of State Hillary Clinton said in the first days of the demonstrations that "It's not America that put people into the streets of Tunis and Cairo," adding that "these revolutions are not ours. They are not by us, for us, or against us" (cited in Hamid & Mandaville, 2013, p. 97) before noting that the government then in place was able to answer to the popular aspirations (Sanger, 2011). However, the evaluation of the situation would quickly change so as to leave room for serious concerns if those in power did not hear the revolutionary aspirations. There were also concerns about the political situation that could come from a redistribution of cards at the highest level of the Egyptian state.

Hence, the first references to the Muslim Brothers were made, reactivating the dual analysis that they inspired at the highest level of US leadership for many years. Faced with the amplification of the protest movement (culminating on Friday, January 25, 2011 during the "day of rage"), the official US position on Egypt, that had until then been a call to the Egyptian authorities, began to outgrow the sole issue of the relationship with whomever is president. This is well illustrated by John Kerry, secretary of state after the departure of Hillary Clinton, who stated that the time had come for a critique of US policy toward Egypt. Hence, in the opinions pages of the *New York Times* dated February 1, 2011, John Kerry warned:

> Given the events of the past week, some are criticizing America's past tolerance of the Egyptian regime. It is true that our public rhetoric did not always match our private concerns. But there also was a pragmatic understanding that our relationship benefited American foreign policy and promoted peace in the region. … The United States must accompany our rhetoric with real assistance to the Egyptian people. For too long, financing Egypt's military has dominated our alliance. The proof was seen over the weekend: tear gas canisters marked "Made in America" fired at protesters, United States-supplied F-16 jet fighters streaking over central Cairo. Congress and the Obama administration need to consider providing civilian assistance that would generate jobs and improve social conditions in Egypt, as well as guarantee that American military assistance is accomplishing its goals … .
>
> Our interests are not served by watching friendly governments collapse under the weight of the anger and frustrations of their own people, nor by transferring power to radical groups that would spread extremism. … For three decades, the United States pursued a Mubarak policy. Now we must look beyond the Mubarak era and devise an Egyptian policy.
>
> (Kerry, 2011, para. 8, 9)

The conditions regarding the departure of Hosni Mubarak and, more specifically, the role of the United States, were still being debated (Cooper, Landler, & Mazzetti, 2011; Marcus, 2011). At the same time, the increasing references made to the main Egyptian Islamist movement were inversely proportional to the US officials' talks. These increasingly insisted on the need for a change of leadership, or even of regime, and less and less on the need for simple reforms. Even though during the months of March and April 2011, some voices could still be heard to warn against a possible rise to power of the Muslim Brothers' leaders (Gerges, 2013a), as the political transition progressed, Hillary Clinton started to explicitly open the door to the Muslim Brothers. In fact, between spring and autumn 2011, Hillary Clinton had many opportunities to echo the need to deal with the Muslim Brothers, recognizing that the reasons underlying the American foreign policy toward certain states in the region should be subject to criticism. For example, this is when several senior diplomats of the State Department and the Pentagon officially said that they were "encouraging ... conversations with an array of opposition leaders, including the Muslim Brotherhood" (Sanger, 2011, n.p.).

The official position of the Obama administration was finally clearly expressed in June 2011 by Hillary Clinton, during a visit to Budapest:

> We believe, given the changing political landscape in Egypt, that it is in the interests of the United States to engage with all parties that are peaceful and committed to nonviolence, that intend to compete for the parliament and the presidency. ... And we welcome, therefore, dialogue with those Muslim Brotherhood members who wish to talk with us.
>
> (Sheridan, 2011, n.p.)

In November 2011, the secretary of state reiterated this position by comparing the opening-up to the Egyptian Islamists to the traditional support afforded to the systems in control, which could be the subject of criticism: "For years, dictators told their people they had to accept the autocrats they knew to avoid the extremists they feared. ... Too often, we accepted that narrative ourselves" (Gerges, 2013a, p. 312).

The Muslim Brothers in power: Taming the revisionist potential

The victories of the Muslim Brothers in the 2012 parliamentary and presidential elections came to validate the Obama administration's approach. Even though the Muslim Brothers still inspired a number of concerns about their defiance toward the United States and the possibility that they could harm US interests in the region, diplomatic engagement and inclusion remained the rule. For example, the year 2012 was marked with high-level meetings between members of the Brothers and US officials. They had regular exchanges, and the US officials were constantly seeking to gather information on Islamist sentiments and analysis while the Arab world was boiling over (Kirkpatrick & Myers, 2012). While John Kerry recognized the Muslim Brothers' victories, the US diplomats in Cairo at the time clearly announced that they wanted to work with the winning party, highlighting (particularly regarding the Islamist movement) that its leaders "have been very specific about conveying a moderate message – on regional security and domestic issues, and economic issues, as well" (Kirkpatrick & Myers, 2012, para. 9). Thus, fears expressed by Jeane Kirkpatrick, former ambassador to the United Nations, a few years before parliamentary elections were dismissed by the official US position that backed openness and the integration of the movement. The former ambassador had stated that "the Arab world is the only part of the world where I've been shaken in my conviction that if you let the people decide, they will make fundamentally rational decisions. But there, they don't make rational decisions, they make fundamentalist ones" (cited in Gerges, 2013b, p. 192). This contrasts with the comments of Assistant Secretary of State for Near Eastern Affairs Jeffrey Feltman, who said:

> We know that parties rooted in religious faiths will play larger roles. We do not yet know what the US relationship will be over the long term with emerging governments, parliaments, and civil society in these countries. We do know, however, that it will be vital that the United States establish and maintain the types of partnerships that help us protect and promote our interests and that give us the ability to help shape and influence outcomes. ... Our support for legitimate governments is the best means of countering violent extremism. The peaceful transitions in Tunisia and Egypt fundamentally undermine the extremist message that violence is the only path for political change. Providing an opportunity for an alternative, non-violent path to genuine political transition de-legitimizes extremist groups and reduces their appeal.
>
> (2012, p. 10)

Echoing these statements, a delegation of representatives of the movement was hosted at the White House in April 2012 to meet the highest US authorities, only a few months after high-level US representatives had been received in Cairo. These US representatives included William Burns, who was responsible for relations with the Ikhwan. The advent of a Brothers majority at parliament and the arrival of Mohamed Morsi's presidency offered an opportunity to verify the relevance of the US policy of engagement with the main winners of the regime liberalization.

At a time when the Egyptian state was experiencing transitional momentum, a relationship was developing between the main state power in the international system and a political-religious movement at the head of the main Arab country. This confirmed unquestionably the duality of the historical position of the U.S. elites toward the Brotherhood, and the continuing presence of this duality was evident in the public statements of the US ambassador, Anne Patterson. Indeed, the months of the Muslim Brothers' governance generated both good reports and distrust. Thanks to the responsibility that the Ikhwan demonstrated on the economic and international fronts, particularly during the Gaza conflict in November 2012 (Gerges, 2013a),[9] the governance garnered a positive assessment; however, distrust arose regarding their ideological framework and their propensity to oppose American values and interests on certain issues. The statements of Anne Patterson are illustrative of this duality. In 2011, she said that she was "not personally comfortable with it enough yet," recognizing their commitment to economic freedoms, but also having concerns about their "less liberal stances on women's rights" as well as about their position relative to the 1978 peace treaty with Israel (Negrin & Abdellatif, 2011, p. 5).

On a more practical level, financial, military, and diplomatic arrangements that had been in force at the time of Mubarak had not changed. For example, the sum of $1.55 billion traditionally allocated for strategic assistance continued to be paid, although US authorities stated that this was intended to finance security efforts in the Sinai region in order to perpetuate the security of the Israeli neighbor (Gerges, 2013b).

Since the coup d'état: Do not close the door again

The period opened by the eviction of the Muslim Brothers in July 2013 produced new tensions within the Obama administration. For more than a year, the Obama administration had been learning how to tame the aspirations of the Islamist movement while at the same time acknowledging the limitations of a policy supporting autocratic regimes. Indeed, this dualism within American Islamist policy was coupled with the need to deal with the regime of Sissi – the man who would become president a few months later (in circumstances consecutive to the arrest of President Morsi and the major Brothers leaders). This problematic relationship with the main face of Egyptian political Islam is found in the words of the same John Kerry who had, two years earlier, outlined a logical criticism about the diplomacy that the United States had been building for years in the Arab world. If the phrase "coup d'état" was not pronounced by any official, the successor of Hillary Clinton said that "Egypt's generals were 'restoring democracy'" (Kerry, cited in Hamid & Mandaville, 2013, p. 97). However, a few days after the army takeover, while there were visible tensions between the two camps, President Barack Obama expressed different feelings in an official statement from the White House:

> We are deeply concerned by the decision of the Egyptian Armed Forces to remove President Morsi and suspend the Egyptian constitution. I now call on the Egyptian military to move quickly and responsibly to return full authority back to a democratically elected civilian government as soon as possible through an inclusive and transparent process, and to avoid any arbitrary arrests of President Morsi and his supporters. Given today's developments, I have also directed the relevant departments and agencies to review the implications under US law for our assistance to the Government of Egypt. United States continues to believe firmly that the best foundation for lasting stability in Egypt is a democratic political order with participation from all sides and all political parties – secular and religious, civilian and military.
>
> (Kaufman, 2014, p. 77)

Repeated by State Department diplomats, this position illustrates the complications that characterize the discourse and the action of the United States. Thus, Elisabeth Jones, assistant secretary for Near Eastern Affairs Bureau, said that:

> Mr. Morsi proved unwilling or unable to govern inclusively, alienating many Egyptians. Responding to the desires of millions of Egyptians who

believed the revolution had taken a wrong turn and you saw a return to security and stability after years of unrest, the interim government replaced the Morsi government. But the interim government has also made decisions inconsistent with inclusive democracy. We were troubled by the July 3 events and the violence of mid-August. The decision to remove Morsi, excessive force used against protesters in August; restrictions on the press, civil society and opposition parties; the continued detention of many members of the opposition; and the extension of the state of emergency have been troubling.

(Jones, 2013)

Marie Harf, the spokesperson of the ministry, said on February 12, 2014:

The United States does not – has not designated the Muslim Brotherhood as a terrorist organization. We have been very clear in Egypt that we will work with all sides and all parties to help move an inclusive process forward. We've also repeatedly, both publicly and privately, called on the interim government to move forward in an inclusive manner. That means talking to all parties, bringing them into the process. We're not saying what the future government should look like specifically other than that it should be inclusive. That, of course, includes the Muslim Brotherhood. We will continue talking to the Muslim Brotherhood in Egypt as part of our broad outreach to the different parties and groups there.

(Harf, 2014)

Thus, in the period immediately after the coup d'état, it seems that embarrassment and a wait-and-see policy were the main features of the US position. "Neither-nor" or, rather, "and-and" was the course taken, dealing with the new regime and sparing the Brothers. If it recognized the, now undebatable, installation of Marshal Sissi at the head of state, American diplomacy remained attached to not completely closing the door to the Muslim Brothers, at least discursively. Hence, they recognized the exceptional nature of the situation in Egypt while, at the same time, noting that mistakes were made by the Islamist movement when it was at the head of government. As the return (temporary or not) of a military regime seemed to signify the end of the Brothers' policy of engagement, it appears that this relationship undeniably illustrates the limits and contradictions of the US policy in this region. Indeed, although US policy still reflects a strong engagement in the Middle East, it now has to deal with huge changes that are increasingly out of its reach.

Notes

1 For an in-depth presentation of the international issues in this region, see Louise Fawcett (2013).
2 Egypt has known a facade of independence long after the official end of the British protectorate in 1922.

3 This institution has produced some analyses that were close to those from the Brookings Institution. See, for example, Martini, Kaye, and York (2012) as well as more essentialist studies about the Islamic fact and the Islamist question (Benard, 2003). For example, in Benard's report, the question of the democratization of the majority Muslim societies is tied up with the question of secularization, as we cannot consider the actors who claim a religious identity as privileged partners. Even more fundamentally, this study draws a typology of the Muslims in the world, dividing them up as "secularists," "traditionalists," "modernists," and "fundamentalists." Put in the "fundamentalists" category, the Muslim Brothers are interpreted as being less compatible with democracy, but also closer to jihadist and terrorist organizations such as Al-Qaida than the moderate actors. Thus, the author argues that there is an ideological and political continuum unifying all the Islam militants.

4 This principle is accepted as the main basis of opposition to the dominant regime in Egypt; namely, a concern for American interests in the area.

5 For an in-depth study of the US academic debates regarding Islam, see Marzouki (2013).

6 On one hand, the work of historian Bernard Lewis tends to accreditate, with the backing of some influential neoconservatives during the presidency of Bush Jr., some acquaintances between Islam and Islamism; whereas other academics, among them John Esposito and Leonard Binder, have for a long time distinguished themselves with a social and political analysis of Islamism. For those of the latter position, Islamism is an identity response to the phenomena of domination and weakening brought about by the experiences of the Muslim countries in the 20th century.

7 Assuming that Islamism represents a potential ally against the systematically violent transnational jihadism, the Bush administration promoted a real "diplomacy of the opposition," which continued to rely on Mubarak's Egypt while keeping the opportunity to discuss and work with his main opponent.

8 On February 11, 2011 ("Friday of Departure"), Mubarak's resignation was announced, and the leadership of the country was entrusted to the Supreme Council of Egyptian Armed Forces.

9 Their role in the fighting and their ability to put pressure on Hamas have been hailed by US officials, to the point that it was described as "positive." See Fawaz Gerges (2013a).

References

Benard, C. (2003). *Civil democratic Islam: Partners, resources and strategies.* Santa Monica, CA: RAND Corporation. Retrieved from www.rand.org/content/dam/rand /pubs/monograph_reports/2005/MR1716.pdf.

Cooper, H., Landler, M. and Mazzetti, M. (2011, February 2). Sudden split recasts U.S. foreign policy. *New York Times.* Retrieved from www.nytimes.com/2011/02/03/ world/middleeast/03diplomacy.html?action=click&contentCollection=Middle%20E ast&module=RelatedCoverage&region=Marginalia&pgtype=article.

Fawcett, L. (Ed.). (2013). *International relations of the Middle East.* Oxford: Oxford University Press.

Feltman, J. (2012). Statement of The Honorable Jeffrey D. Feltman, Assistant Secretary of State, Bureau of Near Eastern Affairs, U.S. Department of State. In U.S. Department of State, *Hearing, May 9, 2012: Assessing U.S. foreign policy priorities and needs amidst economic challenges in the Middle East* (pp. 6–21). Washington, DC: U.S Printing Office. Retrieved from http://archives.republicans.foreignaffairs.ho use.gov/112/74194.pdf.

Gerges, F.A. (1999). *America and political Islam: Clash of cultures or clash of interests?* Cambridge: Cambridge University Press.

Gerges, F.A. (2013a). The Obama approach to the Middle East: The end of America's moment? *International Affairs*, 89(2), 299–323. doi:10.1111/1468-2346.12019.

Gerges, F.A. (2013b). What changes have taken place in US foreign policy towards Islamists? *Contemporary Arab Affairs*, 6(2), 189–197. doi:10.1080/17550912.2013.788869.

Hamid, S. (2014a). *Temptations of power: Islamists and illiberal democracy in a new Middle East*. Oxford: Oxford University Press.

Hamid, S. (2014b). *The enduring challenge of engaging Islamists: Lessons from Egypt*. Washington, DC: Brookings Institution, Project on Middle East Democracy. Retrieved from https://www.brookings.edu/research/the-enduring-challenge-of-engaging-islamists-lessons-from-egypt/.

Hamid, S. and Mandaville, P. (2013). Bringing the United States back into the Middle East. *The Washington Quarterly*, 36(4), 95–105. doi:10.1080/0163660x.2013.861716.

Harf, M. (2014, February 12). Daily Press Briefing, U.S. State Department. Retrieved from https://www.c-span.org/video/?317777-1/state-department-daily-briefing.

Jones, E. (2013, October 29). Testimony before the House Foreign Affairs Committee. Retrieved from http://m.state.gov/md215965.htm.

Kaufman, J.P. (2014). *A concise history of U.S. foreign policy* (3rd ed.). Lanham, MD: Rowman & Littlefield.

Kerry, J. (2011, February 1). Allying ourselves with the next Egypt. *New York Times*. Retrieved from www.nytimes.com/2011/02/01/opinion/01kerry.html.

Kirkpatrick, D.D. and Myers, S.L. (2012, January 3). Overtures to Egypt's Islamists reverse longtime U.S. policy. *New York Times*. Retrieved from www.nytimes.com/2012/01/04/world/middleeast/us-reverses-policy-in-reaching-out-to-muslim-brotherhood.html.

Marcus, J. (2011, February 5). Egypt unrest: US disowns envoy comment on Hosni Mubarak. *BBC News*. Retrieved from www.bbc.com/news/world-us-canada-12374753.

Martini, J., Kaye, D.D. and York, E. (2012). *The Muslim Brotherhood, its youth, and implications for US engagements*. Santa Monica, CA: RAND Corporation. Retrieved from www.rand.org/pubs/monographs/MG1247.html.

Marzouki, N. (2013). *L'islam, une religion américaine?* Paris, France: Seuil. Retrieved from https://ec56229aec51f1baff1d-185c3068e22352c56024573e929788ff.ssl.cf1.rackcdn.com/attachments/original/2/8/6/002594286.pdf.

Mohamed-Ali, A. (Ed.). (in press). *Islamism and foreign policy. Ideology in practice*. Edinburgh, Scotland: Edinburgh University Press.

Negrin, M. and Abdellatif, R. (2011, October 18). US ambassador to Egypt won't sit down with Muslim Brotherhood … yet. *GlobalPost*.

Pinto, M. do Cen. (1999). *Political Islam and the United States: A study of US policy towards Islamist movements*. Ithaca, NY: Ithaca Press.

Sanger, D.E. (2011, February 5). As Mubarak digs in, U.S. policy in Egypt is complicated. *New York Times*. Retrieved from www.nytimes.com/2011/02/06/world/middleeast/06policy.html?_r=0.

Sheridan, M.B. (2011, June 30). U.S. to expand relations with Muslim Brotherhood. *Washington Post*. Retrieved from https://www.washingtonpost.com/world/national-security/us-to-expand-relations-with-muslim-brotherhood/2011/06/30/AGVgppsH_story.html.

Tammen, R.L., Lemke, D., Alsharabati, C., Efird, B., Kugler, J., StamIII, A.C. and Organski, A.F.K. (2000). *Power transitions: Strategies for the 21st century*. Washington, DC: CQ Press.

12 Promoting or resisting change?

The United States and the Egyptian uprising, 2011–2012

Ahmed Ali Salem

After President Barack Obama's electoral victory in 2008, an advisor of the outgoing president, Christian Brose, expressed the expectation that President Obama's foreign policy would resemble that of President George W. Bush's second administration and that the variance between the two foreign policies would be thinner than the variance between the foreign policies of Bush's first and second administrations (Brose, 2009, p. 53). But President Obama was keen to distinguish himself, at least on the surface, from his unpopular predecessor, especially in foreign policy. As he arrived in office, Obama's apparent embrace of "realism" was therefore a clear indication that his foreign policy was the opposite of Bush's, which was characterized as "idealist" (to use International Relations Theory terms), particularly as far as the global spread of democracy was concerned (Cohen, 2016).

Nevertheless, Obama's foreign policy shift was largely in terms of methods and tools, and it did not impact the definition of global American interests, which Obama, as a president-hopeful, articulated in the summer 2007 *Foreign Affairs* issue. In his article, Obama called for the United States to adopt a new vision of world leadership in the twenty-first century, but followed Bush's administration in defining the sources of threats as including weapons of mass destruction, global terrorism, rogue states, the rising powers that could challenge both the United States and liberal democracy, and global warming that would result in new diseases, coastal erosion, and other devastating natural disasters. He described his desired vision of leadership as addressing globally shared concerns of security and humanity, based on past experience, but unbounded by outdated thinking. He stopped short, however, of stating its main characteristics, perhaps purposefully in order not to alienate potential voters.

Interestingly, this vagueness continued after his election as president, and the foreign policy of his first administration (2009–2013) was therefore described sometimes as idealist and other times as realist. This debate was politically oriented: while his critics judged him as no better than his predecessor, his supporters sought to demonstrate his foreign policy distinctions. Both groups, however, failed to recognize the double nature of Obama's foreign policy; that is, its idealist rhetoric and realist action. In this chapter, I highlight this double nature in the case of the Egyptian uprising which began in

January 2011. While Obama praised the Egyptians for bravely revolting against oppression and injustice, his administration backed the ruling military council throughout the transitional period, which lasted until June 2012, thus effectively subverting the revolution.

This chapter is arranged in two sections. The first section traces the salient changes that Obama's first administration introduced in US foreign policy, and reviews the opposing arguments of his critics and supporters as discussed in journals, magazines, and newspapers in the first six months after Obama assumed power. The second section focuses on the Obama administration's policy on the Egyptian uprising and highlights the inconsistencies between its democracy-promoting words and status-quo-entrenching deeds.

Realism and idealism in the foreign policy of Obama's first administration

President Obama's new foreign and defense policy team, notably Hillary Clinton, Robert Gates, and James Jones, alienated many of his electoral campaign supporters, especially those who aspired for fundamental changes, such as liberal democrats who accused Bush's administration of using demo-cratization only as a slogan and endeavoring to promote it only selectively and instrumentally. Also alienated were several of Obama's foreign policy and defense advisors, such as Lawrence J. Korb, Richard Danzig, and Daniel Kurtzer, who were leaning toward liberalism compared to the advisors of Obama's rival in the Democratic Party's primary election, Hillary Clinton, whose team included more original Iraq war supporters (Richter, 2009b). Obama's foreign policy realism began by appointing Clinton as Secretary of State and accepting her nominees as diplomats. He also kept the outgoing Defense Secretary Robert Gates and selected retired general Jim Jones as the National Security Advisor – none had served in his electoral campaign team or was known as a supporter of his campaign rhetoric. The only appointees who had served in his campaign were centralist, such as White House advisors Rahm Emanuel, David Axelrod, Robert Gibbs, and Denis McDonough (Hoagland, 2009). In other words, the spoils of Obama's electoral victory went to the moderates, not his liberal supporters (Richter, 2009b).

One week after her appointment, Clinton announced that she spoke to tens of world leaders who expressed their satisfaction with the new team at the State Department and their efforts to redraw American foreign policy away from the previous administration's practices, which Obama and his new administration continued for months to blame for all foreign policy difficulties (Baker, 2009b). Clinton also announced at her first press conference that the new administration had already begun to review the previous administration's methods of dealing with major issues, such as the ongoing nuclearization of Iran and North Korea (Richter, 2009a). On Iran, Obama called for a new quiet diplomacy, reiterating his old claim that the previous administration had not attempted dialogue with Iran, despite some evidences to the opposite

(Timmerman, 2009). Obama's supporters defended his policy as a good solution to the problems inherited from Bush's administration (Jackson, 2009).

During his first six months in office, Obama visited a number of countries, exceeding the number of visits of any previous president in the same period. To market the new foreign policy to the general public, a top White House adviser claimed that Obama's trips "created a new receptivity to US interests and made America-bashing uncool," and his approach to foreign policy included "a sense of humility" that "was missing" in the past, as former President Bush was perceived as someone who dictated to both allies and enemies (Ward, 2009).

But neither Obama nor his aids hinted to the spread of democracy as a foreign policy goal. His speech to the Muslim world at Cairo University in June 2009 is a good example of this realist policy: while he declared that the United States would respect all law-abiding authorities and groups, even those with which it disagreed, and welcomed every elected and peace-seeking government (Hamzawy & Christiansen, 2009), he made no promise to support the pro-democratization forces in the Muslim world, thus sending a clear message that the United States was reverting to its traditional policy of dealing with the world as is, not upon the wishes of the pro-democratization supporters (Baker, 2009a). This classic diplomacy was based on a realistic assessment of the United States' capabilities, which cannot sustain a policy of reshaping the world in its own image. Accordingly, the maximum that the United States could do to export its democratic values was to enhance them domestically (for example, by closing the infamous Guantanamo Bay in Cuba); promote world trade; and improve its diplomatic relations and exchange of ideas with others (Hadar, 2009).

Hence, Obama appeared as "a hard-headed and unapologetic realist" who recognizes the limits of American power (Dejevsky, 2009) and understands that the United States cannot force the world to submit to its will ("Realism makes a welcome return to US foreign policy," 2009). Believing in gradual change, he wanted to serve American interests pragmatically, defending no ideology. He was compared to the famous foreign minister of the Austrian Empire in the nineteenth century, Prince Klemens von Metternich, who "rejected unabashed power politics, endorsed the idea of an international community with collective solutions, and persuaded liberal states such as Britain to cooperate with their autocratic counterparts" (de las Casas, 2009).

Therefore, his disillusioned political opponents in the pro-democratization camp accused him of hating the political system of the country that elected him (Parker, 2009) and of adopting an anti-American ideology (Glick, 2009). They seized the twentieth anniversary of the fall of the Berlin Wall to remind him that liberal democracy is capable of changing regimes in the right direction (Tomasky, 2009) and called upon him not to confuse spreading democracy and following the previous administration's foreign policy methods, as he could demonstrate US interest in global democratization and, at the same time, adopt new foreign policy methods (Traub, 2009).

But if most supporters and some opponents of Obama's foreign policy found it outright realist, why did some critics call it idealist? The answer lies in Obama's foreign policy rhetoric, which sometimes covered its realism with idealist rationales and aspirations. Thus, former Secretary of State Henry Kissinger, though himself a realist supporter of Obama, criticized him for dealing with every international problem or crisis by delivering a rhetorical and philosophical speech (Atkins, 2009), such as his above-mentioned address to the Muslim world. In promoting international cooperation, Obama also raised expectations of more American involvement in world affairs, which could not be carried out without overburdening the United States financially (Ignatius, 2009). Several prominent realist theorists of international relations warned against this risk. Kenneth Waltz, for example, argued that the inflated defense budget was Obama's greatest, but overlooked, challenge. In his view, the United States was abusing its power and following the trajectory of overwhelmingly strong states in history. For John Mearsheimer, the most dangerous threat that Obama ignored was the real possibility of Mexico turning into a failed state (Avey et al., 2009), restoration of which would require the United States to mobilize huge resources.

Obama was also portrayed as an idealist by the hawks of the Republican Party who were upset at his humility with world leaders, which in their opinion only drew praise from those leaders, not concrete results for the United States (Dilanian, 2009). Conservatives criticized him as naive and unexperienced, and they condemned his simplistic conviction that states and other international actors will change their malign behavior only if they perceive a positive change in US behavior toward them (Usborne, 2009). They likened him to the idealist President Woodrow Wilson who thought that states acted upon the perceived good will of other states, especially the United States (Kagan, 2009). Conservatives also condemned his quiet diplomacy with Iran and bargaining with Afghanistan's Taliban, which they said only raised the demands of US enemies in anticipation of concessions and winning time to achieve their goals (Lambro, 2009).

In short, on the eve of the Arab uprisings of 2011, Obama's administration was its furthest from encouraging the spread of democracy. Its democracy-promoting rhetoric after the eruption of these revolts was therefore not a sign of changing foreign policy toward the Arab countries; rather, it was additional proof of the discrepancies between its idealist words and realist action. Its double-faced position in the Egyptian uprising makes this point crystal clear.

Supporting the status quo while singing for change in Egypt (2011–2012)

Egypt is arguably the Arab state most pivotal to American interests. According to a former US Assistant Secretary of State, the United States has "no more important partner in the Arab world than Egypt" (DeYoung & Fadel, 2012). From a geopolitical point of view, the United States has two long-outstanding interests in the region: first, to secure the uninterrupted flow of oil from the region to American and world markets; and, second, to preserve the regional imbalance of power by supporting Israel and weakening its enemies. Egypt is a key state in achieving both goals: it controls the Suez Canal and is the most powerful state in the Arab camp of peace with Israel. Egypt is also critical to American economic interests; its economic liberalization program introduced a quarter of a century ago integrated its economy in the world capitalist system. Egypt's instability following its uprising in January 2011 endangered all these areas of critical importance to the United States (Sheridan, 2011a).

Before the uprising, Egypt was a classic case of state-as-unitary-actor, which is one of the main assumptions of the realist school of international relations (Viotti & Kauppi, 1987: 6). Interested foreign powers, including allies such as the United States, had to interact only with one actor; that is, President Hosni Mubarak. Egyptian politicians who challenged his monopoly over foreign policy were accused of conspiring with foreigners and undermining Egypt's interests, facing all the political, and sometimes legal, consequences. The United States was not uncomfortable with Mubarak's dictatorship as long as he cooperated with it and served its interests, which he did to a great extent (Broder, 2012: 49).

After the uprising, this scene changed: with no president in office for more than sixteen months, the various players of the foreign affairs game included state as well as nonstate actors, but the main actor was the Supreme Council of Armed Forces (SCAF) – a professional military body that had no political experience whatsoever and which last met during the 1973 Arab-Israeli war. Although the military was the single institution from which all Egyptian presidents had emerged since the formation of the Egyptian Republic in 1953, it was rarely invited to intervene in politics openly. During Mubarak's reign, the military had its own economic and business operations, thus was largely considered the main supporter of the regime. However, during the 2011 uprising, and after more than two weeks of continuous mass demonstrations, the SCAF met without its head, the President, and announced its support of the people's will. This was a critical turning point, forcing Mubarak to resign and delegate his presidential authority to the SCAF on February 11. On March 30, the SCAF issued a constitutional declaration, approved in a referendum and defining the steps to elect a parliament and a president, write a new constitution, and end the transitional period after six months, although the SCAF had pledged to end it earlier. Despite this, the SCAF prolonged the transitional period further and was reluctant to step down and was forced by popular pressures to implement the constitutional steps of power transition, thus submitting the executive power officially to an elected civilian president on June 30, 2012.

US administration's support of the SCAF

The US administration was following these developments closely. At the beginning of the uprising on January 25, 2011, it was caught unprepared for any political leadership change in Egypt (Macintyre, 2011). The US Secretary of State Hillary Clinton expressed her confidence in the stability of the Mubarak regime and said that the Egyptian government was looking for ways to respond to the wishes of the people (NBC News, 2011). Special envoy Frank Wisner also said that Mubarak must stay in office to oversee the transition (Loy, 2011: 28). But on February 1 after a full week of continuous mass demonstrations, Obama broke his silence, expressing his conviction of the need to change and siding openly with the revolutionaries (Obama, 2011a). On February 10, one day before Mubarak stepped down, he reiterated his position more strongly (Obama, 2011b). On the other hand, US officials enticed the SCAF to step in and force Mubarak to step down. The US secretary of defense and the chairman of the joint chiefs of staff both urged their Egyptian counterparts to gently send Mubarak to the exit, restore calm, and preside over an orderly transition ("The ties that bind," 2011). One month after overthrowing Mubarak, Secretary of State Clinton visited Cairo, met SCAF leaders, and announced US support of the steps taken "to lay the groundwork for free and fair elections" ("Obama Administration commends Egypt for orderly transition," 2011).

The SCAF assumption of power was not only welcomed by the Egyptian masses, who simply looked at it as a politically disinterested body that would honestly oversee the transition of power to an elected government, but was also a relief for the US administration for several reasons. First, its head was a close aide of Mubarak, serving as the defense minister since 1991. His leadership was therefore expected to maintain Egypt's strong relationship with the United States. Second, the United States have had strong relations with the Egyptian army since the signing of the peace treaty between Egypt, Israel, and the United States in 1979 ("The ties that bind," 2011).

It is therefore unsurprising that throughout the transition period, the US administration was unwilling to antagonize the SCAF – "the last guarantor of critical US interests" (LaFranchi, 2012) – even when the SCAF appeared reluctant to fulfill its promise to lead a democratic transition and its forces crashed peaceful demonstrations demanding that it hand over power to a democratically elected government. Indeed, one year after Mubarak resigned, the SCAF had already subjected more than ten thousand civilians to military trials, dropped cement blocks onto the heads of peaceful demonstrators from the roofs of government buildings, and stripped women protestors or submitted them to virginity tests (Goodspeed, 2012). In all such cases, the US administration reacted only benignly and verbally with its all too familiar idealist rhetoric.

In November 2011, for example, when Egyptian security forces crashed protestors, killing at least 41 civilians and injuring more than a thousand, senior US officials called their Egyptian counterparts urging restraint, and the White House issued a statement condemning the excessive use of force against the protesters and warning the military to swiftly begin a full transfer of power to a civilian government in a just and inclusive manner as soon as possible (Diehl, 2011). Also, the following month, when the security forces attacked protesters against military rule over the course of several days, killing at least 13 civilians and injuring hundreds, the US Secretary of State expressed deep concerns about that violence and "urged the security forces to respect and protect the universal rights of all Egyptians" ("US urges Egypt to respect rights," 2011). Secretary Clinton also condemned the SCAF's "disgraceful" handling of protests, referring to a brutal attack on women protestors who were senselessly beaten by military police (Beach, 2011). Nevertheless, none of these violations of human rights or SCAF failures to fulfill its democratization promises convinced the US administration to suspend the huge US aid to the Egyptian military or even to link it to SCAF steps to fulfill its promises – a link proposed by opposition leaders in Congress – causing tensions in relations with the SCAF, as discussed below. To the contrary, the US administration continued to supply the Egyptian military with weapons, such as the sale of 125 M1A1 Abrams tanks approved in July 2011 by the US Defense Security Cooperation Agency (de Larrinaga & Wasserbly, 2011).

SCAF protection of US interests

In turn, the SCAF met many expectations of the US administration and frustrated many expectations of the revolutionaries, who typically pushed for changes. Although the SCAF became Egypt's main foreign policy actor, it lacked a new vision of Egypt's foreign policy. Thus, it and the holdover cabinet led a conservative foreign policy and preferred to continue business with the United States as usual, because their worldview and definition of Egyptian interests were like those of the old regime.

When this holdover cabinet collapsed under revolutionary pressures in early March and a new cabinet was formed with the support of the revolutionaries, the SCAF failed to carry through the new government's bold initiatives in foreign affairs, especially those which would upset the United States. For example, the new foreign minister, Nabil El-Arabi, took initiatives to improve Egypt's relations with Iran and Palestinian groups, insisting that Egypt's foreign policy should serve none other than Egypt and that Egypt must restore its previous place of regional leadership (Birnbaum, 2011). Inspired by this positive attitude, revolutionary coalitions, youth groups, professional and business associations, and other unofficial bodies took initiatives to serve what they regarded as Egyptian interests abroad. For example, they organized popular campaigns that visited Sudan, Ethiopia, Gaza, and Iran. But the US administration was not pleased with some of these popular initiatives and Egypt's new foreign policy orientations. Thus, the SCAF removed Nabil El-Arabi, nominating him to the office of the Secretary-General of the League of Arab States. He was elected to that office and began his new career in July 2011.

Another example of the SCAF fulfilling US expectations is its stance on the policy of the minister of international cooperation, Fayza Aboul-Naga, against unregistered foreign funding of civil societies in Egypt, apparently to prevent foreign intervention in Egypt's domestic affairs. Initially encouraged by the SCAF as a response to the US Senate move to link military aid to Egypt to its performance as a democracy (Sheridan, 2011b), Aboul-Naga's policy caused severe tensions between Egypt and the United States, and it was eventually reversed by the SCAF. Specifically, when Egyptian misgivings went beyond typical criticism of American foreign policy (Chick, 2011b) and Egyptian judicial and police officials raided and closed the offices of 17 non-governmental organizations promoting democracy and human rights (such as the US-funded International Republican Institute and the National Democratic Institute), accusing them of receiving foreign funding while failing to register with Egyptian authorities (Collard, 2011), top US officials voiced deep concerns. For example, President Obama spoke to the SCAF's chairman (Richter, 2012), and the Secretary of State warned that this situation could impact all aspects of the relationship between the United States and Egypt, implicitly referring to the Senate-imposed conditions on US aid to Egypt; namely, the State Department must certify Egypt's commitment to preserving peace with Israel, fair elections, and protecting freedom of speech, association, religion, and due process of law (Wan, 2012b). Thus, against all escalatory measures taken by the cabinet, the SCAF ended the crisis suddenly on March 1, 2012 by submitting to the American demands. Upon SCAF instruction, the prosecutor general permitted all American defendants still in Egypt to exit the country (Fleishman, 2012).

While this decision ended the most pronounced diplomatic crisis between the two states, it was decried in Egypt as surrendering to American pressures and making the judiciary a tool in the hands of the military (El Deeb, 2012). Egyptian activists denounced SCAF exploitation of nationalist sentiments and deepening anti-Americanism "by using the case to divert attention from the army crackdown on protests and pro-democracy movements" (Fleishman & Hassan, 2012). Indeed, during the crisis, anti-Americanism was thriving with more than 70 percent of Egyptians pushing for a rejection of US funding (Schenker, 2012). The crisis only deepened the bitterness already felt by many Egyptians toward the United States, which they saw as Mubarak's patron until his fall in 2011 (Fadel, 2012). Many Egyptians were ready to believe that the United States was behind all bad things taking place in Egypt (Sprusansky, 2012b).

One last example of SCAF acting upon the wishes of the US administration concerns Egypt's relations with Israel. During the early months of the transition period, the peace treaty with Israel was at risk because the general attitude among the revolutionaries was against it. As implemented by the Mubarak regime, the treaty symbolized Egypt's total submission to Israel, and therefore many Egyptians demanded its amendment, if not total abrogation. Egypt's revolutionary-supported prime minister once said that the treaty was "not a sacred thing and is always open to discussion" (Myers, 2011). Worried about the peace treaty, US senior officials, including the president, called upon Egypt to respect it. Their worries reached a peak when mass demonstrators, frustrated by the failure of the SCAF to respond to Israeli shooting of Egyptian border guards after an attack on a bus inside Israel, besieged the Israeli embassy in Cairo in August 2011 and called for retaliation (Musallam, 2011). When the demonstrators once again stormed the embassy the next month, the US president and the defense secretary, Leon Panetta, rushed to phone the SCAF chairman, and consequently, Egyptian soldiers evacuated the trapped Israelis. Thus, the Israeli ambassador left the country, and the embassy shut down ("A problem with club Med," 2011).

In addition to respecting the peace treaty with Israel, the SCAF mediated between Israel and Hamas. It brokered a prisoner exchange according to which hundreds of Palestinian prisoners were released in exchange for a captive Israeli soldier – a long-awaited deal indeed. Furthermore, with American help, the SCAF released a dual US-Israeli citizen held on suspicion of spying in exchange for 25 Egyptians jailed in Israel for non-security offenses (Greenberg, 2011). In short, the SCAF removed tensions in US-Egypt relations by blocking or reversing actions taken by cabinet ministers or revolutionary activists on several occasions.

US suspicions of SCAF alternatives – the case of the Muslim Brotherhood

The US administration faced a major challenge during Egypt's transitional period; that is, to preserve a minimum level of integrity and consistency in its policy toward old and new actors in Egypt. It had a special difficulty dealing with the emerging revolutionaries who condemned Egypt's submission to the dictation of the United States and had new visions of how Egypt's foreign policy in general and its relations with the United States in particular ought to be. Secretary of State Clinton once admitted in a testimony to Congress that one of the United States' problems in Egypt was the lack of a single Egyptian voice to converse with, "and I keep reminding myself of that because it is an uncertain situation for all the different players" (Fadel, 2012). To overcome this problem, the US administration reached out to new Egyptian players, issuing an invitation to the White House to presidential candidates and several political activists, especially young people and women, and receiving them warmly. But its approach toward the Muslim Brotherhood was more cautious.

The group had been a player in Egyptian politics to which US administrations paid little attention, but emerged during the transitional period as an electorally popular force. On the one hand, the Obama administration considered it a moderate group, despite its occasional portrayals in American media as "an anti-American, revolutionary Islamist group that wants to wipe Israel off the map and transform Egypt as an Islamist state" (Rubin, 2011: 55). The US administration also rejected the accusations that "the Muslim Brotherhood's commitment to democracy extends only to winning power and its intent is to impose strict Islamic justice at home and a new hostility toward Israel abroad" (Jim, 2012). In turn, the Brotherhood's Deputy Supreme Guide, Khayrat Al-Shatir, told the American (and other) ambassadors in Cairo that it was open to all foreign powers willing to cooperate with Egypt to alleviate its acute economic crises and achieve mutual interests, but not those aiming to serve their own interests at the expense of Egypt's (Al-Jazeera Satellite Channel, 2012). Moreover, the group did not ask the United States to be apologetic about its support of Mubarak's regime provided that US aid to Egypt continued to flow unconditionally as "compensations for the many years [that the United States] supported a brutal dictatorship," according to a senior Brotherhood official (Schenker, 2012).

On the other hand, although the US administration became more accepting of the group, there was hardly any "sea change in US policy towards it," as an expert noted (Jim, 2012). It pursued only "limited discussions" with the Brotherhood in 2011 (Bradley & Entous, 2011), and when the Democratic Coalition, led by the Freedom and Justice Party, an offshoot of the Brotherhood, won 47 percent of all seats in the parliamentary elections between November 2011 and January 2012, the US administration stressed to the group the importance of regional stability and its desire "to see a more inclusive Egypt that respects women and minorities" (DeYoung & Fadel, 2012). In April 2012, only low White House officials received a delegation of the group and its party, which also met with policy experts "to counter persistent fears about the group's emergence as the country's most powerful political force" and to bring down "the wall of mistrust" (Wan, 2012a).

Conservative voices warned that the group's victory could adversely affect US interests and regional stability (Satloff & Trager, 2012) and that the Brotherhood would act in a radical fashion. They blamed the Egyptians and the "policies of Bush and Obama administrations and liberal abdicators who believe any use of freedom is legitimate" (Stephens, 2012). Such anti-Brotherhood voices became louder during Egypt's presidential election in May–June 2012, and the US administration obviously had a similar attitude. Thus, it failed to criticize the measures taken by the SCAF to enhance its power grab, through another constitutional declaration, before eventually transferring the executive authority to the president-elect, the Brotherhood candidate, Mohamed Morsy on June 30, 2012.

Conclusion

Shortly after the eruption of Arab uprisings in early 2011, articles in American academic journals, popular magazines, and newspapers regarded the future of American influence in the Middle East and North Africa in the era of "the Arab Spring" pessimistically. For example, one author questioned whether "the Arab Spring" would be an "American Fall" in the region (Sky, 2011: p. 23). Another author called it an "Arab Winter" and argued that, "the fall of Arab autocrats creates more risks than opportunities for the United States. As Arab political horizons expand, the space for America to pursue its interests may well contract" (Miller, 2011: p. 36). A third found that "the US position in the region, an area of vital interest since the end of World War II, has been weakened" (Smith, 2011: p. 6). This pessimism, however, was premature, not because idealists were correct that the Arab uprisings would democratize Arab states as the 1989 uprisings had in Eastern Europe, but because much of the resulting change concerned new foreign policy actors, not identities – a change welcomed, and partly promoted, by US officials. Since the beginning of the Arab uprisings, the US administration resisted successfully any serious change in the foreign policies of states involved in the Arab uprisings. It had to deal with new actors, to whom it had never paid attention, but with no serious damage inflicted on major American interests in the region, at least in the short run, as it induced and pressured the new actors to play old games.

Strikingly for the pessimists, the US administration was able to navigate relations with Egypt during its transitional period with almost no damage to US major interests in the region. Tamara Wittes, a former US deputy assistant secretary of state for Near Eastern affairs, said that the US administration treated Egypt's new realties with "strategic patience," aiming at not letting disagreements with the interim authorities leave a prolonged negative impact on the relations between the two countries (Sprusansky, 2012a). But many Egyptians resented that the United States only belatedly supported their uprising against Mubarak, and they envisioned a more independent foreign policy and a much smaller role for the United States (Chick, 2011a). The Mubarak regime's submission to the United States made the relations between the two countries an easy target of negative popular sentiments in Egypt. This was evident in the high level of anti-Americanism among Egyptian masses noted shortly before the revolt, arguably because of American "overidentification" with unpopular local dictators (Blaydes & Linzer, 2011: pp. 226–228).

After the uprising, and for the first time in a generation, the United States needed to convince the Egyptian public that an alliance with it is worth preserving (Diehl, 2011). But that required the US administration to meet a major challenge in the post-Mubarak era; namely, to convince Egyptians that the United States had eventually solved the old conflict between its ideals and material interests in the region. In too many occasions after the revolution, US senior officials emphasized the United State's unshaking support for promoting democracy in Egypt, but Egyptians had heard this claim too many times before. A notable example was the 2005 confession of Secretary of State Condoleezza Rice in Cairo that for sixty years, the United States had pursued stability at the expense of democracy in the region, but achieved neither. "Now we are taking a different course. We are supporting the democratic aspirations of all people" (Spencer, 2011). However, deeds did not follow words, and the United States continued to back such notorious dictators as Mubarak. The United States must redefine its interests in Egypt and the region more generally and stop prioritizing stability over democracy; rather, it must support stability *through* democratization – a bold step that US administrations seem reluctant to take.

References

Al-Jazeera Satellite Channel. (2012, February 2). Borderless Talk Show: Political responsibility of Muslim Brotherhood in Egypt [in Arabic]. Retrieved from www.alj azeera.net/programs/pages/9ec68489-1d93-4697-983a-e5ea8ad09ae3.

Atkins, D. (2009, July 11). US yet to profit from soft policy. *The Courier Mail*, p. 66.

Avey, P.C., Desch, M.C., Long, J., Maliniak, D., Peterson, S. and Tierney, M.J. (2009, March–April). Inside the ivory tower. *Foreign Policy*, 171, 84.

Baker, P. (2009a, February 22). Pushing democracy: Handling with care. *The New York Times*, WK1.

Baker, P. (2009b, June 12). Blaming the guy who came before does not work long. *The New York Times*, A16.

Beach, A. (2011, December 21). Cairo's women take to streets and tell military: No more beatings. *The Independent*, 24.

Birnbaum, M. (2011, April 29). Egypt reasserting its role as regional power broker. *The Washington Post*, A08.

Blaydes, L. and Linzer, D.A. (2011). Elite competition, religiosity, and anti-Americanism in the Islamic World. *American Political Science Review*, 106(2), 225–243.

Bradley, M. and Entous, A. (2011, July 1). US reaches out to Islamist parties. *Wall Street Journal*, A06.

Broder, J. (2012, May–June). Unfinished Mideast revolts. *The National Interest*, 119, 49–54.

Brose, C. (2009, January–February). The making of George W. Obama. *Foreign Policy*, 170, 53.

Chick, K. (2011a, May 19). What Arabs want to hear (or not to hear) from Obama speech. *Christian Science Monitor*.

Chick, K. (2011b, August 12). Why Egypt is angry over $65 million in US democracy grant. *Christian Science Monitor*.

Cohen, R. (2016, March 18). Obama's flawed realism. *The New York Times*. Retrieved from https://www.nytimes.com/2016/03/19/opinion/obamas-flawed-realism.html?m cubz=1&_r=0.

Collard, R. (2011, December 29). US "deeply concerned" after Egypt raids NGOs offices. *Christian Science Monitor*. Retrieved from https://www.csmonitor.com/World /Middle-East/2011/1229/US-deeply-concerned-after-Egypt-raids-NGO-offices.

de Larrinaga, N. and Wasserbly, D. (2011, July 13). US poised to supply 125 M1A1 MBTS to post-Mubarak Egypt. *Jane's Defence Weekly*, 7.

de las Casas, G. (2009, July–August). Barack von Metternich. *Foreign Policy*, 173, 28.

Dejevsky, M. (2009, June 17). Critics of Barak Obama's foreign policy need to get real. *The Independent*, 28.

DeYoung, K. and Fadel, L. (2012, January 6). Islamists' wins in Egypt offer test of Obama Policy. *The Washington Post*, A10.

Diehl, J. (2011, December 12). Obama lags in Egypt. *The Washington Post*, A21.

Dilanian, K. (2009, April 22). Administration's foreign policy includes heavy dose of humility. *USA Today*, 5A.

The Economist, (2011, February 26). The ties that bind. 65–66.

The Economist. (2011, September 17). A problem with club Med, 34.

El Deeb, S. (2012, February 20). McCain: Egypt and US "must remain friends". *Christian Science Monitor*. Retrieved from https://www.csmonitor.com/World/Latest -News-Wires/2012/0220/McCain-Egypt-and-US-must-remain-friends.

Fadel, L. (2012, March 7). US seeking a reliable partner in post-Mubarak Egypt. *The Washington Post*, p. A11.

Fleishman, J. (2012, March 1). Egypt says 7 on trial may go. *Los Angeles Times*, p. A03.

Fleishman, J. and Hassan, A. (2012, March 2). Decision decried in Egypt. *Los Angeles Times*, p. A07.

Foreign Policy Bulletin, (2011, June). Obama administration commends Egypt for orderly transition. 21(2), 3–11.

Glick, C.B. (2009, June 30). Ideologue-in-chief. *The Jerusalem Post*, p. 15.

Goodspeed, P. (2012, February 11). A scapegoat wrapped in stars and stripes. *National Post*, p. A16.

Greenberg, J. (2011, October 25). Egypt to release US-Israeli citizen. *The Washington Post*, p. A06.

Hadar, L. (2009, June 11). Obama is the realist, not neocon critics. *The Business Times*, p. 19.

Hamzawy, A. and Christiansen, J. (2009, July 19). Will Islamic opposition movements seize the day? *Daily News (Egypt)*. Retrieved from https://dailynewsegypt.com/2009/07/19/will-islamic-opposition-movements-seize-the-day/.

The Herald, (2011, December 20). US urges Egypt to respect rights. p. 14.

Hoagland, J. (2009, July 12). White House fault lines. *The Washington Post*, p. A17.

Ignatius, D. (2009, July 19). The big decisions to come. *The Washington Post*, p. A21.

The Independent, (2009, June 25). Realism makes a welcome return to US foreign policy. p. 28.

Jackson, D. (2009, April 27). Obama's first 100 days rewrite agenda: Policies show sharp departure from Bush era. *USA Today*, p. 5A.

Jim, M. (2012, July 9). US policy evolving amid Islamist victories. *USA Today*.

Kagan, R. (2009, June 7). Woodrow Wilson's heir. *The Washington Post*, p. A17. [Reprinted in *Canberra Times*, June 12 2009.]

LaFranchi, H. (2012, June 25). US lies low on Egypt, acting behind the scenes. Is that approach wise? *Christian Science Monitor*. Retrieved from https://www.csmonitor.com/USA/Foreign-Policy/2012/0625/US-lies-low-on-Egypt-acting-behind-the-scenes.-Is-that-approach-wise.

Lambro, D. (2009, May 11). "Smart power" stumped: Obama approach isn't making the grade. *The Washington Times*, p. A23.

Loy, F. (2011, May–June). Obama abroad: Ambitious realism. *World Affairs*, 23–32.

Macintyre, D. (2011, December 25). How the West was caught out by the Arab Spring. *The Independent*, p. 32.

Miller, A.D. (2011, summer). For America, an Arab Winter. *The Wilson Quarterly*. Retrieved from http://archive.wilsonquarterly.com/essays/america-arab-winter.

Musallam, Talaat. (2011, September 5). Options of Egyptian response to Israeli aggression. *Al-Jazeera*. Retrieved from www.aljazeera.net/analysis/pages/e4d9808c-dea1-4389-ac16-4ad44cf8b0b6.

Myers, S.L. (2011, September 18). Arab hopes, US worries. *The New York Times*, p. 1.

NBC News. (2011, January 30). Meet the Press. [Quoted in: Foreign Policy Bulletin, June 2011, 4.]

Obama, B. (2007, July–August). Renewing American leadership. *Foreign Affairs*, 86(4), 2.

Obama, B. (2011a). Statement of February 1, 2011. [Quoted in *Foreign Policy Bulletin*, June 2011, 6–7.]

Obama, B. (2011b). Statement of February 10, 2011. [Quoted in *Foreign Policy Bulletin*, June 2011, 7–8.]

Parker, S. (2009, April 27). Obama foreign policy shows change in values. *Korea Times*.

Richter, P. (2009a, January 28). Clinton says world leaders glad of Obama team's course. *Los Angeles Times*, p. A6.

Richter, P. (2009b, February 11). No sure things for Obama advisors. *Los Angeles Times*, p. A14.

Richter, P. (2012, January 21). US voices concern as Egypt continues NGO crackdown. *Los Angeles Times*.

Rubin, B. (2011, December). Navigating the new Middle East? The Obama Administration is lost at sea and on the rocks. *Middle East Review of International Affairs*, 15(94), 50–58.

Satloff, R. and Trager, E. (2012, January 23). How the US should handle the Islamist rise in Egypt. *Wall Street Journal*, p. A19.

Schenker, D. (2012, February 15). Egypt's cold shoulder. *Los Angeles Times*, p. A13.

Sheridan, M.B. (2011a, September 25). Obama faces hurdles in aiding Arab Spring countries. *The Washington Post*, p. A11.

Sheridan, M.B. (2011b, September 30). Egypt cautions US on attaching conditions to military assistance. *The Washington Post*, p. A10.

Sky, E. (2011, summer). Arab Spring … American Fall? *Harvard International Review*, 23–27.

Smith, L. (2011, summer). Middle Eastern upheavals: Weakening Washington Middle East influence. *Middle East Quarterly*, 3–10.

Spencer, R. (2011, April 28). The riddle of Obama and the shifting sands: America's relationship with the Middle East is changing – and Egypt is its test case. *The Daily Telegraph*, p. 21.

Sprusansky, D. (2012a, May). Challenges of Post-Arab Uprising Reconstruction. *Washington Report on Middle East Affairs*, 31(3), 68.

Sprusansky, D. (2012b, May). US-Egypt Relations. *Washington Report on Middle East Affairs*, 31(3), 68–69.

Stephens, B. (2012, June 26). Who Lost Egypt? *Wall Street Journal*, p. A13.

Timmerman, K.R. (2009, May 20). Obama in Wonderland: Myth that "no diplomacy" has been tried. *The Washington Times*, p. A17.

Tomasky, M. (2009, summer). The values that did not fail. *Democracy*, No. 13. Retrieved from https://democracyjournal.org/magazine/13/the-values-that-didnt-fail/.

Traub, J. (2009, summer). The democracy rule. *Democracy*, No. 13. Retrieved from https://democracyjournal.org/magazine/13/the-democracy-rule/.

Usborne, D. (2009, June 16). Has Obama been exposed as an innocent abroad? *The Independent*, p. 22.

Viotti, P. and Kauppi, M. (1987). *International Relations Theory: Realism, Pluralism, Globalism*. New York: Macmillan.

Wan, W. (2012a, April 4). Visit by Egypt's Brotherhood aims to boost image in US. *The Washington Post*, p. A08.

Wan, W. (2012b, February 5). Amid Transition; Egypt's Aid from US is in Peril. *The Washington Post*, p. A13.

Ward, J. (2009, April 21). Axelrod touts Obama's foreign policy strategy. *The Washington Times*, p. A20.

13 Set-up for failure

The Syria-United States relationship

Ethan Corbin

From the Cold War to its rapid descent into destructive civil war today, Syria has played a unique role in Middle Eastern and global politics. When weak, as it was during the twenty-five years following World War II, Syria was an arena in which regional and global powers sought to intervene. When strong, Syria used the few regional and global instruments at its disposal, such as Palestinian armed groups, Iran, or the Soviet Union, to try to impose its will upon the Levant.

While civil war rages in Syria today, the United States remains flummoxed about an effective policy toward the country. Much as it has in the past, the country's weakness has drawn the proxies of all regional great to medium powers, such as Iran and Saudi Arabia. Additionally, it has destabilized its immediate neighborhood and brought in global powers such as Russia and the United States, who are competing for different political outcomes to the Syrian debacle.

Today, US policy toward Syria remains ineffective for three principal reasons, all of which are intertwined and surfaced relatively early in the state's history. First, Syria's modern political form is the result of French neglect post World War I and subsequent defeat at the hands of Israel, which rose to be a key US interest in the region. Second, as the Asad regime made Syrian state interests indistinguishable from its own, the survival of the regime became defined by countering US and Israeli regional interests. Modern-day Syria and its brutal regime exist due to persistent efforts to undo Israel's hegemonic position in the Levant. Third, Asad regime legitimacy and regional position depend on its rejection of Israel and the status quo it imposed on the region in the postwar era. This has led to a Syrian embrace of troubling alliances in Washington's view – both with regional armed groups fighting Israel, often via terrorist tactics, and with Iran, which has been the principal pole of US regional antagonism since the Islamic Revolution of 1979 (Hinnebusch and Ehteshami, 1997).

Since the end of World War II, the United States treated Syria principally as a marginal player, only directly engaging with Damascus in its efforts to wrangle a lasting peace with Arab states and its main regional ally, Israel. Syria was considered a second-tier concern, and its alignment with regional armed groups and its sponsorship of their terrorist tactics locked it into a purgatory imposed by the United States and Israel. Syria never benefited from the spoils of alignment with US regional interests, nor did it feel the full brunt of Washington's ire as every US administration eventually came to the realization that "the Arabs cannot make war without Egypt and cannot make peace without Syria" – Henry Kissinger's famous dictum (Lister, 2011).

In the ebb and flow of the cost-benefit analysis of US foreign policy in the Middle East in the post-World War II era, US-Syrian relations have been unique. Syria continues to be a holdout of the radical states dedicated to rewinding Israeli war gains in the Levant. For this role, it has earned the ire of the United States, though never to the level of Iran or Iraq. The United States has sought to align Syria to its regional interests either through punishment and isolation or through mild incentives – but in the balance between the carrot and the stick, the United States decidedly favored the stick as a means of trying to align Syria to its regional polices and interests. In return, Damascus often chose the use of force, the manipulation of its regional armed group agents, and the auspices of its larger Iranian ally to thwart US regional efforts at a lasting peace between Israel and its neighbors (Leverett, 2005; Seale, 1995; Hinnebusch, 2001; Ma'oz, 1988).

US national interests in the Middle East: What role for Syria?

In the early postwar years, the United States had a nearly myopic focus on two principal interests in the Middle East. First, as the United States worked to implement the Marshall Plan as a means of keeping Western Europe tied to Washington in the burgeoning Cold War with the Soviet Union, it became clear that the uninterrupted flow of Middle Eastern oil would be a key variable to the rebuilding of the European economies aligned with the United States. To guarantee the oil regions of the Middle East remained key suppliers for the West, Washington needed to block the expansion of the Soviet Union into the region.

Syria proved to be an early niggling impediment to these policy goals. Syrian intransigence, for example, was a stumbling block to the plan of US oil giants Socal and Texaco to work with Arabian-American Oil Company (ARAMCO) to transport Saudi Arabian oil to the Mediterranean in the summer of 1945. The Trans-Arabian Pipeline (Tapline) was to serve as the lifeblood of US Secretary of State Marshall's European Recovery Program (Little, 1990a).

Despite concerted efforts by US business and diplomatic interests in Damascus, Syrian President al-Quwwatli refused to allow the pipeline to transit Syrian territory. With Washington's ire piqued, the CIA began to support efforts to overthrow al-Quwwatli; his successor Husni Za'im signed the agreement in May 1949, clearing the way for Tapline to begin fueling Western European economies (Little, 2008, p. 54). Za'im was then quickly overthrown in a coup several months later and executed by his successor, but the transfer rights for the US-designed Tapline remained in place.

In the early bids to block Soviet infiltration into the region, Syria only really came onto Washington's radar during the 1957 'crisis' when it became, for a moment, the center of attention after Damascus expelled several US diplomats in August. The 'Syrian crisis' was sparked by Washington's paranoia that communist sympathizers had infiltrated Syria, were poised for power in domestic politics and in the military,[1] and would thus permit the first real significant Soviet foothold in the region – and right on the border with both Israel and Turkey at that, two key regional US allies (Lesch, 2003).

The test of the Syrian crisis was to see whether the Eisenhower administration would apply its doctrine of aiding those states susceptible to communist infiltration and takeover by any available means, from economic to military (Pearson, 2007).

Washington initially balked at the idea of direct intervention, so it encouraged its allies in Ankara to begin amassing the Turkish army on Syria's border.[2] As rhetoric on both sides escalated, both Moscow and Washington threatened expanded conflict. Washington's subsequent intervention in Syria was not needed, however, as the 'crisis' was settled by Egyptian President Gamal Nasser's decision to send a couple thousand troops into the country.

Not only did Nasser diffuse the situation by getting Turkey to recall its forces from the border, but he also scored a double victory by being perceived as the Arab strongman between the two meddling superpowers and by getting the United States to make a significant shift in its regional policy – where it had previously refused to deal with Arab nationalists, Washington decided to concede to the important role Nasser played in the region and his potential as a key instrument to keep the Soviets out of the Middle East.[3] By doing so, Washington left the Syrian domestic quagmire for Nasser.

Syria as a weak state and of marginal US concern, 1946–1961

Syrian structural weakness at its independence from France is a key variable in understanding Syria's total defeat against Israeli forces in the first Arab-Israeli war and the eventual advent of the Asad regime. Defeat in war during its first years post independence invited domestic political chaos and a revisionist spirit in Syrian regional policy wherein the state would be dedicated to undoing Israeli regional policies, which the United States had pledged to support from the beginning.

Syria gained independence in 1946 from the mandate under which France had ruled since 1920. The modern political reality of the Syrian state did not correspond with many Arab elites' conception of Syria (Bey, 1994). Far from the mythical *Sooriya al-Kubra* (Greater Syria) – encompassing parts of modern-day Jordan, Israel (and the Occupied Territories), Iraq, and Turkey – the new republic was a relative rump state cut somewhat awkwardly into the Levant.

With more focus on Lebanon, the French administration neglected institutional development in Syria, leaving behind an economically and administratively weak state.[4] Relatively bereft of natural resources, leaders could not count on much immediate revenue to jump-start the republic, and the virtual mosaic of ethnic and religious identities[5] left them with little other than the new state as a source of national identity. Almost immediately, the new Syrian state was thrown into a war that would remain a key defining variable of its place in the region to the present.

Israel's decisive victory over the Arab states in the 1948–1949 war introduced a complex security and political variable into the region that continues to challenge the region today – approximately 750,000 Palestinian refugees scattered into camps in all of the surrounding Levantine Arab states.[6] This number is significant when considering the combined population of Jordan, Lebanon, and Syria at the time only numbered approximately 5.4 million (United Nations Population Fund, 1950).[7]

Faced with what they perceived as a growing threat from Israel, a disjointed grouping of Arab states plagued with shifting territorial boundaries and newly displaced Palestinian refugees focused almost immediately on rebuilding their militaries. In the absence of other strong domestic institutions, militaries constantly entered the fray of volatile domestic politics, leading to a protracted era of praetorian politics[8] in the region, particularly in 'frontline' states like Syria.

In the wake of defeat in 1949, Syrian domestic politics soon mirrored regional disorder. The immediate decade and a half witnessed innumerable military coups against the state, failed as well as successful, thus earning the moniker of the 'General's Decade' in the 1950s.[9] As cabinet succeeded cabinet throughout the decade, the military often stepped into the fray: Syria even voluntarily surrendered its sovereignty to align with Egypt in the failed pan-Arab project of the United Arab Republic (UAR) from 1958 to 1961.[10] Perhaps presaging the union's failure, Syrian President Shukri al-Quwwatli stated to Nasser after signing the UAR pact in 1958, "You took a people every one of whom believes that he is a politician, 50 percent of whom believe they are leaders, 25 percent believe they are prophets and at least 10 percent believe they are God" (Heikal, 1973).

Setting up a failed US-Syrian dynamic, 1963–1970

The short-lived UAR soon gave way to the rise of radical Ba'athists in Damascus after Syria seceded from the union in 1961. The 'progressive' wing of the Ba'ath Party came to power in Syria in 1963; the pan-Arab message was subsequently co-opted by a loosely configured cabal centered on several key power players, mostly hailing from Syrian minority groups (Hinnebusch, 2001, p. 43). Stylized as the Military Committee, several key military commanders emerged – Hafiz al-Asad, then commander of the Air Force, was the force behind the substantial Alawi contingent in the officer corps and military intelligence (ibid.).[11]

For US-Syrian relations, the initial policies set in motion by the new radicals in Damascus would have a lasting impact on the bilateral relationship. First, the radical Ba'ath would lead Syria down the path to a disastrous conflict with Israel in 1967 ultimately costing it the Golan Heights, the strategic high ground separating Damascus from Israel. Second, the Ba'ath began an earnest program of support for the developing military wings of the nascent Palestinian nationalist movement. Third, out of the self-destruction of the Military Committee came Hafez al-Asad, the autocratic force that turned the Syrian state into a regional middle power able, at times, to even be a policy *maker*, rather than a policy *taker* – but Asad built his entire regime's legitimacy around a rejection of the Israeli-imposed status quo in the region (Seale, 1995; Hinnebusch, 2001; Ma'oz, 1988).

Asad's unswerving focus on the recovery of the Golan and a broader effort to control the Palestinian movement in his regional policy to counter Israel would at times lead him to the negotiating table with top US officials as well as make his forces the target of US military power, but mostly it left Syria isolated and marginalized over the coming decades. Along the way, Asad dramatically grew the power of the Syrian state, but also sowed the seeds of discontent that would lead the state back into conflict and chaos.

The Asad era and the United States: Stronger state, impossible foreign policy, 1970 to present

Hafez al-Asad took control of Syria after a bloodless coup in 1970. Following over 60 successful and failed attempted coups, Asad was the last man standing after the decades of chaos in the wake of Syria's independence. With the shame of the crushing defeat of Syrian forces in the 1967 war weighing heavy upon his shoulders, Asad set about a program to recover Syria's lost territories and to gain the upper hand in the regional struggle with Israel. As noted above, Asad's refusal of peace with Israel was a key to his regime's domestic legitimacy; and, in many respects, to his regional legitimacy as well.

To achieve his goals, Asad calculated he needed strategic parity with Israel (Seale, 1995). This would mean growing Syrian state military powers significantly. Syria's drive for strategic parity with Israel would lead it firmly into the position of leader of the frontline rejectionist state,[12] aggregating power wherever possible, from rejectionist Palestinian and Lebanese armed groups to vast supplies of Soviet weaponry to an oddly strategic alliance with Iran. All three are key variables to the past and present of US-Syrian relations.

Growing Syrian state power and renewing contact with the United States

Asad's agenda was clear from the outset: growing the Syrian state to be a military power to reach strategic parity with Israel – the most important objective being the re-conquest of the Golan Heights. This policy would lead

Asad into a direct confrontation with the United States, particularly after the 1979 Egypt-Israel peace accord. As Asad consolidated his grip on power over the decade and beyond, however, Syrian state interests and Asad regime interests became one and the same. As Asad became increasingly isolated on the regional and global stage, his intransigence toward the question of resistance of Israeli regional policy hardened, eventually making him the leader or enabler of spoilers to a broader regional peace with Israel.

Asad also viewed the growth of Syrian state power as a means of solving all of Syria's problems, domestic and external. To achieve this, Asad expanded the reach of the public sector and focused on growing oil-related income (both internally and externally sourced) while also seeking a stronger alliance with the Soviet Union for advanced military hardware as well as the technical expertise necessary to help modernize all facets of the underdeveloped Syrian military and economy (Hinnebusch, 2001).

Asad's initial rejectionist fervor resulted in the strategic blunder of the 1973 war, totaling approximately $1.3 billion in rebuilding costs as well as causing the total devastation of Syria's tank and air forces and its batteries of air defense systems, not to mention its strategic alliance with Egypt and another 25 kilometers of the Golan Heights (CIA Directorate of Intelligence, 1973). The Soviet Union responded by resupplying the Syrian forces, even adding to them by including its new, sophisticated Scud surface-to-surface missile to the Syrian arsenal (ibid.). The resupply of hard power weaponry, however, was not sufficient to get the Golan back.

To realign his program after a shaky start, Asad needed a victory. The disaster of the 1973 war showed a need for strategic patience; Israeli forces were only about 30 kilometers outside of Damascus. To stabilize Syria and focus on his regional agenda, Asad knew he needed to stop Israeli forces from being an immediate threat to Damascus. To achieve this, he knew he would need more than Soviet weapons; he would need the help of the United States.

Damascus and Washington under Asad – sticks and carrots

The 1967 war saw Damascus break all relations with the United States. US-Syrian relations had never been close through the entire postwar era until the advent of Asad, and even then they were difficult. As Asad tried to push Syria's post-1973 war agenda of expelling Israeli forces from the Golan and building the power of the Syrian state, Asad realized he needed the assistance of both the Soviet Union and the United States (Seale, 1995).

The early years of dogged Ba'athist intransigence to Israeli regional hegemony were costly to Syria; the most visible signs were the successive losses of territory in the Golan Heights in both wars.[13] While Asad knew he could build Syria to be a disruptive force to Israeli and, by extension, US interests in the Levant, particularly regarding a lasting peace between Israel and the Arab states and a resolution to the Palestinian question, he also knew only US assistance could deliver on his promise of a return of the Golan. While the Soviets could deliver him arms, the United States could deliver him Israeli concessions.

As such, at the end of the 1973 war, Syria moved to reopen diplomatic contact with the United States. In November 1973, via Algerian diplomatic channels, Asad let it be known he was seeking direct talks with the United States. The subsequent visits and negotiations between US Secretary of State Henry Kissinger and Hafez Asad for the disengagement of Israeli and Syrian forces marked the first direct contacts with the United States in the Ba'ath era and the first visit to Syria by a US Secretary of State since 1953 (Kissinger, 1982, p. 760).

Kissinger's plan for Middle East peace in the wake of the 1973 war was to engage an incremental approach which focused on smaller issues first without necessarily considering a predetermined outcome. Kissinger believed this would build mutual respect for either side's interests, allowing for a more credible, lasting peace. Kissinger knew Syria would be a difficult but essential piece to his diplomatic efforts and key to securing US interests of a lasting peace for Israel. As he noted at the time, Syria was "the most intransigent of the Arab regimes. ... Syria considered the state of Israel an illegal creation and, dedicated to its destruction, had not cared much where the borders of that state were located" (ibid., p. 777).

Kissinger indicated to Asad early in their initial contacts there would be no talk of a final settlement; they would, rather, proceed step by step. Kissinger reiterated the strength of working with the United States to Asad by stating clearly: "you'll get better declarations from the Europeans than me. But on the other hand, you'll get more results from the United States" (ibid., p. 778). To move any potential peace process forward, Kissinger knew he had to focus US strategy in 1974 on reconciling Israel and Syria.

From January to May, Kissinger worked to find a means of separating Syrian and Israeli forces and halting the ongoing war of attrition. The intersection of a UN Disengagement force marked a dividing line still manned today. In his memoirs, Kissinger called the settlement a 'down payment' by the Israelis on the broader US-led peace process, believing the disengagement represented a Syrian gain given the balance of forces at the time did not merit it (ibid., p. 1088). The down payment was enough for Asad to jump-start the Syrian state that he would create in his image and that would impose what he considered to be Syrian interests on the region.

Leveraging the gains of the 1974 disengagement

Relieved from the pressures of Israeli forces bearing down on Damascus, Asad focused in earnest on his program of strengthening Syrian power. At least in the short term, Asad's post-1973 power-building efforts were successful. Within a few years, Syria became at least a competent regional spoiler, if not a plausible deterrent to Israeli regional power. Over time, however, Asad's blunders in regional policy, particularly in Lebanon, would increasingly

isolate him. Syria's strength and continued adherence to a vehement rejectionist policy gave it the means to instrumentalize significant control over the
region's Palestinian and Lebanese armed groups. As a result, Syria would
become the leader of the agents dedicated to spoiling US plans for a broader
regional peace.

By the end of the decade following the 1973 war, the Syrian Armed Forces
would boast the most significant missile arsenal among the Arab states:
almost 4,000 tanks, several hundred advanced jet fighters, and even frigates
and submarines for its navy (Dov Tamari, Mark Heller, and Zeev Eytan,
1983; Clawson, 1989). Starting in 1971, Syria began devoting anywhere from
a third to half of its budget toward defense-related expenses (Syrian Aran
Republic, 1970–1983). Syria became the largest recipient of Soviet arms
among Arab states after 1972; by 1983, Damascus was estimated to be
importing well over $3 billion in arms annually and dedicating almost a
quarter of its GDP to its defense budget (Clawson, 1989). It is over this same
time period that Syria began stockpiling chemical weapons as part of its
strategic deterrent policy against Israel.

In addition to spending on new equipment, Asad also grew the manpower
of the Syrian armed forces substantially over the same period. While Syria
went to war in 1973 with 160,000 men, by the time it was hunkering down in
its occupation of most of northern and eastern Lebanon in 1983, its army
numbered 400,000. Internal security services grew exponentially over the
same period, as government spending expanded almost sevenfold over the
course of the decade, and this resulted in a complicated web of seventeen
agencies overseeing domestic security and intelligence matters and hundreds
of thousands of personnel (Syrian Arab Republic, 1970–1983; Hinnebusch,
2001; Mufti, 1996).

After the 1973 war, liberalization measures by Asad and a relative oil boom
caused Syrian GDP to grow by a stunning 12.4 percent from 1973 to 1977.[14]
Along the way, Asad was able to concentrate power under the Syrian executive following a populist authoritarian model (Hinnebusch, 2001). Asad built
his regime on three primary pillars of support – the Ba'ath Party, the ministerial bureaucracy, and the military and domestic security services. In Asad's
state the presidency became paramount, riding atop all three pillars both
legally and politically. As a military commander above all else, Asad used the
military as a principal instrument of power to consolidate his position as
Syria's unchallenged leader; he also ensured his position by constructing an
inner security circle of Alawi military elites and by buying the allegiance of
the Sunni majority through elaborate patronage systems benefiting the urban
upper-class merchant families.

By wresting control of the Ba'ath Party, the military/security apparatus,
and the ministerial bureaucracy, Asad quelled an era of nearly constant
domestic political instability, which in turn allowed him to focus on the
complex regional challenges facing a strong Syria that was still clinging to its
rejectionist position.

From carrots to sticks: The United States and Syria post 1974

As the United States worked to bring Egypt to a separate peace with Israel, Syria ardently began to ensure the other frontline states Jordan and Lebanon did not break ranks with the rejectionist line (Mufti, 1996). Asad also worked to build Syrian control over the Palestinian armed groups to block any US attempts to separate Palestinians from the Arab states in the negotiations for statehood with Israel. Asad's armed group agents would become essential elements of his foreign policy. Asad's vision for the Levant brought him quickly into direct conflict with Israeli and even US forces.

From allies to agents

After its seizure of power in 1963, the Syrian Ba'ath was very quick to support the nascent Palestinian armed struggle, which they wanted to model after the Algerian National Liberation Front. Despite internal party differences, several key Ba'ath Party members worked to build the burgeoning Fatah and smaller groups to become asymmetrical instruments of warfare in their designs for Syria; particularly important were Hafez al-Asad, then air force commander, and Ahmed al-Suwaydani, the head of military intelligence. The informal support soon gave way to institutionalized, structured support – military, economic and diplomatic – for the Palestinian armed groups mounting guerilla operations against Israel (Shemesh, 1988).

The lack of real control over how, when, and where the Palestinian rebels operated, however, was a precipitant of the 1967 war, which devastated the Syrian armed forces (Shemesh, 1988; Sayigh, 1997). While it was the war that Fatah leader Yasir Arafat had wanted, it was the war Asad had feared, as he knew the Syrian state was too weak. The disruption caused by the Palestinian armed groups spread quickly, causing a near civil war in Jordan in 1970 and then steadily breaking down the relative calm in Lebanon via persistent raids south into Israel. Asad learned the dangerous lessons of too much support and too little control of the Palestinian groups. He set about correcting this after Syrian state power grew in the wake of the 1973 war – Asad needed armed group agents he could control, not just allies pursuing a parallel agenda whose reckless use of force would be costly to Syria.

The rapid growth in Syrian military and economic power and the settled internal political cohesion allowed Asad to bring most of the Palestinian armed groups under control incrementally within Syria and stopped them from launching any attacks against Israel from the Syrian border by the mid-1970s. Many groups set up their headquarters in Damascus, such as the Popular Front for the Liberation of Palestine (PFLP) (and its derivatives the PFLP-General Command [PFLP-GC] and the Popular Democratic Front for the Liberation of Palestine [PDFLP]), Al-Sai'qa, and the Palestine Liberation Front (PLF); others such as Fatah were free to operate in the country. All of these groups had limited freedom of action within Syria under Asad; they were tightly controlled when it came to training facilities and were required to cooperate with the Syrian domestic security services. Asad even assigned a special office, Department 235, of the Military Intelligence Directorate to be in charge of surveillance of the groups.[15]

Asad's growing control over the Palestinian armed struggle, however, soon led to a difficult relationship with Yasir Arafat, which would eventually split during Asad's early occupation of Lebanon. Asad's 1976 decision to align with the Maronite Christians to keep them on his Arab side was costly: a domestic Islamist insurgency broke out and his own brother mounted a coup against him – both of which he put down with brutality (Seale, 1995).

Syria's impossible foreign policy

Syria's continued occupation of Lebanon put Asad once again in direct confrontation with Israel and even the United States. Asad's push out of Syria to control the Palestinian groups landed Syria on the United States' first list of state sponsors of terrorism in 1979 due to the tactics the groups used; it has never been taken off. As Syria deepened its control of Lebanon, it solidified its control over the rejectionist wing of the Palestinian armed struggle. Damascus also was present alongside its Iranian allies at the split of Hezbollah from Amal in Lebanon (Norton, 1987).

As Asad's presidency overcame the series of domestic challenges, he hardened his rejectionist position regionally. It is clear Asad was sure of his own legitimacy at home and of Syria's position in the region as the leading frontline state in the struggle against a US-Israeli imposed regional order.[16] To maintain domestic order and regional control over the rejectionist armed groups, Asad needed the power gleaned from his military and domestic security services, but also his alliance with Iran as the Soviet Union progressively faded from being able to support its client states over the 1980s.

During the 1980s, President Reagan's relative inattention to the Middle East crisis brewing around the Lebanese civil war led to a failed rebooting of the peace process under US leadership; the United States was offering a solution no side wanted.[17] Washington's decision to send troops to bolster the Multi-National Force (MNF) peacekeeping mission made US forces the direct target of Syrian- and Iranian-supported armed groups. On April 18, 1983, a Syrian-directed terrorist bombing struck the US embassy, killing 57, including 19 Americans. As the United States doubled down on its presence in the Lebanese morass, US Marines soon found themselves in the crossfire between armed groups and the US Sixth fleet involved in shelling Syrian positions in eastern Lebanon. In total, the United States moved 14 warships off the Lebanese shore; the three-day shelling that ensued, starting on September 18, was the largest US Navy shelling since the Vietnam War over a decade earlier. On October 23 a truck filled with 12,000 pounds of TNT struck a US Marine compound just outside of the Beirut airport, killing 241 of the 350 soldiers present; the action would precipitate the US withdrawal (Fisk, 1990; Freedman, 2008).

With the departure of US forces by early 1984 and the Israeli decision to withdraw to an occupation of southern Lebanon, the country remained in an odd stalemate that would draw on for years more, with Syria holding on to its positions in the north and east.[18] Syria's continued support of the rejectionist Palestinian and southern Lebanese armed groups – from the secular radicals of the PFLP-GC to the more extreme Islamist groups like Hamas and Islamic Jihad – would undermine every serious US regional peace effort ever after. Each of those groups was working in its own way to derail a separate peace between Lebanon and Israel, thereby isolating Syria. Over time, Syria's position would increasingly isolate it even from the more hardline states, who would either make a separate peace with Israel, as Jordan did in 1994, or slowly withdraw their financial support of Syria as the frontline state, as many Gulf states did over time.

During the 1990s, Syrian support for Hezbollah would flourish as a result of its ongoing alliance with Iran and the subsequent disappearance of its Soviet support.[19] As each state became increasingly isolated in the international arena under sanctions, and the target of US regional enmity, their relationship became one of mutual strategic depth – Iran had a bridge to the southern Lebanese Shi'a community and its armed group agent, Hezbollah, while Syria had Iranian financial support to replace lost strategic rent as well as military support against Saddam Hussein's forces that had been pushing up against Syria ever since the Ba'athist split in 1966 (Hinnebusch and Ehteshami, 1997).

As both Syria and Iran continued to reject the US vision of the Middle East in the post-Cold War era, their strategic isolation deepened. President Bill Clinton's administration adopted a harder line against what it termed 'rogue states', or those not willing to toe the line of US-led normative behavior in the international system. In a *Foreign Affairs* article, Clinton's national security advisor, Anthony Lake, referred to them as 'backlash states' and noted that to contain their influence, tailor-made strategies, involving isolation or coercion or combined economic and diplomatic measures, were required (Lake, 1994).

While Iran was identified directly in Lake's article outlining the US position vis-à-vis rogue states, Syria was not. The US administration continued to hold out hope of bringing Syria over to its regional policy, thereby fitting one of the last remaining pieces into the puzzle for its vision of a lasting Middle East peace. The result was no different for Syria, however, as it remained isolated for its intransigence with regards to US policy toward Middle East peace or the victim of direct coercion for feeble efforts to expand its WMD repertoire.[20] The Asad regime was unable to abandon its armed group agents, a key variable to unlocking a new dynamic between Damascus and Washington.

Signs of Syria's growing weakness in the Middle East abounded. The most glaring was the growing indifference of the United States and Israel to Syria's demands in the Syrian-Israeli peace negotiations throughout the 1990s. Asad's last-ditch efforts to negotiate peace with Israel had a blatantly moribund character – regaining the Golan eluded him.

Slowed by congestive heart failure, Asad had been grooming his son, Bashar to assume power, thereby installing a kind of presidential monarchy to preserve the regime he had built over the decades. The young and inexperienced Bashar al-Asad inherited a rentier state that was running out of rent and a regime that made Syria a political pariah both regionally and globally. Further compounding its status was the new Asad's doubling down on Syria's relationship with its armed groups.

Bashar al-Asad embraced the armed group leaders in a way his father had never done before. The former Syrian agents were quickly looked upon as allies, particularly Hezbollah and Hamas. The dramatic shift in Syria's relationship with Hezbollah is emblematic – Hezbollah's leader, Hassan Nasrallah, began to be invited for what resembled official state visits, while Damascus was soon festooned with the image of a new trinity: Iranian leader Ahmedinejad, Syria's Asad, and Hezbollah's Nasrallah. The future of Syria under Bashar would be defined by the state–armed group alliance – it would become a central pillar of Bashar's legitimacy.

Over the course of the George W. Bush presidency, Washington resumed a more distant approach to dealing with Syria. The growth in Syria's illicit trade with Iraq, mainly through subverting the UN Oil-for-Food project, served as both an economic buttress and a political liability. When it became clear Syria was supporting the flow of fighters to the insurgency against US forces during their occupation of Iraq, any serious form of US interest in rebooting the Syrian track of peace talks faded quickly (Naylor, 2007).

More drastic indications of the end of any sort of attempt by Israel and the United States to accommodate or deal with Syria under Bashar became clear with the direct attacks by each on Syrian assets and forces. On September 6, 2007, Israeli jets penetrated Syrian airspace to destroy what Israeli and US intelligence reports claimed to be a nascent nuclear reactor being constructed with North Korean assistance (Hersh, 2008). A year later, on October 8, 2008, US gunships led a commando raid on an insurgent transfer base in Syria near the Iraqi border (Schmitt and Shanker, 2008).

The Obama administration's half-hearted attempt to reboot a Syrian negotiation track failed not too long after US Secretary of State John Kerry's visit to Damascus in 2009. Syria's strategic isolation continued until the weakened state fell into the civil war of 2011 (Alexander, 2013). The revolts were, in large part, a rejection of the state the Asad regime had built in order to serve its regime interest of rejecting Israel's regional position and, in turn, thwarting the US vision for the Levant.

Conclusion

Syria sits at the heart of a region full of vital strategic interests to the United States: the free flow of oil to assure global commerce; the defense of regional allies – particularly Israel – and the pursuit of Arab-Israeli peace; and prevention of the area becoming a wellspring of terrorism or WMD proliferation. After almost fourty-eight years in power, the Asad family continues to vex US administrations, as well as all other regional actors – with Asad earning the moniker of the Sphinx of Damascus. Even before the uprising began in February 2011, Washington participated in various levels of sanctions against the Asad regime for state sponsorship of terrorism. However, various levels of diplomatic, political, and economic coercion by the United States over the past decades have led to very little behavioral change on the part of the Syrian regime and, therefore, have proven to be of scant benefit to US regional interests.

Syria is the only Arab state ally of Iran. Together, the two states have sought to thwart US strategic interests in the region by sponsoring the principal armed groups resisting Arab-Israeli peace (Hezbollah and Hamas today as well as Fatah and the myriad other Palestine Liberation Organization [PLO] groups for decades before). At times, Syria has shown a degree of willingness to align with US interests and bring itself out of regional and international diplomatic isolation – often with the hopes of strengthening its position to regain the Golan Heights in a settlement with Israel – only to squander the opportunity quickly.

The reason for this is due to variables set in motion long ago. The Syrian state was born weak due to relative neglect during its mandate period. The means Hafaz Asad used to pull Syria out of its recurring weakness relied upon sources of legitimacy that drew domestic and regional strength from being opposed to Israeli and, by extension, US policy in the Middle East. Asad's efforts to strengthen the Syrian state and project his version of Syrian interests into the region set in motion a pattern of behavior and alliances that were, and continue to be, fundamentally opposed to US interests in the Middle East.

Throughout its history, a weak Syria has proven to be the bellwether for regional political disruption. As Syria crumbled in domestic political turmoil, regional and global powers sought to intervene in the Syrian vacuum. The current civil war engulfing almost every corner of the country has proven, once again, the regional and global dilemma of Syrian instability. The United States has failed to achieve almost any of its goals as it has tried to negotiate a democracy-friendly regime change in Damascus. Instead, the chaos and destruction of the Syrian war have proven the durability of the Asad regime and its solidified ability to disrupt a regional political order friendly to US interests.

Notes

1 Syrian domestic politics were in fact dominated by the competition between the Ba'ath (pan-Arabists) and the Syrian Social Nationalist Party (SSNP). Thrown into the mix were other competing parties representing a spectrum from royalists

to communists – which both the Ba'ath and the SSNP used to form coalitions to counter each other (Mufti, 1996). See Seale (1966) and Little (1990b).

2 The CIA had been working assiduously on a campaign in Syria to counter the perceived infiltration of Soviet sympathizers in the Syrian government for years – particularly as Damascus had demonstrated itself to be against the Eisenhower administration's regional policies. See Little (1990b).

3 The subsequent policy memo, NSC 5820/1, shifted US policy in the region significantly by undoing the political logic of the Eisenhower Doctrine, admitting the futility of confronting Nasser, and instead moving to use Nasser and his Arab nationalist appeal to the benefit of US main interests. Further, the cost to Nasser of the intervention in Syria soon outweighed the benefits; Syria ended up surrendering its sovereignty to Egypt to form the northern province of the United Arab Republic (UAR). The UAR was the first step in the pan-Arabists' dream of building a new political order, but in reality Nasser had just inherited the unmanageable nightmare of Syrian domestic politics.

4 The French Mandate administration of Lebanon and Syria grossly favored Lebanon, as General Henri Gouraud made it quite clear upon entering the region as the commander of the Army of the Levant and representative of the French government in the Middle East that he intended to carve out a safe haven for the Christian population in the region. Subsequent investments in infrastructure reflected this, allowing Lebanon to modernize relatively quickly at the expense of Syria. See, for example, Khoury (1987); see also Bey (1994).

5 Syria's ethnic and religious makeup is perhaps more easily summed up as a fragile mosaic. Among the Arab population there are Sunni, Alawi and Ismaili Shi'a Muslims, and Christians cohabitating uncomfortably under the pretense of a secular state. The rest of the country incorporates important minority populations of Kurds and Armenians – each with their own irredentist or secessionist yearnings – as well as significant subgroupings of Druze and Circassians. All of these distinct communities within the state combine to set up a unique set of substate pressures that require the Syrian government to focus an enormous amount of attention internally.

6 Figures for the actual number of Palestinian refugees vary; Israel initially claimed far fewer, while Arab states claimed many more. At the time, the UN Relief and Works Agency registered refugees to be in excess of 900,000 (retrieved from: www. unrwa.org/userfiles/reg-ref(2).pdf). The number that has been generally settled upon by all sides in the region today is 750,000 refugees in the immediate aftermath of the war.

7 By country (in thousands): Syria, 3,495; Lebanon, 1,443; and Jordan, 472.

8 A praetorian society can be defined as one in which social forces confront each other directly, with no institutions accepted as legitimate intermediaries and little to no agreement existing among the groups as to an authoritative means for conflict resolution. As a result, the armed forces act as a corporate body to maintain control over government, actively intervening in politics to select or change the government. See, for example, Rapoport (1962, pp. 72–74).

9 After the defeat against Israeli forces in 1949, Syria experienced no less than three successful coups in less than one year. See Kerr (1971).

10 Interestingly, Syria is the only state ever to have voluntarily surrendered its sovereignty to another to which it has no historical attachment. Such a bold move against the status quo of the Middle Eastern state configuration since the mandate era is a clear demonstration of the power of the pan-Arab movement spearheaded by Gamal Abd al-Nasir.

11 Other members of the committee at its outset included Amin al-Hafiz (Sunni), Hammad Ubayd (Druze) and Mohammed Umran and Salah Jadid (both Alawi).

12 The 1967 Khartoum Conference, which came in the wake of the Arab states' defeat in the 1967 war, made very clear the Arab rejectionist position vis-à-vis

Israel. The conference declarations would soon become quickly summarized as the "Three No's" – which were encapsulated in the third paragraph of the Khartoum Resolution: "the main principles by which the Arab states abide, namely, no peace with Israel, no recognition with Israel, and no negotiations with it." As the years progressed and Egypt signed a separate peace with Israel in 1979, Syria would become focused on blocking a separate peace between Israel and the Palestinians, which would only further isolate Syria's regional position and ability to wrangle a settlement to the Golan question.

13   In each of the wars, Syria lost approximately 25 kilometers of the Golan to Israeli advances.

14   World Bank Country Dataset – Syria. The impact of oil-related income was significant for Syria not only due to global price changes in the wake of the oil shocks post 1973, but also due to the investment in and development of a real domestic oil exploration and extraction sector. As such, oil-related income in Syria would eventually make up 50 percent of government revenues. See Hasan and Dridi (2008).

15   The Military Intelligence Directorate was referred to as the Deuxième Bureau until the Ba'athist overhaul of Syria; reference to the Deuxième Bureau remained the common nomenclature for a long time afterward. See Shemesh (1988) and Sayigh (1997).

16   What is and is not considered to be the underlying legitimacy of the Asad regime is a subject of debate. Many authors, even Patrick Seale, who spent a considerable amount of time with Asad as a historical biographer of the Syrian president, come down on the side of the argument that sees Asad and Asad's Syria as being the pillar of rejection against Israeli regional hegemony and the US policies supporting Israel in the region. For example, the following scholars generally support this thesis: Patrick Seale (1995), Moshe Ma'oz (1988), Raymond Hinnebusch (2001), Volker Perthes (1995), Eyal Zisser (2007); Malik Mufti (1996), and Flynt Leverett (2005). However, Lisa Wedeen (1999) warns against attempts to categorize and infer meaning from discussions of legitimacy in the study of authoritarian regimes. Her study of the Asad regime is an enlightening rejection of the common current of understanding of Asad's pillars of legitimacy.

17   The Reagan administration sought to use the Camp David Accords as the founding pillar for its regional peace plan, which translated into a nebulous gray zone between a Palestinian state and total Israeli annexation. Washington officials noted this would mean there would be an eventual political association between the West Bank, the Gaza Strip, and Jordan along with a settlement freeze by Israel and a withdrawal from the occupied territories. Israel has always rejected a full withdrawal, and the Arab rejectionist camp would only accept full statehood for the Palestinians. See Freedman (2008).

18   Syrian occupation of Lebanon did not end officially until 2005, capping 29 years of significant, entrenched military presence in Lebanon. While Syrian occupation began in 1976, it was made 'official' after the end of the Lebanese civil war with the 1991 Treaty of Brotherhood, Cooperation, and Coordination. See Hirst (2010).

19   The Syria-Iran alliance has origins in an early crisis of legitimacy for the Asad regime wherein Asad's Islamic credentials as an Alawi and a Ba'ath revolutionary were questioned. – Alawis had long been perceived as heterodox or even apostate in the region. Iranian Imam Musa Sadr declared a *fatwa* in 1973 pronouncing the Alawi religious tradition to be a Twelver Shi'a derivative of Islam. As such, Asad was given his Muslim credentials to be the president of the majority Sunni Islamic country of modern Syria. See Seale (1995).

20   As already noted, Syria has been under several layers of bilateral and multilateral sanctions for its continued support of Hezbollah, Hamas, and other Palestinian organizations since it was first designated a state sponsor of terrorism in 1979.

Stricter, three-tiered sanctions were imposed by the United States in 2004 when the Syria Accountability and Lebanese Sovereignty Act was implemented as a result of Syria's role in the assassination of Lebanese Prime Minister Hariri. The three major components were: 311 Actions (or Patriot Act, anti-money-laundering measures against the Commercial Bank of Syria); Office of Foreign Assets Control Prohibitions (targeting individuals and entities with ties to terrorist activities); and Commerce Department sanctions. Since the outbreak of the Syrian civil war in 2011, further rounds of sanctions have targeted Syrian government officials and industry.

References

Alexander, H. (2013, September 3). John Kerry and Bashar al-Assad dined in Damascus. *The Telegraph*. Retrieved from www.telegraph.co.uk/news/worldnews/middleeast/syr ia/10283045/John-Kerry-and-Bashar- al-Assad-dined-in-Damascus.html.

Bey, S.M. (1994). *La France et la Syrie: bilan d'une equivoque (1939–1945)*. Paris: L'Harmattan.

CIA Directorate of Intelligence. (1973, December). *Intelligence Report, "Soviet Military Resupplies in the Middle East"*. Washington, DC: Directorate of Intelligence.

Clawson, P. (1989). *Unaffordable Ambitions: Syria's Military Build-up and Economic Crisis*. Washington, DC: Washington Institute for Near East Policy.

Fisk, R. (1990). *Pity the Nation: Lebanon at War*. New York: Atheneum.

Freedman, L. (2008). *A Choice of Enemies: America Confronts the Middle East*. New York: Public Affairs.

Hasan, M. and Dridi, J. (2008, August 1). *The Impact of Oil-related Income on the Equilibrium Exchange Rate in Syria*. Working Paper No. 08/196. Washington, DC: International Monetary Fund.

Heikal, M. (1973). *Nasser Les Documents du Caire*. Egypt: J'ai Lu.

Hersh, S.M. (2008, February 11). A Strike in the Dark: What Did Israel Bomb in Syria? *The New Yorker*. Retrieved from www.newyorker.com/magazine/2008/02/11/a -strike-in-the-dark.

Hinnebusch, R. (2001). *Syria: Revolution From Above*. New York: Routledge.

Hinnebusch, R. and Ehteshami, A. (1997). *Syria and Iran: Middle Powers in a Penetrated Regional System*. London, New York: Routledge.

Hirst, D. (2010). *Beware Small States: Lebanon, Battleground of the Middle East*. New York: Nation Books.

Kerr, M. (1971). *The Arab Cold War: Gamal Abd al-Nasir and His Rivals, 1958–1970*. New York: Oxford University Press.

Khoury, P. (1987). *Syria and the French Mandate: The Politics of Arab Nationalism, 1920–1945*. Princeton, NJ: Princeton University Press.

Kissinger, H. (1982). *Years of Upheaval*. Boston, MA: Little Brown & Co.

Lake, A. (1994, March/April). Confronting Backlash States. *Foreign Affairs*, 45–55.

Lesch, D. (2003). The 1957 American-Syrian Crisis: Globalist Policy in a Regional Reality. In D. Lesch, ed., *The Middle East and the United States: A Historical and Political Reassessment* (pp. 133–148). Boulder, CO: Westview Press.

Leverett, F. (2005). *Inheriting Syria: Bashar's Trial by Fire*. Washington, DC: Brookings Institution Press.

Lister, T. (2011, April 26). Syria: The key piece in a regional Rubik's cube. *CNN.com*. Retrieved from www.cnn.com/2011/WORLD/meast/04/25/syria.role/index.html.

Little, D. (1990a, summer). Pipeline Politics: America, TAPLINE, and the Arabs. *Business History Review*, 64(2), 255–285.

Little, D. (1990b, winter). Cold War and Covert Action: The United States and Syria, 1945–1958. *Middle East Journal*, 44(1), 51–75.

Little, D. (2008). *American Orientalism: The United States and the Middle East since 1945*. Chapel Hill, NC: The University of North Carolina Press.

Ma'oz, M. (1988). *Asad: The Sphinx of Damascus*. New York: Weidnefeld & Nicolson.

Mufti, M. (1996). *Sovereign Creations: Pan-Arabism and Political Order in Syria and Iraq*. Ithaca, NY: Cornell University Press.

Naylor, H. (2007, October 7). Syria reportedly encourages Sunni insurgents. *The New York Times*. Retrieved from www.nytimes.com/2007/10/07/world/africa/07iht-syria.1. 7781943.html?mcubz=1.

Norton, A.R. (1987). *Amal and the Shi'a: Struggle for the Soul of Lebanon*. Austin, TX: University of Texas Press.

Pearson, I. (2007, January). The Syrian Crisis of 1957, the Anglo-American 'Special Relationship', and the 1958 landings in Jordan and Lebanon. *Middle Eastern Studies*, 43(1), 45–64.

Perthes, V. (1995). *The Political Economy of Syria under Asad*. New York: I.B. Tauris & Company Ltd.

Rapoport, D.C. (1962). A Comparative Theory of Military and Political Types. In S. Huntington, ed., *Changing Patterns of Military Politics* (pp. 71–100). New York: Free Press of Glencoe.

Sayigh, Y. (1997). *Armed Struggle and the Search for State: The Palestinian National Movement, 1949–1993*. New York: Oxford University Press.

Schmitt, E. and Shanker, T. (2008, October 28). U.S. Says Iraqi Militant Killed in Syria Raid. *The New York Times*. Retrieved from www.nytimes.com/2008/10/28/wo rld/africa/28iht_ 28syria.17295937.html.

Seale, P. (1966). *The Struggle for Syria: A Study of Post-war Arab Politics, 1945–1958*. London: I.B. Tauris & Co. Ltd.

Seale, P. (1995). *Asad of Syria: The Struggle for the Middle East*. Berkeley, CA: University of California Press.

Shemesh, M. (1988). *The Palestinian Entity 1959–1974: Arab Politics and the PLO*. London: Frank Cass.

Syrian Arab Republic. (1970–1983). *Statistical Abstracts*. Damascus: Central Bureau of Statistics. Accessed from Wagner Library, Harvard University.

Tamari, D., Heller, M. and Eytan, Z. (1983). *The Middle East Military Balance, 1983*. Tel-Aviv: Jaffee Center for Strategic Studies.

United Nations Population Fund. (1950). *Total population by country, 1950*. Retrieved from https://esa.un.org/unpd/wpp/.

Wedeen, L. (1999). *Ambiguities of Domination: Politics, Rhetoric, and Symbols in Contemporary Syria*. Chicago, IL: University of Chicago Press.

Zisser, E. (2007). *Commanding Syria: Bashar al-Asad and the First Years in Power*. New York: I.B. Tauris & Co. Ltd.

14 The United States and Iran

The view of the hard-line conservatives in the Islamic Republic

Hamad H. Albloshi

Since the new American administration's tenure began in January 2017, a war of words has erupted between the United States and the Islamic Republic of Iran. This kind of war is not new between the two nations; it started with the establishment of the regime in Tehran after the revolution of 1978–1979. Formal relations ended between them as a direct result of the hostage crisis, when Iranian revolutionary students occupied the American embassy in Tehran and held American diplomats for 444 days. Negative views toward the United States have existed in Iran for decades. Some Iranians regard the United States as the "Great Satan." An overwhelming majority within the Iranian revolutionary regime shared this hostility toward America. Indeed, the "regime in Iran has always partially defined itself in terms of its opposition to the United States" (Milani, 2010: p. 1).

However, the current war of words is important because it has erupted after a significant improvement in the relationship between Washington and Tehran in recent years: the presidents of both countries had a phone conversation in 2013; Iranian Foreign Minister Javad Zarif shook hands with President Obama in 2015; Zarif met his American counterpart, John Kerry, on several occasions; and both countries, alongside other nations, reached a deal regarding Iran's nuclear program in 2015. Moreover, every March from 2009 to 2016, President Obama released video statements addressing the Iranian people and congratulating them on the advent of their new year, Nuwrūz. His statements showed great respect for the Iranian people, their history, and their culture.

Nevertheless, there are forces within both countries who do not encourage reconciliation. These forces have their own justifications. For example, American conservatives accuse Iran of being a major supporter of terrorism and attempting to be the dominant Middle Eastern power. Former National Security Adviser Michael Flynn stated in February 2017, "the Islamic Republic of Iran is the world's leading state sponsor of terrorism and engages in and supports violent activities that destabilize the Middle East" (Flynn, 2017). At the same time, Iranian hard-line conservatives hold negative views of the United States. This chapter will be a descriptive analysis of these views.

There have been many interesting studies and books about the relationship between Iran and the United States, including Parsi (2007, 2012), Maleki (2008), Yaphe (2008), Milani (2010), Leverett and Mann Leverett (2013), Abrahamian (2013), and Colleau (2016) among others. These works did not deal with the relationship from the viewpoint of the hard-line conservatives in Iran. This group is the most critical of the Unites States. This study will build upon the works mentioned and qualitatively analyse the hard-line conservatives' view toward the United States by relying on three newspapers affiliated with them in Iran: *Shalamchih, Yā Lithārāt*, and *Kayhān. Shalamchih* was a weekly newspaper published from November 1996 to January 1999. *Yā Lithārāt*, was also a weekly newspaper, and its last issue appeared in December 2016. However, *Kayhān*, a daily newspaper, is still currently active in Iran.[1] This chapter covers many issues of *Yā Lithārāt* distributed between April 2015 and December 2016, while issues of *Kayhān* from July 2015 to February 8, 2017 were also analyzed.

Factions in the Islamic Republic of Iran

The hard-line conservatives are part of a competitive system in Iran. It is true that the Iranian regime is not democratic but, at the same time, it is not totalitarian. It is an authoritarian regime with limited pluralism. This pluralism helps different political groups and factions to flourish and compete with each other for power. These factions have different ideological foundations and interpretations of the revolutionary doctrine of the regime. They disagree over the best ways to govern and to construct Iran's relations with the international community. However, they all agree on the importance of protecting Iranian national interests and the Islamic regime.

There are four main factions within the Iranian political system: the traditional conservative right, the moderates, the reformists, and the hard-line conservatives. The traditional conservatives are a result of the coalition between traditional clergy and the Bazaar (traditional businessmen). The moderates are associated with former President Hāshimī Rafsanjani (d. 2017), and they believe that opening Iran to the global economy is necessary. The reformists consist of different political groups which emphasize the importance of civil society, human rights, and political freedom. The hardliners "embrace revolutionary radicalism" and are connected to the Revolutionary Guards, the Basīj, and powerful Ayatollahs such as Misbāḥ Yazdī, and Ahmad Jannatī (Posch, 2005) in addition to a political group known as Anṣār-i Ḥizbullāh. This faction is known as the neoconservatives.

There is no clear definition of Iranian hard-line conservatives. However, scholars agree that this group consists of revolutionaries within the Iranian system who are zealots and loyal to the main principles of the 1979 revolution. For example, Moslem (2002) sees this faction as a loose one "made up of individuals surrounded by cronies who act like a pressure group within the system. While those associated with this faction use similar rhetoric and support each other's actions, by and large they act independently" (Moslem, 2002: p. 135).

Members of this faction believe in the ultimate power of the supreme leader, cultural confrontation with the West, political confrontation with the international community (especially the United States), economic justice, and the preparation for the reappearance of the Mahdi, the Twelfth Shi'a Imam. The only president belonging to this group was Ahmadinejad, though he did have differences with the faction in the last two years of his tenure.

Hard-line conservatives and Iran's foreign policy

Houman Sadri (1997) divides revolutionary leaders into two categories: (1) realists and (2) idealists. Both follow different strategies in their foreign policy approach. Realists understand the limits of their capabilities to change the world. They take the reaction of the international community into consideration while understanding the importance of exporting their revolution (Sadri, 1997). Therefore, "[i]nstead of channeling resources to support national liberation movements, their priority is to build their own country into a model revolutionary state" (Sadri, 1997: 14). In contrast, idealists, also called internationalists, focus more on the external relations of their regime. They believe in their ability to orchestrate other similar revolutions in other countries. Among these idealists, there is a group of radical idealists, who

> have an extreme sense of the mission to export their revolution by any means, even by such interventionist tactics as directly supporting with training and arms the military opposition in other states. ... They do not think in terms of official channels of communication or the relations between governments or states ... but in terms of relations between people or nations.
>
> (Sadri, 1997: p. 13)

Some of these radicals even believe their regime "can take on the world" (Sadri, 1997: p. 13). As a result, these regimes may face international pressures to change their attitudes. However, for the radical idealists, "the isolation of the country by major powers is unavoidable. In fact, they consider the isolation a blessing" (Sadri, 1997: p. 13).

The hard-line conservatives could be regarded as idealists. For them, confrontation with the international community is possible and Iran should strengthen its position among the nations of the world. They assert that during the Rafsanjani–Khatami era, Iran's global position was weakened by the approach taken by those two presidents. These conservatives see the Ahmadinejad's foreign policy as one that brought international dignity back to Iran (Nabaviyān, 2012). This dignity returned because of Ahmadinejad's position toward the West and Israel, in addition to his policies regarding Iran's nuclear program. For example, they believe that the reformist government of former President Khatami had been begging the international community to negotiate with Iran over its nuclear program, but when Ahmadinejad came to power, the main powers of the international community asked the Iranian government to negotiate. To Nabaviyān, a hard-line conservative cleric, this is a sign of Iran's power (*Iqtidār*) (Nabaviyān, 2012).

Therefore, the conservatives disagree with the foreign policy approaches of Rafsanjani and Khatami since the death of Ayatollah Khomeini. One of the main characteristics of the sixteen years of the Rafsanjani–Khatami era (1989–2005) was the normalization of Iran's foreign relations with the international community. Iran's ties with Middle Eastern countries improved, its relationship to European countries developed, and international pressures decreased. This normalization is regarded by the hard-line conservatives as a mistake, as they believe only resistance works against the pressures of the international community (Rasā'ī, 1390 [2012]). Therefore, the Iranian regime should not tolerate any changes to the foundation and values of the revolution (Rastgharī, 1390 [2012]). Rafsanjani was attacked because of his policies, which opened the country to the political and economic influences of the West, and Khatami was attacked because of his moderate instead of radical policies. Thus, hard-line conservative writer Fāṭimih Rajabī believes that the sixteen years during which those two presidents were in office damaged the divine diplomacy of Ayatollah Khomeini (Rajabī, 2007).

The hard-line conservatives on one hand defend the dignity of the Iranian nation and the importance of standing against the world powers and defending the Islamic Republic's national interests. On the other hand, they focus on the importance of the Islamic nation and do not accept the national borders. For example, hard-line conservative strategist Hassan 'Abbāsī believes that Islam cannot be confined by borders or the constitution of the Islamic Republic (*Aparat*, 1390 [2011]).

The nuclear program is the embodiment of the important position that is given to Iranian national interests in the hard-line conservatives' ideology. Since the emergence of this issue, Iranian officials, including the hard-line conservatives, have been repeating the same phrase: "The nuclear program is our right" (Magiran, 1391 [2012], Ra'īs Kumisyūn-i Amniyat-i …). However, different strategies are followed by each group. Hussein Sharī'atmadārī, editor-in-chief of *Kayhān*, believes that the Iranian government should not retreat in the program negotiations because Iran does not need the members of the UN Security Council's (UNSC's) P5+1 group but the P5+1 need Iran (Sharī'atmadārī, 1391 [2012], Khargūsh-i Moscow).

Since the disclosure of the Iranian nuclear program in 2003, international pressure has increased. The Iranians have held long negotiations over the program. These negotiations have sometimes been based on "carrots" and other times on "sticks."

The UNSC has passed different resolutions regarding Iran's nuclear program since August 2006. The level of pressure on Iran increased after each resolution. But Iran has refused to comply and give up its program. Immediately after the submission of UNSC resolution 1747, for example, the former Iranian President Ahmadinejad announced, "Iran will not stop its nuclear activities even for a second [and] the Iranian nation will not forget who supported and who did not support the sanctions" (BBC Arabic, 2007).

In addition to these resolutions, the United States, the European Union, Canada, the United Kingdom, Japan, and France have imposed sanctions against Iran. These sanctions have varied from banning travel of some Iranian officials to suspending trade with the country and eliminating the ability of Iran's Central Bank to trade (MSNBC, 2012). These sanctions increased during Ahmadinejad's presidency, mainly because of his radical attitude and rhetoric toward the international community.

Since President Rouhani's rise to power, he has followed a moderate and pragmatic approach toward the international community. Negotiations resumed between Iran and the P5+1 over its nuclear program, and a Joint Plan of Action was signed by both parties in Geneva in November 2013. Per the agreement, Iran froze portions of its nuclear program in return for a decrease in economic sanctions.

Rouhani continued his efforts to reach a final deal with the P5+1, and in July 2015 the Joint Comprehensive Plan of Action (JCPOA), in which Iran made many concessions, was signed in Geneva. For example, Iran agreed to reduce its stockpile of low-enriched uranium and its centrifuges and to turn one of its nuclear facilities into a scientific centre. In return, the international community reduced nuclear-related sanctions and recognized Iran's peaceful nuclear project (European Union External Action, 2015).

The hard-line conservatives do not believe in the importance of these negotiations. For them, confrontation is the main policy on which the regime should rely. One way to confront sanctions is to use the most effective weapon in the hands of Iran, which is the Strait of Hormuz. The closure of this strait is regarded as an easy step to destabilize the world economy and increase the price of oil. The closure of Hormuz would affect the oil market and harm the United States and other states in the region, especially the Gulf Cooperation Council (GCC) countries, all of whom rely heavily on oil exports to manage their economies. About 90 percent of these countries' oil exports go through the strait. That 90 percent constitutes 75 percent of the oil market. Consequently, the market would suffer from an oil shortage leading to an increase in oil prices (Talmadge, 2008).

Hussein Sharī'atmadārī believes that the United States and its supporters are conspiring against the Islamic Republic of Iran and that oil sanctions are part of this conspiracy. For him, Iran can confront this conspiracy by closing the Strait of Hormuz because the closure is legally based in international law. In addition, he believes that "If Iran is not allowed to sell its oil in the international market, it has the right to prevent others from selling their oil as well" (Sharī'atmadārī, 1390 [2011], Tanginā dar 'Ubūr ...).

Hard-line conservatives insist Iran is under a constant threat. Hassan 'Abbāsī, for example, believes Iran is under threat and that moderate pragmatic foreign policy is not enough to protect the regime. He criticizes Khatami's concept of "dialogue among civilizations" and sees it as a damaging strategy.

Instead, he argues that the Iranian regime must use the same methods as its enemies. In other words, Iran should retaliate and use power to eliminate those threats and pressures. ʿAbbāsī stresses that security should be guaranteed to the Iranian regime and threatens the international powers by saying, "Either all of us are secured, or none of us" (*Aparat*, 1390 [2011]). Therefore, he asserts, "If our honor, esteem, prestige, and entity are spoiled [by the international powers], we will act within and outside our borders" (*Aparat*, 1390 [2011]). He then advocates relying on terrorism because Iran's enemies should be scared; "this is called the holy terrorism" (*Aparat*, 1390 [2011]). For ʿAbbāsī, the United States wants to kill the notion of *jihad*; thus, the current regime is responsible for reviving it, not for discussing the concept of "dialogue among civilizations" (*Aparat*, 1390 [2011]).

Hard-line conservatives and the United States of America

Iran's foreign relations have been unstable since the 1979 Islamic Revolution. However, its relations with Israel and the United States have not changed. Both countries occupy a position in the Iranian regime's political discourse. This discourse remains negative. For example, thirty-eight years have passed since the 1979 revolution, and to this day, those who participate in Friday prayers in many parts of Iran still repeat, "death to US, death to Israel." No one can be sure about the feelings of those people who repeat these slogans against the United States and Israel, but what is true is that the Iranian regime's discourse toward these two countries has been negative for over thirty-five years and these prayer ceremonies are organized under regime supervision. Hard-line conservative clerics such as Ahmad Khatami, Ahmad Jannatī, and Muhammad-Taqī Miṣbāḥ Yazdī lead many of these prayers.

The relationship between the United States and Iran has shifted through different stages. As is well known, Iran had strong ties to Washington during the Cold War because it was an important regional power, along with Saudi Arabia, capable of countering communist influence in the Middle East. The United States had a role in toppling Mussadiq in 1953 and supported the Shah's repressive regime. When the latter was overthrown in 1979, the relationship between the two nations was severely damaged. This happened mainly because of the hostage crisis. Moreover, the United States was among the countries who supported Iraq's war with Iran. The Cold War ended, and the founder of the Islamic regime in Iran died, but the relationship between the two countries has not yet normalized.

There are forces within Iran who believe in the importance of ending animosity toward the United States. For example, former President Hāshimī Rafsanjani encouraged the regime in Iran to start negotiating with the United States in 2012 (DW Persian, 2012). He even criticized the understanding of the "neither West nor East" slogan, believing that it did not mean to cut diplomatic relations with both sides. For Rafsanjani, the slogan meant Iran should be independent but also deal with the world based upon mutual respect and cooperation. He also asserted that he had urged Ayatollah Khomeini, before his death, to end hostility toward the United States (DW Persian, 2012). This pragmatic approach is one of the major reasons behind his disagreement with the hard-line conservatives on foreign policy.

Muhammad Khatami, the former reformist president, also had positive views toward the United States. He had a message for the Americans: he showed his respect for them and their culture in a 1998 CNN interview (CNN, 1998). In addition, he "announced Iran's readiness to gradually normalise ties with the American government" (Moslem, 2002: p. 1).

Furthermore, Zibakalam, a well-known political scientist at Tehran University and supporter of the current regime, has long urged the Iranian government to reconcile with the United States. He had many debates with hard-line conservatives about Iran's foreign policy and its relations with the United States. For example, in a 1997 debate with hard-line conservative journalist and filmmaker Mas'ūd Dihnamakī regarding US–Iran relations, he stated, "I think we should have relationships with any country, including the United States, if it is in our interest" (Shamalchih, 1377 [1998], Guzārishī az Jilisih-yi ...). It can be argued that Zibakalam's position toward the United States remained unchanged for about 20 years; in a recent debate with former parliamentarian Hamīd Rasā'ī, Zibakalam wondered about the benefits that Iran has gained as a result of conflict with the United States (Iran Khabar, 1395 [2014]). On one occasion he asserted that confronting the United States has yielded only negative effects (Iranian Online TV, 2016).

President Rouhani does not go as far as Zibakalam, but he came to power with a discourse that was different from that of the hardliners, especially regarding the international community and the United States. He believes in dialogue between Iran and the United States, and with his famous 2013 phone call with President Obama, he became the first Iranian President since the revolution to talk directly with an American President. The hard-line conservatives did not welcome this step. Upon his arrival in Iran from New York, President Rouhani was faced with a group of radical students demonstrating against the call. They used slogans including "Death to America" (Karami, 2013). The conversation was described as "aberrant" by *Yā Lithārāt*, a weekly newspaper associated with Anṣār-i Ḥizbullāh in the country (*Yā Lithārāt*, 1394 [2015]. Su'ālī bih Nām-i ...).

At the same time, the hard-line conservatives launched a campaign against any rapprochement between Iran and the United States (*Zamaneh Tribune*, 1392 [2013]). Large banners were installed on buildings in Tehran, most designed to illustrate untrustworthy American behavior toward Iran. When President Trump gained power in January 2017, the campaign began again. A banner appeared in Valī'aṣr Square in Tehran, one of the busiest places in the capital, on the first anniversary of the Revolutionary Guards' detention of ten American sailors (Sanger, Schmitt and Cooper, 2016). The sailors were later released, but the incident was important for the hard-line conservatives in terms of demonstrating Iran's power. The banner was described as "the largest banner of the country" by *Kayhān* (*Kayhān*, 1395 [2017], "Qudrat-i Bartar" bar ...).

The campaign was launched because the hard-line conservatives distrust America. Hardliners view the United States as a Zionist regime (*Yā Lithārāt*, 1394 [2015], Siyāsathāy-i Āmrīkāyī ...) and even as "the most traitorous country in the world" (*Yā Lithārāt*, 1395 [2016], Duwlat az Hamīn ...). To hardliners, the animosity toward the United States is deep-rooted, and "it cannot be easily forgotten as a direct result of one negotiation, over one issue" (Akhavān, 1394 [2015]). Thus, this animosity "is not subject to change ... and no one has the right to modify it" (*Yā Lithārāt*, 1392 [2013], Tahdīdhāy-i Pīsh-i ...).

Therefore, nuclear negotiations between the two countries were not seen as an effective tool toward reaching reconciliation. In fact, the hard-line conservatives even believe that "promoting negotiation with the United States is a betrayal of martyrs" (*Shalamchih*, 1377 [1998/1999], Bayāniyyi-i Ḥizbullāh dar ...). One reason for this belief is their insistence the United States will not give up its animosity toward the Islamic Republic of Iran and the Iranians (*Shamalchih*, 1377 [1998], Guzārishī az Jilisih-yi ...). They assert that "American threats against our people are an example of their unforgettable hatred toward Iran" (*Yā Lithārāt*, 1394 [2015], Suʿālī bih Nām-i ...).

This hostility is seen as a tool to disrupt stability within Iran. The hard-line conservatives believe the American government is intent on regime change. They claim the United States was behind the Iran–Iraq War to topple the Islamic regime in Tehran (*Shalamchih*, 1377 [1999], Āqāy-i Khatami ...). The sense of insecurity in the relationship with the United States has been with the hard-line conservatives for a long time. For example, a 1996 issue of hard-line conservative weekly newspaper *Shalamchih* stated the United States would attack Iran (*Shalamchih*, 1375 [1996/1997], Iḥtimāl-i ḥamlih-yi ...).

A massive movement, known as the Green Movement, emerged in Iran in 2009 as a result of the presidential election organized in the same year. The reformists supported Mīr Hussein Mūsavī, former prime minister. The expectation in the country was that he would win. However, Ahmadinejad won and many people believed that the election was rigged in his favor. People demonstrated in the millions and since Mūsavī's campaign color was green, the movement came to be known as the Green Movement. The movement failed to force the regime to withdraw its support of Ahmadinejad, and its leaders have been in house arrest for years.

The hard-line conservatives have long attacked the reformists, but since the emergence of the Green Movement, attacks have intensified. They have been seen as tools in the hands of the United States (*Yā Lithārāt*, 1395 [2016], Duwlat az Hamīn ...). For example, Hussein Sharīʿatmadārī sees the events of 2009 as an "American–Israeli sedition" (Sharīʿatmadārī, 1390 [2012], Qatrih Daryāst ...). Moreover, there is a claim that in 2009, because it did not want to end the crisis in Iran, the American administration convinced Twitter not to close the website for maintenance (*Yā Lithārāt*, 1395 [2016], Duwlat az Hamīn ...).

The hardliners are still cautious about US intentions relating to Iranian politics. For example, in 2015 Muṣliḥī, Ahmadinejad's minister of intelligence asserted that the United States was preparing for another similar crisis (*Yā Lithārāt*, 1394 [2015], Dushman fitnih-yi …). Thus, they believe there is a desire in the United States to create disorder in Iran through the reformists. Moreover, there is a belief that moderates such as a Rafsanjani might welcome American support (*Yā Lithārāt*, 1394 [2015], Pirūzhih-yi Nufūz-i …).

The hardliners view reformists as being in favor of normalising relations with the United States and accuse them of wanting to sign any deal with the American government over Iran's nuclear program, even if the deal harms Tehran's interests (*Yā Lithārāt*, 1394 [2015], Ru'yāy-i Ḥuẓūr-i …). The nuclear deal was a critical moment in the relationship between Iran and the United States, but the hard-line conservatives were not happy about it. Their newspapers covered the issue for months and revealed the hard-line conservatives' suspicions of America's intentions behind the nuclear deal. They believe the agreement was a loss for Iran because "it drastically limited Iran's nuclear industry, it maintained the sanctions that had been imposed upon Iran, and it put Iran's defense forces under supervision"; therefore, *Kayhān* asserted, "we should not have allowed the Americans to make a deal based on these terms" (*Kayhān*, 1394 [2015], Tawāfuq dar …). The nuclear negotiation, which lasted for more than a decade, was faced, in the hard-line conservatives' opinion, with "American efforts to sabotage it." They believe that the aim behind the negotiations was not the objection to the nuclear program, but "to prevent Iran's empowerment" (*Kayhān*, 1394 [2015], Chālish-i 12 …). Moreover, they do not support the Iranian signature on the IAEA's Additional Protocol because it allows "spies to enter the country" (*Yā Lithārāt*, 1394 [2015], Vāguzārī-yi Naqd-i …).

There is an assumption among hard-line conservatives that "the deal did not respect Iran's redlines" (*Kayhān*, 1394 [2015], 180 Darajih-yi …). For them, there are redlines that should not be impeded, such as "the immediate lifting of sanctions against Iran, the refusal of any long-term Iranian commitments, the continuation of nuclear research, and the refusal of unconventional investigations in Iran by any international organisation" (*Kayhān*, 1394 [2015], Mas'ūliyyat-i Tārīkhī-yi …).

The hardliners did not support the government before or in the aftermath of the deal. They continue to be suspicious of Rouhani's negotiating team. For example, Nabaviyān asserted a few weeks before signing the deal, "the nation will not accept a bad deal, and it will delegitimize it." He also claimed that "no member of the negotiation team wanted to defend the interests of the nation" (*Yā Lithārāt*, 1394 [2015], Millat, Tawāfuq-i …). Moreover, days before the deal, hardliners organized an event in Āzādī Square and announced that a statement would be signed by "millions of Iranians" in a mass refusal of the deal. The organizers claimed that 17,000 lawyers signed it as well (*Yā Lithārāt*, 1394 [2015], Rūnimāyī az Imẓāy-i …). Ahmad Khatami, a hard-line conservative cleric, asserted "we will not accept a bad or humiliating deal" (*Yā Lithārāt*, 1394 [2015], Zīra Bār-i Tawāfuq-i ...).

Thus, when the deal was announced, the hardliners were not supportive. One day after the deal, the head of the Basīj students at Tehran University announced, "with or without an agreement, the students will not stop resisting the US" (*Yā Lithārāt*, 1394 [2015], Tawāfuq Bishavad ...). Also, hard-line conservative cleric Ahmad Sālik Kāshānī asserted that "Iran had been cheated" (*Yā Lithārāt*, 1394 [2015], Kulāh-i Gushādī ...).

As previously mentioned, the hardliners see the United States as untrustworthy. They insist America will not fulfill its commitments to Iran. The faction has emphasized this issue on many occasions. For example, Muhammad Riza Naqdī, the head of the Basīj, asserted, "the US will come up with excuses not to respect the deal" (*Yā Lithārāt*, 1394 [2015], "Tawāfuq" Āghāz-i ...). Another official in the Revolutionary Guards said, "the US was unfaithful from the beginning" (*Yā Lithārāt*, 1394 [2015], Bad'ahdī-yi Āmrīkā ...).

To improve public support for the deal, the Iranian government emphasizes its positive effects on the nation's economy. For example, President Rouhani said in a January 2017 television interview that the deal has helped the economy and, without it, the government would only have had a budget to pay salaries and would have been forced to ignore any other projects that would help to develop the country and boost its economy. To Rouhani, the deal has helped the country to export more oil to the international market, which in turn has benefited Iran's economy (BBC Persian, 2017).

However, the hard-line conservatives do not agree. They believe the deal will not improve the economic condition of Iran because the sanction-lifting process is gradual. This means that economic problems will not be resolved immediately (Nūrī, 1394 [2015]). Moreover, an article in *Yā Lithārāt* asserted that only 30 percent of the problems in Iran's economy are caused by sanctions, thus even without sanctions the economy would still be weak (Ibrāhīmyān, 1394 [2015]). Similarly, the same newspaper published a statement by Muslihī in which he declared that only 20 percent of Iran's economic problems are related to the sanctions (*Yā Lithārāt*, 1394 [2015], Tanhā 20 Darsad-i ...). Supreme Leader Khamenei agreed that improving Iran's economy did not depend on removing sanctions, as indicated in a May 2015 statement (*Yā Lithārāt*, 1394 [2015], Qābil-i Qabūl ...). In Khamenei's words, "If sanctions were effective, they would have helped the arrogant powers to reach their goals in the first years of the revolution." Khamenei also believes the regime will continue to successfully resist sanctions (9 *Diy*, 1390 [2011], Agar Tahrīmhā ...).

Moreover, there is an assumption among hardliners that "the people have defeated the sanctions" and that the sanctions are harmless (*Yā Lithārāt*, 1394 [2015], Magar Dunbāl-i ...). Therefore, Iran's dignity should be respected even when it comes to negotiating removal of the sanctions. Hussein Sharī'atmadārī believes sanctions have helped the Iranian regime develop different scientific sectors such as the nuclear sector, the nanotechnology sector, and the space sector (Sharī'atmadārī, 1390 [2012], Chih Kasānī …). In other words, hard-line conservatives see the sanctions and isolation of Iran as a blessing and conclude they will not harm the Islamic Republic.

Some hardliners are skeptical about lifting sanctions against Iran (*Yā Lithārāt*, 1394 [2015]. Khushbīnīhā bih …). Their skepticism is not baseless. Two main actions taken by the United States gave them an excuse to attack President Rouhani. First, less than a month after signing the JCPOA, the US Departments of Treasury and State sanctioned individuals and companies with alleged relations to the Iranian nuclear program. Former Under Secretary of Terrorism and Financial Intelligence David S. Cohen stated, "The Joint Plan of Action reached in Geneva does not, and will not, interfere with our continued efforts to expose and disrupt those supporting Iran's nuclear program or seeking to evade our sanction" (US Treasury, 2013).

Second, about two years after the JCPOA, Congress extended the Iran Sanctions Act against Iran for an additional ten years. The act "targets Iran's energy, military and banking sectors" (Barrett, 2016). Though President Obama did not sign the bill, the action taken by Congress was nevertheless regarded as unacceptable in Iran. *Yā Lithārāt*, for example, asserted, "Four years of promoting for the JCPOA was a delusion … the sanctions have proved that those who worried about the negotiations were correct" (Ṣābir, 1395 [2016]). As a result of this position, hard-line conservatives view Rouhani's foreign policy approach as "begging diplomacy" which will not convince the international community about Iran's right to have a nuclear program (*Yā Lithārāt*, 1392 [2013], Taḥrīmrā bā Tuwlīd …).

As previously stated, upon President Trump's inauguration, a war of words erupted between Iran and the United States. Trump has been against the nuclear deal with Iran and has described it many times as a "terrible" deal (Parker, 2017), "bad," and "suspicious" (Smilowitz, 2016). During the presidential campaign, he even promised to dismantle the deal (Macmillan, 2017). Moreover, Trump issued an executive order in late January 2017 temporarily banning citizens of seven countries, including Iran, from entering the United States (Williams, 2017). As a result, Tehran issued a statement against what it described as "a clear insult to the Islamic world, and especially the great nation of Iran" (Haraldsson, 2017). Others in Iran shared this feeling as well. For example, Teraneh Alidoosti, an actress from the Oscar-nominated movie "The Salesman", boycotted the Academy Awards in protest of President Trump's executive order, describing it as "racist" (Donadio, 2017).

In its statement, the Iranian government declared it would "take reciprocal measures in order to safeguard the rights of its citizens" (Haraldsson, 2017). However, Javad Zarif, in a tweet on January 28, 2017, commented that "Unlike the US, our decision is not retroactive. All with valid Iranian visas will be gladly welcomed" (Reuters, 2017). Days later, Iran welcomed the American national wrestling team to participate in the 2017 Wrestling World

Cup, which was organized in the Iranian city of Kermanshah. The government in Tehran had denied the American team visas to enter the country, but when Trump's order was suspended, visas were issued (PRI, 2017).

The Trump administration's actions against Iran led supreme leader Ali Khamenei to assert that President Trump "represents the real face of America" (*Kayhān*, 1395 [2017], Trump Chihrih-yi ...). Therefore, it can be argued that Washington, with its new administration, has given the hard-line conservatives a legitimate reason to undermine efforts made by Rouhani to normalize Iran's relations with the international community in general, and in particular, the United States. The hard-line conservatives continue to look for excuses to prevent any normalization of this relationship, and Trump's administration may give them what they are looking for.

Conclusion

This chapter has discussed the hard-line conservatives' views toward the United States. In general, the hardliners support hawkish strategies toward the international community. They are idealists and want to export their revolution to the outside world. As this chapter has revealed, the hardliners strongly disagree with rapprochement between Iran and the United States; they believe that Iran should stand against the United States (*Yā Lithārāt*, 1394 [2015], Muqābilih bih Mithl ...) and should not give up (*Kayhān*, 1394 [2015], Sanad-i vienna ...).

Both countries have legitimate reasons to mistrust each other. The rhetoric of some Iranian officials toward the United States is negative, and Iran has taken many actions against American interests in the Middle East. Officials in the United States use negative rhetoric against the Islamic Republic of Iran as well. In addition, the United States has long imposed sanctions on Iran. There is also a demand within the United States for regime change in Tehran. Moreover, Iran is surrounded by American military bases with which the United States could wage war against Iran, and this concerns Iranian officials from all factions.

However, both countries need each other. Iran has important assets throughout the Middle East, and it can use them to benefit the United States. The Iranian regime can use these assets as well to harm American interests. Iranian supporters exist in Iraq, Syria, Lebanon, Yemen, Afghanistan, and other countries. They can be used to fight terrorism, such as the Iranian participation in fighting ISIS or, as was the case in 1980s, to attack American interests in the region. Also, Iran is part of the civil war in Syria, and it can play a major role in ending it. The Iranian regime can similarly use its influence to end political crises such as in Iraq, Lebanon, and Afghanistan. Therefore, the United States has a need for Iran to help solve some of the problems within the Middle East. At the same time, the Iranian regime needs US assistance to fix its economy. Washington can eliminate sanctions against the Iranian regime, encouraging foreign investment in Iranian business. Additionally, Iran needs to be recognized as a regional power, which can be achieved through a deal with the United States and its regional allies.

President Obama's Iran policy was a major step toward normalising relations between the two nations. Building on this policy would have also helped the normalization of the Iranian Revolution; the hard-line conservatives believe that the revolution should continue because it has not fulfilled its task. Moreover, the hardliners believe Iran cannot rely on the international community because it is dominated by the United States, which constantly threatens to overthrow the regime in Tehran. Therefore, they are in favor of creating a vigilant society. In contrast, the moderates and the reformists want to normalize the revolution and the Iranian system. One major step for that is to end animosity toward the United States. In return, they expect a similar warming from Washington.

President Trump's policy toward Iran, however, could jeopardize the efforts to move toward a normalized society in Iran and could strengthen the hard-line conservatives' position in Tehran while weakening Rouhani's position. It can be argued that the harsher the United States becomes toward Iran, the stronger the hardliners in Iran will become.

Iranians show their enthusiasm during presidential elections, and in recent years, they helped two moderate politicians and a reformist to reach power. The relationship with the international community was among many issues that were raised in the campaigns during the 2017 presidential election. The hardliners focused on this issue by attacking Rouhani for trusting the United States and signing the JCPOA. They did not believe that the agreement had positive results on the economy. However, Rouhani and his deputy, Jahāngīrī, stood firm during their campaigns in defence of the agreement.

Despite the attacks on Rouhani and his team, more than 23 million people voted for him in May 2017, and thus he has the chance to govern for another four years. Rouhani supports Iran's engagement with the world; however, he is critical of the United States and its policies in the region. This criticism can be seen as an attempt to present himself as a president who does not bow down to the United States. Rouhani is moderate in comparison to the hardliners, but this does not mean that he will not become aggressive in defending Iran's interests as an independent sovereign nation state and a regional power. His approach is different from his colleagues in the Iranian regime because he does not support confrontation with the international community, and this is one reason for his re-election in 2017.

The results of the 2017 presidential election showed the eagerness of Iranians for a more open and moderate society in relation to the outside world. During the campaign Rouhani asked for a chance to continue the economic and social programs that he and his administration had started in 2013. Iranians gave him this chance, but they want to see positive impacts from these programs. Pressures against Rouhani and the continuation of sanctions imposed on Iran might weaken those programs and, therefore, people's livelihoods. Pressures could strengthen the desire for regime change in the country, but they might backfire as well if they bring a hardliner into power in 2021. This could return diplomatic relations between both countries to the immediate aftermath of the 1979 Iranian Revolution, and more efforts will be needed to rebuild trust between them.

It is true that the supreme leader currently holds the ultimate power in Iran. However, a strong and moderate president can have political leverage within the system to influence Iranian foreign policy and push toward normalising relations and even cooperation with the United States. Shifts may occur within the system, and the president's moderate policies may gain support, especially in the parliament and other institutions such as the Supreme National Security Council.

Therefore, those who view Iran as a unitary actor, regardless of its different political factions, misunderstand the complexity of Iranian politics. They view Iran as similar to totalitarian regimes, and this could lead to misjudgment and miscalculation of the Islamic Republic. It could also delay reform and force undesired change in Iran's policies. The hard-line conservatives in Iran seek excuses to prevent a moderate foreign policy, and their Washington counterparts may give them exactly what they desire.

Note

1   This chapter relies on Persian and Arabic texts and deals with names and phrases in both languages. These phrases have been transliterated based on the transliteration guide of the *International Journal of Middle East Studies* (*IJMES*). Names that were not transliterated based on this guide are commonly used names, such as Khomeini, Khamenei, Ahmadinejad, Rafsanjani, Hassan, and Ahmad, among others. It is also worth mentioning that the names of politicians, authors, activists, intellectuals, and thinkers have been transliterated unless they have their own websites or accounts on Twitter or Facebook that provide their preferred spelling of their names, such as Javad Zarif.

References

9 Diy. (1390 [2011], Diy 3 [December 24]). Agar taḥrīmhā muwaffaq būd. *9 Diy*, p. 12.
Abrahamian, E. (2013). *The coup: 1953, the CIA, and the roots of modern U.S.-Iranian relations*. New York: The New Press.
Akhavān, M.J. (1394 [2015], Murdād 3 [July 25]). Chirā istikbār satīzī taʿṭīl bardār nīst? *Kayhān*, p. 8.
Aparat. (1390 [2011]). Fīlm-i kāmil-i sukhanrānī-yi jālib-i duktūr ʿabbāsī. Retrieved from www.aparat.com/v/f752167fca2ecaf38964ffaff639b8d840967.
Barrett, T. (2016). Senate votes to extend sanctions against Iran. Retrieved from http://edition.cnn.com/2016/12/01/politics/senate-extends-iran-sanctions/.
BBC Arabic. (2007). Iran tukhaffiż taʿāwunahā maʿa al-hayʾa al-dawliyya li-ṭṭāqa al-dhariyya. Retrieved from http://news.bbc.co.uk/hi/arabic/news/newsid_6494000/6494131.stm.
BBC Persian. (2017). Rouhani: Agar barjām ittifāq nayuftādih būd faqaṭ barāy-i ḥuqūq-i kārmandān pūl dāshtīm. Retrieved from www.bbc.com/persian/iran-38484604.

CNN. (1998). Transcript of interview with Iranian President Muhammad Khatami. Retrieved from http://edition.cnn.com/WORLD/9801/07/iran/interview.html.

Colleau, M. (2016). Iran's jenus-faced US policy: The rouhani administration between continuity and change, opportunity and constraint. In S. Akbarzadeh and D. Conduit (Eds.), *Iran in the World* (pp. 33–57). New York: Palgrave Macmillan.

Donadio, R. (2017). Star of Iranian film says she will boycott oscars over Trump's visa ban. *The New York Times*. Retrieved from https://www.nytimes.com/2017/01/26/movies/taraneh-alidoosti-boycott-oscars-trump-iranian-film.html?_r=0.

DW Persian. (2012). *Rafsanjani: Qaṭʿi rābiṭih bā āmrīka qābil tadāvūm nīst*. Retrieved from www.dw.de/dw/article/0,,15856540,00.html.

European Union External Action. (2015). *Joint comprehensive plan of action*. Retrieved from http://eeas.europa.eu/archives/docs/statements-eeas/docs/iran_agreement/iran_joint-comprehensive-plan-of-action_en.pdf.

Flynn, M. (2017). Statement by National Security Advisor Michael T. Flynn on Iran. Retrieved from https://www.whitehouse.gov/the-press-office/2017/02/03/statement-national-security-advisor-michael-t-flynn-iran 3 February.

Haraldsson, H. (2017). Iran responses to Trump's muslim ban by banning US citizens. Retrieved from www.politicususa.com/2017/01/28/iran-responds-trumps-muslim-ban-banning-citizens.html.

Ibrāhīmyān, M. (1394 [2015], Urdībihisht 23 [May 13]). Arzānī nakhāhīm dāsht?! *Yā Lithārāt*, p. 9.

Iran Khabar. (1393 [2014]). Munāẓrih-yi dāgh-i zībākalām wa rasāʾī darbārih-yi barjām. Retrieved from www.irankhabar.ir/fa/doc/news/73857/کآمریکا-سال-37-زیباکلام زیباکلام-چنانچه-ایرانی-نیستید-لااقل-آمریکایی-باشید-ستیزی-منفعتی-مملکت-داشته-رسایی-آقای

Iranian Online TV. (2016). Rudaru 4, Iranian TV debate on American foreign policy, sadegh zibakalam. Retrieved from www.iranianonline.net/watch.php?vid=495afab0f.

Karami, A. (2013). Rouhani greeted, attacked upon homecoming from UN. Retrieved from http://iranpulse.al-monitor.com/index.php/2013/09/2902/rouhani-greeted-attacked-upon-homecoming-from-un/.

Kayhān. (1394 [2015], Tīr 22 [July 13]). Tawāfuq dar chārchūb-i sanad lausanne bākht ast. *Kayhān*, p. 2.

Kayhān. (1394 [2015], Tīr 23 [July 14]). Chālish-i 12 sālih-yi vienna īstgāh-i ākhar ast?! *Kayhān*, p. 1.

Kayhān. (1394 [2015], Tīr 24 [July 15]). 180 darajih-yi ikhtilāf-i dū riwāyat az yik tawāfuq. *Kayhān*, p. 1.

Kayhān. (1394 [2015], Tīr 25 [July 16]). Masʾūliyyat-i tārīkhī-yi majlis inṭibāq-i tawāfuq bā khuṭūṭ qirmiz. *Kayhān*, p. 2.

Kayhān. (1394 [2015], Tīr 29 [July 20]). Sanad-i vienna taṣwīb bishavad yā nashavad: Muwẓiʿ-i Iran ʿalayh-i āmrīkā taghyīr nimīkunad. *Kayhān*, p. 1.

Kayhān. (1395 [2017]). "Qudrat-i bartar" bar buzurgtarīn dīvārnigāri-yi kishvar (akhbār-i adabī wa hunarī). *Kayhān*. Retrieved from http://kayhan.ir/fa/news/95116/ قدرت-برتر-بر-بزرگترین-دیوارنگار-کشور-اخبار-ادبی-و-هنری

Kayhān. (1395 [2017], Bahman 20 [February 8]). Trump chihrih-yi wāqiʿī āmrīkāst: Mardum dar 22 bahman jawāb-i tahdīdāt rā mīdahand. *Kayhān*, p. 1.

Leverett, F.L. and Mann Leverett, H. (2013). *Going to Tehran: Why America must accept the Islamic Republic of Iran*. New York: Picador.

Macmillan, A. (2017, January 24). Trump can have this Iran deal or no Iran deal. *Foreign Policy*. Retrieved from http://foreignpolicy.com/2017/01/24/trump-can-have-this-iran-deal-or-no-iran-deal/.

Magiran. (1391 [2012]). Raʾīs kumisyūn-i amniyat-i millī-yi majlis: 3 hizār milyār dullār bih taqviyat-i bunyih-yi difāʿī-yi kishvar ikhtiṣāṣ yāft. Retrieved from www. magiran.com/npview.asp?ID=2539160.

Maleki, A. (2008). Iran and the United States. In A. Maleki and K.L. Afrasiabi (Eds.), *Reading in Iran foreign policy after September 11* (pp. 215–240). Charleston, SC: Book Surge.

Milani, A. (2010). *The myth of the great satan: A new look at America's relations with Iran.* Stanford, CA: Hoover Institution Press.

Moslem, M. (2002). *Factional politics in post-khomeini Iran.* Syracuse, NY: Syracuse University Press.

MSNBC. (2012). Iranians feel the pain of sanctions: "Everything has doubled in price". Retrieved from http://worldnews.msnbc.msn.com/_news/2012/05/15/1171478 0-iranians-feel-the-pain-of-sanctions-everything-has-doubled-in-price?lite.

Nabaviyān, Sayyid Muhammad. (2012). Jaryān-i Iṣlāḥāt – Jang-i Narm – Lībrālīsm. Retrieved from https://www.youtube.com/watch?v=UFVw23oMlF4.

Nūrī, M. (1394 [2015], 3 Murdād [July 25]). Jāygāh-i iqtiṣād-i muqāwamatī dar duwrān-i pasā taḥrīm. *Kayhān*, p. 8.

Parker, A. (2017, February 2). Trump to Iran: Be thankful for "terrible" nuclear deal. *The Washington Post* Retrieved from https://www.washingtonpost.com/news/post-p olitics/wp/2017/02/02/trump-to-iran-be-thankful-for-terrible-nuclear-deal/.

Parsi, T. (2007). *Treacherous alliance the secret dealings of Israel, Iran, and the United States.* New Haven, CT: Yale University Press.

Parsi, T. (2012). *A single roll of the dice: Obama's diplomacy with Iran.* New Haven, CT; London: Yale University Press.

Posch, W. (2005). Islamist neo-cons take power in Iran. *Institute for Security Studies.* Retrieved from www.iss.europa.eu/uploads/media/analy118.pdf.

PRI. (2017). After a scuffle, Iran welcomes US wrestling team to compete at world cup. Retrieved from https://www.pri.org/stories/2017-02-10/after-scuffle-iran-welcom es-us-wrestling-team-compete-world-cup.

Rajabī, F. (2007). *Ahmadinejad: Muʿjizih-yi hizār-yi sivvum.* Tehran: Dānishʾāmūz.

Rasāʾī, H. (1390 [2012], Bahman 29 [February 18]). Pāydārī hamīshih javāb mī dahad. *9 Diy*, p. 1.

Rastgharī, A. (1390 [2012], Bahman 29 [February 18]). Pāydār bar ʾuṣūlgirāyī. *9 Diy*, p. 3.

Reuters. (2017). Americans with Iran visas welcome to enter country: Foreign minister. Retrieved from www.reuters.com/article/us-usa-trump-iran-immigration-idUSKBN1 5D0E6.

Ṣābir, R. (1395 [2016], Āzar 17 [December 7]). Gulābi-yi barjām javānih nazdih kirm khurdih shud. *Yā Lithārāt*, p. 2.

Sadri, H.A. (1997). *Revolutionary states, leaders, and foreign relations: A comparative study of china, Cuba, and Iran.* Westport, CT: Praeger.

Sanger, D.E., Schmitt, E. and Cooper, H. (2016). Iran's swift release of U.S. sailors hailed as a sign of warmer relations. *The New York Times.* Retrieved from https:// www.nytimes.com/2016/01/14/world/middleeast/iran-navy-crew-release.html?_r=0.

Shalamchih. (1375 [1996/1997]), first half of Diy [December/January]). Iḥtimāl-i ḥamlih-yi niẓāmī-yi āmrīkā. *Shalamchih*, p. 2.

Shamalchih. (1377 [1998], Ābān [October–November]). Guzārishī az jilisih-yi munāẓirih miyān-i duktur ṣādiq zibakalam wa mudīr-i masʾūl-i nashriyyi–i. *Shamalchih*, p. 7.

Shalamchih. (1377 [1998/1999], first half of Diy [December/January]). Bayāniyyi–i ḥizbullāh dar khuṣūṣ masāʾil-i rūz. *Shalamchih*, p. 3.

Shalamchih. (1377 [1999], the second half of Diy [January]). Āqāy-i khatami! mārā az līst-i shuhadā khaṭ bizanīd. *Shalamchih*, p. 16.

Sharī'atmadārī, H. (1390 [2012]). Chih kasānī taḥrīm rā bazak mī kunānd. Retrieved from http://kayhanarch.kayhan.ir/901105/2.htm#other200.

Sharī'atmadārī, H. (1390 [2012]). Qatrih daryāst agar bā daryāst. Retrieved from http://kayhanarch.kayhan.ir/901026/2.htm#other201.

Sharī'atmadārī, H. (1390 [2011]). Tanginā dar 'ubūr az tangih. Retrieved from http://kayhanarch.kayhan.ir/900922/2.htm#other200.

Sharī'atmadārī, H. (1391 [2012]). Khargūsh-i Moscow. Retrieved from http://h-sharia tmadari.blogfa.com/post-209.aspx.

Smilowitz, E. (2016, January 2). Trump: Iran deal was so bad it's suspicious. *The Hill* Retrieved from http://thehill.com/blogs/ballot-box/gop-primaries/264598-trump-iran -deal-was-so-bad-its-suspicious.

Talmadge, C. (2008). Closing time: Assessing the Iranian threat to the strait of Hormuz. *International Security*, 33(1), 82–117.

US Treasury. (2013, December 12). Additional treasury and state designations targeting networks linked to Iranian WMD proliferation and sanctions [Press release]. Retrieved from www.treasury.gov/press-center/press-releases/Pages/jl2241.aspx.

Williams, J. (2017, January 25). Why Trump's "Muslim ban" won't stop the terrorism threat. *Vox*. Retrieved from www.vox.com/policy-and-politics/2017/1/25/14383316/tr ump-muslim-ban-immigration-visas-terrorism-executive-order.

Yā Lithārāt. (1392 [2013], Murdād 30 [August 21]). Taḥrīmrā bā tuwlīd ḥal kunīm nah bā gidāyī-i diplumātik. *Yā Lithārāt*, p. 1.

Yā Lithārāt. (1392 [2013], Mihr 3 [September 25]). Tahdīdhāy-i pīsh-i rūy-i zarif wa rouhani dar new york. *Yā Lithārāt*, p. 4.

Yā Lithārāt. (1394 [2015], Urdībihisht 9 [April 14]). Siyāsathāy-i āmrīkāyī dar iran chigūni ijrāyī mīshavad! *Yā Lithārāt*, p. 10.

Yā Lithārāt. (1394 [2015], Urdībihisht 23 [May 13]). Dushman fitnih-yi buzrgtar az 88 ra ṭarrāḥī kardi ast. *Yā Lithārāt*, p. 2.

Yā Lithārāt. (1394 [2015], Urdībihisht 23 [May 13]). Muqābilih bih mithl bā āmrīkā. *Yā Lithārāt*, p. 1.

Yā Lithārāt. (1394 [2015], Urdībihisht 23 [May 13]). Qābil-i qabūl nīst kih ṭaraf-i muqābil hamzamān bā muzākirāt dā'iman tahdīd kunad. *Yā Lithārāt*, p. 3.

Yā Lithārāt. (1394 [2015], Khurdād 2 [May 23]). Khushbīnīhā bih auwj rasī: āmrīkā muṣammam ast taḥrīmhā rā bardārad. *Yā Lithārāt*, p. 1.

Yā Lithārāt. (1394 [2015], Khurād 6 [May 27]). Ru'yāy-i ḥużūr-i bāzsān-i āzhān dar ta'sīsāt-i niẓāmī-yi iran. *Yā Lithārāt*, p. 7.

Yā Lithārāt. (1394 [2015], Khurād 20 [June 10]). Vāguzārī-yi naqd-i 'istiqlāl wa dar barābar-i 'hīch nisiyyih'. *Yā Lithārāt*, p. 3.

Yā Lithārāt. (1394 [2015], Tīr 3 [June 24]). Magar dunbāl-i sāzish bā āmrīkā hastand kih as shu'ār-i marg bar āmrīkā mītarsand? *Yā Lithārāt*, p. 2.

Yā Lithārāt. (1394 [2015], Tīr 3 [June 24]). Millat, tawāfuq-i badrā qabūl nadārad wa ānrā fāqid-i 'i'tibār mīdānad. *Yā Lithārāt*, p. 5.

Yā Lithārāt. (1394 [2015], Tīr 10 [July 1]). Bad'ahdī-yi āmrīkā az ibtidāy-i muzākirāt namāyān būd. *Yā Lithārāt*, p. 1.

Yā Lithārāt. (1394 [2015], Tīr 10 [July 1]). Rūnimāyī az imżāy-i mīlyūnhā irani pāy-i'Guzārih-yi barg-i millī'. *Yā Lithārāt*, p. 1.

Yā Lithārāt. (1394 [2015], Tīr 24 [July 15]). Su'ālī bih nām-i 'Istikbār sitīzī' dar ṣubḥ-i fardāy-i i'lām-i jam' bandī-yi muzākirāt. *Yā Lithārāt*, p. 7.

Yā Lithārāt. (1394 [2015], Tīr 24 [July 15]). 'Tawāfuq' āghāz-i bihānihhāy-i shayṭānī ast. *Yā Lithārāt*, p. 2.

Yā Lithārāt. (1394 [2015], Tīr 24 [July 15]). Tawāfuq bishavad yā nishavad, dānishjūyān az mubārizih bā āmrīkā dast nikhāhand kishīd. *Yā Lithārāt*, p. 2.

Yā Lithārāt. (1394 [2015], Khurād 27 [July 18]). Zīra bār-i tawāfuq-i bad wa zillat āmī z namī ravīm. *Yā Lithārāt*, p. 5.

Yā Lithārāt. (1394 [2015], Shahrīvar 4 [August 26]). Pirūzhih-yi Nufūz-i āmrīkā savār bar jaryān-i khāṣ. *Yā Lithārāt*, p. 9.

Yā Lithārāt. (1394 [2015], Shahrīvar 18 [September 9]). Kulāh-i gushādī dar muzākirāt sar-i iran raft. *Yā Lithārāt*, p. 2.

Yā Lithārāt. (1394 [2015], Shahrīvar 25 [September 16]). Tanhā 20 darṣad-i mushkilāt iqtiṣādī marbūṭ bih taḥrīm ast. *Yā Lithārāt*, p. 1.

Yā Lithārāt. (1395 [2016], Āzar 17 [December 7]). Duwlat az hamīn laḥẓih dast bih kār shavad: Paygīrī-yi nigāh-i jiddī bih dākhil. *Yā Lithārāt*, p. 6.

Yaphe, J.S. (2008). The United States and Iran in Iraq: Risks and opportunities. In A. Ehteshami and M. Zweiri (Eds.), *Iran's foreign policy from Khatami to Ahmadinejad* (pp. 37–54). Berkshire: Ithaca Press.

Zamaneh Tribune. (1392 [2013]). Naṣb-i gustardih-yi taṣāwīrī dar mukhālifat bā muzākirih-yi Iran wa āmrīkā dar khiyābānhāy-i tehran: Mukhālifān-i diplūmāsī-yi duwlat-i rouhani bā bilbūrd bih ṣaḥnih āmidand, *Zamaneh Tribune*. Retrieved from https://www.tribunezamaneh.com/archives/34929?tztc=1.

15 Losing hearts and minds

The United States, *ideocide*, and the propaganda war against ISIS

Kelly Gleason

The term *ideocide* refers to the action of dismantling and disrupting an ideology with the "hopeful" aim of achieving the death of that ideology.[1] *Ideocide* is always "hopeful" because there is only a slight possibility that an ideology can die. Once an idea enters the consciousness, it never completely leaves. And that is what ISIS is banking on. With no effective messaging campaign by the United States and other entities to thwart its recruiting efforts, ISIS will grow. As it stands now, ISIS will always be present because its online propaganda works (Paganini, 2017). It seductively plants the seeds of its ideology with violent images that promise the glories of the caliphate and a purer Muslim life. That idea of serving a cause greater than oneself is extremely difficult to counter. ISIS promises a community, a sense of worth, and a purpose. The message to counter ISIS must be just as professional and appealing. *Ideocide* is the most important part in the fight against ISIS.

This chapter investigates the capability of the US government's online counterterrorism messaging to fight against ISIS' successful recruiting campaign. To investigate this issue, the following questions drive the chapter: Is the US government's strategic communication and online strategy successful, or has it failed in its efforts to counter ISIS' radical message and social media outreach to potential followers or sympathizers who might join the ranks of ISIS? If so, how? If not, why? To answer these questions, the failures of the US government's strategic communication approach are examined along with how ISIS has dominated the narrative fight. Additionally, the chapter examines how a state actor such as the United States can develop a strategic communications strategy to help in countering ISIS propaganda; the solution proposed here is a reformulation of the United States Information Agency (USIA) but under the possible supervision of a Department of Information. This chapter fits into a larger research debate about the challenges faced by states when adopting communication or information strategies to combat or counter nonstate actors that are promoting violent extremism.

US government mistakes

The core argument for this chapter is that the US government's strategic communication and online strategy and structure exists only in theory, not in practice. The government's efforts have largely failed to deter the target audience from joining ISIS because its strategic communications strategy lacks the structure, plan, direction, and overarching authority to organize and lead a unified effort with predominately Muslim countries in the online fight against ISIS (Winter and Bach-Lombardo, 2016). Due to the government's inability to solve this problem, ISIS has dominated the online arena with its narrative of the violent struggle for the caliphate juxtaposed with imagery of the daily life of ISIS fighters that stresses collective justice, management of material resources, and Islamic purity. This concoction of violent and non-violent narratives resonates with the target audience of susceptible Muslims searching for a higher level of purpose, honor, and belonging. During the Obama administration, the US government did not effectively conduct *ideocide* – the dismantling and disrupting of radical ideology.

There are three main reasons why the US government's online messaging has been largely unsuccessful and unconvincing compared to ISIS' tsunami of daily propaganda. First, the United States lacks integration between the various agencies involved in creating and disseminating online influencing operations. As it stands, online messaging propagated by these agencies is disjointed. Second, there is lack of direction and vision by a steering committee to ensure full-spectrum coordination in synchronizing covert and overt information operations (IO). And third, there is a complete absence of overarching authority to actually enforce a plan for countering online Jihadists.

From 2011 to 2016, the Center for Strategic Counterterrorism Communications (CSCC) was the Obama administration's main answer to fighting online adversarial messaging. The goal of the CSCC was to seek opportunities to work with other organizations to counter violent extremism and to strengthen international collaboration. It sought to find capable foreign non-governmental organization partners who operate in the messaging arena to counter ISIS and other violent extremists, either through support of their own governments or through US government support. The purpose of these engagements was to encourage governments and NGO partners to become active messengers and to coordinate efforts. In the ideal situation CSCC offered itself as a resource, providing assistance to launch the other entities' messaging efforts.

However, according to many experts, the United States was no match for ISIS' propaganda machine. The CSCC, for example, was set up for failure with a meager staff of 50 and an inadequate budget of \$5.15 million.[2] While ISIS was able to produce some 90,000 tweets per day, the CSCC had only completed an estimated 60,000 online actions since its inception in 2011.[3] One of the interviewees who worked at the CSCC admitted that they just did not have the capacity to go toe-to-toe with ISIS when it came to Twitter. Dominating the online information space is all about how many "hits" a message, tweet, or website generates and how widespread communication is.[4] Thus, the CSCC was not set up for success to compete against ISIS' messaging.

A brief history of ISIS and its roots

Before delving into a further analysis on the failure of US institutions regarding strategic messaging, it is first important to understand how the Islamic State handles its own strategic communications. The Islamic State of Iraq and Syria (ISIS) is known by several different names: Islamic State of Iraq and the Levant (ISIL), the Arabic name *Da'esh*, and sometimes simply as the Islamic State (IS). As an intelligence analyst, the author prefers the term ISIS because it is easier to find data in online searches. According to the International Crisis Group (2014), ISIS has come to the forefront of terrorist groups because of its successes in capturing large portions of Syria and Iraq in 2014 (International Crisis Group, 2014). It has demonstrated lethality and combat prowess by quickly defeating large portions of the Iraqi army despite being vastly outnumbered.

ISIS is a nonstate actor and Wahabbi extremist group. According to information warfare analyst Chuck de Caro, the US government has never been adequately set up to deal with an asymmetric foe like ISIS and its online recruiting campaign.[5] ISIS follows an extreme interpretation of Islam, promotes religious violence, and regards those who do not agree with its interpretations as infidels or apostates. It is antidemocratic, sectarian, and militant with a transnational membership, and, despite heavy losses, is constantly recruiting (Rose, 2014).

ISIS came into being in 2003 as a group that resisted the American occupation of Iraq (Woronczak, 2014). With key leaders who were prominent in the Iraqi insurgency in the 2000s, it became well armed and financed (Amnesty International, 2014). Its formal name in the early 2000s was Jama'at al-Tawhid wa'al-Jihad, meaning "the organization of monotheism and Jihad" (Nealan, 2013). The group was also formerly known as al Qaeda in Iraq (AQI) and had close ties to al Qaeda (Kirdar, 2011). ISIS' leader (at the time AQI) was Musab al-Zarqawi, who had proven his leadership skills through fighting NATO after 2001 (Teslik, 2006). Musab al-Zarqawi was a Sunni Muslim extremist, his adversaries at the time being the American forces and Shi'a Muslims. When Saddam Hussein was removed, Shi'a Muslims rose to power, which greatly irritated Musab al-Zarqawi and his Islamic Sunni extremist followers (Abbas, 2014).

During the 2003 US invasion of Iraq, al Qaeda took part in the Iraqi insurgency against coalition forces and Iraqi security forces. Several years later, in 2006, al Qaeda recruited other Sunni insurgent groups. These alliances helped create the Mujahideen Shura Council (and later formed into the Islamic State of Iraq: (ISI)). Zarqawi and his followers were emboldened by their growth in numbers and coordinated many attacks. In 2006, they bombed the Al-Askari mosque, a holy site for Shi'a Muslims (Abbas). Zarqawi was eventually killed on June 8, 2006, when US warplanes dropped bombs on a house in which he was meeting with other insurgent leaders (Knickenmeyer and Finer, 2006). After his death, the group changed its name to the Islamic

State of Iraq and associated less with al Qaeda (Abbas, 2014). On May 16, 2010, Abu Bakr al-Baghdadi was named the leader of ISI, and in 2013 he publicly declared that the group would join forces with the Nusra Front to become the Islamic State of Iraq and the Levant (Abbas, 2014). The Nusra Front, which aligned itself with al Qaeda in the past, has stated on various occasions that it is *not* in fact working with ISIS (Zelin, 2014a).

Aaron Zelin stated that the on-again off-again relationship between ISIS and al Qaeda can be characterized by "distrust, open competition, and outright hostility" (Zelin, 2014b, p. 1). He also noted the impact of this contentious relationship for the global jihadist movement's future. On February 2, 2014, for example, al Qaeda's general command released a statement disavowing itself from ISIS: "ISIS is not a branch of the Qaidat al-Jihad (al-Qaeda's official name) group, we have no organizational relationship with it, and the group is not responsible for its actions" (Zelin, 2014b, p. 5). Zelin added that this was the first time in al Qaeda's history that the group had "publicly disaffiliated itself with a group bearing its name – even though ISIS has not used the name "al Qaeda" since 2006" (Zelin, 2014a). Zelin explained that "ISIS now holds the upper hand, with al Qaeda struggling just to fend off its own decline."[6]

Despite ongoing disagreements with al Qaeda, ISIS' successes have been mostly unaffected. Under Baghdadi, ISIS gained in popularity because it joined the insurgency in Iraq. The insurgency was viewed as a legitimate cause due to the perceived economic and political discrimination against Iraqi Sunnis. ISIS gained even more legitimacy in Syria by joining their civil war. By chance, ISIS joined the insurgency when the Syrian War started in 2011, and in doing so, established a large presence in the Syrian governorates of Ar-Raqqah, Idlib, Deir ez-Zor, and Aleppo (Abouzeid, 2014).

ISIS' original goal was to establish an Islamic state in Sunni-majority regions of Iraq. However, its ambition grew with each success. After ISIS entered the Syrian civil war, its sphere of influence extended to the Sunni majority areas of Syria (Abbas). Baghdadi recognized that ISIS was gaining traction and proclaimed a worldwide caliphate on June 29, 2014. Baghdadi also declared himself the caliph, and the group was renamed Islamic State (IS). Baghdadi's self-nomination as caliph demonstrated that he sought to be the successor of Muhammad as temporal and spiritual head of Islam.[7]

Under Baghdadi, the intent of ISIS is to claim worldwide religious authority over all Muslims and to bring Muslim-inhabited regions of the world under its control. ISIS' current focus is on the Levant region, which approximately covers Syria, Jordan, Israel, Palestine, Lebanon, Cyprus, and parts of southern Turkey. ISIS has since absorbed the terrorist and insurgency groups controlling territory in Sinai and eastern Libya (Abouzeid, 2014). The estimated number of ISIS fighters has fluctuated from year to year. Through 2013 and into 2014, ISIS was also able to grow in numbers in Syria by leveraging the civil war. In September 2014, a Central Intelligence Agency

(CIA) spokesperson stated on CNN that ISIS "can muster between 20,000 and 31,500 fighters across Iraq and Syria" (Sciutto, Crawford, and Carter, 2014). It recruited foreign fighters via its effective information operations and was able to wage an effective mix of terrorism and insurgency in both Syria and Iraq. Former Iraqi President Maliki had inadvertently set the stage for ISIS. After Maliki's defunding and disbanding of the Sunni militia, ISIS brought the former members into its own organization (International Crisis Group, 2013). However, in 2017, the number of ISIS fighters in Syria and Iraq decreased. The US government estimated that approximately 30,000 foreign fighters went to Syria to fight with ISIS, and 25,000 of those individuals had been killed (Chulov, Grierson, and Swaine, 2017).

It should be noted that ISIS could easily get back to the numbers it had in Syria in 2013–2014 if it maintains its successful strategic communication plan for recruiting foreign fighters. But it is of little importance for the larger picture whether ISIS forces increase or decrease in Syria because it wages irregular warfare. ISIS will not go toe-to-toe with a conventional force. The ISIS successes and failures on the battlefield are pendulum-like, thus we should focus on the root of the problem; that is, the ideology.

ISIS' greatest weapon: Propaganda that gets results

ISIS propaganda has the right mix of content and volume. The two different types of content, as mentioned earlier, are, first, the violent acts (also known as gore porn) and, second, the religious and social life of its fighters and their families living a purer form of Islam in a utopian community.

Disseminating gore porn via social media provides ISIS credibility through the display of brute force. This effort has served to recruit fighters and intimidate enemies (Shane and Hubbard, 2014). ISIS' mass media strategy strives to convince all Muslims to struggle and fight for the caliphate, construing this as an obligation to the Islamic religion. ISIS understands the power of the narrative, depicting itself as an agent of change, the true apostle of Islam, a hero of social justice, and a seeker of revenge for true believers who have suffered (Richardson, 2006). Its propaganda reach is worldwide – videos of beheadings have been shown on cable news networks, terrorist websites, and websites like goregrish.com and bestgor.com, which glorify gore and consistently rate ISIS propaganda as their most watched videos (Shane and Hubbard, 2014). It has achieved global television status by employing Twitter, Facebook, Instagram and other social media platforms and sending visceral images that evoke strong emotions. Foreign fighters are used as spokespersons, with images of them as powerful warriors. These recruitment videos are effective for those who want to define themselves as Muslim in addition to pursuing a larger purpose in their lives (Gebeily, 2014).

The second type of propaganda can be categorized as the "normal daily life of ISIS". It is not about fighting or training for war; rather, it involves simple videos about everyday life as part of the ISIS utopia. The optics are the complete opposite of gore porn. The videos show ISIS fighters with their families, taking care of them. Many videos of daily life show the children of fighters playing together, the images always resonating with happiness and hope. These videos humanize ISIS and provide a "slice of life" in an ISIS community.

In Charlie Winter's article "Fishing and ultraviolence," he studies ISIS propaganda presented over a 30-day period. From July 17 to August 15, 2015, he spent two hours a day going through ISIS' Arabic-language support network on Twitter and using combinations of the group's countless designated hashtags as keys. Winter found that in only 30 days ISIS official propagandists had created and disseminated 1,146 separate units of propaganda. Winter noted that ISIS propaganda comprised of

> photo essays, videos, audio statements, radio bulletins, text round-ups, magazines, posters, pamphlets, and theological treatises. … The radio bulletins and text round-ups were released in six languages – Russian, Turkish, Arabic, Kurdish, French, and English. After grouping the different language versions of the same item together there were 892 units in total.

Winter discovered that the propaganda was overwhelmingly about "normal" life. On one particular day there were 50 pieces of propaganda, 32 of which were about civilian activities, described by Winter as "a plastering workshop in Mosul, newspapers being distributed in Fallujah, pavements laid in Tal'afar, telephone lines fixed in Qayara, cigarettes confiscated and burned in Sharqat, and even camels being herded in Bir al-Qasab" (Winter, 2015).

This mix of violent and daily life propaganda caters to a wide target audience. For example, a young uneducated person who is curious about ISIS might want to know about everyday life in ISIS and the possibility of meeting a significant other and starting a family. Once they come to view ISIS as providing a community setting, they might escalate to violent videos. Or it could be completely the other way around with, for example, an educated person getting drawn into watching ISIS gore porn and wanting to know more about ISIS and, thus, starting to watch the daily life propaganda videos. The viewer soon realizes that the ISIS utopia provides the whole package they have been searching for.

According to Clint Watts and William McCants, ISIS has an advantage over journalists in terms of directing what types of messages are put out about the conflicts in Iraq and Syria, because journalists are unable to work in the war zones. Hence, ISIS has become the sole provider of coverage for these conflicts, a situation that allows it the opportunity to manipulate the truth. Foreign fighters relay back to their communities the methods of their participation – whether by beheadings or other forms of execution of Iraqi soldiers – via social media (Watts and McCants, 2012). Even potential recruits can begin their training by communicating with fighters on the ground through Facebook. The 'wannabes' live vicariously through the experiences of fighters, and this becomes a form of virtual military basic training in what to expect (National Public Radio, 2014).

ISIS' media productions are also professionally polished and have the same qualities as Hollywood-produced commercial films. The beheading of James Foley, for example, was designed for an American audience. It had a well-spoken English narrator, lighting, and music to accompany the heinous acts. All of ISIS' heavily produced info-entertainment, including sleek recruitment videos, strive for the perception of legitimacy and omnipresence, inspiring recruits from all over the world (Mackey, 2014).

In addition to using a professional video production crew, ISIS understands that bombarding the target audience works to its advantage through sheer volume. Eric Schmitt recently stated in his analysis of ISIS propaganda that the Islamic State and its supporters are producing as many as 90,000 tweets and other social media responses every day (Schmitt, 2015). This number of tweets is so impressive that it drew speculation from other reporters, who eventually verified that such a quantity of tweets is indeed possible (Pundit-Fact, 2015). The expert and author J.M. Berger also argued, in testimony before Congress, that by late 2014 there were at least 45,000 Twitter accounts being used by ISIS supporters. Berger also defended the claim that 90,000 messages a day is likely a conservative number and said that the figure would include both supporters and actual members of ISIS (Greenberg, 2015). That said, he also offered two other cautionary notes. First, "the numbers are driven by a small number of high over-performers, probably fewer than 2,000 accounts that often tweet in bursts of 50 or more tweets per day as part of a deliberate strategy". Second, "deceptive techniques such as the use of bots and purchased retweets [are employed] to inflate these numbers". Berger said that while he took steps in his analysis to eliminate as much of this noise as possible, he had probably not identified all of it (Greenberg, 2015).

In general, ISIS is able to win the Twitter battlefield because it employs social media strategies that magnify and dictate its message. ISIS has many Twitter accounts and apps, the most successful of which is "The Dawn of Glad Tidings" (commonly known as "Dawn"). The app is like the Drudge Report and CNN rolled into one, providing the latest news about ISIS. Users can sign up through the Internet or on their smartphones for the app, which posts tweets to users' accounts. Content is controlled by ISIS social media headquarters, and tweets are spaced out so that Twitter's spam detection is not triggered. The application, which debuted in April 2014, saw its highest posting activity of 40,000 tweets per day when ISIS took over Mosul, Iraq (Berger, 2014). ISIS also has its members tweet using certain "hashtags" at different times of the day so that they trend on the social network. These efforts enable manipulation of popular Arabic Twitter accounts like @ActiveHashtags, which used to tweet each day's top trending tags before it was recently suspended. If ISIS could land a hashtag on @ActiveHashtags, for example, then one tweet averaged 72 more retweets. As the original tweet gained exposure, it went viral for the day. This process of manipulating Twitter is still conducted throughout the day with different images and propaganda messages (Berger, 2014).

ISIS propaganda is complex, multi-layered, and demands an entity that can handle it

ISIS is a complex enemy because it is neither decentralized nor centralized. It has the correct mix of both models to make it a lethal propaganda machine. In many instances, the elimination of leaders/members of a decentralized organization only makes such an organization even stronger (Brafman and Beckstrom, 2006). In the case of an extremist organization such as ISIS, every death caused by an infidel emboldens ISIS members in their cause and motivates budding Islamic extremists to commit jihad for the caliphate. Hence, America must concentrate its efforts on the narrative, not just a kinetic or ground solution. In the words of information operations strategist Chuck de Caro:

> If you want to effectively fight an insurgency, you have to do it from two different fronts: You have to fight it kinetically through violent means, but more importantly, you have to fight it through non-kinetic powers of information operations. In fact, the kinetics of warfare need to support the non-kinetics to defeat an insurgency. The problem has always been that the non-kinetics have supported the kinetic strategy, and not the other way around.[8]

Many US information operation (IO) strategists have agreed that the primary solution for fighting a decentralized insurgency is the narrative. However, the American strategic communications community (SCC) is not ready to embrace a counterinsurgency propaganda strategy. According to one US Army public affairs officer, "as it stands now, the SCC is diffused and disorganized. No one office is in charge of the SCC. Instead, almost every agency has its own concept of how to implement IO against Islamic terrorists."[9] For example, the Central Intelligence Agency is possibly tackling the ISIS propaganda on an international level; the Federal Bureau of Investigation could be reviewing propaganda that entices Americans to join ISIS; and Homeland Security might be reviewing what new ISIS propaganda would incite individuals to come to the US and conduct terrorist acts.[10] Each agency has a different message for possibly the same target audience. Jay M. Parker of the National Defense University also asserted:

> You will get a variety of answers of what the strategic communication community is. And there is the problem: Everybody is involved, and each entity has its own understanding of what the problem is. During my time in the psychological operations and strategic communication community,

I have come to the conclusion that there is no central United States node or hub for strategic communication strategy. The strategic communication community is like the current media environment – heavily decentralized – which results in counter-productivity and decreased effectiveness. Which, at its best, is reactive and not proactive.[11]

Whereas the United States has designated departments for different sectors of society such as commerce, labor, treasury, and transportation, there is none for information. Without any overarching entity to govern the strategic communication strategy, the message America is presenting to its target audience is confusing and incoherent.

No one is in charge of strategic communication coordination

As part of the research for this chapter, interviewees were questioned about who is in charge of the strategic communication online strategy; answers ranged from "I don't know" to "there is no one in charge" or "everyone is in charge to some extent." According to interviewees from the Central Intelligence Agency (CIA), National Counterterrorism Center (NCTC), Department of Defense, and Department of State, there is no all-encompassing infrastructure or approved approach that dictates the grand scheme of how to conduct online counter-messaging against ISIS. A senior US Army Public Affairs officer explained the mess of the US government's haphazard strategic communication structure:

> Every organization does their own form of what they consider to be "strategic communication" or "public diplomacy", which means there are no parameters to reference. It is quite possible for one organization to be conducting an online information operation, its message possibly affecting that of another organization conducting its own information operation simultaneously. The problem is that no particular entity has authority over the other. Thus, there is a lack of coordination for effective communication.[12]

The US government desperately needs a plan, direction, and leadership to provide the enforcement necessary to conduct the online fight against ISIS. At one time, the US government had the United States Information Agency (USIA), which adequately provided worldwide public diplomacy (Fitzpatrick, 2008). The USIA's mission was to develop and present America's public diplomacy and explain US foreign policy to publics abroad. The USIA was not mired in traditional diplomacy that was concerned with relationships between international leaders. Instead, it focused on direct communication with citizens of other countries (Fitzpatrick, 2008).

Unfortunately, in 1999, the USIA was discontinued because the Clinton administration and certain members of Congress decided it had served its purpose and was no longer needed. Since the United States had won the Cold

War, less attention and money was being allocated to foreign affairs. Funding was greatly reduced; staff was cut. This marginalization of the USIA resulted in fewer public diplomacy actions and a smaller American presence. Eventually, when the USIA was no more, its operations were absorbed into the Department of State, and broadcasting became the task of the Broadcasting Board of Governors (Fitzpatrick, 2008).

The demise of the USIA was a mistake because the Department of State is ill-suited to conduct long-term public diplomacy and other strategic communications initiatives (Nakamura and Weed, 2009). America needs an updated version of the robust USIA structure that takes account of social media, which did not exist at the time when the USIA was active, to assist in countering the many extremists groups that have proliferated today. A model such as the USIA would allow other countries to be more involved in countering ISIS' online propaganda. Imparting credibility to others would help reduce the stigma attached to a message where the US government is its sole originator. According to a senior Department of State official, the lack of coordination stems in part from the dismantling of the USIA.

When the USIA was dissolved into the Department of State, the original mission of the USIA was submerged. Its resources were cut up and divided into different offices in a way that diminished the effectiveness and unity of the budget, resources, and planning. The budget that once belonged to the USIA was now divided between six bureaus that focused on six different regions: Africa, East Asia and the Pacific, Europe and Eurasia, Near East (North Africa and the Middle East), South and Central Asia, and the Western Hemisphere. Think of these bureaus as you would combatant commands. Each one of them is very powerful, and each has an autonomous history. These bureaus are some of the most powerful entities in the Department of State because they make policy, they meet with embassies, they develop budgets for the embassies, and they speak on behalf of the embassies. These bureaus have clout with the inter-agencies of the Department of State. The problem with dissolving the USIA and giving portions of the public diplomacy budget and assets to each of these six bureaus is that each bureau did something different with it. In essence, each bureau conducted its public diplomacy differently than its sister bureau. They organized public diplomacy differently, they spent their public diplomacy money differently, and their programs were different from each other. It was like a centrifugal force had thrown off all of the common planning techniques that the former USIA had organized and planned for as the single overarching actor for public diplomacy.[13]

This example qualitatively depicts the certain challenges of strategic communications and public diplomacy at the highest levels of the government. Twenty-nine interviews conducted by the author on the topic corroborated a similar sentiment about how detrimental losing the USIA was to the government's ability to carry out a more unified strategic communications plan.

A lack of credibility

The US government's attempts at developing propaganda to fight ISIS at their own game have not been up to par. In 2014, for example, the Department of State developed a campaign that they posted online as "Run, do not walk, to ISIS Land." It was graphic and sarcastic because it used ISIS' own violent propaganda and poked fun at it with sly text. At the beginning of the video, the phrases "useful new skills" and "crucifying and executing Muslims" are presented next to a film of prisoners being killed, four beheadings, people being hanged in front of a crowd, and bodies being heaved over a hillside. It is not humorous; it is just gruesome. This video used irony, and that is a tricky approach because sometimes the message can be lost on the audience if they do not pick up on the cues. At the end of the video, the Department of State emblem is shown.

There has been an audience for this video. The Global Engagement Center (GEC) still has it up on YouTube and it has had over 900,000 views. The unit within the Department of State that was directly responsible for the video was the Center for Strategic Counterterrorism Communications (CSCC), which was later replaced by the GEC. Albert Fernandez, the former Director of the CSCC, stated that the purpose of the video was to use ISIS' gruesome propaganda against it and send the message that ISIS, rather than being a worthy cause, is degrading and inhuman (Miller and Higham, 2015).

The CSCC has to be applauded for at least doing something. There had to be a starting point. There have been other attempts, but "Run, do not walk, to ISIS Land" is the most memorable. However, most Muslims that the author interacted with for this research do not like it as it lacks credibility because of the association to the Department of State. Ideally, any propaganda needs to be perceived as coming from a predominately Muslim country.

Thus, in addition to the issue of the lack of a central coordination body for a communications strategy, the US government also runs the risk that its messaging lacks credibility among a target audience that is predominately Muslim. As part of the research, the author interviewed Afghanistan Senior Prosecutor Haqyar Habibullah. Haqyar is a prominent attorney in Afghanistan and his primary role is to prosecute high value-targets that are pulled off the objective by Afghan and US combined special operations units. Haqyar expressed that any online message that has a connection to the US government and is aimed at influencing Muslims will fail because it will be viewed as a message from the "infidel" or an "apostate." This line of logic can most certainly be applied to the US propaganda war against ISIS as well.

According to Haqyar, there must be an appealing online counter-message to dissuade prospective followers from joining an Islamic extremist group, especially one such as ISIS that has made headway into Afghanistan. He also reinforced the point that any counter-message should not be perceived as originating from the United States since most groups will be skeptical of the message as America is not predominately Islamic. According to Haqyar, the counter-message would be more convincing if it is perceived as originating from a "Muslim brother" Islamic nation, such as Jordan, Iran, Iraq, Libya, Morocco, Pakistan, the United Arab Emirates, Tajikistan, or Saudi Arabia, rather than from an "infidel-infested" country. Haqyar affirmed many times over that the United States must not take credit for any form of propaganda. He explained that one way to avoid the American stigma is for the United States "to secretly provide funding and video production training to Islamic countries." He stated that the transfer of funds should be done in a manner that does not draw the attention of critics who would want to discredit the online counter-messaging campaign. Haqyar further argued that the money could be fed through the American embassies to civil societies and media relations groups that are trying to present the peaceful Islamic voice but do not have the resources or funding to effectively do so.

Finally, Haqyar advocated that the counter-message must present the peaceful passages of the Islamic religion. He suggested that an online message that presents the kindness and warmth in the Qur'an would be well received by "disenfranchised Muslims who are mostly illiterates." The counter-message must not be observed as a war on Islam, but rather a war on those who seek to twist the Islamic religion to benefit their own cause. Most importantly, Haqyar insisted that this plan be put into action now because ISIS is still at a stage where it can be managed in burgeoning areas such as Egypt, Libya, or Afghanistan.

Countering the narrative: Possible strategies and approaches

During the interviews for this research, the participants shared possible strategies and approaches moving forward. These ideas came from individuals who understood that the present strategic communication approach is not working and that the United States' adversaries are winning the online influence war via their violent social movement.

As argued by some, the CIA has the correct culture and infrastructure to influence and inform the target audience of disenfranchised/susceptible Muslims against joining an Islamic extremist group (Miller and Higham, 2015). Within the CIA's organization is the Open Source Center (OSC) (Ensor, 2013). The OSC provides analysis of open-source intelligence materials and is also tasked with improving the availability of open sources to intelligence officers and other government officials (Naquin, 2007). Examples of open-source intelligence is information that can be collected from public, unclassified material such as newspaper articles, radio broadcasts, TV news shows, or blogs.

The reporter Kimberly Dozier conducted an interview with CIA spokesperson Jennifer Youngblood during which she explained that analysts are "scattered throughout US embassies worldwide to get a step closer to their subjects" (Dozier, 2011). The CIA's Open Source Center representatives collect information available from the Internet, databases, press, radio, television, video, geospatial data, photos, and commercial imagery and present it in a format palatable for wide distribution (Central Intelligence Agency, 2010). As one interviewee explained, the OSC has the correct architecture for conducting online influencing and informing campaigns. Within each of the global regions of concern for the Department of State is an embassy with an OSC branch (US Department of State, 2015). Each office consists of a director, a deputy director, and a large group of local employees who speak the local language. Their job is to monitor all media for that region (Naquin, 2007). They produce hundreds of thousands of reports that are quality controlled and then transmitted over the Open Source system to US government employees at an unclassified level. This is an amazingly useful tool. The OSCs have connections to the local media and are using local people who understand the culture and language. Certain regions also monitor ISIS and jihadi websites for the benefit of the intelligence community. The OSC could become a part of an apparatus that counters terrorist messaging more successfully.[14]

Better public diplomacy

According to a focus group conducted by the author with counterterrorism specialists, to conduct a successful counterterrorism communication program, there must be a light side and a dark side.[15] The light side is what public diplomacy does at the embassy level, with press interaction and cultural programs.[16] Concerning the dark side, if the United States were to engage in the influencing of individuals, and that was construed by some as being intrusive, these practices may then be considered classified. Effective influencing directed at a target audience is somewhat of a classified activity that cannot be performed by a public affairs officer at an embassy. The OSC would be best suited to lead *both* the light and the dark sides of informing and influencing. The OSC would most certainly resist, arguing that these new tasks detract from what they were originally set up to do. Currently, the OSC is responsible for the light side of the CIA's work. It must now go one step further by using the connections it already has to start counter-messaging and creating propaganda that influences target audiences.

Through the research interviews, it also became apparent that the National Security Agency (NSA) needs to be added to any new or coordinating structure for combatting online jihadists.[17] This agency has forged the strongest links with private industry such as Google, Microsoft, and Apple. According to the author Ori Brafman, this is a key connective node, and it is important because any competent organization in today's environment needs to be technologically current. An organization also needs to measure readership and be able to pivot and change as new technology comes along. The NSA has the nimbleness and culture to move quickly, and it can link up with a technology giant. If US information operation strategists wait on government contracting to do this, America could be waiting for years and have substandard results.[18]

Establish a Department of Information (DoI)

Based upon dozens of interviews conducted over several years, it is strongly recommended that the President of the United States (POTUS) sign an executive order creating a Department of Information (DoI). Here, The author is not advocating for something similar to the Ministry of Truth in George Orwell's *1984*, but rather an organization that coalesces the talents and assets of the United States to effectively counter adversaries' online messaging, or acts as an *ideocide*, in addition to favorably presenting America around the globe. The proposed DoI would be an updated version of the former USIA with an emphasis on dominating the influence sphere of the Internet, resulting in the disruption of Islamic extremist messaging or, again, acting as an *ideocide* against the proliferation of radical ideologies. The DoI would provide overarching supervision and authority to properly and effectively counter adversarial online propaganda. Figure 15.1 is a diagram of how the DoI might operate.

The DoI Director would answer directly to the White House on the strategic communication strategy. The Director would not be affiliated or represented by any particular US agency because the DoI's mission would not fall under another agency's agenda. Moreover, if the Director is appointed from another US government body, s/he would have to sever ties with it to ensure that the DoI would not be influenced by the culture of the said agency. The DoI's mission would be guided by the National Security Strategy. The DoI's objective would be to ensure target audiences are influenced via unclassified and

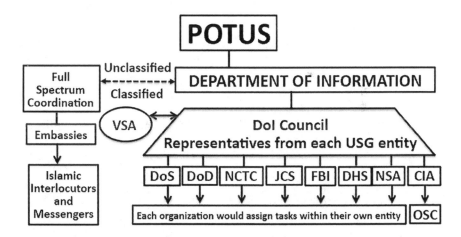

Figure 15.1 Department of Information

classified messaging in the best interest of the United States. To achieve this mission, the DoI would have authority over all US government and military messaging apparatuses. Main representatives from every organization, to include the Vice Chairman of the Joint Chiefs of Staff, would be part of the DoI Council, ensuring synchronization to achieve full-spectrum strategic communication. Because every US government organization has some form of messaging capacity, each would be included on the DoI Council. The council's pursuit of full-spectrum coordination programs would require both proactive offensive messaging and defensive counter-messaging to dominate the information space. The primary focus in this information space would be online messaging.

The DoI would be responsible for developing, directing, and enforcing the strategy for combatting Islamic extremist propaganda. The strategy would be based upon consultation and compromise among the representatives from each US government entity. The full-spectrum strategy would be broken into two sections: overt and covert operations.

Overt Operations

The unclassified portion of the strategy would entail that every agency present and facilitate cohesive messages to avoid diffusion and to lessen the confusion of common target audiences. The council would agree upon the tasks that each agency would undertake, and it would evaluate their successes. The council would also be a medium for members to exchange ideas and practices so that successes could be repeated by other organizations.

An additional DoI unclassified task would involve creating a leaderless, domestic-based public outreach program entitled Volunteers for Safe America (VSA). The goal of the VSA would be to enlist the public's help in countering Islamic extremism messaging. Citizens and private industries would become the decentralized messaging arm of America. The participants would be guided by the DoI council's goals, and the US government would provide the needed funding and grants. The end result of this type of approach is the American public becoming more engaged in countering violent extremism by helping to level out the propaganda advantage ISIS currently sustains with its own decentralized messengers.

The National Security Agency (NSA) has strong relationships with industries that would greatly assist in messaging. The NSA's Commercial Solutions Center (NCSC) invites business and industry professionals to increase the marketability of commercial information assurance (IA) products by having them tested and evaluated through the National IA Partnership. The NCSC could partner with the DoI and include other industries into the mix to assist with the production and distribution of messaging. In conjunction with the DoI, the NCSC Industry Support Team would host forums to afford vendors the opportunity to discuss new technologies along with their possible applications to the goal of countering ISIS' propaganda.

According to some of the author's interviews, the NSA has established relationships with leaders of Google, Facebook, Twitter, and others in the entertainment industry. These prominent connections must be exploited. Many talented Americans outside of the government realm show interest in wanting to help defeat ISIS. The crux is that the United States is currently void of a program that would allow these individual industries to contribute help. We need to extend an invitation and begin the cultivation of these possible decentralized nodes of power.

Covert Operations

The CIA would handle the classified aspect of DoI's strategy. The CIA has the correct culture and infrastructure to influence and inform the target audience via online social media. The CIA would work with the DoI in developing propaganda through the embassies and the CIA's Open Source Centers (OSCs). As already mentioned, these are located in different Department of State-designated regions throughout the world (Ensor, 2013). Though not designed to be an influencing arm of strategic communication, the OSCs have the ideal mix of creative individuals with local language skills, and established relationships with decision makers in the media. The OSC is already studying ISIS through its analysis of open-source material. But in order for it to morph into an influencing apparatus, it will require more resources so that it can broaden its roles and responsibilities. The adaptation of the OSC's current function is a necessary step in developing effective online messaging.

Without question, implementing the DoI is risky and bold – but it is also necessary. It empowers US government entities, industries, and individuals to direct their messaging resources and talents to better fight an enemy that is indeed authoritative and oppressive. This innovative institution would provide the plan, direction, enforcement, and overarching authority and leadership that is *desperately* needed to combat ISIS' successful online recruiting propaganda. The DoI should be created with longevity in mind as it can be used to counter all adversarial communication, not just ISIS. The United States has yet to present compelling and meaningful communication to defeat its enemies via messaging – yet it has the resources, talent, and foreign relations to be a forceful and influential presence. The DoI would demand that America's diplomatic, informational, military, and economic powers come together and collaborate to create a unified front that *ideocides* ISIS' most powerful weapon: the narrative.

President Donald Trump's administration recognizes the need for a bold move in the cyberspace arena. During President Trump's visit to the Middle East in May 2017, he met with Saudi Arabia's King Salman and they inaugurated the Global Center for Combating Extremist Ideology. The center in Riyadh will monitor and combat Islamic extremist messaging. It is too early to tell whether or not this will have any impact on the messaging fight. Certainly, this is a step in the right direction, but it is still not enough.

Disclaimer

The views expressed here are those of the author and are not an official policy or position of the National Defence University, the Department of Defence, or the US Government.

Interview sources

Interviewees for this chapter were represented by some of the following agencies but ultimately represent personal opinions and not official government policy:

Central Intelligence Agency
National Counterterrorism Center
Department of Defense
Center for Strategic Counterterrorism Communication
Department of State
National Defense University
Government of the Islamic Republic of Afghanistan
US Military Psychological Operations
Asia Society
NYPD Counterterrorism Bureau

Notes

1 This is a term created by the author.
2 Interview with a Center for Strategic Counterterrorism Communications (CSCC) member who requested anonymity.
3 Interview with Ambassador Henry Ensher, former Vice Chancellor of the College of International Security Affairs, speaking in a personal capacity.
4 Interview with Chuck de Caro, author, information warfare analyst for the Department of Defense, and advisor to the Department of Defense's Office of Net Assessment.
5 Derived from multiple interviews with Chuck de Caro in 2016.
6 Aaron Zelin gave a lecture on the "Online Jihad Environment" at the College of International Security Affairs on March 17, 2015. Zelin is the Richard Borow fellow at the Washington Institute, where his research focuses on how jihadist groups are adjusting to the new political environment in the era of Arab uprisings and Salafi politics in countries transitioning to democracy.
7 Aaron Zelin, lecture on the "Online Jihad Environment" at the College of International Security Affairs on March 17, 2015.
8 Interview with Chuck de Caro, January 15, 2015.
9 Telephone interview with US Army public affairs officer, January 21, 2015.
10 Interview with Chuck de Caro, January 15, 2015.
11 Interview with Dr. Jay M. Parker, January 18, 2015.
12 Interview with a senior US Army Public Affairs Officer, January 17, 2015.
13 Interview with Department of State official, January 28, 2015.

14 Interview with Department of State official, January 28, 2015.
15 Focus group with members of the Central Intelligence Agency (CIA) and National Counterterrorism Center (NCTC) in April 2015. The views expressed are personal opinions and not official US policy.
16 Interview with Department of State official, January 28, 2015.
17 Ibid.
18 Ibid.

References

Abbas, H. (2014, December 23). ISIS Eyes Influence in Pakistan: Focus, Fears and Future Prospects. *Jinnah Institute Policy Brief.* Retrieved from http://jinnah-institute .org/policy-brief-isis-eyes-influence-in-pakistan-focus-fears-future-prospects-2/.

Abouzeid, R. (2014, June 23). The Jihad Next Door. *Politico Magazine.* Retrieved from www.politico.com/magazine/story/2014/06/al-qaeda-iraq-syria-108214.html#.V UaoIDdgPzI.

Amnesty International. (2014). *Ethnic Cleansing on a Historical Scale: Islamic State's Systematic Targeting of Minorities in Northern Iraq.* London: Amnesty International Ltd.

Berger, J.M. (2014, June 16). How ISIS Games Twitter. *The Atlantic.* Retrieved from www.theatlantic.com/international/archive/2014/06/isis-iraq-twitter-social-media-stra tegy/372856/.

Brafman, O. and Beckstrom, R. (2006). *The Starfish and the Spider: The Unstoppable Power of Leaderless Organizations.* New York: Penguin Group.

Central Intelligence Agency. (2010, July 23). INTelligence: Open Source Intelligence. Retrieved from https://www.cia.gov/news-information/featured-story-archive/2010-fe atured-story-archive/open-source-intelligence.html.

Chulov, M., Grierson, J. and Swaine, J. (2017, April 26). Isis faces exodus of foreign fighters as its "caliphate" crumbles. *The Guardian.* Retrieved from https://www.theg uardian.com/world/2017/apr/26/isis-exodus-foreign-fighters-caliphate-crumbles.

Dozier, K. (2011, April 11). CIA Open Source Center follows foreign Twitter, Facebook accounts. *Huffington Post.* Retrieved from www.huffingtonpost.com/2011/11/0 4/cia-open-source-center_n_1075827.html.

Ensor, D. (2013, November 8). The Situation: Open Source Intelligence Center. *CNN.* Retrieved from www.cnn.com/2005/POLITICS/11/08/sr.tues/.

Fitzpatrick, K. (2008). The Collapse of American Public Diplomacy: What Diplomatic Experts Say about Rebuilding America's Image in the World; A View from the Trenches. *United States Information Agency Alumni Association Survey.* Hamden, CT: Quinnipiac University. Retrieved from www.publicdiplomacy.org/Fitzpatrick20 08.pdf.

Gebeily, M. (2014, June 25). How ISIS is Gaming the World's Journalists. *Global Post.* Retrieved from www.globalpost.com/dispatch/news/regions/middle-east/iraq/140625/ ISIL-ISIS-internet-twitter.

Greenberg, J. (2015, February 19). Does the Islamic State Post 90,000 Social Media Messages Each Day? *Pundit Fact.* Retrieved from www.politifact.com/punditfact/sta tements/2015/feb/19/hillary-mann-leverett/cnn-expert-islamic-state-posts-90000-socia l-media-/.

International Crisis Group. (2013, August 13). Make or Break: Iraq's Sunni and the State. Middle East Report No. 144. Retrieved from www.crisisgroup.org/~/media/

Files/Middle%20East%20North%20Africa/Iraq%20Syria%20Lebanon/Iraq/144-ma ke-or-break-iraq-s-sunnis-and-the-state.pdf.

International Crisis Group. (2014, June 20). Iraq's Jihadi's Jack-In-The-Box. Briefing No. 3. Retrieved from www.crisisgroup.org/en/publication-type/media-releases/2014/ mena/iraq-s-jihadi-jack-in-the-box.aspx.

Kirdar, M. (2011, June). Al Qaeda in Iraq. *Center for Strategic and International Studies.* Retrieved from http://csis.org/files/publication/110614_Kirdar_AlQaedaIraq_Web.pdf.

Knickmeyer, E. and Finer, J. (2006, June 8). Insurgent Leader al-Zarqawi Killed in Iraq. *The Washington Post.* Retrieved from www.washingtonpost.com/wp-dyn/conte nt/article/2006/06/08/AR2006060800114.html/.

Mackey, R. (2014, June 20). The Case for ISIS Made in British Accent. *The New York Times.* Retrieved from www.nytimes.com/2014/06/21/world/middleeast/the-case-for-i sis-made-in-a-british-accent.html?_r=0.

Miller, G. and Higham, S. (2015, May 8). In a propaganda war against ISIS, the US tried to play by the enemy's rules. *The Washington Post.* Retrieved from www.washingtonpo st.com/world/national-security/in-a-propaganda-war-us-tried-to-play-by-the-enemys-ru les/2015/05/08/6eb6b732-e52f-11e4-81ea-0649268f729e_story.html?tid=sm_fb.

Nakamura, K. and Weed, M. (2009, December 18). *US Public Diplomacy: Back- ground and Current Issues.* Washington, DC: Congressional Research Services. Retrieved from www.fas.org/sgp/crs/row/R40989.pdf.

Naquin, D. (2007, Winter). Remarks by Doug Naquin: Director, Open Source Center. *CIRA Newsletter*, 32(4). Retrieved from http://fas.org/irp/eprint/naquin.pdf.

National Public Radio. (2014, September 6). Interview with Clint Watts by Scott Simon. ISIS Runs a Dark Media Campaign on Social Media National Public Radio. Retrieved from www.npr.org/2014/09/06/346299142/isis-runs-a-dark-media-c ampaign-on-social-media.

Nealan, P. (2013, July 3). A Short History of AQI/ISI. *SOFREP* [Special Operation Forces Report]. Retrieved from http://sofrep.com/22373/a-short-history-of-al-qaeda-i n-iraq-aqi-isi/.

Paganini, P. (2017, June 1). ISIS Publishes Detailed Guide on How to Use Services Like Craigslist to Lure Non-Believers to Their Death. *Security Affairs.* Retrieved from http://securityaffairs.co/wordpress/59624/terrorism/isis-guide-online-services.html.

PunditFact. (2015). What is PunditFact. Retrieved from www.politifact.com/punditfact/.

Richardson, L. (2006). *What Terrorist Want: Understanding the Enemy, Containing the Threat.* New York: Random House.

Rose, T. (2014, October 31). ISIS Strikes Resumption of Lebanon's Civil War. *Breibart News.* Retrieved from www.breitbart.com/Big-Peace/2014/10/31/ISIS-Stokes-Resum ption-of-Lebanon-s-Civil-War.

Schmitt, E. (2015, February 16). US Intensifies Efforts to Blunt ISIS Message. *The New York Times.* Retrieved from www.nytimes.com/2015/02/17/world/middleeast/us -intensifies-effort-to-blunt-isis-message.html.

Sciutto, J., Crawford, J. and Carter, C. (2014, September 12). ISIS can "muster" between 20,000 and 31,500 fighters, CIA says. *CNN.* Retrieved from www.cnn.com/ 2014/09/11/world/meast/isis-syria-iraq/index.html.

Shane, S. and Hubbard, B. (2014, August 31). ISIS Displaying a Deft Command of Varied Media. *The New York Times.* Retrieved from www.nytimes.com/2014/08/31/ world/middleeast/isis-displaying-a-deft-command-of-varied-media.html?_r=0.

Teslik, L. (2006, June 8). Profile: Abu Musab al-Zarqawi. *Council on Foreign Relations.* Retrieved from www.cfr.org/iraq/profile-abu-musab-al-zarqawi/p9866.

US Department of State. (2015). Countries and regions. Retrieved from www.state.gov/countries/.

Watts, C. and McCants, W. (2012, December). US Strategy for Countering Violent Extremism: An Assessment. *Foreign Policy Research Institute.* Retrieved from www.fpri.org/articles/2012/12/us-strategy-countering-violent-extremism-assessment.

Winter, C. (2015, August 1). Fishing and Ultraviolence. *BBC.* Retrieved from www.bbc.co.uk/news/resources/idt-88492697-b674-4c69-8426-3edd17b7daed.

Winter, C. and Bach-Lombardo, J. (2016, February). Why ISIS Propaganda Works. *The Atlantic.* Retrieved from https://www.theatlantic.com/international/archive/2016/02/isis-propaganda-war/462702/.

Woronczak, A. (2014, June 17). ISIS Born From Occupation of Iraq, Not Syrian War. *The Real News Network.* Retrieved from http://truth-out.org/news/item/24419-isis-born-from-occupation-of-iraq-not-syrian-civil-war.

Zelin, A. (2014a, February 4). Al Qaeda Disaffiliates with the Islamic State of Iraq and al-Sham. *The Washington Institute.* Retrieved from www.washingtoninstitute.org/policy-analysis/view/al-qaeda-disaffiliates-with-the-islamic-state-of-iraq-and-al-sham.

Zelin, A. (2014b, June). The War between ISIS and al Qaeda for Supremacy of the Global Jihadist Movement. *Research Notes*, No. 20. Washington, DC: The Washington Institute for Near East Policy. Retrieved from www.washingtoninstitute.org/policy-analysis/view/the-war-between-isis-and-al-qaeda-for-supremacy-of-the-global-jihadist.

16 An imperial design or necessity of political economy?

Understanding the underpinnings of a Trump administration

Tugrul Keskin

No foreign policy – no matter how ingenious – has any chance of success if it is born in the minds of a few and carried in the hearts of none.

Henry Kissinger

Domestic policy can only defeat us; foreign policy can kill us.

John F. Kennedy

Political economy of foreign policy

Unlike the European colonialist powers, the United States only reluctantly entered world politics after World War I; however, its perceived imperial foreign policy strategy towards the Middle East began in earnest following World War II. The establishment of a "cohesive" approach to foreign policy coincided with the needs of the United States in the post-World War II era, specifically the needs of the US domestic political economy based on car manufacturing, industrialization, and urbanization. It also aligned with the outcomes of President Franklin D. Roosevelt's New Deal policies that pushed for the creation of a modern capitalist economy (Hamby, 1992) and the emergence of a military-industrial complex (Dunne & Sköns, 2009). US interests in the Middle East were driven by the needs of the domestic American political economy rather than the political design of imperialism per se. However, the form of imperialism that emerged as driven by a nation's material needs became a core element of US foreign policy throughout much of the 20th century. Indeed, since the late 1940s, US foreign policy has swung back and forth between the poles of hard and soft power. Its "hard power" approach used military and economic activities to influence the behavior and interests of other political and national entities, while "soft power" was used through such means as "humanitarianism" and other forms of public diplomacy programs. Its greater embrace of soft power foreign policy elements, including the promotion of Western concepts of human rights, democracy, and freedom, came into greater focus following the 1979 Islamic Revolution in Iran and later with the collapse of the Soviet Union. At the same time, we also saw the emergence of the neoliberal economy, characterized by increased privatization and the deregulation of markets. Though in contrast to prior strategies of deploying hard power as the primary tool of foreign policy, neoliberalism and the spread of US humanitarianism abroad worked in tandem with both domestic and global US interests. US foreign policy is therefore not materially different from that of other imperial powers in that it is rooted in, driven by, and adapts to the demands of the domestic political economy.

Who designs US foreign policy?

Formulation of foreign policy is not a simple process in a globalized and interconnected world. Especially after World War II, economic dependencies have become the core driver of foreign policy design in policy makers' circles, specifically inside the Beltway in Washington, DC. The United States is a modern state with advanced and complex political structures and institutions created to enhance the national interest. Therefore, the way that the United States formulates its foreign policy is more unique and also more recently formulated than the foreign policy of the rest of the world. Also, the variety of different social, political, and economic actors that have played vital roles in the formation of US foreign policy since World War II is unique. There is no single architect of US foreign policy; rather, multiple actors and institutionalized power holders and interest groups design foreign policy (Domhoff, 2006). As some portray it, US foreign policy, especially in the Middle East, is formulated and influenced by a powerful Israeli lobby or by other political actors and interest groups (Mearsheimer & Walt, 2006). These viewpoints are imaginative conspiracy theories.

Others believe that US foreign policy is formulated through a complex process of negotiation and discussion between business circles, social and political interest groups, and the bureaucratic civilian and military elite (Mills, 1956). Additionally, in the 1980s, with the emergence of neoliberal economic structures, we began to see an additional group of scholars participating in the formulation of US national security interests and foreign policy: think tank scholars (Haass, 2002). However, it is important to note that these think tank scholars are also a product of and linked to groups such as corporations, ethnic lobbies, and many other special interest groups. All of these social, political, and economic actors and stakeholders are a core part of the national establishment inside the Beltway.

The more that the United States is perceived as being empire-like, the more US foreign policy increases in complexity in response to transformations of the domestic political economy. Therefore, in the process of policy formulation, new institutions and approaches emerge from the struggle for justification of existing foreign policies and their outcomes. This was the case, for example, right after World War II, during the Vietnam War, with the emergence of neoliberalism in the 1980s under the Reagan administration, in the 1990s post-Cold War era, after September 11, 2001, and with the emergence of

China as a global power. However, there was a convoluted process of transformation to the existing policies, because foreign policy does not change in a short period of time and requires lengthy processes of discussion and brainstorming as communications take place between the state institutions and the stakeholders involved in domestic politics.

When looking at the politics of today, the victory of Donald J. Trump in the 2016 US presidential election was considered surprising by many liberals in the United States and also by foreign stakeholders; but this was not an unexpected result for those who follow American demographic trends and who understood the power and interests of the American middle class in the rural areas and small towns. Since the implementation of neoliberal policies by the Reagan administration, American society, and particularly the middle and lower classes, have been struggling to adapt to the challenges of economic liberalization. Over time this has led both to the outsourcing of American middle-class jobs to developing countries with cheap labor, lowering the cost of products, and to an astonishing number of immigrants coming to the United States since the 1984 census. It was in this economic context that Walmart was created and consequently swept the "white"-dominated American towns from Ohio to Tennessee. Today, Walmart provides low-cost products to those who were once part of the American middle class, and every city and town with a predominantly middle-class population has a Walmart store. Relatedly, when a Walmart retail store opens in a small town in the United States, it means that another mom-and-pop store will be closed (Basker, 2007). Most importantly, a young small-town native is more likely to move to a bigger city to find a job or educational opportunities, where the competition for economic resources is now harsher than it was from the 1950s to the 1970s (Moberg, 2011). Additionally, they encounter social and political obstacles as a result of social globalization and increasing diversity. Therefore, we are not able to understand the transformation of American society today, and Trump's victory, without examining the development and growth of companies such as Walmart and their direct relationship to class and ethnicity in the United States.

Domestic changes in American society have tremendous implications for US foreign policy. Trump is not an insider of the Beltway, and he definitely is not a part of the establishment in Washington, DC. Almost all US presidents have failed to recognize or address the economic problems of the middle class and to manage the social integration of "whites" into the globalized big cities. While many American presidents have tried to "liberate the world" through "freedom" and democratization programs, in the process they have failed to adequately address the negative consequences of neoliberal globalization within American society.

Trump's victory is a product of these circumstances. However, as mentioned before, US foreign policy is designed largely inside the Beltway (Moor, 2014) by a cadre of powerful elite who work within a civilian and military bureaucracy, as well as in corporations, think tanks – to include such individuals as Francis Fukuyama and other neoconservatives – and as part of interest groups and lobbying firms, and with retired government officials. None of these groups care to know (Hanson, 2016) about the concerns of the "white" middle class. This is exactly the group of people that Trump is concerned with and that he was catering to with his election rhetoric of bringing back American jobs for the American middle class. It is important to note that this powerful group also includes established organizations such as the Council on Foreign Relations, CNN, business conglomerations, and others who benefit from the status quo of a neoliberal American foreign policy. It is unlikely that Trump will be able to act independently to change US foreign policy while navigating the power structures and managing critique from the power elite in Washington, DC, who are frequently perceived as controlling state institutions.

Neither Bill Clinton nor George W. Bush nor Barack Obama paid much attention to the trend of outsourcing American jobs to other countries because they were too busy collaborating with the winners of globalization (Shivani, 2016). Donald Trump and his strategists identify with the frustrated masses, and their victory in the 2016 US election is a result of the domestic frustrations of the "white" middle class.

US foreign policy: From the Cold War to the post-Cold War era

Following the early stages of US foreign policy characterized by American missionaries and Woodrow Wilson's utopian worldview, which we see between 1913 and 1921, one of the first US foreign policy engagements with the Middle East began during Harry Truman's administration between the years 1945 and 1953. Truman's doctrine was born during the Cold War era and in the context of a post-World War II Middle East. European colonial powers started to withdraw from the region as a result of independence movements and the weakening military force of the old colonial Britain. As a relatively young global power challenged by the Soviet Union, the United States needed to maintain its presence in the region to contain the communist threat as well as to control the petro-political economy in order to meet domestic market demand. Hence, Truman established solid relations with Mohammed Reza Shah Pahlavi of Iran (Tristam, 2017) and Ismet Inonu of Turkey. Turkey had joined NATO in 1952 (Council on Foreign Relations, 2012) and in the 1953 CIA-supported coup (Dehghan & Norton-Taylor, 2013) brought Mohammed Reza Shah Pahlavi to power again. In the 1930s and 1940s, the map of the Middle East was reconfigured based on the political economy of a US national security strategy. The American-based California-Arabian Standard Oil Company, or what is known today as the Saudi Arabian Oil Company (Aramco), was established a year after the Kingdom of Saudi Arabia declared independence. Interestingly, oil was discovered in the Kingdom in 1938, and it officially became a member of the United Nations in 1945. On the other hand, the State of Israel was founded in 1948 and Truman's administration recognized Israel immediately after its independence was declared in order to influence the new state.

In the 1950s, the North African states began to obtain independence from the colonial powers. One of the most important was Gamal Abdel Nasser's Egypt, and the Arab Republic of Egypt was founded in 1953. Five Middle Eastern countries – Iran, Turkey, Saudi Arabia, Israel, and Egypt – became the center of US foreign policy for the following decades.

During the Cold War era, the United States established military bases and strategic alliances throughout the Middle East in order to facilitate its interests in these locations (Ashley, 2012). This is similar to what took place in Latin and Central America. However, the 1979 Islamic Revolution in Iran led to a shift in US foreign policy during the Reagan presidency. During the Cold War era, the United States had not taken sides between local actors amidst the various ethnic and religious conflicts; however, this strategy changed after 1979 and during the Iran-Iraq War. The United States slowly but steadily changed its objectives in the Middle East by using local actors rather than just Middle Eastern state institutions; for example, by collaborating with Middle Eastern NGOs and media organizations as well as local ethnic, religious, and opposition groups in order to advance a new US national security strategy (Chomsky, 1991). However, the Gulf War between 1990 and 1991 accelerated the US grand strategic plan for the region, one that was based on the combination of a humanitarian approach and the use of hard power to advance US foreign policy objectives. As a result, the United States openly began to support and train local ethnic, religious, and opposition groups against the fragile authoritarian states. It is important to note that the feudal or semi-capitalist social structures of Middle Eastern societies had not yet generated modern forms of political opposition parties; therefore, religious and ethnic opposition movements were dominant actors in the political arena at the time.

On September 11, 2001, the terrorist attacks against the United States dramatically changed US foreign policy objectives toward the region and led to the creation of another plan related to the Greater Middle East Initiative (Ottaway & Carothers, 2004) for regime change in the region. "Islamic" terrorism became the main focus of US national security strategy during the George W. Bush era between the years 2000 and 2008. The 2003 Iraq War was a result of this long-term national security strategy, as policy makers in Washington targeted fragile authoritarian states in the region. Therefore, the Iraq War was not just a neoconservative plan, but rooted in some of the larger US national security interests of the post-Cold War era.

Donald Trump's political team: Former generals and the economic elite

In order to understand and predict future relations between the United States and Middle East and Muslim-populated countries under the Donald Trump presidency, one must closely examine Trump's 2016 election campaign speeches, the composition of his national security team, and how he has dealt with the Middle Eastern leadership and nations during the first part of his presidency. In doing so, one should be realistic concerning how much he will be able to affect change given the amount of influence that prevailing domestic and international actors and institutions will have on his approach to the Middle East. Most of these actors (Itkowitz, 2014) have a complex relationship with the power elite in Washington, DC, but Trump and his initial national security political appointees do not have a similar harmonious link to the DC establishment.

Additionally, according to some scholars, US national security interests are shifting towards a prioritization of Asia (Manyin et al., 2012) and away from a Middle East-centric foreign policy. However, in addition to the security interests fueled by the US needs for a growing political economy, China's rising influence in the Middle East, the fight against terrorism, providing security assistance to Israel (Mearsheimer & Walt, 2006), and the Kurdish issue remain at the center of American foreign policy objectives in the Middle East. Nevertheless, Trump holds very different views from the administrations of Bill Clinton, George W. Bush, and Barack Obama on issues concerning the Middle East. For example, in an interview before the election, Trump harshly criticized George W. Bush's plan for the occupation of Iraq, Obama's policy toward Syria, the nuclear deal with Iran, general US foreign policy toward Saudi Arabia, and, most importantly, foreign interest groups and lobby activities in Washington, DC. According to his election rhetoric and slogans, Trump's foreign policy approach reminds us of Patrick J. Buchanan's perspective on Iraq and the Middle East generally (Buchanan, 2003). Trump appears to hold a more libertarian approach than the rest. However, the complex process of US foreign policy formulation and the long-established national security strategy might not be easily changed or shifted by Trump and his national security team.

In the beginning of Trump's presidency, he appointed some very "controversial" civilian and military bureaucrats to his cabinet. For example, one of his most trusted advisors, Michael Flynn, a retired military general and former director of the Defense Intelligence Agency, was selected as national security advisor (Vladimirov, 2016). Additional close advisors and appointees included Reince Priebus (Chief of Staff), Steve Bannon (Chief Strategist), Sean Spicer (White House Press Secretary), James Mattis (Department of Defense), Alabama Senator Jeff Sessions (Attorney General), Kansas Republican Mike Pompeo (Director of CIA), and Rex Tillerson (Department of State). Almost all of these people have little or no relationship with the bureaucratic liberal establishment inside the Beltway and have very different foreign and domestic policy approaches and perspectives from the existing players within the foreign relations bureaucracy. They are also not similar to neoconservatives. Consequently, these selections ruffled the feathers of the editor of the conservative *Weekly Standard* and neoconservative Bill Kristol, who harshly criticized Trump's administration. In some ways, the neoliberal response to Trump's policies and selection of cabinet members has been similar to the liberal response. Trump's "nativist" and ethnonationalist approach has been criticized by both sides of the political spectrum because they all originate from the power elite inside the Beltway. For instance, both sides equally questioned Russian interference in the US election as a "domestication process" towards Trump's policies (Cillizza, 2017; Kristol, 2016).

Trump then lost several of his initial political appointees: Michael Flynn, Sean Spicer, Reince Priebus, Steve Bannon, Anthony Scaramucci, and Sebastian Gorka. The Washington elite has tried to implement their own team within the Trump administration, and H. R. McMaster has now replaced Flynn as a new national security advisor. Unlike Bannon and Flynn, "Lt. Gen. H. R. McMaster, President Trump's new national security adviser, is considering a reorganization of the White House foreign policy team that would give him control of Homeland Security and guarantee full access to the military and intelligence agencies" (Baker, 2017, para. 1). A silent proxy war is being waged inside the Beltway, and this has turned into a public and open struggle between the establishment and Trump's team of outsiders. In this context, actors from the establishment – liberals, neoconservatives, and classical Republicans alike – are all equally unhappy with Trump's independent policies.

Since McMaster became national security advisor, Trump's foreign policy approach has shifted closer towards that of the Republican establishment. One of his first foreign visits, for example, took place in Saudi Arabia (Applebaum, 2017), where he met with Saudi Arabia's King Salman and Egyptian President Abdel Fattah al-Sisi (Reuters, 2017). This visit helps demonstrate that Trump has discarded some of his campaign rhetoric and started to use some of the more established strategies and pillars of US foreign policy. Trump's rhetoric on Iran has also been mostly silent since McMaster became the new dominant strategist in the Trump administration – but even this might change. Most of Trump's close associates are not happy about McMaster's role in formulating foreign policy. As a result of the complicated power struggle within Trump's cabinet, Steve Bannon resigned from his role at the White House (Colvin & Lemire, 2017) and returned to his famous Breitbart News Network, albeit temporarily. Trump and his strategists have nevertheless attempted to build their own national security network within the administration, very similar to what the neoconservatives had tried to do. However, the neoconservative movement has been working with the establishment in Washington, DC for more than half a century, whereas Trump and his team, even though they have better relations with local nativist groups throughout the United States, are newcomers.

One of the first tests for Trump's foreign policy in the context of the Middle East can be seen in the Turkish case, specifically in relation to the Gülen Movement and the Kurdish issue. For example, Flynn wrote that we must understand that "Turkey is vital to US interests. ... Gülen [a rival of Erdoğan] portrays himself as a moderate, but he is in fact a radical Islamist" (Flynn, 2016, paras. 2–3). He concludes his article by saying, "The forces of radical Islam derive their ideology from radical clerics like Gülen, who is running a scam. We should not provide him safe haven. In this crisis, it is imperative that we remember who our real friends are" (Flynn, 2016, para. 21). (What is also interesting is that another one of Trump's close, albeit unofficial, advisors is Newt Gingrich, a history professor, long-time Washington insider, and member of the Ataturk Society of America, who is also not a fan of the Gülen Movement and his followers [Romig, 2012].) As Flynn's evident concern with Turkey shows, the Gülen issue will be on the negotiating table between the Trump administration and the Turkish State/JDP-AK Party.

With regard to the Kurdish issue, this might be a problem that is partially resolvable. A new administration might be able to change US strategy on the issue, which has so far been directed towards supporting the Kurds against Iraq, Syria, Iran, and Turkey. In addition, the newly appointed CIA director, Mike Pompeo (Central Intelligence Agency, 2017) is a hardliner and strongly opposed to Obama's Iranian nuclear deal (Times of Israel, 2016). This new group of US policy makers is very much like the old Middle Eastern political elite, who are secularist and both pro-US and pro-EU. Consequently, the conservative and pro-Muslim Brotherhood Erdoğan and current Turkish government might face certain challenges with Trump's emerging foreign policy priorities. Pompeo, for example, is likely to continue to use the Kurds against Iran, in addition to other Islamic groups and movements.

Will Trump be able to change US foreign policy?

In the first year of the Trump presidency, we have witnessed unprecedented resistance against the Trump administration by the power elite inside the Beltway. The elite have been inseparable from Washington's bureaucratic structure and institutions since the Cold War began and have a complicated network extending from the US government to think tanks, lobbying firms, and the powerful liberal media. Over the last several decades, US foreign policy and national security interests have been designed and formulated by these groups of people, who should be considered an interest group.

Regardless of who becomes US president, the elite work to educate and "domesticate" any incumbent on their strategic role and viewpoints. In so doing, they try to impose their agenda on domestic and national security strategy formulation. None of the presidents, as individual actors, are as powerful as this group, and all are influenced by them. At times, members of the elite have emerged from the neoconservative side of the spectrum, whereas in other cases, they followed a liberal humanitarian agenda. These elite interests occasionally overlap with the interests of the American middle and lower classes, and sometimes they contradict them. We should remember the Farewell Address given by Dwight D. Eisenhower in 1961 regarding how the elite tried to influence him on military spending. As a war hero from a military family and a hardcore Republican and white man, even Eisenhower ironically complained about the elite's influence and power in Washington, DC, and saw this power as a threat to the real interests of the American people. Indeed, his speech is not that different from the 1956 book by critical sociologist C. Wright Mills on the power elite. Also of note, Eisenhower was an insider, unlike Trump and his team. I believe that Trump is not as powerful as the

Washington elite and will be marginalized through media and the liberal elite by the end of his term. Therefore, he must use a different strategy to implement any policies that could potentially benefit the American middle-class groups that he claimed to champion during his 2016 election.

References

Applebaum, A. (2017, May 21). Trump's bizarre and un-American visit to Saudi Arabia. *The Washington Post.* Retrieved from https://www.washingtonpost.com/new s/global-opinions/wp/2017/05/21/trumps-bizarre-and-un-american-visit-to-saudi-arabia /?utm_term=.df731326e92a.

Ashley, S.P. (2012, August 30). Cold War politics in the Middle East. *E-International Relations Students.* Retrieved from www.e-ir.info/2012/08/30/cold-war-politics-in-the -middle-east/.

Baker, P. (2017, February 22). McMaster may reorganize Trump's foreign policy team once again. *The New York Times.* Retrieved from https://www.nytimes.com/2017/02/ 22/us/politics/hr-mcmaster-trump-foreign-policy.html.

Basker, E. (2007). The causes and consequences of Wal-Mart's growth. *SSRN Electronic Journal.* doi:10.2139/ssrn.950882.

Buchanan, P.J. (2003). Whose war? *The American Conservative.* Retrieved from www. theamericanconservative.com/articles/whose-war/.

Central Intelligence Agency. (2017). About CIA: Mike Pompeo. Retrieved from http s://www.cia.gov/about-cia/leadership/mike-pompeo.html.

Chomsky, N. (1991). After the Cold War: US foreign policy in the Middle East. *Cultural Critique*, 19, 14–31. Retrieved from http://www3.nccu.edu.tw/~lorenzo/Choms ky%20Middle%20East.pdf.

Cillizza, C. (2017, July 8). Trump totally changed his tune on Russian hacking today. Why? *CNN.* Retrieved from http://edition.cnn.com/2017/07/07/politics/trump-putin-russia-meddling/index.html.

Colvin, J. and Lemire, J. (2017, August 18). Strategist Steve Bannon resigns from Trump administration. *ABC News.* Retrieved from http://abc7ny.com/politics/steve-bannon-resigns-from-trump-administration-abc-news-reports/2322093/.

Council on Foreign Relations. (2012). US-Turkey relations: A new partnership. *Independent Task Force Report* No. 69. Retrieved from https://www.cfr.org/report/us-tur key-relations.

Dehghan, S.K. and Norton-Taylor, R. (2013, August 19). CIA admits role in 1953 Iranian coup. *The Guardian.* Retrieved from https://www.theguardian.com/world/20 13/aug/19/cia-admits-role-1953-iranian-coup.

Domhoff, W. (2006). *Who rules America? The triumph of the corporate rich* (5th ed.). New York: McGraw Hill.

Dunne, J.P. and Sköns, E. (2009). The military industrial complex. Retrieved from http s://core.ac.uk/download/pdf/7170012.pdf.

Eisenhower, D.D. (1961, January 17). Farewell radio and television address to the American people. *The American Presidency Project.* Retrieved from www.presidenc y.ucsb.edu/ws/?pid=12086.

Flynn, M.T. (2016, November 8). Our ally Turkey is in crisis and needs our support. *The Hill.* Retrieved from http://thehill.com/blogs/pundits-blog/foreign-policy/305021 -our-ally-turkey-is-in-crisis-and-needs-our-support.

Haass, R.N. (2002, November). Think tanks and US foreign policy: A policy-maker's perspective. *US Foreign Policy Agenda*, 7(3), 5–8. Retrieved from http://photos.state. gov/libraries/vietnam/8621/translations/ej112002.pdf.

Hamby, A.L. (1992). *Liberalism and its challenges: From FDR to Bush*. New York: Oxford University Press.

Hanson, V.D. (2016, July 5). Washington's hollow men. *National Review*. Retrieved from www.nationalreview.com/article/437454/american-elite-and-american-people.

Itkowitz, C. (2014, May 14). Which foreign countries spent the most to influence US politics? *The Washington Post*. Retrieved from https://www.washingtonpost.com/blo gs/in-the-loop/wp/2014/05/14/which-foreign-countries-spent-the-most-to-influence-u-s-politics/?utm_term=.cd1b92c3cd83.

Kristol, W. (2016, July 24). Putin's party? *The Weekly Standard*. Retrieved from www. weeklystandard.com/putins-party/article/2003473.

Manyin, M.E., Daggett, S., Dolyen, S., Dolyen, B., Lawrence, S.V., Martin, M.F., … Vaughn, B. (2012, March 28). *Pivot to the Pacific? The Obama administration's "rebalancing" toward Asia*. Washington, DC: Congressional Research Service. Retrieved from https://fas.org/sgp/crs/natsec/R42448.pdf.

Mearsheimer, J. and Walt, S. (2006). The Israel lobby. *London Review of Books*, 28(6), 3–12. Retrieved from https://www.lrb.co.uk/v28/n06/john-mearsheimer/the-israel-lobby.

Mills, C.W. (1956). *The power elite*. New York: Oxford University Press.

Moberg, D. (2011, April 28). Wal-Mart's shocking impact on the lives of hundreds of millions of people. *Alternet*. Retrieved from www.alternet.org/story/150781/wal-ma rt's_shocking_impact_on_the_lives_of_hundreds_of_millions_of_people.

Moor, A. (2014, March 15). US foreign policy is led by politics inside Washington's Beltway. *The National*. Retrieved from https://www.thenational.ae/us-foreign-policy-is-led-by-politics-inside-washington-s-beltway-1.589485.

Ottaway, M. and Carothers, T. (2004). *Policy brief: The Greater Middle East Initiative: Off to a false start*. Washington, DC: Carnegie Endowment of International Peace. Retrieved from http://carnegieendowment.org/files/Policybrief29.pdf.

Reuters. (2017, May 21). Trump praises Sisi, says he hopes to visit Egypt. Retrieved from www.reuters.com/article/us-usa-trump-saudi-egypt-idUSKBN18H08H.

Romig, R. (2012, January 26). Newt and Atatürk. *The New Yorker*. Retrieved from https://www.newyorker.com/news/news-desk/newt-and-atatrk.

Shivani, A. (2016, June 6). This is our neoliberal nightmare: Hillary Clinton, Donald Trump, and why the market and the wealthy win every time. *Salon*. Retrieved from www.salon.com/2016/06/06/this_is_our_neoliberal_nightmare_hillary_clinton_donal d_trump_and_why_the_market_and_the_wealthy_win_every_time/.

Times of Israel. (2016, November 18). Trump's CIA pick Pompeo anticipates "rolling back" the "disastrous" Iran deal. Retrieved from www.timesofisrael.com/trumps-cia-pick-pompeo-anticipates-rolling-back-the-disastrous-iran-deal/.

Tristam, P. (2017, August 18). The US and the Middle East since 1945 to 2008. *Thoughtco*. Retrieved from https://www.thoughtco.com/us-and-middle-east-since-1 945-2353681.

Vladimirov, N. (2016, November 16). Report: Trump to pick Michael Flynn for national security adviser. *The Hill*. Retrieved from http://thehill.com/homenews/administration/ 306506-retired-lt-gen-michael-flynn-reported-to-be-national-security-advisor.

Acknowledgments

This volume grew out of a conference on American foreign policy and the Middle East hosted by the Graduate School of Social Sciences at Maltepe University, Istanbul, in the spring of 2016. We are deeply grateful to the hosts and participants of that conference and the subsequent submission of updated and edited chapters for the completion of this volume. Additionally, we would like to thank the many other authors who were solicited separately and who contributed additional chapters to help round out the many complex elements and debates on US foreign policy in the Middle East. Certainly, it is important to note that the views expressed here are those of the authors alone. They do not represent official policy, nor do they represent any government entity.

We would also like to thank our respective universities for their continued support of these important academic and policy-relevant endeavors. First, thank you to the Chancellor of the College of International Security Affairs at National Defense University (NDU), Michael S. Bell, and to the Academic Dean/Interim Chancellor, Charles B. Cushman Jr. Thanks and appreciation also goes to the leadership of Shanghai University and the Centers for Global and Turkish Studies. We are similarly grateful to Andrew C. Hess, Hassan Abbas, and Timothy Luke for their invaluable professional insights and support. Fantastic intern and copy-editing support came from Srijoni Banerjee, William Chim, Alex Iverson, and Logan Cotting.

We are deeply appreciative of the editorial team at Routledge, including editor Robert Sorsby and his assistant Claire Maloney. We would also like to thank the editors of the Routledge Studies in US Foreign Policy series, John Dumbrell and Inderjeet Parmar. Additionally, we would like to thank the two blind reviewers who provided excellent comments to enhance the overall scope and content of the volume.

Last, we would like to thank our respective families for their unwavering love and support.

Index